OLYMPIC
OBSESSION

OLYMPIC OBSESSION

The Inside Story of Britain's Most Successful Sport

Martin Cross

breedon **books**
PUBLISHING

First published in Great Britain in 2001 by
The Breedon Books Publishing Company Limited
Breedon House, 3 The Parker Centre, Derby, DE21 4SZ.

ISBN 1 85983 233 4

Printed and bound by Butler & Tanner, Frome, Somerset
Cover printing by GreenShires, Leicester

Contents

Foreword

by Alan Green

I'M ASKED frequently what's been the best broadcasting moment of my career. Naturally, given that I devote an overwhelming amount of time to the sport, the assumption is that it will relate to football. To a World Cup, a special goal or those thrilling climactic minutes of the 1999 European Cup Final in Barcelona. At a pinch, they might accept that it has happened in an Open Championship, or Ryder Cup, golf being another one of those sports that I'm so fortunate to be associated with. But no, my proudest moment in commentary arose not in football nor in golf, but in rowing.

Years on, I still feel tears welling up thinking back to that Saturday on Lake Lanier when Steven Redgrave and Matthew Pinsent crossed the line to win the Olympic gold medal in the coxless pairs. Despite my advancing age and a feeling that I now ought to really know better, I remain an intensely emotional Irishman, especially prone to crying on occasions like that. I cried unashamedly. You see, whatever commitments I had in football during that year, describing another Manchester United 'Double' or the European Championship, I'd known that my 1996 would climax with *that* race on *that* lake and, however subconsciously, I'd been preparing for *that* moment for many months. A moment that represented sporting history. Redgrave winning his fourth gold in successive Olympic Games. I couldn't afford to mess up and I admit that emotions that morning were determined as much by my relief that I hadn't as the fact that Redgrave and Pinsent had won. I remember, too, looking to my right to remind myself of one of the main reasons why the commentary had gone so well. Martin Cross.

It was scarcely a year since I'd met Martin. I'd been in China and Hong Kong with the England football squad during their preparations for Euro '96. Arriving at Heathrow off the long flight from the Far East, my instinct was to grab a shuttle to Manchester to get home. Instead, I was scheduled to fly back in the direction I'd come from, to Zurich, en route to my first ever regatta at Lucerne.

It was September 1995 when it was first suggested to me that I should commentate on rowing at the Atlanta Games. Initially, I shuddered at the thought. Rowing? What did I know about rowing? Nothing. Nothing at all. It took me quite a time to even entertain the notion that I could commentate on the sport. All will be well, they said, you'll have Martin Cross alongside you.

When I first saw him outside a café by Lake Lucerne, only a couple of months before we were due to fly out to the States, I had my doubts. I remember he looked rather scruffy, carrying a haversack and half-kitted out in rowing gear. Was this a potential broadcaster or an ageing oarsman in front of me? As it turned out, Martin was both and those doubts lasted oh, all of a few seconds.

We gelled immediately, a chemistry quickly forming that ensured an excellent working relationship and a lasting friendship. At the heart of it was mutual respect. He rated me for what I'd done in broadcasting and I could hardly fail to admire what he'd achieved in a boat. We knew that we could learn off each other and that's precisely what happened. That morning in Georgia, I was totally confident of my ability to describe the details of the race and Martin knew he was able to supply, succinctly, the whys and the wherefores.

I'm still learning from Martin. Although he's moved to television, we remain in close contact. I still advise him on aspects of broadcasting. He still teaches me about rowing. I can't think of anyone that could do it better. It's not merely his knowledge, although the term 'encyclopaedic' wouldn't flatter him. It's that you feel his passion for rowing in every breath, with every word. And his obsession with the sport over the last quarter of a century has embraced all its key figures: Redgrave, Pinsent, the Searles, Foster, few have been untouched by Martin.

Perhaps my own love for rowing and the people who populate it, however surprising to outsiders, might have developed without him. It's simply that I doubt it. Enjoy this book as much as I will.

Introduction

'MAD is he? Then I wish he would bite some of my other generals,' was George III's reported comment to the Duke of Cumberland in response to the latter's complaints about the unconventional approach of General Woolfe.

I knew that any attempt of mine to write an account of a sport with which I have been closely involved for over 30 years would be a challenging task. I even suspected that trying to combine this job together with that of piecing together an autobiography would be somewhat daunting. But doing this, at the same time as endeavouring to weave the lives of others into an already complicated pattern, has seemed at times like madness.

So to create some sense and give some clarity, I decided to pick out 14 strands from my own life (one for each chapter). Some of these strands you might expect to see in any sporting biography: getting hooked on the sport; winning an Olympic gold; my 'rowing after-life' as a TV commentator. Others perhaps appear less often: resentment, hero-worship and emotional break-down are just three examples. This done, I begun to feel more confident about the quality of the image that might emerge.

But as I began to write, I felt that the strands I was using somehow needed more strength and colour (perhaps this was not surprising, from someone who had chosen rowing – unique of all team sports). So to weave the sort of tapestry that I wanted, I attempted to entwine the strands of my own life with similar ones drawn from other's lives. I chose 14 people, who I thought had gone through similar experiences to myself. So for example, Steven Redgrave's life between Atlanta and Sydney contrasts with my own attempts to carry on past my 'sell by date'.

Some of these people may be less familiar to you, like Adrian Cassidy. But it was my intention that you would be able to hear the sound of their voices, perhaps almost as clearly as I heard them, as they told their own tales to me. It was for this reason that I chose to travel the world from Leipzig to Toronto, to interview them in detail. Wherever possible, I have used their own words, as recorded and transcribed by me.

So by now you might have guessed that this is not a sporting biography in the traditional sense. In some ways, it is almost easier to describe what it is not. You will find many of the world's greatest sportsmen and women spoken of here. But this is not a book about rowers. It has the glint of Olympic gold and exudes more than a hint of the excitement of the world's greatest sporting extravaganza: But it is not about the Olympic Games. You will learn the inside story of Britain's most successful sport. But you would be wrong to think that this was just a book about British rowing.

In the end, though, it is for you to determine whether the images that have emerged on the tapestry are clear ones. Whatever you decide, I hope that the experience of reading *Olympic Obsession* will have evoked in you some empathy with the passions that rowing has kindled in me and many others; even if it is only a fraction, the read will have been well worthwhile.

Website: www.olympicobsession.com

Acknowledgements

UNTIL I had tried it, I viewed writing a book as a rather solitary occupation, rather akin to single sculling. I realise now that this is not so. As I write these acknowledgements, it is surprising just how many persons have, at one time or another, made up part of the crew that has brought *Olympic Obsession* to publication. They all made a difference, especially when at times it seemed I was battling alone against wind and tide; then there were always people prepared to help out and lend their 'weight' to the oars.

Chief among those is Anton Rippon at Breedon Publishing. Anton's love of sport and his enthusiasm for bringing sporting tales to a wider audience have been inspirational. His support, both as publisher and editor, has been immense. Many others have helped with various aspects of the book. Chris Dodd's assistance, particularly his ideas as to how parts of the text could be improved, was invaluable, as were the suggestions of David Tanner, who read through a draft of the book. Others have read sections of the draft and made suggestions. In this respect I am especially grateful to Adam Clift, Pat and Moira Cross, Alan Jones, Harry Mahon, Jonny Searle and Anita De Frantz. Any mistakes that remain are my responsibility alone.

Providing good images of rowing is a very specialist skill. I have been fortunate in having the help of several individuals, who spent a considerable amount of time researching through their back catalogues for the right shots. Chief among these is Peter Spurrier, whose insights through the lens have been an inspiration to me. Dominik Keller has continued to provide the sport with wonderful images of rowing; in this respect, they are yet another legacy of Thomi, Dominik's father and FISA's president, sadly departed in 1989. Again, Richard Bennett spent hours trying to find 'just the right shot'. Others have allowed the use of photographs from their own collections, notably John Shore, David Tanner, Adrian Cassidy, Pat and Moira Cross (again!) and Richard Budgett. Stewart Hill and Mrs J. Axton helped me discover and understand the wonderful paintings of Thomas Eakins. Stefan Klasener showed me just how powerfully words and images can combine

My thanks are also due to Alan Green, a man who spends his life using words to convey the excitement, spectacle and raw emotions that sport produces. He was kind enough to take time out from his huge range of commitments to write the foreword to this book as well as to read through a draft.

It's difficult to quantify the wonderful effect that even a few moments of someone's time and thought can have on the process of writing. Throughout the book there have been many prepared to do just that. Sue Oldham, the wonderful Life Trainer, started the whole process going in

1997. Annette Green gave me the confidence to write my own story and the belief that people would read it. Glen O'Hara – an incomparable historian – showed me how I could put the skills of a historian towards researching and constructing this book. Jorg Weissig showed me wonderful hospitality when I travelled to Leipzig. Pete Sheppard, John Beattie, Ian McNuff, Jon Searle, Teresa Cross, Pete Spurrier, Garry Herbert, Campbell Ferguson, Richard Boulton, Vic Russell, Pat Sweeney, Mike Teti, Jurgen Grobler, Johan Blondelle, Marnie McBean, Peter Hoeltzenbein, Daniel Topolski, Paul Townend, Rachel Cugnoni, Janet Thomas and 5JT, Pat Talbot, Jo Iredale, David Hughes, Stuart Coulter, Penny Croucher, Catherine Cross, David Craggs, Sue Cross, John Walsh, Pam, and especially Tamsin, were all willing to provide help when it was needed.

Olympic Obsession could never have been written without the help of the 14 people who allowed me to try to fathom out what it was that made them tick and how this – and they – might relate to me. None of them ever sought to influence what I wrote. I hope it is clear from the pages of this book that I hold all of them in the greatest possible respect. My special thanks are due to Jon Searle, Harry Mahon, Anita De Frantz, Shannon Crawford, Siggi Brietzke, Chris Clark, Andy Holmes, Greg Searle, Matthew Pinsent, Tim Foster, Mike Teti, Steve Redgrave, Adrian Cassidy and Miriam Batten.

Thanks must also go to those at Hampton School who have shown me consideration and understanding in allowing me the space and time to pursue my 'Olympic Obsession'. In particular, my three headmasters, Gavin (where ever you are), Graham Able and Barry Martin. Likewise, those long-suffering colleagues of mine in the History Department: Jon Cook, Ken Rice, Maurice Xiberras, Ed Wesson, Richard Worrallo, Ed Kendall, Dave Clark and Ed Wild. But most of all, as far as School is concerned, those pupils of mine who have had to tolerate their history teacher's eccentricities over the years.

But of course, the greatest burden has fallen on the shoulders of my family and it is to them that I am eternally grateful: to Natasha, Lara and Frank for putting up with their dad taking up so much time on the word processor when he could have been playing with them, or they could have been playing their own games on the computer. Finally (yes at last), the thanks I owe to my wife, Chris, are immeasurable. I won't even begin to list the number of areas in which she has given advice, support or inspiration. I know that for her, at times the writing of *Olympic Obsession* has been a painful experience. But this part of my journey along the river of life has been all the more rewarding because we have been able to make it together. It is for this reason that I respectfully dedicate *Olympic Obsession* to Chris.

Barn Elms to Barcelona

DO YOU ever find that it's only when you've been doing something for a long time – years maybe – that you begin to look back and work out what it was that made you become so involved in the first place. I don't mean the nostalgic 'Those were the days' type of reminiscing; no, a far more profound glimpse, the sort that leaves you questioning the kind of person that you are, or have become. Often, those insights occur when you realise that something you have done for a long time has to end. With me they started at my last Olympics, in Barcelona. It wasn't just that at 35, I knew that my fourth Games would be my last; no, with me there was something, or rather somebody else.

Jon Searle was then just 23. I'd known him for 11 years and watched him grow from the cocky little schoolboy who sat at the front of my history classes, through his first awkward strokes in a boat, to a potential Olympic champion. It was a journey that years before, a teacher of mine, Jim Clark, had watched me make. As I waited for Searle's Olympic final to begin, my mind wandered to back to how Clark, himself an international oarsman, must have felt when he watched me in the '84 Olympic final. That day too, the lake was still and silent, just like the water now on the Banyolas course.

The reeds round the lake stood tall and still, basking in the heat of the mid-morning sunshine. Away in the distance, you could see the white, snow-covered tops of the Pyrenees, and closer still, the reflections of their tree-covered foothills on the surface of the lake. It was a scene that invited feelings of serenity but I felt uneasy. Perhaps it was the thought of racing in my own final just two hours away. But there was also something else; just then, I couldn't work out what it was.

The crackle of the loudspeaker disturbed my thoughts. Searle's race was under way. At first, the boats were just distant dots as they left the 2,000 metres start line some three minutes earlier. But as they passed the 1,000 metres mark, I could just begin to make out the crews. Five seconds ahead and creaming the rest of the field were the imperious Abbagnale brothers from Italy. Their technique as perfect and precise as the magical Azzuri that brought the football World Cup back to Italy. The Italians were flying towards their third Olympic gold medal, with what seems like an ocean of clear blue water between them and the rest of the field.

That included Jon Searle, rowing with his younger brother Greg. The split times showed they were 4.8 seconds behind the Italians at the halfway point. I remember feeling a brief moment of relief that my former pupil would not become an Olympic champion like me; as if somehow their triumph could diminish my own status in the sport. Then I remembered the words of the Searle's cox, Garry Herbert. When we had spoken about his race the previous evening, he'd said, 'Mart, I know we can give them five seconds at 1,000 metres and still beat them.' Garry and I had both been taught at the Cardinal Vaughan School. As a young boy, he'd felt inspired by the photograph of my crew racing in the 1984 Olympics, that had hung in the school lobby. The realisation that somehow I was responsible for at least a small part of what was going on out there made me feel hungry for a British triumph.

With 500 metres left, though, what Garry promised hadn't happened. Even though they were now challenging for silver, I was sure they'd left it far too late. But I had not taken into account the Searle magic. As the metres ran out and the clock moved into injury time, Greg Searle, in the stroke seat, sensed the urgency of it all and upped the tempo. His brother Jonny, dreadlocks streaming behind him, responded. This was the kind of race he loved; rowing a crew down in the last few metres. I knew that lying prone in the bows of the boat, Garry would be screaming at his crew for more, his voice tinged with the certainty that they would find something extra and catch the boat in front of them.

The Italians in the stands were behaving like a soccer crowd screaming for the final whistle to blow while they were still ahead. With just 100 metres to go the Abbagnales must have begun to smell the scent of the bouquets that are awarded to the champions. Then it happens. With centimetres left – the killer touch. Just as Solskjaer's injury-time goal in Barcelona would win the European Cup for Manchester United, so the Searles' last few desperate strokes snatched the gold medal away from the Abbagnales. I was on my feet exploding with the crowd, arms in the air: 'YEEES!' In the boat the exhausted brothers find the energy to celebrate, arms punching the air. Maybe Ferguson's players must have thought they had the monopoly on unlikely wins in Barcelona. But it had all been done before.

Youth had had its day. With unashamed sentimentality, pictures floated into my mind of the time when the Searle brothers first came into my life;

fresh-faced schoolboys, looking for a sport to make their own. When he first stepped into a boat, the 13-year-old Jonny Searle had seemed so small and spindly. Somehow, it seemed incredible that, such a boy had just become an Olympic champion. That thought jolted me back to reality. I realised that I had a final of my own to race. I began to move back to the boating area. But as I wandered along the path, I found it hard to stop my thoughts drifting back to the day when I, like Searle, had stepped into a boat for the first time. It was on a summer's day in London over 20 years ago now.

The tide had been flowing out for some hours, leaving great swathes of sloping shingle banks exposed. The silvery grey tideway seemed a long way from the high bank where we stood at the apex of the first bend of the Putney to Mortlake Boat Race course. Sprouting out of the concrete slabs of the long Fulham wall on the opposite bank was the Eric Millar Stand of Craven Cottage, home of Fulham Football Club. A crowd of excited 13-year-olds, clustered round the heavy wooden hulls of the 'tub' fours, the smell of their freshly varnished planks mingling with the characteristic scent of the Thames. Barn Elms Boathouse has launched many a young person on their rowing career, although I'm not sure that many of them would have thought it was as an important a moment in their lives as I thought it was in mine.

The sense of anticipation was high as we carefully wheeled these craft down the concrete ramp, across the crunchy pebbles and slimy stones and slipped them into the river. Stepping out of the water and into the boat felt like an adventure and a kind of release, as I sat there, gently floating, and supported by this great river. I grasped the smoothed handle of the long oar gently and waited to move off, out from the bank and into the stream of life. I had been waiting for this moment for many months, for it was not only a boat that I was launching but also a new life.

It seems a pretty grandiose claim to make for a 13-year-old. But then, that's how I felt. I doubt that was the case for many among the crowd of schoolboys clustered around me on the Putney towpath on that day. Like the characters in the film *The Usual Suspects*, if you scratched the surface you'd find they were all there for similar reasons. 'Failed' soccer players were mixed in with swots, labelled 'unathletic'. Gangly, uncoordinated youths, who couldn't catch a ball, tagged along with disaffected adolescents, who didn't seem to fit in with any group. Like them, I was desperate for two things: acceptance by my peers and to find a sport that I was good at. But for me, it seemed more pressing because my dad was Head of PE.

Twickenham, 1963: Football was not my sport. But at six years old I used to imagine that one day it would be me, playing soccer for the Vaughan on those pitches behind me. Maybe my dad did too. Perhaps that was why he took this picture.

Pat Cross, whom I idolised, had come into education by a circuitous route. He was the eldest of two children, born in East Ham in 1923. His father drove a crane in the London Docks and his mother was a pious lady of Irish descent. It was a joy to her that Pat Cross announced his intention to become a priest. He left Britain in 1937 and spent nine years training at the English College in Lisbon. But to his mother's disappointment, he could not realise his vocation and was promptly called up. Following his National Service and a spell at teacher training college, his first job was at the Cardinal Vaughan School in Kensington, which he joined in 1952. When I arrived, he was already something of a fixture (he was to stay there until 1988). Pat Cross the teacher was larger than life, popular with his colleagues in the staff room and generally liked and respected by the boys. He'd been a good sportsman too, representing his regiment and college at soccer. He was a figure to look up to in every sense of the word.

The 11-year-old boy that I was then, felt very proud to have a dad like him but also daunted; I fell well short of all the standards that I used to measure my father's 'greatness'. I was a failure at football. The only time I got to play for the school, I scored a fantastic goal but it was in the wrong net. I had forgotten which way I should have been kicking! There weren't any other sports at which I felt remotely good at either. I wasn't a particularly good runner and shied away from gymnastics in PE.

This view of myself as a someone who had little sporting talent, or skill, remained embedded deep in my consciousness. It still surfaces occasionally – even now. My confidence was not helped by my studies either. I was not particularly gifted academically. English, maths and languages were poor, the only saving grace was my enthusiasm for history. In short, I did not measure up to the burden of my (and I imagined my dad's) own expectations of the kind of student I should have been.

It wasn't that I had an unhappy childhood, or anything like that. Born in 1957, I was the eldest of three children. My sisters, Catherine and Teresa, arrived in 1960 and 1962 respectively. In order to pay the mortgage, my dad had to hold down a variety of second jobs, as a petrol pump attendant, or a night school instructor. So as soon as my youngest sister was old enough to go school, my mother, Moira, had to return to work. She had an extraordinary energy and many talents, which ran from organising trades unions at British Airways, through acting to painting scenery in amateur dramatics. In many ways, she was an inspiration and my biggest supporter. But the volatility of her father's Celtic temperament and her mother's obstinacy made her a frustrating person to live with on occasions.

My dad used to tell me that she worshipped the ground that I walked on. It was something that I couldn't see then. Now, it's a different matter. If you were to visit my parent's house you'd notice two shrines: on one side of the room a little grotto to the Virgin Mary, with statues and holy pictures; and on the other, one to me, complete with photographs, trophies and certificates. I'm sure that Mary has long forgiven my mother for making my 'shrine' the bigger of the two, although I'm not sure my sisters have the same tolerance. According to them – and I've no reason to doubt their view – at home I was an uncouth, morose and even monosyllabic big brother. But this wasn't how I remember myself at school

There I felt more than a little timid and lonely. The one bright spot on the horizon was rowing. In 1968, Pat Cross took advantage of the Inner London Education Authority's boathouse on the Thames at Putney to introduce the sport to the school. If ever there was an argument for publicly-funded rowing centres, then Barn Elms was it. I was to be one of five Olympic medalists who started their rowing there. Such dreams were then even beyond my father, but by 1970 the Vaughan was producing its first competitive crews.

The standard was not particularly high; my father's colts four could generally win a race or two at regattas before getting knocked out by the more established rowing schools like St George's, or Bedford Modern. It was when I was taken to watch his crew race at Peterborough regatta in 1970 that I made my first acquaintance with the sport. My father, no doubt mindful of my 'failure' as a soccer player, reminded me that I could start rowing when I reached the third year, at the age of 13. From early on, I therefore had it imprinted on my mind that I would be a rower. This would be my sport: my dad had said so…

The trouble was that for a long while I was poor at rowing, everything felt awkward. The blade would frequently dive well below the surface of the water, my hands and forearms ached and, most annoyingly, I did not seem to be able to do anything in time. But if I couldn't row that well, I had to learn to work with others. I could plainly not go off in my little dream world and do my own thing. On the football pitch, I could run up and down and watch the game from afar, maybe getting the odd kick, without ever disturbing too much the game for the other 21 players.

In rowing it was different. My blade had to come through the water at

Row Ridding Farm, 1968: Dad and me on the Lake District farm where I spent most of my childhood holidays.

the same pace, or in the same way as everyone else's. If not, the chances were that either my back would impale itself on somebody else's slower-moving oar handle behind me, or the person in front of me would catch their back on mine. This was a great incentive to try to move together. So here I was in a group of people, who were totally reliant on me performing, as I was on them. We were all learning a new skill from scratch. I may have felt awkward and unsure but it was apparent, in the early stages, that most others felt the same. I therefore stopped regarding myself as less good than others and begun to look at myself in a new light. What's more, being involved in rowing threw me together with boys that I would not normally have associated with.

Derek Bond was one of the tough lads in my year. He was popular and bright; generally a good person to be around. I'm not sure that before I started rowing Derek and I had ever really strung more than a couple of sentences together in three years of school. We were to become firm friends and successful international rowers. Not long after we had begun to row together, I was getting hassled by some boys a year older than me. Derek jumped in to the rescue, informing them that if they wanted to bother me, they would have to deal with him first. I never got any trouble again. It was the first time that anyone had ever done anything like that for me. It was a powerful sign that with rowing my fortunes were changing.

But if I had found some new friends and was on the way to being accepted as part of a group, I was still a long way from being anything approaching a decent schoolboy rower. For all my father's enthusiasm, his coaching skills were rudimentary. If I was to progress further, something dramatic needed to happen, without which, in all probability, I would have long since drifted into rowing's obscure backwaters. In September 1971, a new teacher arrived at the Vaughan.

Jim Clark was an unusual appointment for the post of assistant PE teacher at the Vaughan. Most unusually, he was not a Roman Catholic, or even vaguely religious. Although long hair was the fashion of the time, his was just the wrong side of respectable. He was fresh out of teacher training college at Chester. My father liked him at once, not least because Clark was an international rower of some repute, aiming for the 1972 Olympic Games. No doubt my father must have had my interests somewhere close to his heart when he appointed him

With Clark's appointment, not only had I gained an inspirational coach but also a streetwise role model. From the impressionable age of 14, I was weaned on stories of the world of international rowing. Clark was rowing in the Thames Tradesmen's coxless four, who were on course for Olympic selection. They deliberately cultivated a rebellious image to goad rowing's stuffy establishment, cocking a snoop at the conventional public school or Oxbridge rowers from clubs like Leander. Their long hair, colourful language (they called the Bishop of Chester all sorts of four-letter words for disqualifying them at Henley) and outrageous kit, made them powerful role models to an impressionable adolescent like me.

Almost immediately, I was led into the world of international rowing. After each of Clark's races, I was given blow-by-blow accounts: where pushes had come, how the boat had felt and, if they were racing Cambridge, how they'd 'stuffed those stuck-up public schoolboys'. Already, by the time I was 15, I was living in a world of East German and Russian super-rowers. It was one that I desperately wanted to join.

More than that though, in my adolescence Clark provided a strong sexual image. His nickname at school was 'Man Clark' because he had been spotted kissing his fiancée outside school one day. On the way to rowing sessions, he would tell me of what the 'lads' had got up to the previous night and come out with advice for dealing with girls like: 'Remember your ABC; always be cool.' Cool was the very last thing I was with girls, either then, or now. But I felt that I was genuinely being initiated to a world which I needed to understand and this was a part of growing up, which was never 'taught' at school.

That process was accelerated by Clark's suggestion that I join his club. There, I was an innocent little scout, pitched into a world of cussing and swearing gas fitters, chippies and engineers, all coming down to the wooden shack on the Kew Meadows side of Chiswick Bridge that was then home to Thames Tradesmen's Rowing Club. I learnt more there in a week about relationships with adults, than I had in years with the Boy Scouts (although I would not have recommended any of my new club mates for the post of Scout master). George Hooper, the club chairman, a rotund and burly man, who was proud of the fact that he had never been in the stewards' enclosure at Henley – with 'those bloody toffs' – used to take a group of us youngsters out in an old 'tub' four at weekends. It was not really training, more messing about in boats; it was the best way to learn about rowing.

At the same, Clark was introducing us to basic weight and circuit training. I threw myself into it with all the zeal that I could muster. Now I had a goal to aim for, a coach and role model to guide me and the determination to get there. Quickly, my run times got faster until I was in the top two or three in my year. By the summer of 1972, there was nobody who could beat me round a 'commando' circuit. My body started to fill out, I began to feel and look like a sportsman.

It was during that summer that I won my first 'pot', rowing in a novice

The Tideway, 1972: I looked and felt the most awkward rower in an undistinguished Cardinal Vaughan four racing in the Schools Head. Left to right: Paul Holland, me, Janusz Pietraszewski, Derek Bond, Aiden MacMahon.

eight for TTRC at Horseferry regatta, beating a crew from St Paul's School. From there, Derek Bond and I moved quickly through the junior ranks. It almost felt pre-ordained; how could it be other with Clark as my coach?

His last year at the Vaughan was to be 1974. Then he was rowing in a new British 'super eight', made up of oarsmen from Thames Tradesmen and the socially more exclusive Leander club. The press made much of the social mix at the time. But the rowers couldn't care less. They were under the spell of the legendary Czech coach Bohumil Janousek. 'Bob', as everybody knew him, was a big, thick-set man, who spoke English with a heavy Eastern European accent. He was a man of few words. He hardly ever praised his athletes from whom he always kept a respectable, distance, never mixing socially. But he had a good sense of humour with a laugh that sounded like a donkey's bray. His rowers worshipped him. Clark talked about him in hushed tones: it is hardly surprising that to this day, Janousek remains one of the most charismatic people that I have come across in rowing.

Those were the pre-Redgrave days when British crews used to get beaten by just about everybody. Janousek changed all that. That summer I went to watch his eight (with Clark in it), at the Lucerne World Championships The memory of that large number one, on top of the bows of that beautiful wooden Karlisch shell moving through the field, is one of

21

the most indelible memories of my life, up there with England winning the World Cup. I had travelled to Switzerland, with my tent, to see my hero win Britain's first medal in world rowing for ten years. Everybody said it wouldn't happen. But I knew it would. I fell in love with the beautiful Rotsee course; I knew one day, I would get the chance to race on it in British colours.

But if it was going to happen, it would have to be without Jim Clark – he was moving to a better-paid job at another school. What's more, Derek Bond was over the age limit to race as a junior in 1975 and there was nobody suitable for me to row with at my school. In those days, there was no junior rowing squad system; if you didn't have a school crew, you didn't get in the team.

But then, David Tanner came to the rescue. These days he runs British International Rowing. Then, he was an ambitious Head of History at Ealing Grammar, for whom success on the water was as important as promotion in the classroom. To make up a four, he needed another man. Trouble was, he hadn't done his homework. Tanner thought he had made a coup of getting Derek Bond – who he thought was the stronger out of our pair – to complete his line up; instead he got me.

There was no hiding the disappointment on the faces of the Ealing boys when I turned up on the first day of training in September 1974. It wasn't as if I was exactly ecstatic. Without Jim Clark, I felt like I'd had a magic talisman removed. I wasn't sure that I could do it either under Tanner's guidance, or on my own. As I stepped into an Ealing boat for the first time, I felt more lonely than I had for a long while in rowing.

Perhaps it was this that gave me the motivation to prove myself among my new crew mates. Certainly the competition inherent in the squad system that Tanner ran at Ealing was very conducive to the type of hard training sessions that I liked. Soon it became clear that there were four of us significantly better than the other members of the squad. John Beattie, Ian McNuff and Robin Roberts and I were all very evenly matched in the boat, even if we did have different abilities in running, soccer, or circuit training. I was not to know then that we would spend the next seven years rowing

Kensington 1973: Derek Bond (left) and I, display a season's silverware outside Cardinal Vaughan School. Our medals were for winning the National Junior 16 pairs title. Some of the silverware was won in composite crews with Thames Tradesmen's RC.

together, or that our friendships which were built then would last a lifetime. For me, they quickly became a point of reference in a rapidly changing world.

John Beattie, who looked the image of Joe 90, was a county class swimmer, who came into rowing late mainly because he had gotten fed up of watching boys who he thought were lesser sportsmen than him go up on stage to get pint tankards on Monday morning assemblies. I was always jealous of John's abilities at other sports, particularly soccer, and often in awe of his lightning fast brain which he used to squeeze any advantage out of an opponent. John had an innate sense of rhythm and with his 'magic foot' (in a coxless boat the rudder is attached to one of the rower's shoes which requires very sensitive movements), he always steered the boat on a better course than our opponents.

Robin Roberts was the biggest and strongest of the four of us. So even now, it's difficult to make sense of his death from a brain tumour at the age of 42. He didn't shine at any sport, although I suppose if Ealing had put out a rugby team then rowing would have lost him to the scrum. Robin had a very calm, even temper and liked nothing better than to row long strokes at low intensities for miles and miles during the winter. I always felt particularly at ease with his presence behind me in the boat. When things got frenetic, or the conditions rough, Roberts was like a port in a storm.

Ian McNuff was the rebel in the boat. His Afro-style hair-do set him apart from most other rowers of the time – junior, or senior. An only child, he was a talented sportsman and musician. There was just a hint, which I never got to the bottom of, that he'd mixed with a group of scallies in his early teens and been lucky not to get his fingers burnt. Rowing seemed a bit of a pathway to respectability for him, and his intensively competitive nature was ideally suited to the sport. When he stopped rowing, he lost no time in switching his energies – with some success – to the struggle for a top job in National Westminster Bank. Both he and I were well matched in the gymnasium and in running-speeds – significantly faster than the others. We were room mates and I was his best man. For me, he was the brother that I never had, although I sensed that my need for his companionship was greater than his.

There could not be a bigger contrast between my old coach Jim Clark and my new one, David Tanner. The former a champion rower, with an intensely strong physical presence, the latter looking like a bespectacled academic, not remotely athletic. What saved him from educational, or

Ealing, 1975: Schoolboy heroes. Our four – pictured here just after our Henley victory – had won almost everything we had entered. We pose in front of Ealing School with coach David Tanner.

academic, obscurity was his ambition, organisational flair and determination to push his abilities in other areas. He had an intimidating presence as a teacher. (I have seen more than one sixth former quail at his implicit threat that their UCAS reference might not be quite what they expected). In 1974, he was only 27. Perhaps it was his school-masterly manner, as much as my inability to guess older people's ages, which made me think that he was then already 49 years old. But then David is nothing if not an enigmatic character. I could not have remotely guessed, when I met him, that he would become one of my closest friends and that our personal and professional relationships in rowing would continue to the present day. In the sport of rowing, both of us had found an outlet for our personalities that it would be difficult if not impossible to let go of in later years.

Together, the five of us were a potent mixture. By the start of the season I had done enough to show that I could stroke the boat. It was where I wanted to be; the glamour seat. Stroke always gets a mention in the press, where other members of the crew miss out. Moreover, there's always the suggestion that the person who strokes the boat is just that little bit harder, or tougher, than the rest. This isn't always the case but at the time, I certainly allowed myself to believe it.

We achieved some outstanding results through our junior season. We were comfortably the fastest schoolboy four, ahead of a crew from Hampton School. But more than that we proved fast enough to beat many of the best men's fours racing that year. Although not Jim Clark's four, who beat us by some distance at the National championships. It was in that race, that I felt that I had really come of age, as I sat in the lane next to my schoolboy hero for the first time.

John was as sharp as ever while the six boats in the final were sat together on the start. There was a bit of a crosswind, making aligning difficult. Normally, if they are slightly off course, rowers indicate, by raising their hands, to the distant starter located in a tower up to 50 metres away. But John, perhaps conscious of the international boat's apparent nervousness next to us, raised his hand and shouted a loud 'no' as our boat began to drift slightly off course. Jim's crew took this for the 'go' and rowed off, only to be awarded a false start. It was the last thing they wanted,

Henley, 1975: The 'Ealing' four on the way to taking the Visitors' Cup. From left to right: John, Ian, Rob and me.

Montreal, 1975: The champion GDR junior four (none of whom I have ever seen since), pose with our four. From the right: Robin, me, John and Ian. Shorts were not team issue then, hence the variety of styles on display.

particularly as they had to race a fast Cambridge four. Now, I was no longer the budding protégé but a bothersome opponent. Under his breath, as they re-attached themselves to the start, Jim called us a 'bunch of wankers'. I felt proud of John's actions and of the implicit complement that Jim's remarks implied – it was only what he would have told me to do in the same circumstances.

Although we lost that race, we were more fortunate against other college crews, winning the Visitors' Challenge Cup at Henley Royal Regatta. This was a mighty achievement for any schoolboy crew. We went from there to win a silver in the final of the World Junior Championships, rowing through the field from last place to snatch the medal on the line. The East Germans were out in front. Perhaps without that country's seeming perpetual sporting domination of rowing – a significant part of which we now know was achieved with the use of drugs – we might have been less pleased to have finished second. But it was a fantastic result which left us hungry for more. That autumn McNuff, Beattie and I approached Tanner to coach us as a senior crew, with an aim of achieving full international honours. Roberts felt that he wanted to take his life at his own pace for a while and stopped.

So now, we were the new kids on the block, cocksure and not a little arrogant. Bond moved back into the boat to replace Roberts. Even then our ambitious aim of achieving selection for the senior team at the World Championships within two years seemed a formality. Almost everything in our lives was directed to that end. I cut my roots, switching from the proletarian atmosphere of TTRC to the more bourgeois surrounds of London Rowing Club at Putney. The latter offered us exclusive use of a new German boat; at Tradesmen, we would have to compete for a boat with another crew. So we became the flagship of a club that was the London home to many Oxbridge graduates looking to continue their rowing.

The atmosphere, although pleasant, was decidedly more snooty than at TT. I felt awkward leaving my first club. But then it was easy to be seduced by a club which had superior facilities and fantastic contacts at the Henley Royal Regatta. That year, we dined in the stewards' dining tent, guests of 'Farn' Carpmael, president of LRC. No doubt, old George Hooper would not have approved. But then sentimentality and sporting success do not usually go hand in hand. London gave us a tremendously stable and supportive environment within which to train. In our first year as seniors, we won the Wyfold Cup at Henley, a tough event for senior rowers. The following season we secured selection for the senior World Rowing Championships in Amsterdam. Our tenth place finish did not dampen the feelings that we had arrived in the international rowing world proper.

That year, Jim Clark won a silver medal in the pairs. In years to come, I knew that without his influence, the closest I would have got to international rowing would have been the slipway at Barn Elms. But there I was, clocking up a fourth Olympiad in Barcelona.

It was Jon Searle's first Games and already he had become an Olympic champion. From then on, I became more aware that when I looked at Jon Searle the rower, the more it was like looking into a mirror and seeing a reflection of a something that looked like a younger version of myself. He was a successful junior international who, like me, had gone on to achieve senior success. He seemed to have a youthful arrogance, or certainty that his own innate racing ability was better than that of his opponents – or sometimes, for that matter, his crewmates; that too was familiar. Both of us loved spending time in each other's company, more often than not exchanging the latest gossip on rowing's relationships: who was going out with who, or which crew had been faster than another on a recent training piece.

We both shared something of a crusading zeal to right wrongs or abuses in the way the sport was run, something which had gotten both of us into trouble. The urge to rebel was never far from the surface in each of our characters. In a way, we were both rebels. But one of the most intriguing things we shared was the fact that we were both motivated and inspired by a teacher while we were in our teens: with me it was Jim Clark; for Jon Searle, it was Martin Cross.

Although we had spent a few years as colleagues and even crew-mates in senior teams, I had never thought to ask Jon about the influence I had on him as a youth. It was not until I had stopped international rowing, and Jon was training for Sydney, that over breakfast after an outing I asked him who his first rowing hero was. With a big grin and a hint of awkwardness, he said loudly, 'You.'

For a moment, the redness in our faces must have matched each other. I remember laughing to ease the tension I felt; as I did so, Jon told me why it was that he had held me in such esteem.

I had been teaching Jon at Hampton School for almost six years, when I competed in the Los Angeles Olympics. Now, well into his second year of rowing, Jon relished the chance to watch his teacher on television challenge

Henley, 1976: The last stroke of the final of the Wyfold Cup. It was one of my hardest Henley races. This view of the river banks, packed with spectators and the lack of any bends, explain why so many rowers make Henley the focus of their season.

for a gold medal. More that 15 years later, the images of my crew rowing through the mist on California's Lake Casitas were indelibly etched on his mind. I begun to realise that the race and medal ceremony had a huge impact on him.

But it went further than that. Jon went on to explain: 'Do you remember when you did that assembly after you came back?'

As he said it, a long-forgotten image came into my mind of hundreds of exuberant children in front of me, clapping like mad while I held a medal aloft like a captain who has just won the FA Cup, displaying it to his supporters. Then, I had felt a strange mixture of exultation and sheepishness. Now, as Jon spoke, I felt much the same things. He went on: 'I felt this intense pride that I actually knew somebody who had won the highest honour in sport and I suppose from that moment on, I had an intense desire to do the same. The funny thing was that for weeks afterwards, I would go to sleep and in my head would be a picture of you crossing the line.'

There haven't been many occasions in my life when I've realised that something I've done has made a real difference to the way somebody else saw themselves; that day in the café was one of those moments. I think we both looked a bit embarrassed, the way people sometimes do when they've connected on a different level beyond that of their normal relationship; to release the tension, I asked Jon if he wanted another cappuccino. I knew that I wanted to talk some more and wanted a bit of time to reflect.

As I got up from the table, I found myself thinking about Jon as a youngster. Most rowers don't dream of winning an Olympic gold medal for as long and from as early in their careers as Jon Searle did. Perhaps that powerful urge helped him and his brother close the seemingly impossible distance between them and the Abbagnales?

The funny thing was, when I first came across him, at Hampton, I never had him marked out as a rower, let alone potential Olympic champion. I remembered him as a thin spindly, little boy; all arms and legs, who only just squeezed into the bow seat of the school eight during his first season as a 13-year-old. Then, there was no indication that he would be anything other than just another rower who hadn't made it at soccer, cricket, or his father's game of rugby.

I could see that if he wasn't immediately a star, starting rowing had helped to take away his adolescent conviction that he was 'no good at sport'. Maybe it had also given him the chance to make friends and connect with his contemporaries in the way that it had helped me? One thing was clear: when he turned 15, and a growth spurt kicked in, he moved from being one of the weakest to almost the strongest rower. That year, his crew won the School's championships. Success at Junior International level followed, with a fairly seamless transition to the senior team.

By the time I was walking back to the table with our drinks, I felt certain of the similarities between my own beginnings in the sport and his; even down to the relationship with his coach, Steve Gunn. Steve was one of those rowing-mad bachelors who seem to spend every spare hour they had coaching on the river or urging the boys on in the gym. Like Jim Clark, Steve had was an exceptionally strong and outspoken character. More important, for the first time, under Steve Gunn, Jon felt as if a teacher was treating him like an adult. His previous coaches, Tony Creber and Jules Fox, had hardly ever swore at him (at least not to his face). With Steve that changed; it became part of the rhetoric of a training session. I'd felt the same when Jim Clark began to coach me at school.

The conversation flowed easily for another hour as we compared how our schools and coaches had influenced us as we got older. We agreed about most things, especially Hampton School.

Unlike the Vaughan, which had little background or rowing tradition, Hampton has produced more junior internationals than any other school in

Lake Banyolas, 1992: The Searle brothers charge past the Abbagnales in the final strokes of the Olympic coxed pairs final.

31

the country. Dan Topolski, the famous Oxford coach, once wrote of Hampton boys: 'There was always something special about them, they always had something of the underdog with the chip on their shoulder, or the canny street fighter about them.' Jonny Searle fell into both these categories.

More than anything, Hampton fostered the spirit of the underdog; the small, plucky street fighters from a minor independent school, up against the 'big guns' of the likes of Eton, Radley and St Paul's. Jon's choice of clubs after school perpetuated this. Searle chose to remain a member of Molesey Boat Club, Hampton's base on the Thames. With most of the British internationals rowing out of Leander, training out of Molesey was like being a member of a rebel outpost. It was a spirit that Searle revelled in, much as I did while a member of TTRC, although I think with him it ran deeper.

If you cut Jon open, I suspect you would find that at its core, his heart was yellow and black, the colours of Hampton School and Molesey Boat Club. I reminded him of the time we raced together in the eight for the worlds in '91. Jon Searle was rowing at '4', right behind his brother, Greg at '5'. In a crucial race, we were trailing; our race plan hadn't worked. Then I heard Jon say to Greg: 'Come on Greg, let's you and me go for a Hampton 50 stroke burn; just the two of us...go now!'

Hampton figured too, when in the following year Jon was looking for someone to coach him and his brother in preparation for the Barcelona Olympics. He turned to his old school coach, Steve Gunn, then Head of Sixth Form at Hampton. For Jon, victory with Steve Gunn as his coach in the Olympics was almost like reliving his schoolboy triumphs at Henley and the National Schools. Steve continued to coach Searle for another four years, up to the Atlanta Games. I always thought that Searle's very public display of annoyance on the medal rostrum at Atlanta – it reminded me of a petulant child – was as much about his feelings of having let Steve Gunn down, as it was of finishing third behind the French and Australians.

This was one thing over which Jon and I disagreed: perhaps I was taking the psychoanalysis a bit too far? Once he told me that he didn't want to delve too deeply into his mind and the reasons why he was a great rower, for the fear that if he discovered 'the truth', he might then lose the magic ingredient which had made him such a success.

There is no doubt that Jon had something special. Big as he had been among schoolboy crews, in the world of international rowing he was a comparative shrimp. During tests on the Rowing Machine, or 'Ergo', which measures power output, he nearly always came bottom of the squad. Usually in training and often during the early-season regattas, his performances were nothing out of the ordinary.

But on the big occasion, like the Olympics, during racing he somehow seemed to come alive. When the pressure was on, he'd become like a demon, an aggressive racing brain combined with an innate ability to motivate his crewmates. This was especially the case in the second half of races when his crew needed to produce something extra. Jon's gift allowed him to be the catalyst for some incredible performances. Usually the person that Jon was inspiring was his brother, Greg.

Their age difference had meant that they were never able to row together while at school but for years Jon had dreamt of them rowing in the same crew. This was one aspect of Jon's life that was very different to mine. In my years at school and beyond, I had always missed the closeness that I suspected a relationship with a brother might bring, Instead, I looked for this with my crewmates. However, knowing Jon, I realised that having a brother did not always bring the chance of filial bliss.

His 'kid' brother, was much bigger in stature and stronger too. While Jon was trying to explain away his poor ergo scores, Greg was breaking world records on the machine. To his credit, Jon never seemed to allow this to outwardly bother him, but there was no doubt it lurked in the background.

More than ever, that day in the café, I came to understand that the brash, sometimes cocky personality that I'd always come to associate with Jon's character was as much there as a kind of shield to protect his own sensitivities as it was the nature of the man.

That fact came home to me again a year or so later, after the finals of the 1999 World Rowing Championships in St Catherine's, Canada. Jon's route on the comeback trail had won him a seat in the British coxed four. It wasn't an Olympic class boat. But a good result at the World Championships would give him a real shot at the Olympic team.

He rowed a tremendous race, his crew taking a silver medal behind the boat from the USA. Garry Herbert, (his cox from Barcelona), and I were commentating on the race for BBC television and were thrilled with the result. I was looking forward to an easy post-race interview for *Grandstand*. I couldn't have been more wrong. It was like the Atlanta medal ceremony take two. Searle (and the rest of the crew) were extremely fed up that they hadn't won gold; what's more, they looked it. I was prepared to do an upbeat piece about Jonny Searle back on the medal trail and there was this face full of gloom. Searle and his crew mates knew that anything less than gold would make his route back into the Olympic team more difficult.

Just then, the image of his pair triumphing in Barcelona flashed through my mind. Without thinking, I asked him about the possibility that he might again strike up a pair with his brother. It was a fair question from a BBC interviewer but not from a friend and former teacher. We both knew that as much as Greg would like to row with Jon again, the coaches were almost certainly likely to want Greg to row with a rower who they thought better; someone bigger and stronger than Jon. He fluffed his response to the question terribly. I felt guilty, as after the interview he asked for his response to that question be edited out.

So for the Searle brothers, Sydney was never going to be Barcelona mark two. Their inspirational cox, Garry Herbert, was now a television commentator. Steve Gunn had travelled to the other side of the globe to coach in New Zealand. For Jon, the realities of 'life' had set in: work, relationships, babies made matters more complicated than they'd been in his previous two Olympiads. But in 2000, nothing seemed to dent his determination, not only to win a place in an Olympic boat but to win another gold medal in Sydney.

But fate intervened. Just six weeks before the key spring trials, which could have won him an Olympic place, he skidded off his black Triumph motorbike and broke his right arm. The plaster was due off only days before the trials: it was 'game over'. But Jon refused to give up. He insisted on training with his plaster cast, using only his inside arm to hold the blade. One arm rowing is not the most comfortable way to enjoy the sport, as I found out to my cost when I agreed to row a few outings with him in a pair.

Incredibly, Jon somehow managed to race at the trials, just a few days after his cast came off. His pair, though, with veteran Richard Stanhope, was beaten into last place. In reality, all hope of an Olympic selection was gone. In vain, Jon tried to throw his hat in the ring as a single sculler – never his strong suit – but was well off the pace. By May, even he had to admit defeat. However, the Olympics were too powerful a draw for him to ignore. He took a vacation to see his brother race and was lucky enough to pick up some work as a television pundit.

As he stood by the side of Penrith Lakes watching the Olympic finals, it would have been hard for him not to think back to that day in Barcelona some eight years previously. Then it had been my turn to stand and watch

Lake Banyolas, 1992: Jonny and Greg Searle are captured together with cox Garry Herbert on the Barcelona victory raft moments before the presentation of medals. I was moved by the almost childlike tenderness in their embrace.

the sport crown new Olympic champions. Now it was Jon's. I've no doubt that he believed that it could have been him out there on the lake, if circumstances had been a little different. Truth was that the necessities of life had caught up with the young rebel. It was now his turn to face the fact that his moment of Olympic glory had come and gone.

Harry's Game

IN 1977, tired and hot from my exertions after finishing fourth in the 'B' final, I got out of my boat oblivious to anything except the desire to get to the finish line and watch the top coxless fours race for the gold medal. Next year, the 'worlds' would be in New Zealand and I imagined that I would be in the 'A' final, playing with the big boys. I pushed through the crowds and found a good spot to see the closing moments of the race. To my surprise, the New Zealand boat ran the Olympic champions from East Germany surprisingly close. As I watched the crews slumped over their blades, the sound of brief congratulations floated back to me from across the water. To those forced, breathless almost grunted noises, was added the sound of a man standing next to me. In an unmistakable Kiwi drawl he shouted to his crew, 'Good race guys,' then continued to watch the scene in silence. At the time, I didn't know who he was, or his name, Until I saw somebody pat him on the shoulder and say, 'Well done Harry.'

Even then, with a balding head and greyish beard, Harry Mahon had more than a passing resemblance to Obi Wan Kenobi, the character played by Alec Guinness in the film *Star Wars.* These days, the likeness is even greater: lines on his weather-beaten face suggest wisdom born from years of intent study of the movement of rowers and their craft. Off the water, he is a man of few words. But in a way, this adds to the mystique because on the water, his speech flows endlessly, like the awareness of a boat's movement that he is trying to unlock in the minds of those he coaches. When I hear him coach, I can't help thinking of Obi Wan's wish, 'May the Force be with you.'

When you see Mahon's crews race at their best, it is easy to understand why so many rowers and coaches feel drawn towards the man who seems to know how to unlock this hidden power. If you want to know what I mean, watch a video of the British eight winning a gold medal at the Sydney Olympics. Mahon's boats seem to ghost along, apparently effortlessly. There is the movement, fluidity and style of a Brazilian soccer team at its best, the awesome speed of a Michael Johnson. Yet they have a gentleness of touch like Tiger Woods, as he chips in from 60 feet. It is enough to send shivers down your spine, as his crews propel their fragile shells across water in a way that is almost magical.

As you've probably gathered by now, these days I am one of Mahon's disciples. But back then as I prepared for the new season in 1978, there was nothing that Mahon could have taught me. I didn't need 'The Force'. Speed in rowing came through effort or trying more. If in doubt 'pull harder' was my catch phrase. It wasn't my style to pay much attention to such subtleties as the feeling of the boat. I played to my strengths, rowing a longer stroke, hitting a harder catch, or pulling a stronger finish. To put it in football terms, I reckon that Graham Taylor would have loved me; work-rate was the key; fancy passing would never have been a substitute for the long ball. With all due apologies to David Batty, I was out of his mould, rather than that of a cultured Zidane.

In the winter of 1977, there was little to challenge the way I perceived myself, that was until Derek Bond announced his retirement one night at the start of a gym session. The arrival of Dave Townsend was to break the cosy little relationship that we had developed in our crew. 'Tosser', as his friends and foes alike knew him, was already a rower of some repute, having competed in the Montreal Olympics. He was three years older than us, although sometimes it seemed like 30. There was no doubt that Dave was a mature, sensible and ambitious man. His public school education, let alone his flat and job (he was president of the London University Students' Union), marked him out from us grammar school boys – we still lived with our parents. With Dave around, it was as if we were now rowing with a 'grown-up'. What's more he had a clear idea of how he wanted us to row. Harry would have approved.

Dave spoke the language of 'The Force', urging me to be more discerning about the way the boat moved in between strokes, or be less brutal with the way my blade entered the water at the start of the stroke. To me this felt disturbing. Not only was I less sure about relationships in the boat, but the efficiency of the way I rowed (of which I had always been pretty sure) was now being called into question. Rowing in the key 'three' seat, just behind me, Dave was the 'playmaker' of the crew. It was his job to set the boat up with his poise, length and rhythm. He had an ability to reproduce the same movement every stroke, with a kind of metronomic efficiency. Now I can see that his style was the perfect foil to my aggressive 'pull-harder' approach – when the synthesis worked, we went fast. Those days, I wasn't so understanding.

This was especially the case when, during outings, he would come out with, 'Crossy, Let's try a little less hard and get more run out of the boat.'

Lucerne, 1978: Our four with Dave at '3' paddling over a perfectly still Rotsee. I love this photograph; to see why just turn it upside down.

Now in rowing this is generally a pretty useful comment; like the advice of the golf pro who advises his pupil to try hitting the ball less hard and then sees the ball go further. But golf was never my game (I still try and smack the hell out of the ball). So Dave's advice usually fell on deaf ears. What's more, I often saw it as a challenge. My whole rationale was to try harder; it's not surprising that on occasions the tension between us boiled over into open conflict on the water.

Over Easter 1978 we were training on the beautiful Lake Sarnen, six kilometres long and surrounded by snow-capped mountains in the heart of Switzerland. The first piece of work hadn't been so good. During the few minutes rest, Dave started making suggestions about changing rhythm for the second piece. I went on the attack straight away with a reply that contained lots of four-letter words and the assertion, 'If YOU would pull harder, we might go faster.'

On this occasion the president's diplomacy deserted him. Apart from the personality clash, my way of rowing was probably challenging his own perceptions of what it meant to be 'hard'. So Dave weighed in with the riposte, 'If you stopped to think about your rowing for just one second...'

Our slanging match, which stopped short of blows, was interrupted only by the necessity to start the second piece, with me muttering under my breath, 'Match that you soft bastard.' I set off as hard as I could go for a piece which should have been at half-power. Dave, rather than just row at

Two crews that played Harry's Game to perfection: *Above,* Lucerne, 1982: New Zealand winning the World Championships by a street. I like to see the relaxed expressions, even though the crews are working flat out. *Below*, Great Britain, pictured during their repechage win, their best row of the Olympic Regatta.

half-pressure, picked up my gauntlet and was pulling as hard as he could. Neither he nor I let up for the whole 20-minute piece, our grunts and groans echoing around the mountains of the Bernese Oberland. At the end we were both exhausted. Ian and John, rowing in the bows behind us, were smiling, having rowed at the correct pressure throughout. After that, I never doubted how 'hard' Dave could be and, rather grudgingly, thought I needed to listen to him a bit more.

By the first races of the 1978 season something was clearly working. We were much faster than the previous year, beating all the boats from Western Europe. The press started to take note of our performance. We were featured in a *Guardian* article entitled 'Ealing Four Sketch a Bolder Canvas'. It concluded with a quote from Jim Clark. He'd subbed in for a few outings in the winter and been impressed with what he'd experienced. 'Let the hero have the last word,' it started. 'They're good and strong, yes, I think they'll make the final in New Zealand'.

It seemed a reasonable aim to try to make the 'A' final. It was clearly too soon to aim for a medal. The East Germans were as fast as ever but even they had been beaten by a new Russian combination. Then there was the New Zealand four, silver medalists from the previous year when they were coached by Harry Mahon. Surely on their home waters they would be too difficult for us to beat?

Matters hadn't been helped by an illness of John Beattie's, which necessitated us missing both Henley and Lucerne regattas. This meant that we would be travelling to the Southern Hemisphere without the vital experience of top competition. At the time, though, all this seemed secondary to the excitement of a trip of a lifetime. None of the World Championships that I've been to remotely rivals the 'Karapiro Experience'. For me, it was simply the best championships ever.

It helped enormously that we would start our training camp on the less testing waters of Sydney's Paramatta River. Sydney Rowing Club were to be our hosts for a month. We were joined there by teams from the USA and Canada, with whom there was more than one amorous liaison (as usual the Canadian team had far more women than men). I lost my heart to a 17-year-old spare called Cathy Lund. Unfortunately, after a promising start walking along Manley beach, my John Travolta impersonation on the dance floor at the Sydney Rowing Club party failed to impress her; neither did the obligatory white shirt and matching trousers that I'd bought in the Harrods sale.

Despite my efforts to dance like an extra from *Saturday Night Fever*, Sydney Rowing Club was a fantastic place to train. Even in those pre-*Neighbours* days, it was a lot more romantic to have Sydney Harbour Bridge and the Opera House down river, than Tower Bridge and the Tower of London. Perhaps Australians training on the Thames thought differently? But when you have come with mud-laden feet from the slimy River Thames, the pleasantly hot spring climate, combined with the greeny blue shade of the Paramatta, almost turned rowing into a different sport. What's more, there was a hint of adventure lurking up in one of the river's creeks, where sharks were said to lurk around the discharge of a meat factory. At that time you were lucky if you could even spot a fish in the Thames. At the rowing club there were tables laden with fresh fish for every meal. Oysters for breakfast became the norm.

Gradually, through the camp our speed improved. We won the warm-up regatta at Penrith. The finish was signalled with a shotgun blast as the leading crew crossed the line. Legend had it that a jealous coach once tried to sink the opposition's crew with a well-aimed blast. That night, our normally staid and sober coach, David Tanner, got blind drunk at the party following the regatta. Legend has it that he waltzed round the dance floor with a slot machine, rather than dance with Penny Chuter, who was then coaching Jim Clark. Tanner's was the only coach's face missing from the team photograph the next morning. But he had done his job. Our boat was vying for speed with the World Championship double of Baillieu and Hart and the silver medal pair of Clark and Roberts. As the team moved to Lake Karapiro for the World Championships, we were expected to put in a strong showing.

Visiting New Zealand was a bit like being in some rural English backwater where time had been suspended for 30 years. Everything seemed green; there were no motorways to speak of – it was like driving on the Isle of Wight. Sheep and cattle seemed to abound everywhere. The famous rowing clubs that I'd heard of just seemed to be little more than tin shacks, unlike the grand buildings of London, or Leander rowing clubs. I wondered how on earth this little island could have produced such fantastic rowers.

While staying in Hamilton we came across our first Maoris. They seemed to be among the town's 'down and outs'. In Australia, the only Aborigine that I'd seen was a guy working cleaning out a cage at Sydney Zoo. In the days when Cathy Freeman wasn't even a glint in her father's eye, it was clear that in Australia racial prejudice against the Aboriginal population was fairly rife. But somehow I hadn't expected to see it in New Zealand with the Maoris.

Nevertheless, the atmosphere around the regatta course was the friendliest and most enthusiastic that I have ever experienced. For the opening ceremonies, the Maoris were back in their more familiar ceremonial roles. The mood was markedly different to any other regatta or championship. Even the normally reserved athletes from Eastern Europe

Sydney, 2000: The Olympics came to Penrith 22 years after I first rowed there. For everyone except Andrew Lindsay, the Olympic eights final is still in progress: Australia and Croatia charge, but somehow, above the noise of the crowd, the British bowman hears the sound of the finish buzzer.

seemed to loosen up, although we knew that of the KGB and Staazi informers and agents were still in evidence. Even they must have been entranced by the atmosphere around this distant lake at the opposite end of the world.

But if anybody thought that its remote location would prove a problem to draw the New Zealand sporting public, they were wrong. The size of the crowds were phenomenal. For the opening ceremony of these championships there was no racing, just a row-past, yet an unprecedented 14,000 people turned up to watch. That day set the tone for the championships. Security was relaxed and there was almost a carnival atmosphere in the crews' boating area.

Tension returned for our first race. We drew the in-form crew from the USSR. That meant that we would almost certainly have to race again in the repechage round to make the final. At halfway, after a good start, I wondered what on earth was going on. We were leading the race and the Russians were nowhere. I kept waiting for a push to come from them. But it never materialised. We crossed the line first in a state of absolute delight, our season's objective achieved in one row. What we later found out, was that the Soviets were playing the 'repechage game'. Short of race practice, they had calculated that their speed in the final would be enhanced if they had a second race in a subsequent round.

So the Soviets were a different prospect in the 'A' final. Their power was phenomenal, not least because they were all monstrously big men. Valeri Dolinin, who rowed in the 'two' seat, was like a character straight out of a Dostoevsky novel; he drank vodka like water whenever he got the chance. If I thought my rowing was rough and ready, I had only to look at the brutal way he and his crewmates performed. Their blades buried far too deep in the water, bodies all over the place, but for some reason (I suspect that drugs may have had something to do with it) they could fly.

We never saw them in the final. They were so far in front after only 250 metres. Dave, who had not seen them go, later told me that he assumed we were leading and it was us or the East Germans for the gold medal. Reality set in, though, when the 'East' took off with 500 metres to go, just failing to catch the tiring Russians on the line. Nevertheless, we held off the Czechs, French and the young West Germans (the New Zealand crew had failed to make the final) to take what was a pretty brilliant bronze medal. It was by far the biggest crowd that I've ever raced in front of and they cheered us to the rafters when we were presented with our medals. Thirty-four thousand Kiwis cheering a British medal sounded fantastic.

They weren't so enchanted with their eight's bronze medal in the last race of the regatta. Harry Mahon's crew had failed to fulfil the burden of expectation placed on it. This was hardly surprising. Mahon favoured keeping his silver medal four together from the previous year. But the selectors didn't think anything counted unless it was the eight. All week the crowd had drunk from cans of lager emblazoned with New Zealand's gold medal eight from the '72 Olympics. The Kiwi crew couldn't even drown their sorrows without feeling guilty.

A crew that Harry Mahon would have been proud of was the British pair of Jim Clark and his partner John Roberts in the coxless event. These two were the smoothest pair around. Johnny Roberts was rowing's Paul Gascoigne of his era – silky skills in the boat, minimal training, interspersed with plenty of beers. They took silver behind the East German Landvoight brothers. Three years from leaving school I had joined Jim on the medal podium.

At the age of 21, I'd achieved all that I'd ever wanted from international rowing – to win a medal. In those days 21 was a pretty tender age to pick up a medal. It was almost too much to contemplate. In fact, I didn't take it off for over a week. The other thing that remained glued to my body was an East German racing singlet. You couldn't swap them as you traded your vests with the other teams – the 'Easties' were forbidden to trade them. But some of them, desperate for hard currency would sell theirs quietly. I paid £15 for mine.

As the curtain fell on the regatta, to the spectacular sights and sounds of two enormous Maori war canoes paddling up the course, I stood alone by the lake and was moved to tears by the haunting sound of the Maori horns and chants. They were the same cries as Cook's sailors had first heard when they were homeward bound from their Polynesian paradise over 200 years earlier. Perhaps they were similarly moved, as they, like I, felt the magic of a moment that would never be repeated.

Success brought its rewards, but they were pretty thin pickings. A slot on *Grandstand* and an invitation to a couple of sports award lunches. Of course, we were shoved at the back of the room. Successful rowers like us realised that we were only minor stars in the sporting firmament. But to us, it still felt like heaven. For the first time we were rubbing shoulders with 'real' sporting personalities. Seb Coe, Ron Greenwood and Sharron Davies were all there.

But the most significant award we received was a grant from the Sports Aid Foundation. This charity, started by sports enthusiasts like millionaire shipping tycoon Eddie Kulukundis, for the first time enabled British athletes to take on the state-funded sporting might of Eastern Europe. The sum of £4,000 was a relatively huge amount of money for its day and enabled us, not just to eat properly but to spend valuable time away on still-water training camps. The debt owed by British sport to the founders of the SAF is immense.

That level of funding enabled us to focus exclusively on our goal of a medal in the Moscow Games. But before that, lay another World Championships, in Yugoslavia.

It was a country that I never really understood. As a historian, I knew it was formed after World War One. But I never appreciated the polyglot nature of its nationalities. As far as I knew, one Yugoslav was the same as another. While out drinking a coffee during the championships, I got into conversation with a waiter. To my surprise, he insisted that he was Serbian not, Yugoslavian. Then, I wasn't even aware that Bled was in an area of a different culture; that of the Slovenians. It was to be another decade before Yugoslavia was torn apart by a brutal war and Slovenia was to win its freedom. But in 1979, there was not even the merest hint that this might be in the future.

Since World War Two the Serbian strongman Marshal Tito had kept the diverse nationalities together with a mixture of Communist government, flavoured with a hint of capitalist economics. Tito spent his summers by the shores of Lake Bled where the championships were to be held. He built an imposing villa on the lake's eastern shore.

When you take your first look around the lake of Bled, you can see why he chose that location. It is one of the world's most beautiful and spectacular lakes, let alone rowing courses. Nestling in the heart of the Slovenian Alps, it is dominated at one end by a castle perched on top of a sheer cliff face which plunges dramatically into the deep blue water. Towards the finish, the focus shifts to a beautiful little pine-clad island. From among the trees rise the whitewashed walls and spire of a church. In summer tourists are ferried around it gondola fashion. Sometimes they are lucky enough to see a bride and groom returning after their marriage.

In this most romantic of locations you can just about squeeze a 2,000 metres course into the lake, so the start is tight up against the town-end of the lake. From the many hotels and cafes, tourists sip their cappuccinos and could almost reach out and touch the rowers sitting ready to begin their races. It all adds to the atmosphere of an unforgettable venue to which rowers love to return.

The World Championships had last been held in Bled in 1966. Then, according to legend, the New Zealand eight had written off a grand piano in the midst of an infamous last night binge. But if there were to be any more virtuoso performances from the Kiwi competitors in 1979, Harry Mahon was not going to be the conductor. For us, winning a bronze medal had been a huge success; for Mahon's eight it had been akin to a sporting disaster – one for which Mahon had to face a different kind of music. He was dropped.

In fact, New Zealand did not even send a crew to race in our event. We still faced the East Germans (out to avenge their defeat) and the Soviets (who seemed to have lost none of their speed) and there was a fast crew from Czechoslovakia. During the season we had been beaten by all these crews. There were no fairy stories this time in the first heat. We had to qualify for the final the hard way.

Winning a medal the year before might have made me more relaxed about our prospects of repeating it in Bled. In fact, the reverse was true. I was desperate to prove to others and myself that we were 'worthy' medalists – that the previous year's result hadn't been some kind of fluke.

At 500 metres in the 'A' final the odds looked against us. We were lying in fourth place behind a rampant East German four, the powerful Soviets and a new Czech crew who clearly had our measure. It was then that luck began to play a role. Dolinin, from the Soviet crew, had been having back problems all year. In order to race the final he had to have a cortisone injection administered to him by the Swedish team doctor. It may have affected them because just before the 1,000 metres their steering became erratic and the inevitable happened; one of their blades caught a plastic buoy. The resultant 'crab' lost them half a length. They were 'on the ropes' and we 'caught them with a few', launching a massive 'push' to take us clear of them to within a few feet of the second-placed Czechs on the line.

It was bronze again and, what's more, we were the only medalists from the British team. I felt enormous relief. Winning a medal at Karapiro was obviously no fluke. Next year there was the Olympics in Moscow. Another bronze would do nicely. I don't ever remember even thinking that we would ever aspire to the gold medal. The East German crews seemed untouchable. Looking back, if we were to move out of the bronze age, something more might have been needed. Maybe Harry might have had the answers?

But in 1979, I hardly knew Harry. Then it was more of an event to have a meaningful conversation with a New Zealand rower than it was with a Russian. To me, Harry was just some Kiwi coach with a beard. Even when his crews really burst upon the world's stage during the early 1980s, I never got to know him. Of course, I saw the results of what he did. In 1982 and 1983, I watched from the sidelines as his eights took the world title by storm. It wasn't the fact that they won, it was the way they did it, moving with deceptive ease. The following year the New Zealand coxless four won the gold medal in the Los Angeles Olympics. To me, they were the best crew in the Games and though coached by Brian Hawthorne, they rowed in the inimitable Mahon style. But still Harry remained just a face on the New Zealand team.

It was when he came to Europe as the new Swiss national coach that I eventually got to know him a little. Not that it was easy. Having a meaningful conversation with Harry seemed to be about as easy as trying to interview Kenny Dalglish on one of his bad days. There were a few 'yeahs', 'nopes' and 'maybes' – and that was about as far as conversations with me, or anyone else – as far as I can gather – went.

It wasn't until 1997, when I went out with him in a launch to hear him coaching Greg Searle, that I got the surprise of my life. He never stopped talking.

Was this the Harry Mahon that I knew? I listened, enthralled to his dialogue: 'Keep those hands moving out, stretching out and separating...

Feel you are sitting there and the boat is sucking you towards it, rather than the opposite way round... No, too quick for the boat... Steady with it... Steady with it... Better... Hold your shoulders back and just sit there and watch your handles go away from your body. Now you're feeling the boat underneath your feet, running through the water... our hands are leading you, the water that's running under you is telling you when your handles will arrive at your feet... That was good... Yeah, three in a row, where you picked it just right...' I suppose that on the page, the dialogue might look dry, or sound like drivel. But for me in the boat then, it was like discovering Mozart for the first time. Not only could I see the effect that his coaching was having on Greg; it was also the way I was starting to look at the sport at that time in my life.

By then, I'd long retired from international competition but was still plugging up and down the river in my single. My motivation? Apart from that which you'll read about later, I wanted to turn my David Batty into a Zinadine Zidane. Now my body was getting too old to thrash through each training session, I needed to find a way of thinking that I could still improve. I begun searching for 'The Force'.

It is said that there is a purpose behind each relationship that we have; that others are sent along to teach us something about ourselves. Whether you believe that, or not, Harry came along at the right time in my life. I suppose that one way of looking at it might be to see the extrovert inside of me, drawn to unravel the world inside the mind of his introvert. Whatever, I began to watch him coach more often and listen to his story. Through it I would learn something that I never suspected: that relationships and communication were of profound value in Harry's life. It was just that, unlike me who chatted to all and sundry, he gave himself to others through his coaching.

So it was little surprise to learn that Harry did not see his demotion from the team in 1979 as anything but an opportunity. Rather than mope at chances lost, he settled down to work with a group of raw but exciting young rowers. They were future World and Olympic champions like Chris White, Shane O'Brien and Roger White Parsons. When he got hold of them, they did not amount to much but once they learnt to play Harry's Game, the East Germans and the rest of us would trail in their wakes.

Harry developed his philosophy early in his life, when rowing was just one of the sports that he played and coached at the school where he worked. He might have made a New Zealand international if he had been bigger, but lightweight rowing was not in vogue then. He left New Zealand in 1969 for a geography and environmental studies teaching post at Ridley College, Canada. He was there for five years.

First and foremost, Harry was a laid-back teacher who liked to enjoy his work. His lessons sounded to me like they were out of the ordinary. He often used to take his students on the bus into Toronto to sample the feel of a big city, rather than teaching Environmental Studies from a book (I can't imagine Chris Woodhead would have approved).

His outlook as a coach was similar. Rowing was to be enjoyed, not just for the sheer sense of exhilaration from moving through water but also for the relationships that it developed. It mattered to Harry that he got on with those that he was coaching. He needed to bond with his charges; rowing was fun and relationships were important to him. Seeing him coach on the water, it is not hard to understand why. He puts so much of himself into the process of coaching rowing technique, giving people the same rhythm and sense of movement, it is almost as if he is giving them a gift of himself.

It was in St Catherine's that Harry struck up a life-long friendship with the great Canadian coach, Neil Campbell, who was also a teacher at the school. They were to be rival coaches in the 1984 Olympics. On that occasion, Campbell's crew got the better of Harry's. The styles of their two Olympic eights were completely contrasting, Campbell relying on a much more aggressive, power-based style of rowing, while Harry's eight – world champions for the previous two years – just ghosted along effortlessly. True to form, the New Zealanders cruised to victory in the heat. On that form, I thought the gold was a formality.

The trouble was that Harry probably did too. Over-confidence must have played a part when, in the final, the Canadians blew them away. The memory of that loss still troubles Harry deeply. If his eight had failed to win, at least he could draw solace from the brilliant gold won by the New Zealand coxless four who simply rowed away from an outstanding field looking as though they weren't really trying. It was the Mahon philosophy at its best. For many, they were the outstanding crew of the regatta. However, these were the men that Harry had rejected, so in a way their triumph also brought reminders of what should have been for the eight.

Harry seemed to lose his way in New Zealand after that result. The following year brought little joy for him, with two fourth-place boats. In 1986, Harry's four returned to the medal rostrum with a silver but he was clearly looking for other challenges. He found it by moving to Europe to become the Swiss national coach.

Harry made an immediate impact there, particularly in the more challenging crew sculling boats – the double and quadruple – which require the highest level of expertise in the sport. The Swiss were used to working hard to make a boat move fast. Harry wanted them to do the opposite. He worked on a lot of exercises at very light pressure, where they would just reach out and put their blades in the water. At first, their natural inclination was to begin driving back but Harry made them wait until the inertia of the boat's movement had to be overcome. Then, he allowed them to move their bodies back. To the scullers, once this technique was grooved in, it was as if the boat was moving without really any effort. Then, Harry allowed them to increase the pressure. With their new technique, they felt as if they were moving as fast as they were before Harry came, but for much less effort.

So much of Harry's work is based on timing the stroke to perfection, to achieve apparently effortless movement. He draws his inspiration for this from many sources. For him the top-class practitioners of other sports are a rich seam to be mined. Perhaps it is because of his own love of running that his favourite memory relates to the time he was running around a Swiss lake and some Kenyans overtook him. Harry was immediately struck by the way they seemed to ghost past, silently, effortlessly, their feet making no sound at all as they touched the path. Harry is no mean runner. But these Kenyans passed him as if he was standing still. It is the way that he wants his crews to row.

Greg Searle got a chance to sample the Mahon magic when Harry began to coach him in 1997. That year, Searle became the first British single sculler for almost 40 years to medal at a World Championships. But Harry's achievement that year was set against a backdrop of his own personal battle against cancer.

In the spring of 1997, Harry was diagnosed as having cancer of the colon which had metastasised into his liver. His condition necessitated an immediate operation to remove the tumour. His doctor told him that he only had a year or so to live. Harry's response was typically combative: 'No mate, more like ten to 20.' It didn't seem that way during the first World Cup regatta that he attended in Paris that summer. In great pain, he was forced to return home without watching Searle race.

But if you haven't already guessed it by now, you won't be surprised to know that Harry is an exceptional man. He was determined to apply the same natural, rhythmical principles which he used to coach rowing to the treatment of his disease. After an initial treatment of chemotherapy, he chose to adopt a more natural, holistic approach to healing, relying on his body's natural mechanisms. This was no surprise for a man whose whole creed of rowing is focused on the natural rhythms and movements of the body. He became fully conversant with the literature of gurus such as Bernie Siegel and Louise Hay. After a training session with Searle during the World Championships, he would more often than not have his head stuck in one of these books. Harry experimented with all kinds of healing techniques, including a faith healer.

On the evidence of the scans, these seemed to be working; the growths in his liver were shrinking. What struck me was the way that this man had gone about life with his cancer. It was almost as if it wasn't there. In fact, he refused to change his lifestyle in the least, coaching as many crews as he could in a day, as well as fitting in his runs. During that year, I found myself spending more time with Harry. I often found that I compared my own way of dealing with illness – or for that matter any of life's turmoils – unfavourably with his. In a way, I suppose through talking to him I hoped to learn about how I could change the way I thought about my self.

We sat next to each other on a transatlantic flight: a mad dash to New York for Greg Searle's stag night in October 1997. As usual, the conversation started off with sport before moving on to something a little more deep.

He had his head buried in a copy of *Black and Blue*, the autobiography of David Kirk, the All Blacks scrum-half. On the fly leaf I saw that Kirk had inscribed the book with a personal dedication to Mahon. After half an hour or so, he motioned to me to read a passage. It was when Kirk was describing the difference between the great international scrum-halves and the rest. Not surprisingly, it was all to do with timing and 'feel'. Kirk wrote of the split-second within which a scrum-half must release the ball before the forwards crush him. The ordinary players feel how rushed they are, while the great ones experience the moment fully. It is as if, for them, time is standing still. For them, there is no rush, no pressure, only effortless movement and motion.

This was all music to my ears. I was sitting next to the person who I regarded as the most gifted coach in the world, who was more than happy to talk about his craft for the next few hours. It was as if a person reading their favourite novel had suddenly found themselves sitting next to the author.

As we talked I began to feel more comfortable with him and I sense him with me too. I found myself trying to probe further into the Mahon psyche.

'You know Harry, that your athletes see you as some kind of guru, don't you? How do you feel about that – them sort of hanging on your every word?'

He was silent for a while before a reflective, 'Yeah,' broke the silence. Before I could speak, he went on, 'I feel I'm... really responsible for what might happen to people. If I stop to think about it, like now, I find that quite a heavy burden.'

I pressed him further. 'So what is your gift then Harry, that all these people want to benefit from?'

He answered with an evasive 'I don't know.'

'But you know that you have a gift don't you?' His eyes looked up and to the left, as if he was recalling moments in his long career

'Yeah, yeah... well... that I seem to be able to... [turn] just about any group of people that I might coach on the water into something that somebody else might have been trying harder and not managed to do.' Once again he fell silent for a few moments, as if he was struggling to admit to himself, let alone to me, that he *was* special. It reminded me of the first time that I'd tried to propose to my wife. I wanted to say the words but they just wouldn't come out. Then, like

The Tideway, 2000: Harry Mahon captured in a typically laid-back pose during Cambridge's preparations for the Boat Race.

me, he tried again. 'I've just got this… yeah, I've just been lucky, I guess, that I seem to be able to move people on to another level.'

So that was about as much as I was going to get from the great man himself about his talents. It was all down to luck. He is even more downbeat about the levels of skill that he is teaching. He doesn't think that it is a sport with a particularly high skill level. For him the world's greatest rower would never match up to the All Blacks scrum-half. In fact, he is confident enough to believe that he could teach anyone who has ever ventured out on to Serpentine how to row. He assured me that if he gets hold of someone who hasn't been exposed to rowing before and gives them the basics, they end up saying, 'So is that all rowing is?'

I felt deflated when he said this. That this was all he thought of a movement that I'd spent my life trying to master. Perhaps I'd made it seem much more challenging than it really was. But even so, I couldn't understand how someone who thought of himself as an 'artist' could coach this 'simple' sport with as much drive and enthusiasm as Harry did. It was almost as if he sensed my next question before I'd even formed it.

'I don't know quite what it is you're looking for me to say Martin, maybe a psychologist would work me out. But since I've been ill, I've begun to realise what it is that I've done with all these people that I've coached, that there has been a real purpose to it.'

'You mean it's all down to the guys you've coached?'

'What I value are people really… it's what I coach for actually. You know, when it comes down to it, rowing's just another avenue for meeting people.'

When it comes down to it, there is hardly anybody in the rowing world who hasn't got a good word to say about Harry. When you consider how much of himself he has given them, it is hardly surprising. But even though he has many friends, there are only a few that would confess to knowing him really well. Since his struggle with cancer he has mellowed a little and become more reflective (he admits that when he was first in New Zealand he was a pretty hard person to live with). But now he is clearly a man to whom friendships and relationships are very important.

He is adamant that his illness has not affected the way that he coaches. Perhaps these days, he does not have the same energy that he used to. In the spring of 1998, he ran the London Marathon in around four hours. He was hoping for a quicker time but his reaction to treatment made this impossible. By the summer of 1999, things were not looking so good for Harry. His scans indicated that the tumours in his liver were no longer in remission.

What's more, he needed a dose of steroids, just to attend the Vienna World Cup regatta. I was with him cycling up and down the bank, following the races. His face was yellow and his eyes bloodshot.

The news on the water wasn't good either. Greg Searle's season had been adversely affected by a series of injuries. He and Harry had yet to discover the sparkle of their old relationship. By Henley regatta, his friends were predicting that Harry would not see the World Championships. But perhaps they didn't know the man. As a result of a radically new type of chemotherapy, Harry was able to recover sufficiently to spend the summer giving his expertise to the British eight. Their coach, Martin McElroy, was a Mahon devotee and jumped at the chance to have the great man along to most sessions. In St Catherine's, Mahon looked like a different man.

The first time I saw the British eight training on the course, it took my breath away. Their stroke looked so long and connected, the rhythm so effortless. They were moving so quickly that they were travelling far more between strokes than I could remember. Then the image of that Kiwi eight in 1982 flashed into my mind and I knew that the Mahon magic had been at work again. Their brilliant final row, where they won a silver medal, was testament to the inspiration of a great teacher.

That winter, Harry carried on life much as normal, coaching at Molesey and Cambridge. For the summer he had different plans. Mahon was determined to be in Sydney and to get the British eight moving better than it had ever gone before. His relationship with the eight's coach, Martin McElroy, was crucial and almost unique in the world of top-class sport, where fragile egos usually get in the way of two coaches working together for any length of time. But the young British coach knew that Harry's technical expertise was vital if the eight was to develop sufficient speed to challenge for a gold medal. On top of that, McElroy was happy to add to his own skills by having Harry in the boat alongside him and he allowed him the time and space to make his own distinctive input.

During the season, Mahon timed his chemotherapy sessions so as not to miss crucial races or key training sessions, and gradually the eight began to fly. Wins in Vienna and Lucerne were offset by defeats in Munich and Henley. But by Sydney the crew was clearly moving better than it ever had done. There was an effortless ease about the way they raced. On the pick-up, the blades disappeared below the surface of the water more quickly and smoothly than any of their rivals. A brief hiccup during their opening heat, which saw them lose to Australia, was merely seen by Harry as an opportunity to remind them how things should be done in the next race. Throughout the week, Harry continued to work ceaselessly on their technique, not just on the water but also by having each man row perfect strokes on his beloved Row-perfect ergometer before they went out to race or train.

Harry watched the final from the coaches' van which drove alongside the race. It is difficult to extract from him exactly how he felt during those five minutes or so, when the British eight moved effortlessly out into a lead which they were never to relinquish: joy at the result, satisfaction at the way in which it was won, or maybe relief that he had laid to rest his demons of 1984, when his Kiwi crew failed to medal? All Harry will admit to was feeling pretty pleased for the boys and Martin that he had helped them achieve something that had been their goal for a long while.

Harry is never far away from the river. Although a virus laid him low following his return from Sydney, he is still prepared to teach anyone to row who asks him. He was heavily involved in Cambridge's preparations for the 2001 Boat Race, which saw them triumph after the race was controversially restarted. Through it all, he remains unassuming. He shuns the fact that he has been an inspiration to others, offering other cancer sufferers support, comfort and company; Helen Rollason, the BBC television sports presenter, was just one of the people who was particularly appreciative of Harry's help in coping with her illness.

That brings me to the C word; the 'Big C' as John Wayne used to call it. This was meant to be a chapter about technique, about Harry's unique gift for teaching people how to row. I wanted all you non-rowers – well, if I'm honest, rowers as well – to read it and understand something unique about the way of the man with a blade. I suppose on one level that's what it does. But this chapter is not really about that at all. It's about how a man's life has been changed by cancer – not for the worse but for the better.

Since he was diagnosed, Harry has had the 'best life': he's found love with his partner Sarah; in other relationships there's been a richness, that he's never quite before experienced; he's achieved a lifetime's ambition of coaching an Olympic champion eight. Let's face it, how many people get off the telephone to a man whom doctors have given a few weeks to live, and instead of feeling down experience something of the wonder that life has to offer? Lance Armstrong in his autobiography *It's Not About The Bike* wrote that, given the choice between winning the Tour de France and having cancer, he'd choose the latter. Does it make sense? What would you choose? I never understood that sentiment until I saw that with Harry, cancer was not a death sentence, rather a gift that life brought him. It's only now, that I can begin to understand what it really means to play Harry's Game.

Politically Correct

I HAD always been a day-dreamer. At school, while the teachers droned on about chemistry equations that I didn't understand, I would stare out of the window, look up to the clouds and fantasise about being a fighter pilot. As 1980 approached, windows and clouds still had the same appeal, but my dreams had changed. What's more, now they were almost so close that I could almost reach out and touch them. I dreamt of being in the Olympic Games, of walking through that gateway to the Moscow village and drinking my fill of the Olympic spirit within. There were no medals involved in this fantasy, just to be there was enough.

Anita De Frantz had a dream too. Her parents had been part of Martin Luther King's Civil Rights movement. King's vision of children being judged 'not by the colour of their skin but by the content of their character' had inspired their daughter to try to become the first black female Supreme Court Justice in the history of the USA. But before she could do that, there was a smaller but no less powerful dream of an Olympic medal to be won in Moscow.

But the war the Russians were fighting in Afghanistan, and the resulting campaign to boycott the Olympics, was a rude awakening. It catapulted us into increasingly bitter and desperate fights to salvage the shreds of what remained of our dreams. The trauma of those struggles changed our lives for good and politicised us both. It led De Frantz to being 'just a heartbeat away' from the most powerful position in the Olympic movement. As for me, I set off on a similar messianic path to make sure that such a trauma would never happen again. Perhaps my experiences during that year should have prepared me for the view as I stood on the steps of the Olympic Stadium in Moscow on the eve of the opening ceremony. But then surprises seemed to be what 1980 had in store for me.

The serried ranks of elite Soviet troops walked slowly over the carefully manicured turf of Moscow's Lenin Stadium. In just 24 hours, the Games of the 19th Olympiad would begin. Each of the khaki-clad soldiers was carrying a mine detector, sweeping it precisely and methodically over every

Moscow, 1980: Soviet troops minesweep the turf of the Olympic Stadium the day before the opening ceremony. I was unceremoniously ejected from the stadium moments after I took this picture.

blade of grass. With Soviet soldiers in Afghanistan being killed by the Mujaheddin or maimed by their mines, no one was taking any chances.

To Ian McNuff and myself, who had sneaked out of the Olympic village to look at the venue, it seemed preposterous that anybody in a security conscious Moscow could have laid a mine under the turf. But there it was, proof that the battles being waged in the mountains around Kabul were reverberating as far as the Olympic arena. Nobody was taking any chances. No sooner had we glimpsed the view than we were being ushered none too gently out of the stadium by KGB officers in black leather jackets. Our athlete ID cards did not impress them. The following day Moscow airspace was closed for the duration of the opening ceremony, while a massive military presence surrounded the stadium.

In fact, none of this should have seemed remarkable to an athlete who had struggled long and hard against the collective will of the West's political leaders for the right to participate in the Olympic Games. Especially as the politicians played dirty. Images of burnt children – supposedly the victims of Soviet napalm attacks – were sent to many of us. Employees of the civil service, police and armed forces were told that if they went to the Games it would be at the expense of their jobs. Geoff Capes, Britain's premier shot putter, had to resign from his job as a policeman in order to attend Moscow Games.

When the first news of the Soviet invasion and the possible Western boycott of the Games began to filter through, I was not concerned. There was time enough for the Soviets to finish their business and respond to President Carter's demands to leave. At that stage not even the Americans, far less Brezhnev and his advisors, thought that the Red Army would be embroiled fighting Afghan guerrillas for another six long years.

The Olympics had weathered participating countries' warlike actions before. Neither the Soviet invasion of Hungary nor the British and French invasion of Suez halted the 1956 Games in Melbourne. Perhaps the only outward sign was the bloody water polo final between the USSR and Hungary, as the latter team sought to exact revenge. In 1968, when the 'Prague Spring' was withering in the full heat of the Brezhnev doctrine, Red Army tanks once again rolled into another country. It did not affect the Games, neither did the police massacre of demonstrators in Mexico City just before the opening ceremony. Even the blood of the 13 Israeli athletes shot in Munich had stopped the Games only for a day.

But the political survival of the US President was what was at stake here. The lifeblood of Jimmy Carter's administration was ebbing away. His presidency was already mortally wounded by the hostage crisis in Iran, where supporters of that country's religious leader Ayatollah Khomeini had kidnapped the staff of the American embassy in Tehran. What's more, it was election year. Carter desperately needed the transfusion of popular support that appearing firm might bring. By playing the tough guy against the Kremlin's aggression, he could win votes from his hard-line Republican opponent, Ronald Reagan.

In Britain, it was an ideal opportunity for Margaret Thatcher, the 'Iron Lady', to make an impact on the international stage. So, with Carter, she rang the alarm bells, warning of the dangers of not resisting Soviet expansion. Of course, the war in Afghanistan was nothing of the sort. But it was a familiar melody to the British Government's ears. What's more, they expected us athletes to dance to their tune. They couldn't have been more wrong.

In the spring of 1980 I did not yet have the kind of loathing for Thatcherite policies that I was to develop subsequently. But the events of that year went some way to pushing me in that direction. The Conservatives did not have the first clue about the workings of British sport. Their sports ministers have generally been a lacklustre breed. The unfortunate incumbent in 1980 was Hector Monroe. Eager to provide alternative possibilities for the staging of the Olympic Games, his department made a crass offer to stage the track and field programme at the Crystal Palace, a stadium whose capacity was a paltry 18,000. It was laughable. Really, they couldn't care less about the Games, far less the athletes, so it was hardly surprising that the Government found few British athletes willing to consider even a boycott.

I was then part of a rapidly growing athlete organisation that was trying to put pressure on anybody and everybody to attend the Games. When the House of Commons debated the British boycott, the galleries were full of track-suited athletes, listening intently to the arguments. Labour's Shadow Minister of Sport, Denis Howell, did us proud. For the Conservatives, Monroe was denied his appearance at the dispatch box for the closing arguments, his place was taken by that political heavyweight, Michael Heseltine.

If one Conservative Sports Minister was conspicuous by his absence, a future holder of the post was making his presence felt. When his place in the Games was in doubt, he showed far more courage in standing up to Margaret Thatcher's demands than he did over her ludicrous football identity card scheme in later years. With his prowess in the spoken word the Hon Colin Moynihan more than made up for his lack of inches. He held both the presidency of the Oxford Union and the cox's seat in the Blue boat. The mental agility required in the cut and thrust of debate mixed well with his aggressive competitive instincts (he also won a Blue in boxing) to make him a great cox. He was sure of a seat in the Olympic eight and was determined that his party's prejudices should not stand in the way of his glory.

Moynihan set about organising an athlete campaign to lobby both MPs and officials to ensure that they got the message that most British sportsmen and women wanted to go to Moscow. Even so, when the Government began to mount pressure, sport's governing bodies began to waver. Thatcher, invoking the ghost of Churchill, cast the Soviets in the mould of the fascist aggressors of the 1930s. The Iron Lady would stand fast as the guardian of liberty and protect Afghanistan.

So those of us who were arguing for the Games to continue were being cast in the mould of the hated Thatcherite bogeymen, namely Neville Chamberlain and his fellow appeasers of the 1930s. Archie Nisbet had competed in the coxless fours at the 1936 Berlin Olympics and he was among those arguing passionately for a boycott. Nisbet saw Hitler's Games as an enormous propaganda coup for the Nazis. For him, Brezhnev was another Hitler, which was slightly ironic since Brezhnev had fought in World War Two against the Nazis. If Nisbet could have had his way and reversed history, Jesse Owens would have been nothing but a footnote in its pages.

But of course, the argument was about more than just sport triumphing over political repression. If the Conservative Government had been prepared to institute economic sanctions against the Soviet Union, then my stance against the boycott would have been difficult to maintain. It was this inaction, more than anything, which undermined the Government's claim to hold the high moral ground. What's more, by the summer it was clear that the Games would go ahead in Moscow, even if it was only the Eastern Bloc athletes who turned up. In any case British sportsmen and women were unwilling to fall on their sacrificial swords for a government that patently cared so little for sport. It wasn't that athletes were blind to what was going on in Afghanistan, or politically naïve, rather they were more aware that, if a boycott did occur, it would do nothing for the people being bombed in Afghanistan. In the end, we knew that sport was important in the USSR but expendable, as Chernenko's boycott of the Los Angeles Games was to show four years later.

It was in this light that the decision of the British Olympic Committee as to whether they should send a team to the Games assumed crucial importance, not only for the Games but also for the Olympic movement itself. Ominously during that summer, the number of national Olympic committees deciding to boycott the Games had grown ever larger. The West German NOC, with the level of financial support that it received from the federal government, was hardly in a position to defy them. One by one the Olympic committees voted for a boycott. The great German sculler Peter-Michael Kolbe would miss his chance to renew his rivalry against Pertti Karpinnen of Finland. Norway's boycott meant that the legendary Hanson brothers had now sculled their last race together.

As they boarded the plane to come to Europe, Harry Mahon's New Zealand crews were told that they weren't going to compete in the Games. Perversely, Australia's rowers only learnt of their NOC's decision to attend the Games while 30,000 feet over Thailand en route for Europe. But of course, the crucial absence as far as the Games were concerned was that of the USA. And without British attendance, the Games would become just an extension of the Spartakiade; the Eastern bloc's Games.

So, as British attendance at the Games became vital to their credibility, the pressure to pull out became intense. It wasn't surprising that sports with a strong Establishment connection, like shooting, equestrian and yachting, voted not to attend the Olympics whatever the result of the British Olympic Association vote. As usual, the athlete's opinions were largely irrelevant to these associations. Malcolm Cooper, who was to win a gold medal for shooting in the 1984 Olympics in Los Angeles, didn't even have a chance to state his own opinion. It was this aspect which I found so frustrating. To me then, sports administrators were generally a bunch of 'old farts' who would naturally be on the side of the Conservative Government. I was enraged that athletes were so impotent on such a key decision. We had spent years training, often just for the Games. We were generally used to being invisible to most of the administrators. But when they began to stop us racing – without even listening...!

Rowing was, of course, another 'Establishment' sport. But with a difference; there was no danger that rowers would not be heard. In a packed meeting at the Amateur Rowing Association's offices, there was not one rower who did not want the chance to go – or at least decide for themselves. Listening to that vote was the ARA's representative on the BOA, Chris Davidge. In his day, Davidge was a charismatic stroke-man who had been to

Moscow, 1980: This picture, taken by the author in the desolate surroundings of the Olympic Village symbolised the loss of the soul of the Games due to a pointless boycott. The only flags flown in the village were those of the Soviet Union and the IOC.

three Olympics including the Games in 1956 just after the Soviet invasion of Hungary. I had hardly ever spoken to him, but through sources in the BOA I knew that he was strongly in favour of a boycott. Through this athletes meeting we worked to neutralise his views on the Council of the ARA. Consequently they voted to support the Games.

There was one more hurdle to pass, though. The BOA was crucial. Here Davidge continued to press his case for a boycott, despite the clear opinion of the sport he was representing. But those then on the BOA were made of sterner stuff. Robert Watson, hockey's representative, argued passionately in favour of attending, even though his sport had earlier decided to boycott. In such a climate, standing up in favour of going was a brave option. In the end, Watson and others carried the day; we were going to Moscow.

But the boycott had removed much of the gloss from taking part in the Olympic Games. The bonanza of free kit, that the British team had received in Montreal four years earlier, never materialised. With the political pressure on, many of the BOA's sponsors withdrew. What's more, in a move that created much resentment, athletes had to leave immediately after their event. Perversely, it was during this time that we could have let 'ordinary' Russians know our opinions about the war which their country was fighting in Afghanistan. Those of us who did take the opportunity to question our Soviet interpreters about the war had some lively conversations. Their expectation was of a war, key to their national security, that would soon be over. There were many questions to us, too, about the British 'occupation' of Northern Ireland, and American support for the fascist government in Chile.

But the overwhelming feeling of Muscovites was that they were overjoyed to see the British. Many, seeing our tracksuits, just came up to say 'hello'. In some cases they even offered small gifts. I still have a gaily painted wooden spoon from one Russian who told me how pleased he was to see the British team in Moscow. I was genuinely touched by their reaction. Even, too, with the rather 'official' telegrams from tractor factories in Siberia, or collective farms in the Ukraine, thanking us. At least somebody cared about us.

But in other ways, Moscow was a culture shock. I saw my first all-female gang of navvies. They were covered from head to foot in mud and dirt while fixing a hole in the road. For other women, notably Moscow's prostitutes, the Games meant a complete upheaval. They were rounded up and exiled for the duration. There was no doubt that the streets were quiet. But the scare stories of mass evacuations of children were probably untrue. In summer, many of the better-off Muscovites headed off to their dachas. Every so often, though, the overriding impression of greyness was broken by a splash of colour from one of the huge murals that occasionally filled the whole sides of buildings. The men depicted were huge Stakhanovite figures with rippling muscles like Arnold Schwarzenegger, banner or hammer in hand, exhorting the workers to greater efforts. The women were focused and determined by the men's sides, yet not reliant.

The KGB were in evidence too. I was none-too-gently moved on in Red Square – tourist loitering seemed not to be an acceptable pastime. Other athletes, like the former Olympic champion Chris Brasher, reported being followed as they went out of the village exploring Moscow's suburbs. But for me, nothing could take away the experience of walking into the Olympic village for the first time.

It's a bit like being on a Club 18-30 holiday where everything is free. Thousands of young men and women, all superbly fit and healthy, with hormones oozing out of every pore. The 24-hour cafeterias, with their mountains of food, were buzzing through the night and there was endless entertainment for those who felt bored. We even had the Bolshoi Ballet come to give us performances (although the ever-present disco was probably more popular). All this is combined with incredible sports facilities and free tickets to watch any of the other sports.

It's an unreal world, a kind of sporting nirvana. At dinner you might find yourself sitting next to one of the world's greatest, or most famous athletes, like Alberto Juantarina, the Olympic champion at 400 and 800 metres, or Nelli Kim who sat next to me on the bus travelling to the gymnastics.

At times I almost forget why I was there, what all the struggles had been for – to race!

By the morning of our first heat I had definitely 'lost the plot'. My head was stuck in a book almost right up until we boated. Afterwards I realised that it was my way of ignoring or side-stepping the tension which I felt. On the start I was too relaxed and we 'bombed', coming in a long way behind everybody. For the repechage, though, things were different. I ensured that I was 'psyched-up', pacing around the boathouse like a caged tiger. And, with what was probably our best row ever, we won a place in the Olympic final.

All the 'old firm' were there from the Eastern Bloc that we'd raced during the previous two years, plus a fast Swiss crew who had beaten us on

Moscow, 1980: The boys in Red Square. From the left: John, me and Dave. Because of the boycott, athletes were supposed to return home immediately. Somehow, David Tanner wangled another three days' stay out of the BOA for us to play tourists. It was bliss.

each occasion that they had raced us that season. It was still a very strong field in a regatta that had clearly suffered from the boycott. In the end, though, it was between us and the Czechs for the bronze medal. Unlike the previous year we were to prove the stronger in the last 500 metres. We won a bronze medal, our third in so many years. The medal ceremony was the first occasion that we had the opportunity to get out of the boat and shake the hands of the other crews. In all other rowing championships, second and third-place crews had to stay in the boat to receive their medals.

In the middle of the East German national anthem (played for 11 out of 14 medal ceremonies that day), Ian McNuff puked up on the red carpet. Earlier, Dave Townsend had announced his retirement, while John Beattie couldn't stop grinning; his 'magic foot' had steered us straight down the lane in a difficult Moscow crosswind. As for me, I had achieved all that I ever wanted from sport. At that moment I didn't care what happened to me for the rest of my rowing career. I had been 'famous for 15 minutes'.

But in reality the boycott gave me new goals and a sense of purpose within the sport. I had come within a whisker of being denied the chance to compete in Moscow at all. But for thousands of other athletes that nightmare had become a reality. What drove me on was the fact that the pathways through which athletes had been consulted about the boycott were so informal and tortuous that there was no guarantee that something similar might not happen again. I felt very messianic about it. Governing bodies should not be able to treat their athletes in such dismissive fashion.

So, from Moscow onwards my mission was to make sport's governing bodies appoint athlete representatives to their boards. Eventually this road took me to achieve the office of athletes' representative on the Council of the British Olympic Association as well as rowing's international governing body, FISA. At times my progress was so fast that I even had delusions that I might be suitable for a place on that 'holy of holies', the IOC. But when the British position fell vacant, the only person who thought I might be remotely suitable was me. In reality, although athlete representation had come a long way, I was light years away from being anyone with real power in international sport.

That much was made clear to me in no uncertain terms as I walked up to the normally welcoming lobby of Birmingham's Hilton Hyatt Hotel in October 1990. It was blocked by uniformed police. Behind them hotel security guards formed a solid phalanx. Outside in the rain, a small crowd of people jostled to gain admission through the metal detectors. Two South American women, dressed in furs, wearing expensive jewellery and laden with bags of shopping, flashed their passes to the uniformed men and gained admittance. A journalist without the correct security clearance was less successful and was being quietly but insistently ushered away. The signs looked ominous for me as I struggled to the top of the steps. Through the glass doors I could see a crowded lobby full of well-dressed people. I felt conspicuous and out of place in my tracksuit – like when I'd once turned up to the ballet in jeans and T-shirt, only to discover that it was a Royal Gala performance. Of course, I should have known better. This was not just any sports meeting; these people and their retinues were from the blue bloods of the sporting aristocracy, the International Olympic Committee. I was seeking an audience with its leader, the most powerful man in the sporting world, His Excellency Juan Antonio Samaranch.

Despite me having a prior appointment, I carried no security clearance. I had to wait outside for over an hour, and then another hour in the lobby. A few familiar faces appeared, to make me feel less uncomfortable. Dick Palmer, the cheery Welshman who in Moscow had been the only member of the British team allowed to march in the opening ceremony (holding not the

Union Flag but the IOC banner as a protest at the Soviet invasion). Since then he had run the British Olympic Association. Palmer was an athlete's man through and through and I trusted him. But despite the efforts of people like him, I still felt unwelcome. That feeling did not change when I met President Samaranch in his large suite of rooms at the top of the Hyatt. The former Spanish ambassador to Moscow looked relaxed in an open-necked shirt and pastel yellow sweater which set off his tanned complexion. It was the first time I had ever seen him when he was not wearing a suit.

At first he was genial enough. I was just another athlete come to pay homage. In his hand he held a small box; the obligatory gift. The conversation was small talk: what I'd done in the Olympics; the recent achievements of other British athletes. He began to press the gift, a small enamel box celebrating the 1908 Olympics held in London, into my hand, when I realised that he had no idea that I was there to take issue with him over the direction that he was leading the Olympics. Immediately his appearance grew far more businesslike. His features drew into a frown as he listened to my objection to the inclusion of tennis, which I felt devalued the Olympic gold medal because the world's top players chose not to attend. He dismissed all my points without any hint of a willingness to compromise. At that meeting, I lost any notion of idealism that I might have held about what was driving the Olympic movement; now it was clear that IOC was driven simply by the power of the dollar.

But even in an organisation such as the IOC, there are exceptions. One of them was also in that same hotel in Birmingham. As it happened, she had argued strongly in favour of tennis being admitted to the Games. But on more than one issue she too had found herself isolated from the Samaranch line. But for the Moscow boycott of 1980, she would probably have been sitting as a judge in a New York court rather than arguing sports politics with the 'fat cats' of the IOC. Like me, she fought against the political establishment in order to attend the Moscow Games. It was a struggle that changed her life. But all this was far away from the mind of the young woman who in the fall of 1979 prepared to realise her Olympic dream.

These days Anita De Frantz's time is at a premium. Mostly she is on a plane travelling between one sporting meeting and another, spending little time in her Californian home. We caught up to chat over old times during the World Rowing Championships in Cologne, which she had just flown into from Seoul following an IOC meeting. I had really got to know her through my time on FISA's Council. In the days of the Moscow boycott, we just spoke on the phone a few times. Otherwise I knew of her because she was one of the only black women to row in the World Championships. If you didn't know Anita by name, then it was a fair bet that you knew of the black woman who rowed at 'two' in the American four.

In the years after Moscow, whenever I met a member of the IOC they would often ask, 'Do you know Anita,' in almost reverential tones, as if knowing De Frantz was some kind of honour. Perhaps on the IOC, where women, let alone black women, aren't exactly at a premium, they realise what a special person that she is. In fact Anita was one of the only IOC members to emerge with anything like credit from the infamous exposé on the IOC, *Lords of the Rings*.

Anita does carry some kind of aura around with her. Perhaps it's because she seems so out of the ordinary for the position she holds. A member of IMG, the international sports marketing agency, once remarked to me that 'unless she loses a few pounds and smartens up her act, she's no chance of making it to the top job in the IOC'. Although she occasionally wears a jacket and skirt for meetings, most of the time she dresses down. Her T-shirts and old trainers are definitely not de rigueur for an IOC member, let alone a potential president. However, it is that which makes her so refreshing. She clearly prefers spending her time among the athletes rather than officials, so in conversation it was easy to lapse into the familiar jargon of 'old rowing buddies'. However, Anita is politically astute with a mind that is razor sharp. She never lets slip an injudicious phrase or comment. I got the feeling that even if she disliked Samaranch, you would never get to hear of it. But as we began to talk about her preparations for the Moscow Games, she became animated as she remembered the events that changed her life.

In 1979, Anita De Frantz exchanged her lucrative position in a Philadelphia law firm for a $4,000-a-year job at Princeton University. She figured that at least it would give her room and board; enough to live on while she trained with her pairs partner 'Coz' Crawford, an engineering student at the Ivy League college. After Anita had won a bronze medal in the Montreal Olympics of 1976, she asked her coach John Hooten if she had what it took to become an Olympic champion in Moscow. Anita had such confidence in his opinion that his answer of 'yes' was enough to put her relentless legal ambition on hold. She figured that she could wait a little longer to become one of the 'Supremes'.

The Olympic ideal had come into her life from an early age. When she was seven, her father told her of his wish that together with her brother,

Montreal, 1976: Anita De Frantz (third left) on her way to winning an Olympic bronze in the coxed fours event.

they would become the first Afro-Americans on the US swimming team. For him, it would be another victory over the racist allegation that 'black people can't swim'. Her father was secretary of the National Association for the Advancement of Coloured People. His life-long struggle for black equality started with the attempt to secure desegregation of the student accommodation at Indiana University. De Franz's mother was one of the first five women of Afro-American descent to live in the newly-desegregated housing. With parents whose relationship was forged in the heat of the Civil Rights struggle, it is not hard to find the source of Anita's ambition.

By 1976, at the age of 24, she had established herself as the first black woman on the US rowing team. It gave her a national profile that, together with her parents' willingness to speak out against injustice, made her a natural spokesperson for athletes. When the United States Olympic Committee needed a female athlete to sit on its board, Anita seemed an ideal choice. By 1978, she had also secured a key role in the Carter administration, serving on the Presdient's council on physical fitness and sports. She helped with the drafting of the Amateur Sports Act. With a world silver medal that year in the American women's four, there seemed to be nothing that could go wrong for Anita. But 1979 was an *annus horribilus*. Feuding among coaches, sickness among the rowers and, most of all, the serious illness of her father conspired to produce a poor result in the Bled championships. With her ambition of a gold in Moscow still burning bright, it was not where she intended to be. As the Olympic season began, she determined to travel to Princeton to row with Crawford in the coxless pair.

It was at a friend's birthday party in Princeton in January 1980 that she caught the distinctive southern drawl of President Jimmy Carter announcing, 'We may not send our spectators to the Olympic Games in Moscow.' Alarm bells started ringing; she immediately phoned some of her contacts in the White House. Her worst fears were realised. Carter was about to announce, 'We are not going to Moscow.' Even after all these years, the anger still burned fiercely in her eyes when she remembered the sense of betrayal that she felt then. She was enraged, especially with Carter's use of 'we'.

'Where were "We" when I was freezing my tail off on the river training to go to these Games?'

At a stroke, her political patron had turned her Olympic dream into a nightmare.

But Carter's proclamation could not by itself stop an American team travelling to Moscow, Anita knew as much from her involvement with the Amateur Sports Act. It stated that the US was supposed to send a team unless the athletes faced 'severe physical danger'. Clearly, their safety was not an issue in Moscow. What was more, talk of withdrawing passports was hot air. That could not be done unless there was a state of war in existence. Carter therefore had to ensure that the USOC voted not to send a team. His administration set about applying the necessary pressure. Although the USOC received no federal funding whatsoever, the large corporations that paid for the team were persuaded to withdraw their support for 'patriotic' reasons. Any support to individual sports programmes was withdrawn pending the vote of the USOC and briefings were given on the imperative to boycott by no less a sports expert than the Chairman of the Joint Chiefs of Staff. Members of the USOC became convinced that they were assault troops in the front line of the Cold War. Despite the arguments put forward by the athletes, they did their patriotic duty and voted not to go.

The US administration was waging war on anybody who wanted to argue in favour of going to Moscow. De Franz's argument that it should be up to the individual athletes, combined with her refusal to admit defeat, made her a prime target. Her telephone was tapped. What's more, her public profile as athlete spokes-person saw her become the target of a vicious hate mail campaign. In what she considers to be a politically-motivated decision, her family was targeted. A lawsuit was filed against her father, alleging that he had embezzled funds from his practice. It was later proved that they had been taken by his chief accountant in order to pay for his wife's cancer treatment. Eventually the charges were dropped but only after a great deal of pain for her and her family. She nevertheless set about the battle with all the ardour of her parents' battles against racial intolerance. At last Anita had a cause that she could call her own.

But the Establishment ensured that she was blocked at every turn. At a White House meeting of athletes she thought she would have a chance to put her arguments in person to President Carter. Naturally, the invitations were staged so that out of the 200 or so that attended, there were only 15 so-called dissidents. Eventually Anita was called to address the meeting. As she stood up to make her pitch, someone called, 'The President of the United States.' The meeting rose and did not applaud as Carter walked in. She stood there in stunned frustrated silence. She had been set up. Carter made a speech, then immediately left the meeting. Anita had no chance to make her points. Afterwards at the press conference she was even asked, 'Why, as a patriotic American, didn't you applaud the President?'

Her options were blocked at every turn. She took the USOC to court but as luck, or careful planning, would have it, the judge had literally fought the Communists during the Korean War. Not only that, but he had lost an arm doing so. He seemed to show little interests in the legal niceties of the case. To him there was an important principle at stake which he articulated in his closing remarks. He said, 'Sometimes you're asked to serve your country. Sometimes you're asked and don't come home. Other times, as in this case, you're asked not to leave your country. Surely you can serve?'

Like me, though, Anita knew that 'serving her country' had nothing to do with boycotting the Games. As in Britain, American trade with the USSR remained unaffected.

Convinced that right was on her side, Anita looked at the possibility of taking the case to the Supreme Court. The votes would be crucial. Four judges were very conservative and likely to support Carter's boycott call. The other five were more liberally-minded and might listen. But again Anita found her attempts blocked. Whizzer White, one of the justices who might have been sympathetic to the athlete's cause, had to excuse himself from the case; his daughter was on the US women's hockey team. They, with the rowers, had been the most vociferous opponents of the boycott. As a result, the votes did not stack up.

Even then Anita was still unwilling to admit defeat. The Olympic Charter made it possible for an international federation to enter a team with the backing of that country's individual sports association, in this case the USRA. She contacted FISA president Thomi Keller, who said that he'd be delighted to enter the American rowers if he received clearance from the USRA. It was withheld.

As she finished telling me of her unsuccessful campaign against the American boycott, she had an air of sadness about her. 'You know, to this day I don't know how many rowers would have travelled to Moscow if we'd have won. It would have been very scary to go against the patriotic grain.'

But she reserved her biggest regret for not insisting on a face-to-face meeting with the US President. 'I wanted the satisfaction of him [Carter] having to look me in the eye and tell me why I couldn't go. You see, he never dealt with any athlete who was really affected.'

I asked her about Carter's White House reception for the Olympic team.

'Yes, I went. It was an all-expenses-paid weekend in Washington and my father was all excited about meeting Ed Moses's dad.'

I must have looked surprised. As if in answer to my unspoken question, 'Wasn't that giving in?' she said, 'All the rowers, were dressed in T-shirts protesting the boycott. We gave out stickers too. That was really the start of my campaign to ensure that it never happened again.'

Anita never stopped fighting, although in 1980 her time as an international oarswoman was over. For one thing, travelling for another four years in the close proximity of over 30 women was not something that she relished. Besides, there was still that other cherished goal of the Supreme Court. Perhaps if she had gone on to realise her potential in Moscow, the route to legal glory would have been clear? But Anita had unfinished business. Although she would take another six years to recognise it, the trauma of the boycott campaign had effectively ensured that her future would lie within Olympic sport. If her drive to reach the top in the legal profession can be believed, then there was only one place that she could feel content: no less a position than at the top of the IOC.

But then she was hardly flavour of the month with the members of the USOC, some of whom she called 'medical miracles' – men who could walk without the aid of a spine. In addition, her political connections were gone. Even though Carter did lose the election to Reagan, the Republicans had no reason to favour what they saw as a rabble-rousing Afro-American lawyer. Ultimately, though, Anita and others would ensure that the US boycott would be seen for the mistake that it was. When that happened, Anita was back in favour. Whether it was people trying to say 'sorry', or whether they just admired her spunk is open to question. But those in favour of the boycott – for example the chairman of the Los Angeles Olympic Committee, Peter Uberoth, the organiser of the 1984 Los Angeles Games – now found Anita's potential star quality too great to ignore.

California, 1999: Anita De Frantz. At the time of writing, she had just declared her decision to stand for election to the IOC.

Although he had some misgivings over her ability to court controversy, in the end the chance to have a talented female *and* black Olympian involved proved too big an opportunity to pass up. Southern California had a high proportion of black Olympians. Moreover, Anita would prove a valuable link with African sports leaders who needed to be persuaded to resist Moscow's tit-for-tat boycott of the 1984 Games. So Anita was lured out to California where she proved to be a superb asset.

The financial success of the Games gave Anita another problem. She was ready to move back to Washington to pick up her legal career when an opportunity arose to run the Los Angeles Amateur Athletic Foundation, the body responsible for allocating the surplus raised from the '84 Games. In effect it would give her a wonderful opportunity to play a benevolent aunt to hundreds of kids, either supporting them through to Olympic standard competition, or giving children the chance to develop their personalities through athletic competition.

The opportunity to work with kids trying to learn through sport proved too tempting. It was what she had done with her father from her fourth birthday in the pool near her Indianapolis home. Whenever she talks about this project, which she still runs, her eyes light up as if it is this work that she cares about more than any other.

In a revealing moment she explained one of her favourite stories. She remembers a scared little girl in the marshalling area, waiting to swim a 50 metres dash at the ninth annual summer swim. Anita, remembering how at that age she had felt frightened before races, went over to reassure the child, promising to stand at the end of the pool during the race. The child finished, with a struggle in the last 20 metres. As she got he breath back in the water she asked Anita, 'Did I do enough to make the final?'

Anita replied, 'D'you know honey, I was so busy watching you, I didn't watch how anyone else did.' The girl was upset. Anita, remembering her own disappointment at never winning a gold medal, tried to empathise with the girl, attempting to cheer her up and added, 'Don't worry, the best I ever did was a bronze medal.'

The girl replied, reaching up out of the water – in a wonderful role-reversal – to hug Anita and comfort her by saying, 'That's OK, you did your best…'

Given her incessant drive, it's clearly a message that she still feels in need of hearing.

In 1986, though, Anita still had visions of a legal future. That was until the chance came to join the elite members of the IOC, as one of the two American representatives. She still remembers the excitement that she felt when her name was first touted as a possible replacement for Julian Roosevelt. However, her appointment was not a foregone conclusion, for Peter Uberoth had a strong claim. But a few IOC members were unhappy at the way his book on the '84 Games *Made in America* had criticised them. What's more, despite his claims in the book to have opposed the boycott, he was hardly active in that campaign. De Franz's profile and pedigree in the Olympic movement meant that, after him, she was the obvious choice. The IOC had already recognised her struggle against the boycott at its Baden-Baden congress in 1981 where she was awarded the Olympic Order. Once again her talents, gender and race had placed her at the head of the field.

But the IOC is not known for appointing firebrands. It is one of the most conservative organisations in the world. A self-perpetuating oligarchy whose constitution was based on a similar organisation, Henley Royal Regatta. Its numbers include several members of Europe's royal families; Samaranch himself was a member of Franco's fascist government in Barcelona. Youth is largely conspicuous by its absence. These people act and are treated like the aristocracy of world sport. Their homes are five-star, they travel first-class with VIP receptions. Anita herself acknowledges that the IOC is not an organisation known for its dynamic nature. Many members rarely speak in debates. What had happened to the woman who was so subversive in 1980, that the state had to have her phone tapped? Had the risk-taker changed, or mellowed?

Inevitably the answer is 'yes', although Anita would not think so. Within the IOC she is viewed as one of its most vocal members, although that is hardly claiming much. But, undoubtedly, she does speak her mind. In 1989, during a debate on drugs in sport, she suggested that not only athletes but also coaches and administrators guilty of using steroids should be banned for life. It was an exposed position to take and the debate on that issue went on for over two hours, with over 20 IOC members speaking – the Olympic equivalent of an all-night sitting in the House of Commons! Anita lost the vote, but her star was rising. It was hard for an articulate black woman not to be noticed in the male-dominated world of the IOC. What's more, with the huge importance of American television money to the income of the Games, it would not be long before Anita found her way on to the executive board.

The outspoken woman from Indianapolis has long since developed an ability to know when not to press lost causes. She is not known for outbursts in meetings. In 1993, the sport of rowing was ripped apart with controversy over the decision to admit three lightweight events to the Olympic regatta in place of open-weight categories. Anita did not favour granting lightweights Olympic status. In the all-important executive meeting, though, Anita abstained from voting as she was 'conflicted'. But Anita is more proud of the influence that she wields on a wider stage. When Moscow's local government wanted to turn the Olympic rowing course and its facilities to other uses, she was approached by the centre's directors. Her approach to the Mayor of Moscow clearly carried enough clout.

Certainly, she seems very popular among the rank and file IOC members, although they are practised in saying one thing and voting in the opposite way. But there are few IOC members who could boast to having sampled the delights of being a rower doing a European tour 'on the cheap'. She still remembers, with glee, the time a team-mate's bunk in Essen's military barracks collapsed on her. While many IOC members insist on limousine travel, she relishes the opportunity to 'rough it', probably as an opportunity to get back to her roots.

At least that was what I felt as she was crammed into the back of my battered Ford Escort. She was dropping into a nearby rowing meeting on her way back from an IOC meeting in Korea en route to California. My mud-caked car spluttered along the A4 before expiring in the darkness just the other side of Slough. Anita was clearly shattered. But there was no hint of complaint, just a shared hilarity about the incongruous circumstances. The fact her athlete's roots run deep is an important weapon in the De Frantz armoury.

But she can still be embarrassed by the IOC's blunders. When the Salt Lake City bribe scandal broke early in 1999, the US press scented blood. Anita had her background and finances examined with a fine tooth-comb. I could not have imagined any IOC member less likely to have been involved in any bribes or irregularities. Yet every night, after the long meetings in Copenhagen, I saw Anita spend anxious hours on the telephone or internet, seeing what charges she might have to rebut. There is no doubt that, following the scandal, the IOC will change for good. Athlete opinion, basic morality, let alone the red faces of the IOC's multi-million dollar sponsors, demand it. Samaranch will be gone after Sydney. Those who wish to lead sport's most powerful organisation in the 21st century are making their pitch.

It is not a job that Anita openly courts. But then, rather like the Papacy, nobody does. There is an assumption that the best candidate will be arrived at by some kind of mysterious consensus. I knew all this and stopped just short of asking her a direct question about her ambitions to run the IOC. Instead, I asked if she was satisfied with her present responsibilities in sport. The diplomat in her began to outline the tremendous satisfaction that she got from her job with the Amateur Athletic Foundation of Los Angeles. Then she stopped and the rower who led the boycott campaign looked at me. She knew what I wanted to know.

'If you're asking me do I want to be president of the IOC... maybe, maybe.'

I took that as a strong affirmative, about as clear a 'yes', as you might expect from a member of the IOC executive board.

That would be a rich prize indeed. Her parents would recognise it as the fulfilment of Martin Luther King's visions that he articulated so unforgettably on the steps of the Lincoln Memorial in 1963. Perhaps if it doesnt come, Anita will turn her attentions back towards Washington; her Democratic connections are once more impeccable. But I have a sneaking suspicion, that if she could turn the clock back, she would exchange it all for a victory over Carter in the boycott campaign and a seat on a plane to the Moscow Olympics, way back in July 1980.

Postscript

As chapter endings go, I was pleased. More than two years after I interviewed Anita in 1998, I sent her a draft to read. There seemed no immediate logic as to why I did so then, although I now realise it was serendipity. At the time Anita was undecided if she would put herself forward to replace Samaranch. Two weeks later she wrote back:

'Martin. I want you to know that I am going to run for the Presidency of the IOC... I do believe that reading your text solidified my resolve. I know it won't be easy but, this time, I get to decide to go to Moscow!'

I was bowled over by her letter. But I never really understood her reference to Moscow until a few weeks later. The IOC session to elect the president could have taken place in any of the beautiful locations around the world. But no – almost exactly 21 years after the opening ceremony of the Games that Anita missed, the election will take place in Moscow.

In some way, the course of her life over the last two decades now seems clear. Her path changed irrevocably back in 1980. Now, on 16 July 2001 – win or lose – it will change forever once more. As conclusions, or beginnings go, it would not be politically correct if I had ended this chapter in any other way.

Heroes

BEFORE I left the medal stage in Moscow, with the strains of the East German national anthem still ringing in my ears, I shook hands with Siegfried Brietzke for the first time. It was pretty perfunctory, as greetings go. I suspect it meant a lot more to me than it did to him. That's because he was my hero. Yes, he was up there on a par with all the heroes of my youth: Bobby Moore, Geoff Hurst, President Kennedy and... Siegfried Brietzke. Kind of strange. He wasn't even my first rowing hero. As an impressionable schoolboy that had been my old teacher, now team-mate, Jim Clark. But by 1980, Jim seemed to be more a friend than hero. No, by 1980 the tall blond East German was firmly number one. After all, he'd just won three Olympic golds on the trot. Before Redgrave amassed his four that was enough to top the *Guinness Book of Records*.

I suppose it was love at first sight. But then I was an impressionable 16-year-old. It was even Jim Clark who sort of 'introduced' us. He told me to watch out for a 'tasty' new East German four at the Lucerne World Championships. As I stood on the edge of the Rotsee and watched this crew win by a mile, I immediately identified with the figure at stroke, Brietzke. Even from the edge of the lake, his striking blond hair marked him out from the others in the boat. To me, it seemed like it was he who was setting the shell's remarkable pace and flow, somehow, dragging the others along with him. It was what I aspired to do.

So it was that Brietzke became my rowing hero. He didn't know it then. In fact he wasn't to know it for another 25 years. His picture was still on my bedroom wall when I lined up against his crew for the first time in 1977. After 20 strokes they were out of sight. The picture came down after that – it had to – although for me, Brietzke never lost his place as a rowing god. We raced each other for another three years – he always won. The funny thing was, in all that time we never spoke or even nodded. Just that brief handshake on the medal rostrum at the Moscow Olympics. But that was it – hello and goodbye all at once.

Not that I forgot him, I supposed that he was living in some kind of Socialist sporting Valhalla. But in those days, East Germany seemed about as impenetrable to me as the home of the gods had once appeared to mere mortals. That all changed in 1989 when its walls came tumbling down. The

Moscow, 1980: The Olympic victory ceremony for coxless fours. I did not see
Siegfried Brietzke (fourth left) for another 19 years.

East German system collapsed. It changed the lives of all those international
sports stars forever. At a stroke, they lost their hallowed status, not to say
their jobs. Hundreds left and Jurgen Grobler, who was to become
Redgrave's coach and mentor, was among them.

In the years that followed, the meticulous documentation of the Staazi
files began to lay bare the fear and abuse on which much of East German
sporting success had been built. Even Grobler was revealed as having given
information to the Staazi. All of a sudden everything that East Germany ever
did in sport was being called into question. Was the man who I had made
my hero only that good because he took performance-enhancing drugs?
Had he too supplied information to the Staazi? As the story became news, I
found myself defending the triumphs of my sporting hero. After all these
years, I did not want Brietzke to be knocked off his pedestal.

But what was I doing, defending the reputation of a man who I had
never met? A man whom I'd made practically immortal without ever
knowing? To make sense of it all, I had to go back to the autumn of 1980.
Then, as Brietzke's rowing career faded away and dawn was breaking over
that of his record-breaking replacement, Steven Redgrave, I prepared to row
with Jim Clark, my teacher and, more importantly, my first rowing hero. It
is one thing to put someone on a pedestal from a distance, like Brietzke. It

is quite another having them sitting behind you in the same boat, especially when you fail to deliver. The trauma of the year that followed, after promising so much, was to change forever my perspective of sporting heroes.

With the retirement of David Townsend following the Moscow Olympics, our four was bereft of a natural asset: a powerful rhythm-maker to sit in the 'three' seat and dictate the pace of the boat. There were two options: a young, inexperienced Henley winner called Andy Holmes who promised much but had yet to deliver at the top level; and Jim Clark. Clark's had been an illustrious career with four silver medals. But the sheen had begun to wear off after he had spent two largely fruitless years sculling with Chris Baillieu. The partnership had run its course with their failure to win a medal in the Olympics. Baillieu would now try the single, while Jim, just turned 30, looked for something else.

He had trained with us for a brief spell in 1978 when Dave Townsend was injured; then the boat had flown. Now, with his experience and hunger to revive the success that he had once known, Jim seemed the ideal replacement. For me, it seemed like a dream come true. My first glimpse of international rowing had been of Jim's crew in the Munich Olympics. I had been weaned on his stories of races won and lost on far away lakes. It was because of him that I was now in the international team. His place in the boat seemed like a natural progression, almost a fulfilment of all that had gone before. In reality, Andy Holmes never had a chance and it is only with hindsight that I could see how wrong that decision might have been. The niggles started to creep in early. Whereas McNuff, Beattie and Townsend had been benevolently tolerant of my wayward timekeeping, Jim was not. Partly this was due to the pressure of his job at Latymer Upper School. What annoyed him was that most mornings, I had only to fall out of bed.

I had started going out with Amanda, the youngest daughter of Pat and Eileen Brennan. They looked after London Rowing Club, where we were based, and had a small flat above the club. Their three daughters, who often helped behind the bar, always stood out in a club which was then and still is open only to male rowers. Amanda was the most attractive and timid of the three girls. It was not an ideal environment for someone of her character to live in. Her long dark hair, svelte figure and striking brown eyes marked her out from her sisters. In particular, it was her air of seeming unapproachability that was so beguiling. It had taken me some time to even get to talk to her, let alone ask her out.

By the winter of 1980, we had been dating for almost two years. Her interests of art and drama were completely different to mine, although I would learn to love both. What was more, she couldn't stand rowing. So it was faintly incongruous that after outings, someone who ate, slept and drank the sport would rush upstairs to the flat, sit by her as she did her homework and talk about anything else except rowing. Perhaps it was that sort of refuge that I was looking for. Amanda shared a room with her sister Rebecca. Amazingly, she put up with me sleeping on the floor, next to Amanda's bed, most nights. This was especially since I generally had to be up at the crack of dawn for a training session. But although I had only a few steps to negotiate down to the boat bays, I still contrived to turn up late for outings.

I suspect that if it had been just the lateness, Jim would have been able to cope. But of course, there was more. The boat never had the same feel to it as when Jim had rowed with us in previous years. Notably, the balance during the recovery was erratic. In addition, we tended to apply the power in different parts of the stroke. I was known for my no-nonsense direct but rustic application of pressure at the catch. Jim prided himself on a much smoother application of power at the catch and a more rhythmical 'feel' on the recovery phase. In a sense, it was the same contrast as that which had existed between Dave Townsend and me, except that I could always tell 'Tosser' to get lost when he started exhorting me to 'allow the boat to run more', or not to 'bash it so hard'. This wasn't possible for me with Jim.

For a start, he had been my teacher only a few years previously. The pull of the pedagogue-student relationship was far stronger than that of team-mate or friend. What's more, I thought that he clearly knew what he was talking about. Ever since he had coached me at school, he had been trying to smooth out my rough edges. Now, he was doing it again, except it was from the seat behind me, not from the coaching launch. Of course, I desperately wanted to think that I was rowing more smoothly, or at least could aspire to. When it didn't happen, I fell into a morose silence. I wasn't to know that, at the time, Jim's back was giving him serious problems; that it was touch and go whether he would carry on at all. In fact it was probably this injury, as much as anything, which made him appear tetchy. What I did know then was that the dream of rowing with my hero was turning sour. The situation gave rise to all my old stereotypes about 'not being good enough'. In addition, I was clearly no longer the 'leader' of the crew, as I had once imagined myself to be.

Verase, 1981: The pressure of rowing with one of your heroes. Jim Clark, rowing behind me in the '3' seat (second left). The photograph was taken by our coach David Tanner, with whom I was in a 'strop', hence my cap pulled down over my face.

But the tension on the water contrasted markedly with the mood off it. There, the camaraderie produced a synthesis between us that was rarely present in the boat. Perhaps it was a way of breaking the tension. Certainly our Easter altitude training camp to Johannesburg was one to remember. After having annoyed the 'Right' with our participation in the Moscow Games, the next year we did the same to the 'Left' by visiting apartheid-ridden South Africa.

It was inexcusable really. Nelson Mandela would be locked away for another nine years while poverty, violence and discrimination were the lot of almost all South Africa's non-white population. Officially, they weren't even inhabitants of their own country. The Group Areas Act made them natives of a string of homelands, meaningless dust-blown territories within South Africa's borders. They were only let out to work, although their presence was then supposedly invisible. Soweto, a black township of several millions next to Johannesburg, was not marked on any map. Officially, it didn't exist. Neither did any black sportsman in South Africa's international teams. Although the sporting boycott hit the rugby-loving Afrikaans particularly hard, the South African Government would not change their policies because of it.

But sport was an important means of drawing the attention of the world outside to the evils of the South African system. Sonny Ramphael's South African Non Racial Olympic Committee was busy banning sportsmen and women who tried to ply their trade in the face of apartheid, and yet we went. Not quite oblivious to all the evils of apartheid – I had to teach them for GCSE lessons at school – but certainly unaware of individual suffering. We went boldly, stating that sport and politics didn't, or at least shouldn't, mix. After the political interference that meaninglessly destroyed the Moscow Olympics it seemed like we were flying the flag of politically-free sport. Perhaps we were, although on reflection it doesn't seem a particularly principled thing to have done. All that could be said in our defence was that we took part in no official competitions (a fact which caused us to be omitted from SANROC's infamous sporting 'Black List' published later that year).

Our experiences with the experiment of altitude training were inconclusive – we never did it again. But seeing the reality of apartheid brought home to me the evil of the regime like nothing else could. The most shocking thing was seeing our host family's black maid, together with her baby, sleeping the night on the concrete floor of the dog kennel. She was working late because, as a result of our visit, there was too much housework to get through and she couldn't get back to her township. Our hosts (who looked after us wonderfully) were transgressing the law by letting her stay the night in a 'white' area as much as she was breaking the infamous Pass Laws by not returning to her township. If found (there was always the hint of a suggestion that the Afrikaans family next door might inform) the maid would lose her 'right' to stay in the squalor of the Johannesburg township. She would be thrown back in to the economic nemesis of the Bantustan (black homeland) whence she came.

It felt like there was a kind of nemesis waiting for us on our return. The boat continued to feel lifeless and the tension boiled over with an ultimatum to me from Tanner to 'get my act together' or else I might be out of the crew. My 'sloppy' approach had been identified by Jim as a factor in our poor performance. The chastisement at first amazed, then shocked me. Had my old crewmates, Ian and John, agreed to this? I felt isolated and vulnerable in a unit where I'd previously felt so secure. Despite the warning, nothing really changed. The season dragged on despite winning a bronze medal from

Lucerne, 1982: It's not often that Steve Redgrave – or me – had to fight to keep ahead of the umpire's launch but we were outclassed in the final of the Quadruple Sculls.

a poor row at Lucerne regatta. But in August something happened during the pre-World Championships training camp on Lago Di Varese in Northern Italy. For some reason (to this day I don't know why), the boat began to fly.

Rowing is often one of those infuriating sports in which things seem to happen for no apparent reason. Our times improved dramatically, so much so that we were the quickest boat in the team. It seemed like the whole year had just been a long nightmare from which we had just emerged. The boat was flying and at last I was rowing as smoothly as Jim wanted me to. We began to enjoy ourselves on the water, stealing several plastic ducks which Italian hunters used as lures to attract their prey. We tied them to our rudder lines and rowed off with them attached to the boat, howling with laughter as the plastic family bobbed along in our wake. What was even more funny was that another coach, Richard Ayling, had his rubber dingy shot at by an irate hunter who wanted his lures back. It tickled us that the hunter had blamed Ayling, rather than us, for stealing them.

It was therefore with enjoyment and anticipation that I crossed the Alps travelling to Munich, that year's venue for the World Rowing Championships. The course was one that I was looking forward to rowing on immensely. As a 14-year-old I'd received a postcard from Jim, with a picture of the enormous grandstand, purpose-built for the 1972 Olympic

Games. Almost uniquely among rowing courses, the water was crystal clear. It added a slightly surreal feel to training because you could see the bottom of the lake while rowing along.

On my postcard Jim, had written that 'the competition was incredibly fast'. Now with the retirement of Brietzke, the field in coxless fours seemed wide open. But from the very first session on the Olympic basin, the relaxed 'feel' of the boat that we'd had in Italy, had disappeared – almost as magically as it had appeared a fortnight earlier. There was no discernible reason for it. Something had changed but we didn't know what. For my part, I begun to feel uncomfortable in the boat, leaning away from my rigger. That particular sensation was my bête noire, haunting me whenever things felt uncomfortable. My confidence began to evaporate. It should have been no surprise that we were duly knocked out of the finals by a mediocre Spanish crew and trailed in a lowly tenth place. But despite everything, I wasn't expecting it.

It was the first time that I had ever 'failed' in rowing. What's more, it had happened with my hero sitting behind me. There was no one else to blame but myself. I was inconsolable. At that moment it seemed like all my previous results counted for nothing; I was a rowing failure. I couldn't find solace with Beattie, McNuff and, least of all, Jim; they were all in their own private worlds. As far as the rest of the team was concerned, dealing with a people in a boat that has 'failed' is about as easy as trying to find words to comfort a person who has lost a close relative. Without conscious effort, you assume pariah status.

It was more marked that year because the team did well. The eight, coached by Penny Chuter, won a silver medal. At one moment, during the last '500', it seemed possible that they might have won the gold. For me, in my self-centred way, that would have been unbearable. I felt relieved as the Russians won. The coxed four, with Andy Holmes on board in the 'three' seat, failed to win a medal but in a glorious manner: they lead the world for 1,250 metres in the final. Even the young quad, with Steven Redgrave in his first senior World Championships, finished higher than we did. As Jim pointedly said to me at the course, when I tried to assuage him about the following year's prospects, 'You can't come back from that!' He was right, at least in the sense of our four. The bonds that had held Tanner, McNuff, Beattie and I together since our schooldays had snapped.

I had already determined that I would not row in the national squad coached by Chuter. For a brief moment, in the winter of 1981, it looked a possibility that David Tanner, with Bob Janousek's help, might run a rival eights squad. The wily Czech turned up once to an early winter gym session, full of disaffected rowers like myself. There was much rumour and intrigue as to who would go with what camp.

One weekend, when our 'rebel' eight finally took to the water, we passed the 'official' squad eight on the water. Then we could see for ourselves who was with Chuter. I was shocked. Both John Beattie and Jim Clark had – there seemed no other way of putting it at the time – gone over to the 'enemy'. I don't know whose 'defection' hurt the most, Beattie's or Clark's. But it was a death blow to our infant rebel crew. McNuff stopped rowing to concentrate on his job, while most of the 'rebels' went into the squad.

As for me...? I had all sorts of approaches to come into the fold. Richard Ayling, Penny Chuter's assistant, spent a Sunday afternoon trying to persuade me to join the squad. It was a fruitless task. I had already made up my mind that rowing with Jim was something I couldn't face again. We didn't stop being friends. Indeed, in later years I would often run to him for advice and help. But our relationship had forever changed. I'd seen my schoolboy hero as a fallible human being, rather than the superhuman person that I'd placed on a dais.

In addition, I felt guilty. This was my fault. If I'd have rowed like Jim wanted me to, then perhaps he would still have been up there on a dais, rather than a rower at the unsuccessful end of an illustrious career. Now, I realise that seeing Jim off his pedestal, although difficult, was no bad thing. Not least when I began to realise that my choice of heroes said far more about my own values and self-worth than it does about those of my 'hero'. But at the time, I didn't have that awareness.

From 'Hero to Zero' is an process that keeps today's tabloids busy. Witness the demolition of British sporting heroes like Gazza, Alan Shearer or even Tim Henman. Sometimes it is the sort of journalism which shames the press. On other occasions, I have to admit, it is compelling reading. But when you're in the middle of it – let alone the cause – it's a painful process. Most great sportsmen and women have to go through that process. It's rare that anyone, with the exception of people like Bobby Charlton or Jack Nicklaus, attains that iconic status which puts their reputation beyond reach of the press. A long career usually always ends with a flop or two. So after shedding one hero in 1981, it maybe wasn't surprising that I turned to another.

Although Steven Redgrave's iconic status lay in the future, even in those early days there was still something of an aura around the 19-year-old Marlow giant. Much of this rested on the expectation of what was to come. Both he and his coach, Mike Spracklen, thought he was good enough to win the single sculls at the 1988 Olympic Games. But although he promised much, Redgrave's forays into the world of single sculling as a junior had not been spectacular. In a crew boat he seemed much better, although even in the double sculls with Adam Clift they threw away a certain gold, losing to an East German boat which contained the eventual winner of the single sculls in Seoul, Thomas Lange. Yet few denied that Redgrave's was a raw and exciting talent.

In 1982, Spracklen's chosen vehicle for Redgrave to learn his craft on the international stage was the quadruple scull. It was a fast technical boat with the advantage of allowing Redgrave to train in his single, while having the company of his crewmates. The friendships forged between the young group of scullers that formed the basis of Spracklen's sculling group, men like Adam Clift and Eric Sims, still run deep. Their humour was rough and ready, with more than a hint of the practical joke about it.

When Adam was going out on his first date with a local girl, Steven and the 'lads' bought several packets of condoms, putting them in Adam's car. They made sure that they were invisible to Clift but not to his date. In addition, they had stuffed a few condoms in each pocket of his jeans. That evening, whenever he was pulling out his money to pay for petrol, or cinema tickets, a wad of condoms would fall on the floor. Adam never did say if this encouraged or put off his-partner for the evening. But, much to Steven's amusement, they never saw each other again.

It was into this environment that I entered. I was very much an outsider but Mike Spracklen was glad to have a measure of experience among his young group. The others were too, although I sometimes felt that as the only person who had won World Championship medals, Steven and I were often competing, like wary stags, sizing each other up before claiming rightful possession of the territory. There was no doubt that, in Steven's eyes, the Marlow reach belonged him.

Although we never actually fought – our duels were kept to races on the water – there was an understandable tension. It was made worse because I never had the raw speed to compete with Redgrave in the single. The only way that I could keep up was by racing at a higher stroke rate than the one which Spracklen set. This was something that used to annoy Steven (who

Lake Sarnen, 1983: Approaching the end of the lake during an evening training session just before the World Championships. Our base there was the idyllic Hotel Waldheim.

lived and died by completing the programme as it was laid down). Often he would shout out in frustration at me across the river, as he caught sight of my higher cadence. But even so, it was almost impossible to better him on a stretch where he knew the position of every bush, current and eddy.

I wasn't the only one who'd get frustrated. Adam, a faster sculler than me, had often tried to better Steven. Then, just as Adam was getting an advantage, a despairing Lancashire voice would scream out expletives as he got stuck in a bush that Steven had somehow just managed to avoid. Sometimes the rivalry between Adam and Steven did spill over off the water. Once, the two of them went for each other on the lawn of Spracklen's house where they used to boat from. In a desperate effort to separate them, Mike leapt on Steven's back. But the big man kept on, whirling around the garden with his coach clinging on to his back. For Adam, as he later recounted with a satisfied smirk on his face, 'It slowed him down, so I had the chance to really catch him with a few!'

But the rivalry was helping my sculling to improve, although for a long time it looked as though our quad would not be good enough to make the final. Even worse, the eight, which I had rejected – with Jim on board – looked certain medalists. After an ignominious performance at Vichy regatta, Malcolm McGowan, the 'seven' man in the eight, taunted us with the refrain, 'Ten lengths down in a blue Carbocraft', which he sung to the tune of *Yellow Submarine*. Redgrave replaced me at stroke for the next race in Duisburg although it made no difference. But somehow, by the World Championships, we had found some speed. Steven and I played musical chairs again, so I stroked the boat. We ended up making the final – just! The eight finished an ignominious ninth and last place. It was Jim Clark's last race.

It was our final race in the quad too. By then, Steven thought he'd done enough to break through in the single scull. The poor result for the eight meant Chuter was out and Tanner returned. Under his guidance, John Beattie, Ian McNuff and I returned to row in a four again. But the results in following year's World Championships were hugely disappointing, particularly as it was the year before the Olympics. My crew finished in a distant sixth place, while Steven was humiliated, being eliminated early from the competition. He spent the latter stages of the week whizzing round the giant water ski tow, next to the Duisburg course. There was, as yet, no sign of the heroic feats that he was to achieve.

In Duisburg, heroes seemed in short supply. East Germany weren't so dominant any more. None of the new breed of champions that year seemed to measure up, as Siegfried Brietzke once had for me. The gold medal coxless four from West Germany had come up through the system, just like me. They were my age. In fact, when I had won my first bronze medal, they finished a distant sixth. The values and standards of my youth seemed to be changing quickly. I could not be sure of myself any more.

With hindsight, it was during those years that I began to 'grow up', certainly in rowing terms. During the forthcoming Olympic season I would once more have to fend for myself. Ian McNuff would give up for good, David Tanner once again became *persona non grata*, while Jim Clark had finally thrown in the towel a year earlier.

But for all my new-found maturity, I found I still needed heroes. With no-one to relate to, my thoughts turned back to the stroke of the East German four. On occasions I found myself either trying to mimic his own inimitable style, or knowingly talk about the races he'd won to other rowers. I presumed he was now happily retired behind the Wall in East Germany; he was of course, Siegfried Brietzke.

It was not until I let go of the sport some years later that I got a chance to come face to face with him. But how circumstances had changed. Documentation about East Germany's use of drugs to achieve sporting

success was revealed daily. The charts showing exactly what drugs East German champions like Marita Koch (whom I'd watched win Olympic gold in the 400 metres) had been taking. The cost of this abuse began to be revealed in cases like that of the triple Olympic champion swimmer Rica Reinisch, who told of how she was fed pills from the age of 12 and now suffered from ovarian cysts and heart problems. The evidence was clear that some East German athletes who were worried about the effects of these drugs on their bodies had refused to take them and had then been thrown off the team.

On top of all this were the revelations that many East German athletes had been agents of the secret state police, the infamous Staazi. They reported faithfully on every aspect of the lives of their team-mates: who they talked to or slept with; what they said about the political system; whether they mixed with foreign competitors whilst travelling abroad. Even something as innocuous as exchanging a racing shirt was looked on as a serious misdemeanour. After having an affair with another team member, Harold Jahrling, an Olympic champion oarsman – now a coach in Australia – was punished by being thrown off the World Championship team.

The revelations threatened to dog British preparations for the Sydney Games. In 1998, Jahrling's former coach, Jurgen Grobler, then coaching Steven Redgrave, was linked with the Staazi (it was emerging that many former East German athletes and coaches had similar connections). In addition, Jurgen must have been closely involved with the doping programme – despite what he told Steven on his arrival in Britain in 1990. I don't blame Jurgen for his lack of candour on that occasion, nor would I seek to judge a fine coach through his involvement with a system which left little choice. But while acknowledging that it was difficult for any individual to stand up to the doping abuse, this news began to leave huge question-marks in my mind about the integrity of the medals that the East Germans had won – some of them at my expense.

Yet despite all this, I still found myself wrapping up the achievements of the East German rowing team in some kind of magic and mystique. I still have an affection for Jurgen and his achievements, both in East Germany and Britain. Perhaps in a way, it was still hard to knock my heroes off their

Duisburg, 1983: A disconsolate look, as we walk our boat off the course following our sixth place finish in the World Championships. I am leading the crew off, Ian's face is partially obscured by the rigger.

pedestals. As I finally travelled to Leipzig to meet Siegfried Brietzke in the spring of 1999, 1 wondered whether that spell might finally be broken.

It was my first visit to what was the former East German state for ten years. Then I had been struck by the drab, ordinary, rather colourless nature of the streets and buildings. Nothing could have prepared me for the scale of the change that has happened since reunification, than my arrival in the magnificently restored railway station of Leipzig. The huge concourse contained some spectacular pieces of modern sculpture, while the floors beneath contained a massive shopping centre.

And now the parking lots contained none of the little Trabants, of which I'd seen so many on my last trip. They were the sort of Ford Cortina of East Germany – a car for the masses. It could seat four people in absolute discomfort while chugging along the autobahns at a sedate 50mph, emitting a highly noxious exhaust from its two-stroke engine. The waiting list for that car had been ten years, unless you were an Olympic champion in which case it was only two. When reunification came, people used the profits from the exchange of their worthless Ost Marks with the all-powerful Deutsch Mark to buy Volkswagens, Audis and BMWs. The Trabants disappeared overnight. Now the station car park contained the brands from the west of Germany and plenty of other makes, like the new green Mazda of Jorg

East Berlin, 1971: Jorg Weissig's 'Sonny Boy' Siggi with his engaging smile.

Weissig, the man who had come to meet me. Weissig was Brietzke's former coach.

Jorg had since returned to live in Germany after a spell of coaching in Belgium. It was with his help that I had managed to trace my former hero, who had agreed to travel back to his old training centre in Leipzig to meet me. Clearly 'Siggi' (for that was what everybody, including our four in the 'old days', seemed to call him) still had a particularly close relationship with his old coach. It must have been because of that relationship that Siegfried, who now lived in the north of Germany, had agreed to drive nearly 400 kilometres to Leipzig the following morning. Why else would he come that far to talk to a man he had never met?

In the evening before Siggi arrived, Jorg and I talked a lot about the 'old times', when East Germany was the foremost rowing nation in the world. Leipzig had become the top centre and Jorg had coached its top crew, containing Siggi. He showed me a lot of his old photographs, of Siggi when he started rowing as a lad of 17. Although he looked only 14, his features were unmistakable, always fixed in a smile under that mop of bright golden hair. If I wanted to learn about Siggi, it was clear that Jorg had many of the answers. As midnight approached, I set about the conversation with relish.

Jorg had been involved in all aspects of Siggi's career. In an effort to attract talented youngsters to the Leipzig training centre (at that time in competition with others all over East Germany), in 1968, he had appeared on the nation's top Christmas television show, asking for youngsters of 16 and over to come to Leipzig and try rowing. The thought drifted into my head of Mike Spracklen going through a comedy routine with Morecambe and Wise just to get hold of the young Steven Redgrave. However, in East Germany, the recruitment of sporting stars was serious stuff (the nation's prestige depended on it). The 16-year-old Brietzke, who clearly had wanderlust (he had planned to go to sea), was almost immediately hooked and applied to join Weissig's scheme.

It must have been an exceptional crop of youngsters that came along with Siggi. Within a year, six of the original 100 had won gold medals at the World Junior rowing championships in Ioanina, Greece. The following year, Jorg put together four of his 19-year-old prodigies in a crew to race the then undefeated world and Olympic champion coxless four from SC Einheit Dresden, stroked by Frank Forburger. In a sensational result, they won by five seconds (although this verdict was reversed at the East German trial a month later). In soccer terms it was like putting the FA Youth Cup winners up against the winners of the European Champions League and expecting the youngsters to emerge victorious. But these boys were clearly no ordinary youths and it wasn't long before 'Weissig's Babes' were to leave their imprint on the world of rowing.

They did that in no uncertain fashion, rowing with Mager in a pair. Siggi became Olympic champion for the first time at the Munich Olympics. Two years later, Jorg put together his famous four and they were unbeaten for the next three years. Siggi won his second Olympic gold in Montreal. During the Olympic semi-final, Siggi's crew decided to try to record a time under six minutes, then a world record. They stormed down the track in five minutes 53 seconds, breaking the then world record by almost double figures. It was a breathtaking performance, one which perhaps only Redgrave could match today. Their record stood for over 14 years.

In all these crews Siggi was at stroke. To me, it seemed that he had to be the East German equivalent of Steven Redgrave. As I listened to Jorg telling me Siggi's history, I was waiting for something that indicated just how highly my hero was regarded in East German rowing. But in the small hours of the morning, my illusions about Siggi's status began to be slowly deflated.

Apparently it was Semmler who was the strongest man in the crew (it was with him that I had surreptitiously exchanged shirts after the Moscow Olympics). He was better at sculling, weights and track and field than Siggi. When they formed the four, Semmler thought that these qualities would make the stroke seat his own. But he was disappointed. What he did not possess was the guile to decide which tactics were the best to employ for the race.

Semmler sounded a bit like me; tried too hard, technically less than adept. I thought then that such a man could never have been my hero. It would have been like looking in the mirror. No wonder I had chosen Siggi, the man who was technically more adept (a quality which I hadn't possessed). Although Siggi wasn't a Redgrave-type figure, he nevertheless did have the important ability to lift the crew with a smile. Siggi was a 'sunny boy', never complaining at any training load, always motivated, whatever the circumstances.

As our conversation drifted off in the early hours of Saturday morning, I went to sleep in Jorg's study, packed with Olympic memorabilia. I dreamt of races won and lost in far away climes, of East German rowers in their distinctive racing singlets, and of meeting my hero after all these years, wondering what he looked like and if indeed, at the end of it all, he would still be my hero.

The door bell rang at 9.30 on Saturday morning and a tall man, wearing jeans and an open-necked shirt, stooped as he walked through the door of the flat. He still looked fit, no older than his mid-30s. Although fair, his hair had lost some of its blond colour. On his face was that rather broad but youthful smile. Whatever else he had become, Siegfried Brietzke was still a 'sunny boy'. As we shook hands our eyes met and as we held each other's gaze there was more than just the look of two old rowers – ancient combatants – meeting after a long while. I could see in his eyes a kind of searching look, as if he too had also been wondering what the purpose of his long drive here had really been.

As we eased round Jorg's kitchen table, where the coffee and that dark bread of which the Germans are so fond was in plentiful supply, I had my first disappointment. Although he remembered the crew that I raced in, he did not recognise me. When I looked up to see his face, the smile had gone. But I didn't see any trace of regret, just a matter-of-fact look in his eyes. For the first time I was aware of the same sense of distance and unapproachability that I'd felt when we used to race. As we started to talk, I felt distinctly awkward.

It seemed easier to start the conversation by talking about the experiences that we had in common. In New Zealand, for instance, I remembered the smile and wave that he had given me as we both watched the closing ceremony immediately after the finals. It was the first time that he had acknowledged me and I was surprised that he could give me such a cheery greeting when he had just lost a key race. We had won a bronze medal, while they had taken the silver, losing to a brutal but effective Russian crew. For a seemingly invincible four, it was a result that seemed so out of character. As his mind remembered that distant race, I could see in his eyes that even after all these years, it was a result that still rankled: the master tactician and strategist had been found wanting. My confidence began to return. The man was only human after all. When he waved at me that day, he must have been seething inside. I recognised that if I wanted to know the real person who was my hero, I had to look beyond the 'sunny boy' and to what feelings were camouflaged by that broad smile.

Part of what it was hiding then was his intention to give up. That season, was his eighth in international competition. At the tender age of 26, Siggi was tired of racing but, most of all, tired of training. There were no recriminations, no dramatic statements at the end of the race, like Redgrave's in Atlanta, just a realisation that he had had enough of the massive training load that Jorg's schedule demanded of them.

Redgrave, Pinsent and company had been doing the same programme (and more) since Grobler arrived in Britain. But 20 years ago it was a phenomenal load. Three sessions a day, covering something like 50 kilometres on the water and over an hour of weights in the gym. Sometimes, to ring the changes, Jorg brought along a top cycling or swimming coach, so the crew could listen to a different voice and learn a different skill. But it was all too much for Siggi, who had married in 1973. His young son saw little of his dad. He felt he had won everything that the sport had to offer. Unlike Steven, he clearly did not think in Olympic cycles. For him, the Moscow Games, then only two years away, were an Olympics too far.

Ultimately, though, it was the advocacy of Jorg that won through. A month later, as the crew stopped by the side of the river in Leipzig to mull over their decision, their coach argued forcefully for them to continue for just two more years. When Siggi spoke of the time that he wanted with his family, Jorg argued that, as a triple Olympic champion, the grateful state would be bountiful to him. But in the end it was the frustration of finishing on a losing note that drove Siggi and the crew on. As Jorg walked away to let the crew make their decision, he must have known that there was only one option.

It was in the Moscow Games that Siggi had his best performance. They had to row with a sub on board. Mager, Siggi's pairs partner, had an infected finger and was not allowed to row with it. They chose to race with Jurgen Thiele, an inexperienced youngster from their club. It was an impressive display of club loyalty. The crew really wanted to swap Thiele for the bigger and more powerful Doberschutz, then rowing in the eight. The coach of the eight agreed to let Doberschutz go but would not take Thiele in return. Rather than let their young club-mate go without a vest, they rowed with him and beat the Russians by some four seconds.

This must have been Siggi's crowning moment. With three consecutive Olympic gold medals, more than any other rower, he was now a hero of the East German state, to be feted at banquets and ceremonies all over the Democratic Republic. I asked him how it felt to be a hero. It was as if the word was anathema to him. He flatly denied that he had ever seen himself this way, or even that other people had.

It was hard for me to understand this, unless he was being self-effacing.

I knew that after the Olympics, the state asked him to speak in many schools, precisely because he was a sports hero, so I pressed him again: how did it feel to be a hero for these young people? He answered in English, without waiting for interpretation. 'Nein, never a hero.' With a rather Germanic type of explanation, he replied that at Leipzig he was in an optimal situation, with a good group of people. For him, success was the logical consequence of the training programme.

It was extraordinary that such a successful rower could fail to see that he was a hero for at least the young people that he spoke to. But for him the word itself had more powerful connotations. For him to be an Olympic champion (even three times over), clearly felt like nothing extraordinary in a country where Olympic success was regarded as the norm. Contrast the 50 gold medals that East Germany won in the Moscow Games with Britain's three. Perhaps it was the consequence of being schooled in the ways of a deeply collectivised state, where the needs and sometimes the personality of the individual was always secondary to the needs of the many. In some ways, the sport of rowing must have been an ideal metaphor for this model of society. Or perhaps it was just that I was unwilling to see my hero as he really was?

There are those today who see East German sportsmen and women as demons, rather than heroes. Sharron Davies, among others, is on record as demanding recompense for her silver medal won in the 1980 Olympic Games because her opponent's performance was steroid enhanced. If I wanted to see Siggi in his true light, then I had to grasp the nettle and ask him about steroids. Papers revealed since 1989 had shown that the entire East German rowing team of 1980 were on the doping programme lists at the Leipzig institute and the Sports Medicine Institute in East Berlin.

It was hard for me to ask the question. I suppose I still thought that the drugs were not really the reason for his success. So I asked the question in a de-personalised way: 'Has all the recent publicity about drug taking in East German sport detracted from your success?' It was as if he was waiting for that very question. It was one of the only times that he didn't wait for the interpreter before answering.

'Nein!' came the unequivocal response.

There was no way that he was going to put even the smallest part of any of those medals down to anything except the hundreds of thousands of kilometres that he had rowed, or millions of kilos that he had lifted in the gym. Both he and I knew that the effects of steroids in rowing were not as dramatic as they were in other sports such as swimming, sprinting, or the throwing events. They were used chiefly to aid recovery between sessions.

But his defence was ferocious. He said that the GDR was a small country and had to fight the richer countries where drug taking was also a problem (although I have never known of anybody who took drugs in British rowing). He became articulated. Although he hadn't thought of himself as a hero, he did see himself as an astronaut, someone who was constantly having to be at the service of science, which was trying to push the boundaries of the body to its limits in the service of the state. The scientists had 'not only experimented with drugs'. But in the closest that he came to showing any remorse, he concluded his eulogy by agreeing that 'maybe the scientists made mistakes'.

I could buy the analogy of Siggi as 'The Right Stuff'. Both Kennedy in America, and more so Kruschev in the Soviet Union, had used their astronauts as soldiers in a proxy war fought between the super powers. Sometimes, they were expendable. So it was with the GDR, who did not have access to the technology of the Space Race; instead they used sports stars. But I was left feeling that although the scientist made 'mistakes', Siggi accepted what it was that the scientists were trying to do. I was sure that he had willingly taken performance-enhancing drugs.

Even so, I was not salivating at the prospect of seeing my Olympic bronze upgraded although I know others, who felt cheated of better colour medals, that would relish the prospect. Even Siggi's admission that he had taken drugs had not dented my admiration for his and his crew's incredible athleticism. In rowing at least, the equation that drugs equals you win; no drugs equals you lose, is false.

Of course there was a more disturbing aspect to all this. Siggi may have seen his body as something to be placed in the service of the state. But others didn't. Those who did not want to take the little blue pills that were given them by their coaches were told in no uncertain terms that unless they did so, they would be off the team and lose all the substantial privileges that the state gave to international athletes. Most accepted silently; their lifestyle was too good to do otherwise. But there was something Orwellian about supporting a state which proclaimed to the world its zeal in the fight against doping, then forced its athletes to take them.

Naturally the whole doping campaign was carried out in secrecy. Only those in the position to know, like the chief coaches, were probably aware of the full extent of doping abuse. Staazi records, now housed in the

Gauck Institute in Berlin, detail the extent of discussions on doping in rowing. But each rower has much more on their files than just what drugs they took. Some have two: their blue file for information that informants gave on them; and a yellow folder for the information they gave about others. I wanted to ask Siggi if he had been a Staazi informer. Judging from the scale of the organisation this would have been quite unremarkable. Most informants tried to make the unpleasant task of reporting on their team-mates as painless as possible by divulging only the most mundane of details. Yet face to face across the table in that kitchen, it was a question that I could not ask. The answer lies buried (for those who want to look) in the Gauck institute.

Perhaps it was because I already suspected what the answer might be. He was a fairly unapologetic advocate of the Socialist state. Someone who was prepared to extol its virtues to others. That much was said to be the duty of each rower. In a remarkable passage from *Rudem*, the East German text book on rowing, athletes are told it is their duty to engage in political discussions 'in the boathouse' after training sessions. Somehow, I could not imagine Siggi and company discussing the latest Trabant production figures after they had finished their third session of the day.

But Siggi was not alone in eulogising East German Socialism. No less a person than the great East German sculler Thomas Lange was praising the benefits of the East German system on West German television in 1989, just a week or so before the Wall collapsed. Clearly it was a traumatic time for those in privileged positions in the East. In the weeks after what was called 'The Change', Lange's estranged father, reputed to be involved with the Staazi, shot himself. Now those athletes, without the state safety net, had to find whole new ways of supporting themselves.

But Siggi had to go through this trauma twice. When he finished rowing in 1980, he tried to make a name for himself as a coach. For the first time in his life, the smile did not work; he could not pass on to others the secrets of his own success. It was a painful lesson for the 'sunny boy' to learn. He was touring round East German schools, playing the 'hero', while in reality he felt a failure.

This was a side of the man that I had never before seen. There was the person who lay behind the smile. For him, living up to the image of a hero was impossible while his personal inadequacies were laid bare before him. Oddly enough, I began to warm to this person. His pedestal was not so high now and we held each other's gaze as he told me the end of his story.

He left coaching in 1986, to take up a post in the Scientific School of Leipzig, which lasted until 'The Change'. Then the triple Olympian was left to his own devices in the new Germany. It seemed useless holding on to the same values. Initially, he voted for the PDS (the successor to the East German Communist Party), but soon began to realise that capitalism is best run by the capitalists. He will vote for the conservative CDU next time.

It took a long time for him to find employment. In 1993, he managed to talk his way into a secure job, negotiating deals to buy land for a company building gas pipelines. Much of his work was with clients in the old East Germany; it was clear that his firm was looking for someone who understood their ways. Since then he has began to find the happiness and security that he felt when he was rowing. Siggi bought some land and built his own house during weekends and holidays; the work ethic is still very strong. But as for the sport he left behind, he doesn't row or train now – he hasn't the inclination, or time – and his only exercise now is walking the dog.

With the end of Siggi's story, the search for my hero was over. It was mid-afternoon now and he glanced at his watch – there was a long drive ahead of him. Almost before I knew it, he was saying his goodbyes. We shook each other's hand and looked into each others eyes. The same questioning look was no longer present in his. In mine, I guess that he saw a more understanding gaze than the one which had greeted him a few hours earlier. At last, in that instant, my hero was off his pedestal, or rather I had begun to understand why it was that I had placed him there. Then he was gone.

It was only when he had left that I began to curse the fact that I'd forgotten to get a photograph of the two of us together to show Ian and John back home. In that instant, I recognised that I had once again become the young rower, while the gas salesman in his late 40s was for me once more the rower who raced like the wind. As I turned back towards the kitchen table, I found my face breaking into a broad smile.

Fool's Gold

I NEVER really wanted to be an Olympic champion in 1984. Well, at least not at the start of the season. A medal, yes. Silver would do, but bronze would be fine also. If it was in a crew with my old friends, so much the better. Sure I might have dreamed about winning. But from where I sat in the boat, it was a pretty unrealistic dream. For one thing, Olympic champions were people who were made of different stuff to me. Then it was the decathalete Daley Thompson, or swimmer David Wilkie. Now it's Michael Johnson, or Steven Redgrave. Clearly superhuman. Sort of… better than me – if you know what I mean. The fact that a British boat hadn't won an Olympic gold since 1948 didn't help much either.

But at 8.30 in the morning of 24 July 1984 I had a gold medal round my neck, while I looked up at the Union Flag being raised to the strains of *God Save the Queen*. 'What the hell am I supposed to feel?' I thought, as a televised image of David Wilkie's tears during his medal ceremony in 1976 refused to leave my mind. Of course I was pleased, like a climber who's just completed the ascent of a mountain that he thought he'd never climb. But it wasn't long before the view from the top of Mount Olympus became threatening. I was up in the clouds, among the sporting gods, feeling like I didn't belong.

It was a crazy year, the experience of which changed me for good. Since then I've been trying to come to terms with what happened. For years I would look at the medal and think, 'I'm not worthy.' It's hardly surprising. Whenever I showed it to people they acted as if it. were a sacred host, speaking in hushed tones. A few brave, or cocky, ones tried it on – Neil Kinnock did before the 1992 General Election but it didn't seem to help him much.

Sometimes it takes something – an event or a meeting – to give you a fresh perspective on something that's happened in your life; make you look at things in a different way. With me it happened in that same year that Neil Kinnock wore my medal. I met a woman, a spare on the Canadian Olympic team, called Shannon Crawford.

That summer she unexpectedly became an Olympic champion; she found herself on the Olympic victory podium, the place that all sportsmen and women long to be. Yet as Shannon looked at her medal amidst all the fanfares, photographers and celebrations around her, she felt it was something that she didn't deserve. Maybe it was because I felt I'd helped her through some difficult times during the Games that I thought I understood just a small part of what she was feeling that day.

Whatever, it was since that day that I began to look afresh at my own status as an Olympic gold medalist – perhaps I had never really tried to look that hard before? But for the first time, I felt I knew an Olympic champion whose experience, in some way, seemed to mirror my own. Understanding what happened to Shannon Crawford that year helped me to make some sense of the feelings I had. But as the 1984 season dawned, that awareness was far away as I prepared to renew my Olympic Obsession.

The year started badly. I wasn't exactly flavour of the month with the new team of coaches led by Penny Chuter. It was hardly surprising really. I'd spent the winter months trying to smash their selection policy. Penny had the idea of forcing everyone into the national squad – if you didn't join, you wouldn't go. It meant that my idea of a pair with my mate from the coxless four, John Beattie, was a non-starter, no matter how fast we were. With a group of disgruntled and former rowers I instituted the International Rowers and Scullers Club with the idea of putting pressure on the ARA to change the policy. I spent the winter running to meetings after training or getting reluctant rowers to sign petitions. It all came to naught – nothing changed.

It got worse. All that fuss meant that I was Public Enemy Number One with Penny Chuter. She wouldn't let John and I use squad equipment, so we had to borrow an outdated boat from Hampton School. Such was the ill feeling between us that at the first set of trials Penny and I nearly came to blows. One of the seats in my pair was broken. I had pinched a seat from a spare squad boat. Penny caught me and her resentment at my politicking boiled over. She grabbed me by the collar and raised her hand as if to strike me. We were pulled apart. Looking back, it was handbags at 30 paces, I suppose. But the menace and frustration in her face were real enough then. What's more – and I don't suppose the argument was an ideal preparation – Beattie and I lost the trials. There was nothing for it but to eat humble pie and go into the squad.

We were kept well away from the eight which was run by Graeme Hall. They were mostly the 'touchy feely' kind of rowers. To me, making an eight with that lot would be like filling a football team full of skilful players like Matt Le Tissier and Steve MacManaman and expecting it win – you need your Battys and Keens to provide some backbone. So as a 'hardman' for whom training was everything and technique secondary, Hall wasn't interested in me and I was consigned to the coxed four group with all the other 'problem rowers'.

An odd lot we were, too. There was Andy Holmes, a bit of a loner but hard, although nobody wanted to row with him so he paired up with Paul Wensley, a young hopeful who nobody thought would make the cut. The 6ft 7ins Richard Budgett cut a ludicrous figure in the boat. The first time he saw him race, Hall laughed at his technique. But like golf's Jim Furyik, whose swing breaks all the rules, Budgett got results. His partner was the cerebral Tom Cadoux-Hudson. They'd won a bronze in 1981 and wanted to relive their glorious moment together. But Tom was now a full-time medic (he fixes people's brains these days) and couldn't get time off to train. Redgrave, in the midst of his odyssey to win the single sculls in Seoul, made up the group. We all knew he didn't want to row. In fact, our coach Mike Spracklen was Redgrave's coach and mentor too. While he raced us in his single, which was slightly slower than our pairs, we regarded him as cannon fodder.

But we all knew what his potential was in a rowing boat. So did Penny Chuter, who was playing a careful game with Spracklen. She allowed Mike to think that if Steven was fast enough in a single she'd send him, if not (and Penny was pretty sure he'd be too slow), then there was always the coxed four. So now Mike realised that if Steven was going to make the singles grade, he would have to drag his sculling speed up to scratch by racing our pairs. Within the group there was resentment against Steven for thinking that he was good enough to be the single. None of us, except Mike, thought that he would make the grade by himself. In those days he'd yet to win a senior medal and there were questions about his racing temperament still to be answered. So within the group there was not a lot of love lost. We all wanted to knock the hell out of each other. Mike gave us plenty of opportunity. We seemed to race every session, a different boat winning each time. It didn't make us friends but after a few weeks there was a bond of mutual respect and a shared antipathy towards the eights group whom we thought were having an easy time

But as the moment of selection grew closer for the Olympic four, I was still obstinately wanting to shun the four and stay in a pair. Mike partly encouraged this hope. At the start of our Easter training camp in Sabaudia, just south of Rome, there was a pre-season warm-up regatta with some good opposition. We were to race in three pairs and the single, although by entering us in different events on different days, Mike kept us apart. John and I won our race, rowing through an Italian pair in style. We were presented with an enormous golden goblet, complete with a fake marble stem and base. Such was our glee, that night that we bought champagne and offered the cup round to the rowers in the eights group. We hoped it would taste bitter.

However, the celebrations turned out to be something of a wake for our pair. The next day Spracklen and Chuter were determined to select their Olympic crew. We went through a torturous procedure, the like of which I'd never experienced before. Perhaps it was because Mike and Penny could still not agree on the final personnel that each of us were asked to write down our preferred boat and crew. Everyone else, except Steven and I, put down a four. By now there was little doubt about Steven 's potential and all the other rowers' permutations included him at stroke.

Redgrave chose the single, I stuck to the pair with John. It was as if I had been offered a place in a Premiership football team, only to turn it down for something in the lower divisions. Mike and Penny wouldn't believe I could be so obtuse or bloody-minded. I was summoned to the Land Rover where the two coaches were deliberating. As I lifted myself into the passenger seat, an Olympic gold medal was the last thing on my mind. It was the constant battles that I'd had with the coaching team throughout the winter which were uppermost in my mind. Bloody-mindedly, I determined not to give way.

They told me that I had to choose a four with me in it. After a few moments of prevarication I said, 'OK. Me, Holmes, Budgett and Beattie.'

'What, no Redgrave?' Spracklen asked.

'He wants to do the single and his heart's not in the four.'

They then quizzed me about Beattie versus Cadoux-Hudson. In my mind Beattie was better. Or at least, Cadoux-Hudson hadn't proved himself any better than Beattie in our races. But I sensed that the 'nod' was going Tom's way and bluntly stated, 'If you put Tom in the crew over John, I won't row in it. I'll go off and do a pair with John and you can do what you like to us.' They told me to leave. Fifteen minutes later they came out and announced that they had selected a four, which had three people in it: Cross, Holmes and Budgett. Beattie, Cadoux-Hudson and Wensley would have to race for the last seat. Their idea was to race over 1,500 metres three times, each with a different bow man. The crew with the fastest time would stand. But everybody thought the idea ludicrous. It was hardly a fair scenario to the last man in. Another mutiny set in. The whole group refused to row any trials, insisting that Mike and Penny just pick the crew they wanted. Later that day the four, with John Beattie at bow, took to the water in preparation for Mannheim regatta, three weeks hence.

As for Steven, he was allowed to continue in his single on the proviso that on the Sunday, Steven would come into the four at stroke for what was in effect a trial.

A grimy dock off the inhospitable River Rhine was the location for one of Europe's top regattas. It was an unlikely venue for the definitive selection of Britain's Olympic crews. Factory chimneys belted smoke into the air, which left you with a horrid sulphurous taste in your mouth after a race. Coal dust swirled around the goods sidings along the dock. To make matters worse, the course was 150 metres shorter than the usual 2,000 metres. After the last stroke you had to dig your blades into the water and making an emergency stop to avoid hitting the wall at the end of the dock. Accommodation was rough and ready, in a German army barracks. Henley or Lucerne were a million miles away. But the good burghers of Mannheim seemed to have secured enough sponsorship to attract the world's best.

On the Saturday racing, our four (sans Redgrave), had a good win against the previous year's silver medalists from West Germany, whom we rowed down in the last 500 metres. Winning an international regatta again felt great. I was sure that we could win an Olympic medal now. We saw Redgrave finish a distant but vaguely respectable third in the singles behind Karpinnen and Kolbe. That afternoon, as we rested in the barracks, we determined that we wanted nothing to do with Redgrave. For us a medal was enough. The thought that we might make it gold with Redgrave didn't enter our heads. But we still had to go through with the 'trial'. That night Steven stepped into the boat at stroke for a practice paddle. I moved back down to the bow seat to accommodate him. Budgett and Holmes stayed in the 'two' and 'three' seats. Beattie remained in the barracks.

It was an incredible sensation. The four with Steven in was dynamite. I could hardly keep up with the pace that he was setting in the two practice starts that we did. There was a brutality about the attack we now had on the catches that I had never experienced before. I thought, 'My God! This is what it feels like to row in a gold medal boat.' We were non-committal when John asked us how it had gone. But the next day, as he watched us demolish the West Germans in the first few strokes, it was clear that Penny had got her Olympic four, that Steven would not be in the single and that John would have to look for another boat.

In those few hours my thoughts had shifted into another paradigm. I had just rowed a radically different race pattern to anything that I'd done before, in racing, or in training. Steven's power was awesome. He clearly had set out to show us just how good he was. But we had risen to his challenge. Behind Steven, Andy needed no urging to show him that he could match his power. 'Budge' was crazy enough to follow any lead and row flat out until he dropped. In the bows I felt that I rose to the occasion and could add something to the pace of the boat. In effect our rowing horizons moved to another level. Previously, it was enough just to think of winning a medal. Now, anything less than gold would be a failure. All of a sudden, I was supposed to beat the best in the world, not just finish an honourable second or third. To do this, I had left my friend and crewmate, John Beattie, on the bank. For the first time as I started out on the slopes of Mount Olympus, I began to look back at the view. Underneath the brash exterior, I began to feel a little unsure.

But I wasn't the only one in that position. The favourites for the gold in our event that year were the coxed four East German boat with Harold Jahrling, the double Olympic champion, in the bow seat. But the East German Olympic champions looked as though they might miss the one event for which they spent all their time training. Chernenko, the ageing Russian leader, was determined to extract revenge for the US-led boycott of the Moscow Games. There seemed a distinct possibility that Eastern Bloc countries would miss the Los Angeles Games. In an effort to at least race them once, we decided to travel behind the Iron Curtain to face them at Grunau regatta in East Berlin. In a borrowed boat, which felt a little uncomfortable, we lost to the East Germans but beat the rest of the Eastern Bloc, including the Russians. But we'd done enough to feel confident about taking on Jahrling and company if they came to race at the Lucerne regatta, where we would have our own boat.

By the time Lucerne came around, the boycott was confirmed. On the day that East Germany finally announced that it would not be going to Los Angeles, I was interviewed by BBC television news. Questions were now being asked as to the real value of medals won at an Olympic Games boycotted by the world's most powerful sporting nations. By now I was well and truly on the gold medal quest – you could hardly be on anything else with Redgrave at stroke and Spracklen coaching. By this point I was just climbing upwards without bothering to look down. So, with as much conviction as I could muster, I asserted that the value of an Olympic gold was such that it could never be tarnished. But in the back of my mind was the fear that the East Germans wouldn't turn up at Lucerne. For an Olympic gold to really mean something in 1984, there was no doubt that our four

Lucerne, 1984: The traditional rowers' victory celebrations after our world record-breaking win against East Germany. We sent cox Adrian Ellison into the Rotsee.

would have to hope, that we would beat them so convincingly and in such a manner that our claim to be worthy of the status of 'true' Olympic champions (should we win in LA) would be recognised.

All the East German crews (but none of the Russians) turned up for the Rotsee regatta. For such a fanatical sporting nation, the Soviet-inspired boycott was a disaster. Promises of a Spartakiade-type event meant little to their athletes compared to the Olympics. Of course, the athletes had no choice but to support the boycott; generally they were too closely watched by the Staazi to register any differing opinions. But for now the Rotsee regatta would be their Olympic finals. They had come to prove that any medals won in LA would be at their expense. Conditions for the Saturday finals were fast.

Before the race Steven asked me what I thought a fast time would be in the conditions. With one eye on the programme, with the record set by another East German crew at 6 mins 12 secs, (in rowing, Rotsee records are the nearest things to world records) I cautiously reckoned that 6.13 would be an excellent time. Although I had many second and third-place medals on the Rotsee, I had never won there before. Although confident about our speed, I still couldn't quite imagine standing on the same podium where the East Germans had always stood ahead of me.

And as the race progressed it looked as if I'd still have to wait. A fast American four led at 500 metres, with us third behind the East Germans. By 1,000 metres the 'East' had moved through into the lead, while we were just level with the US. It had been a fairly ordinary start. But then we started to

Whitton, 1983: Amanda, photographed by me.

surge and by 1,250 it was clear that we would take the 'East'. With 500 to go, I looked across at Jahrling and we were past them, opening up over a length of that clear greenish Rotsee water between us and them.

I'd won races before, but this was different. For the first time I was beating the East Germans – and their top boat too! I gave myself the luxury of looking back at that distance before the finish and savouring the feeling. We crossed the line over a length and a half ahead in a new Rotsee record of 6.07. All at once I was now no longer looking up to the summit of Mount Olympus and those sporting gods – I was up there with them, enjoying the view. With one race we had rowed ourselves into the position of favourites to win the Olympic title. If we did win (and there were plenty of Lucerne winners who failed to do that) then our gold medals would indeed be a valid currency.

But rowing wasn't the only thing changing in my life just then. I was in the middle of an affair. Ann Callaway rowed at seven in the women's eight. The final-year medical student was tall, lithe and seemed to exude an air of self-confidence. I was unsure about my relationship with Amanda, who was then in her final year as a drama student at Dartington in Devon. Because of my training load, I had not been able to visit her as often as I used to in previous years. We had unavoidably grown a little more distant. She had become active in the hard left organisation Militant Tendency and begun to question whether she could ever marry someone with political views as dubious as mine. In my own mind, it was clear that when she finished her course and arrived back in London for good, it would be decision time for our relationship. Whatever the logic (at the time there was not much rational thought going on in my mind), I had gotten myself into the deceit and deception of a triangular relationship; although Ann knew about Amanda, the latter knew nothing of Ann.

In the days before I left for America, the deception became harder as Amanda came back to London and moved back into my flat. I justified it by thinking that, after the Olympics, everything would be much clearer and I could make a decision as to who I really wanted to be with. In any case, Ann had indicated that she was not willing to be part of a triangle when the Games finished. I began to see myself in a different life, capable of things that previously I had not believed I could do. As the team gathered at Heathrow for the flight to the Los Angeles, Amanda, who'd taken a job in one of the airport shops, came over to say goodbye to me. She looked radiant and seemed happy that her fellow workers knew that she had a 'famous' boyfriend going off to the Olympics. We kissed and embraced. As she waved and walked away, I was struck by the contrast between her demure manner, her slim delicate figure with her long hair tied neatly in a pony tail and Ann's more muscular, robust frame.

The two women seemed worlds apart both in looks and temperament. In a way, Ann seemed to reflect the lifestyle I aspired to, that of a potential Olympic champion, someone at the top of their métier. As a consequence, I rationalised that Amanda belonged to the person that I thought I was trying to leave behind. I did not for one moment imagine that such a transformation would be so difficult, or painful. But as we jetted out of Heathrow on 4 July 1984, those realities were easily put aside as I prepared to enter the dream world of the Olympic Games.

Being an athlete in preparation for the Games, it is often hard to keep a grip on reality. The scenery already seemed so familiar from countless television programmes. The highway patrolmen complete with Ray Bans on their Harley Davidsons, who accompanied our coach, seemed far more romantic than their British equivalents (probably because the television show CHiPs was popular at the time). Andy Holmes, a Cadillac fanatic, loved the whole thing. We spent a few hours trying to find him a pair of California plates from a breaker's yard, for his 'Caddy' back home.

America's West Coast was well and truly in the grip of pre-Games fever. We seemed to be feted wherever we went. Everybody, from the shopping mall assistants to the socialites who threw parties for us in their homes, wanted to know an athlete in preparation for the Olympics. Our training camp was held in San Diego. We were based right on the ocean and in between training sessions spent long afternoons on the beach. It was a wonderful location where very night we watched the sun sink into the Pacific.

Our sense of being something special was enhanced by the unusual training pattern that Mike Spracklen made us adopt. The Olympic regatta would have to be held early in the morning, as by 11am the strong sea breeze made the course unrowable. It meant that we would probably race at eight in the morning. To be properly warmed up it meant (by Spracklen's reckoning) that we would have to rise at 3am, take a light breakfast and travel down to the course for a first paddle at 5am, just as the dawn was breaking, and take to the water for the second outing at around 7.30am, just when we would be boating in the Olympic regatta. It was a regime that we would stick to throughout the three weeks of our stay in America. It was surreal in itself: going to bed at seven o'clock on a warm, balmy evening and then walking across the turf of the athletic track, with the sprinklers going full blast, in the middle of the night. What's more, none of the other boats kept to the same times, so we really believed that we were doing something special.

There were several underlying tensions that I tried to put to the back of my mind. What I would do about Amanda was one of them that was easy to hide. Another that wasn't so easy to mask was the atmosphere between myself, Steven and Mike. Much of this was due to the sparring between Steven and myself as to who was the crew leader. As stroke, Steven was in the most responsible and powerful position in the boat, although from the bow seat – and as the most experienced rower in the boat – I got to make important calls as to when to make extra efforts, or to raise or lower the rate. To wind Steven up, or to release the tension on myself, I would contrast my experience and medals with his lack of success.

But Steven never tired of pointing out that the standards that I had settled for were 'second best' and that what had been good enough in the past was now no longer applicable. It was a challenge to me and everything I stood for. He wanted me to change my mind-set to that of a potential Olympic champion, rather than just a medalist. Looking back on it, he was right. Maybe he sensed that unless I changed in some way, I would always be good for second or third place but never the top spot. At the time, though, it was the cause of a massive row in the middle of Lake Otay during training.

But once we moved into the Olympic village on campus Santa Barbara, with only a few days to go before the opening heat, we knew that we were moving very fast. The rest of the crews seemed to know it, too. Maybe it was just my imagination. Other rowers seemed to look at me with more respect, as if to acknowledge that we were favourites for the gold.

We duly acknowledged this in the first heat with a win against a new American crew. The American four were a different unit to the ones that we had raced in Lucerne. We'd now beaten practically everyone in the regatta. The problem was that the victory set up a week of inactivity and waiting. All we could do was lose the event. Whenever anyone asks me what it's like to be favourite for an Olympic gold, I think of the fear which I felt during that never-ending week. It built inexorably, day by day.

The only relief were the sessions on the water together with the mindless hours spent on the arcade games in the village and the chats I had with Cathy Lund, an old girlfriend on the Canadian team. We both had to sneak away from our respective partners, just to be able to talk. It was something I needed to do, not least to unload my worries about Amanda and Ann. But whatever light relief that these sessions brought, there was always the reality of that race.

The night before the final, Spracklen called us together to discuss the race plan. He and most of the crew were of the opinion that we should play a reprise of the first heat. Dominate the race from the first few strokes, throw in a massive early challenge and then move away from the expected American riposte from 1,000 metres in. I was the only dissenting voice. To my mind we were better off playing to our strengths: a measured first 1,000, then a devastating finishing burst. It had never let us down yet. But Spracklen's plan it was.

That night, I did not sleep. The tension was now almost unbearable. It did not seem to affect Budgett, my room mate. His rhythmic breathing (venturing on snoring) lasted most of the way through a long night. The 3am wake-up call came as some relief but then there was the collective silence of the crew to cope with, through breakfast and on the hour-long drive to the course. We were all wrapped up in our own thoughts; if anything, the tension grew. There was a momentary release as we took the boat on the water for our warm-up paddle. But the nerves returned again as we retired to out tent to await the race time.

As if that wasn't enough, the weather conspired to make matters worse. Unusually at 6am, the course was shrouded in a thick mist. If it did not lift by 7.30am, the race would have to be postponed. It was almost unbearable. As we lay in our tent, the expectant hum of the 16,000-strong crowd across the lake, stirred more butterflies.

Every so often the Olympic anthem, which prefaced all medal ceremonies, rang out through the public-address system and brought the possibility of a gold medal tantalisingly to mind, only to be replaced by the nerves of what lay ahead.

At the last moment word came through that the course was clear enough. As our shell hit the water, the burden of almost all of my doubts and worries magically lifted as we settled into the familiarity of our pre-race routine, a routine which we had done every day for the last four weeks. Bursts normally rowed at 36 hit 40 strokes per minute; the release of the collective tension was palpable.

For what seemed like an age we waited on the start. But by then I was entirely focused. The race plan even worked well. By 250 metres we were in the lead. As we pushed to move away, the Americans started coming through us like an express train. By 500 they were half a length up and beginning to push away.

Panic bells started ringing in my mind; then I started to read the race. Our race plan was now history. We had to react and quickly. I decided to call the race myself, taking over from the pre-arranged pushes that Adrian had planned to call. With 500 metres to go we checked the Americans' move and as the remnants of the mist began to envelop us, I was worried. We had virtually given our all to get back on even terms. There seemed nothing left to give; the Americans had taken up our challenge with relish and flung back the label of favourites in our faces. My legs were screaming at me to stop. For an instant, I even contemplated the silver medal.

That thought produced a powerful response. It was as if I had to purge myself for even allowing it to cross my mind. Immediately I called for the last big push. 'This one's to be Olympic champion.' At that moment I wanted it so badly. I drove my legs down even harder, daring them to throw me more pain. From the boat's reaction I knew I was not alone. Over the year, let alone the last week, we'd endured so much agony to win that bloody medal. The Americans were rowing better but we wanted it more.

Lake Casitas, 1984: Our Olympic four powers off the start during the first heat of the Games, while Steve takes his usual early glance at the opposition.

For the first time in the race we began to gain on them, but ever so slowly. With 20 strokes to go, we were through the Americans. With five strokes to go, I knew I was an Olympic champion.

We crossed the line and I felt... nothing! That's not supposed to be in the script I thought as I slumped down over my oar. Ahead of me, 'Budge' and Andy had their arms raised in triumph; Steven threw-up over the side of the boat. I sat there, immobile and emotionless for some time.

Then I heard the shouts of John Beattie. 'Martin... Martin.' He had run round the end of the lake and was calling my name with an exuberance that I'd never heard before. I erupted into an orgy of shouting and joy; a dramatic release of all the tension and expectation of the past few weeks. As I looked at John, almost in homage to our old four, I imagined that our places could have been reversed, with him in the boat and me running round to salute him.

After the medal ceremony I wanted us to paddle to a quiet corner of the lake to savour the moment as a crew, but the others wanted to get back to the celebrations on the bank. I suppose, for me, that wish was as much as about trying to prolong the magical feeling that I was experiencing. I thought that when I returned to dry land, things would never be the same again. Even in my moment of triumph, the question of Ann or Amanda drifted into my mind.

Lake Casitas, 1984: My dad 'watching' my Olympic final. He spent almost the entire race like this.

Ann and I planned a week's vacation to the Grand Canyon after the closing ceremony of the Games. When I told Amanda that I would be late back, there was no hiding the disappointment in her voice. It cut like a knife into my conscience. Whatever I might have thought, being an Olympic champion was not a palliative for personal angst.

Not that I didn't enjoy all that bit of being 'famous for 15 minutes'. Being in the village with a gold medal for the second week of the Games is like being a kid in Disneyland who gets put to the front of the queues on every ride. The medal, I never let go of it. On some occasions it was almost as if I had to look at it to believe that we'd won the race.

It wasn't hard to see why. I began to think, 'What me, Olympic champion? There must be some mistake.' Then I'd look at the medal and think, 'No, it's true.' My mind was telling me that it was only very special people who won gold medals. But when I looked at myself in the mirror I just saw plain old me, not some Olympic God, like a Coe, a Brietzke, or even a Redgrave. Yet there was I with this large, heavy gold object around my neck. So it was that I began to rationalise that there were different types of Olympic champions: the worthy or great champions like a Redgrave, or a Coe; and a kind of second-class sort, which included people like me.

My personal life exacerbated this kind of schizophrenia. On the one hand, I was now a 'hero', certainly in the eyes of the rowing world and my family (if not the wider sporting public). To my mind, a relationship with Ann Callaway would represent the fulfilment of this kind of lifestyle. But on the other hand, the 'loyal' and 'honest' me (the way I had always previously viewed myself) increasingly began to see the 'new' me as something of a philanderer who had cheated on his girlfriend. Reconciling the two views of myself became a struggle and one with which I was intensely uncomfortable. It became much worse when I returned home.

Returning home I felt like I'd come back from inter-galactic travel. The world I'd left behind had changed. As I turned the corner into Belgrade Road, I noticed a no-entry sign in the middle of the road with a policeman standing next to it. 'Must have been a bit of trouble round here,' I thought. Then I saw the bunting and a large banner slung across the road saying, 'Welcome home Martin.' At the same time loudspeakers fixed to lamp-posts began to blare out the theme from *Chariots of Fire*. My neighbours (the ones that only spoke to me when I parked my car in front of their drive) had closed the road and organised a street party for me. I whispered, 'Beam me up Scotty,' but to no avail. There was no escaping the celebrations.

It was a wonderful idea but the fact was I was waiting with dread the arrival of Amanda later in the afternoon. She was conspicuously absent from the party. The separation lasted for an excruciating month, with a Portuguese holiday in the middle. It was a nightmare for us both: two

Hampton, 1984: 'Welcome home Martin'. The residents of Belgrade Road meet me in more congenial circumstances than they had previously been used to.

people who had previously been inseparable but who were now unable to speak, but still both hanging on to the shreds of the relationship that we'd once had.

In the end, I made the break with Amanda on the pavement outside my flat. It was ironic that Chris Dodd from *The Guardian* had just come to interview me about my Olympic experiences. Amanda waited as I awkwardly relived the year. When Dodd left, she asked if I wanted her to leave. I waited an age before I heard myself whispering, 'Yes.' She turned and walked out of my life. That night I didn't sleep. I spent half of it outside Ann's flat and the other half outside Amanda's.

The next morning, looking like a dog, I had to start a fun run in my new capacity as a 'local hero'. It was an incongruous experience because the last thing I felt like was an Olympic hero. I went into a semi-reclusive state, avoiding my rowing friends and turning down offers of appearances on television shows like *Super Teams*, or *The Krypton Factor*. It was my way of wearing sack-cloth and ashes.

But towards the end of the year I occasionally started to remove my hair-shirt. I phoned up the BBC television programme *A Question of Sport* and asked if I could appear.

Lake Casitas, 1984: A thin mist still hangs over the lake while Mike Spracklen joins in our victory celebrations.

'Martin Who?' came the response at the end of the phone. Obviously my name was not going to get me on the show, so I played my joker.

'I'm an Olympic gold medalist,' I responded.

'Did you row in *that* four?'

'Yeah, that was me.'

They didn't want me, but they wanted my medal. Still, I enjoyed making the programme. I got to meet some really famous people and my team won too.

When David Coleman did his little 'two-way' interview with me during the show, we talked about my bronze in Moscow and the gold in LA. In a perceptive moment – a rarity on *A Question of Sport* – he asked me which one I had enjoyed the most. 'Moscow,' was the reply.

'What? You preferred winning the bronze to becoming Olympic champion?' His voice sounded slightly incredulous.

For a brief moment I sat back and thought of the year I'd had and all that had gone on with Ann and Amanda. 'Yeah, life was a little less complicated then,' I replied.

Was it some quality of Amanda's that I first saw in Shannon Crawford's face some eight years later in 1992? I was with the British squad, training on

Casitas, 1984: I think that the first person that I embraced after the medal ceremony was my dad (who is wearing that rather incongruous Disney hat). My mum insists it was her though (see page 251).

Lake Sarnen in Switzerland. The powerful Canadian women's squad shared the same venue. Shannon was one of two 'spares' travelling with the team to cover for injuries.

I was at once struck by Crawford's detached air. Her whole face and demeanour seemed somewhat aloof, as if she was somehow detached from the proceedings around her. Perhaps it was the challenge of getting to know what lay behind the impassive exterior, or maybe I just felt sorry for her as a 'spare'. I knew that being 'on tour' was a lonely occupation and that being there as a spare is even more challenging. In rowing, unlike football, spares hardly ever get used in races. At worst, you might end up as a sort of glorified bag carrier for the rest of the team, spending the time wishing injuries on another squad member.

We talked under a large umbrella, sheltering a joint barbecue for the two teams. It was still raining hard as I asked her what she thought of the members of her team.

'Oh, they seem so "Other worldly" to me,' she replied.

'What, even now you're one of them?'

'I'm not. I'm the spare.'

I didn't understand why Shannon was dealing with her membership of the Canadian Olympic team in this way, but that much became clear when she told me how and why she got involved with the sport.

She never had the remotest thought that she might one day aspire even just to try for the Olympics. Shannon saw herself as a plodder. Before rowing, she had tried out other team sports like volleyball but seemed to lack the co-ordination to play well enough. She took up rowing to fill a hole in her life.

Working as a nurse in theatre was a demanding and sometimes traumatic job. It was not something that Shannon wanted to do for the rest of her life. Marriage and family were her priorities. But despite the social life around the rowing club in Toronto, relationships didn't seem to be happening. So increasingly rowing, rather than her job, or projected family, became more of a priority. So Shannon just plodded along, gradually getting better and better without really noticing it.

In many respects it was the ideal sport for a 'plodder' (or so it seemed to Crawford). She would always do the training load that the coaches set. Like the tortoise who had continued to stick at the sport while the other hares fell away. She was no technician, the finer points of the sport seemed to pass her by. When coaches talked to her about technique during outings, she would nod, as if she understood what they were saying, when in reality she didn't have a clue. Every so often, though, an 'occasional glimpse' of what it could feel like when she and her crew moved smoothly on through the water came along out of the blue. Remarkably, it kept her going.

The person who never did anything that was 'out of the ordinary, or re-markable', left Ontario on New Year's Day 1992. She could hardly believe what she was doing as she drove to Victoria on Canada's West Coast for Olympic trials. Al Morrow, the Canadian women's coach, had assembled an exception-ally strong group of women and put them on a mammoth training programme.

The group was structured around the twin powerhouses of Kathleen Heddle and Marnie McBean. In 1991, spearheaded by them, the squad achieved unprecedented success at the World Championships in Vienna. Never before had Canadian rowing had so many top-class athletes. It was now the nation's top sport for the Barcelona Games

It was quite a culture shock for Shannon, the plodder, now in the company of these seemingly incredible athletes. She had no real expectation of making the national team; to do so would mean that she would have to oust a world champion from her seat. But somehow, as the cuts were made in the squad, she always seemed to squeeze in. Before the final selection race in June, Shannon was still hanging on in there. But she knew that she had no chance of making the Olympic team proper. Even to make the 'spare',

Lake Casitas, 1984: Me, wearing my Olympic gold, enjoying the racing and the company of my two sisters. Catherine is on my right and Teresa on my left.

she would have to beat Kelly Mahon, who had won a gold medal as stroke of the Vienna eight.

She was almost apologetic when she told me that she'd won her seat race, as if she was somehow detached from the significance of her victory, even though its result was clearly of great importance to her. I found myself thinking that this woman has a really complex character. Of course, I hardly needed a degree in rocket science to work that one out (the same could be said of almost every woman I've ever met). But as the rain started to ease, I began to sense that what had begun as my attempt to 'rescue' the spare, was now starting to provoke challenging thoughts in me. After all, I must have seemed 'other worldly' to her but at the time in my life, I felt pretty 'ordinary', even compared to some of the people that I was rowing with – let alone to the Redgraves and Pinsents of this world.

We had to leave Sarnen the next day, so I never got the chance to talk any more. But during the Barcelona Games we would spend many hours chatting, gossiping, in the cool of the air-conditioned food tent, or under a shady tree outside. We were away from home and both enjoyed the flirting and listening to stories from each other's past. But strangely, Shannon told me nothing of the turmoil that was then going on in her mind over the composition of the Canadian eight.

As the Games drew closer, Shannon's worst nightmare was that one of the eight might become injured, meaning she might have to race in the Olympic regatta. Jenny Doey, the stroke of the coxless four, doubling up in the key 'six' seat of the eight, had experienced a summer of protracted back problems. She had already missed Amsterdam regatta, for which Shannon was called to stand in. Al Morrow thought that Doey might be fit for the Games although it had became increasingly obvious to all involved with the Canadian squad that the chances against this were rising.

For Shannon, the fact that it was Jenny Doey made it worse. She was a supremely talented rower and highly popular with everyone on the team, including Shannon. Being one of the longest-serving members of the team meant that everybody thought that Doey, more than anyone, 'deserved' a chance at gold.

As she thought about the possibilities, Shannon's confidence wobbled, thinking (irrationally) that if she did have to race then she might end up making a mistake, causing the favourites to lose. But more than that, the realisation that Shannon, would probably end up with a gold medal proved daunting. She was afraid that some people might think that she was in some way undeserving of the honour; that she just got lucky and 'got a ride' in the boat. I suppose at heart she was as much afraid of judging herself by those standards. She tried to rationalise that it wasn't her fault; she just happened to be in the role of spare. But as to the feeling that she had an absolute right to be in that boat: that was submerged in a sea of doubts.

For a long time I knew nothing of all this. Al Morrow insisted to his rowers that not a word leaked out. It was on the night before the first heat that Morrow told his crew that Shannon would row in Jenny Doey's place. Up until then, there had always been the possibility of pretending that something wouldn't happen. When reality set in, everybody was pretty emotional – Jenny wouldn't be getting her gold. It proved too much for Shannon, who quickly left the team meeting; she didn't want the rest to see her tears.

At the time, I was sitting watching the moon rise over the lake when I saw her walk by. I could see that she was upset, although she wasn't going to tell me why. My first impulse was to rescue her; tell her everything would be all right, that her frustrations at being the 'spare' among a bunch of certain gold medalists would pass. But she didn't want to talk. So I found myself telling her how I'd felt when I'd won my gold; of the fruitless years that I'd spent feeling like a 'second-rate' Olympic champion. A lot of stuff came out then; things that I was conscious of never having articulated to anyone before. It was almost as if I was starting to shed a load which I had been carrying for many a year.

So instead of being the rescuer, I found myself being the rescued. That was at least until we parted company. She had remained silent for most of the time and I suppose I felt a bit uncertain, so I asked her to imagine how she might actually feel, if she got called to 'sub' in the eight.

'You might feel you have problems now Shannon, but that'll be nothing to what you'll feel next Sunday if you get called on to sub into that eight. Then you'll be standing on that medal rostrum with a gold medal round your neck that you feel doesn't belong to you.'

She looked at me with a long hard stare, during which I could have sworn that the expression on her face changed from angst to relief. Perhaps it was that, for the first time, her biggest fear had been articulated by somebody and after that, it didn't seem so threatening.

The Canadian eight comfortably won their first heat and qualified directly for the final. As we had to do in 1984, it meant an interminable wait. Shannon coped in the way that she was used to; focusing on the day-to-day tasks. Al Morrow had been very careful to set a routine and race days were therefore supposed to be like any other. There was no big 'pep' talk, just a few words checking that the women 'knew what they were doing' and his wish to 'have a good row'.

Through it all, Shannon knew what she was doing, what her role was and although she was, in reality, 'scared to death', the routine and her ability to detach herself meant that she could imagine that she was merely an observer, seeing these things happen to somebody else.

Her memories of the race (it was a boiling hot day) are few. On the start the American crew in the lane next to her were linking themselves together in a symbolic embrace; each woman joining her hands with the person in front and behind her, almost as if they were at prayer. In the lane on the other side, the Rumanians engaged in their deep-breathing exercises, sounding like racehorses snorting before the 'off'. Down the end of the course awaited a packed grandstand and nine Olympic gold medals, one with the name Shannon Crawford metaphorically engraved on it.

Her mind was supremely focused in the race. Shannon's only memories were the sound of cox Leslie Thompson's voice and, just a couple of feet in front of her in the boat, the sight of the braid which tied Marnie McBean's hair in a neat ponytail. She was completely unaware of the course itself. When they crossed the line she could only compare it to the 'foolish and

Lake Banyolas, 1992: A pensive Shannon Crawford (sixth right) contemplates the arrival of Jenny Doey on the medal rostrum.

elated' feelings that she had experienced on her very first win at Canadian Henley; in a way, not knowing quite what she should do with herself.

During the ceremony she never really looked at her medal at all, except that she was amazed at its weight when it was placed around her neck. But there was one moment of doubt on the stage. Jenny Doey was ushered down to the medal rostrum for symbolic photographs with the victorious crew. The significance of this was not lost on any of the medalists on the stage, least of all Crawford.

Shannon knew that it was an appropriate and fitting moment for a woman who had got so near to being an Olympic champion. For an instant, she dreaded that she would have to take off her medal and hand it to Doey to wear for the photographs. Thankfully, one of the other women (she doesn't know who), passed theirs forward for the photos. The rest of the morning passed in a blur, as it does when there is so much joy and celebration, so many interviews to be given.

I did not see her until about three hours after her victory. We embraced and for the first time that day Shannon burst into tears, She whispered quietly, 'You're the only person here who knows how I really feel.'

I felt pleased and a bit embarrassed. I can't remember if I said anything in response. Just a silent hug would have expressed more than any words

Lake Banyolas, 1992: Jenny Doey at least got to feel what it was like to stand on the Olympic podium wearing a gold medal. Luckily, Marnie McBean (fifth right) loaned her the medal for the photograph, much to Shannon Crawford's relief.

could. But knowing my propensity to fill silent moments with something, I'm sure I came out with something corny. In a way, I hope I didn't because it was one of those moments that stay fixed in your memory, long after they have happened.

Shannon's international career did not begin and end with the Olympics. While most of the women gave up, the following year she pressed on and won a bronze medal in the 1993 World Championships, rowing in the 'two' seat of the women's coxless four. This, as much as anything, gave her the opportunity to turn her back on the sport and move towards her cherished aim of raising a family. She married Bruce Coreley. They now live in Toronto with two little boys.

There is little in their home now to suggest that Shannon is an Olympic champion. It is not her style; she much prefers the low-light to the limelight. She is content to be a wife and a mother and prefers not to dwell on her Olympic triumph. Now it is a 'closed chapter', something that she once did ' by herself'. But for the future, there is the prospect of telling her children, when they are old enough to understand, that once she achieved something that really meant a lot to her. In time Shannon may even come to savour the view from the lofty heights of Mount Olympus.

Resentment

IT WAS the New Year's Honours list that really got to me on the first day of 1985. There I was, waiting in anticipation for my MBE, which I then thought an Olympic gold surely warranted. What came after rowing's first gold for almost 34 years? Nothing! A scan through the newspapers revealed that hockey's Roger Self, their team manager, was awarded an MBE and they only got a bronze! I was denied even the notion that I might refuse to accept the honour (as I didn't believe in the honours system). I thought the whole thing was typical of the Establishment. Either the Tories couldn't care less about sport, or else rowing's 'heavies' had messed up (probably both, I thought). After that, 1985 was open season for just about every kind of resentment going.

Maybe you can still feel the resentment oozing out of me now, after all those years. If I'm honest with myself, deep down, I'm sure that part of it is still there, although now, in recognising it, I'm able to understand much more of what was going on then.

There's no doubt that it was powerful stuff. Boy, did I enjoy it. Having something or somebody to resent was quite a motivation. Politically, I drew much then from a deep resentment of the Tory government, especially over their treatment of the miners during the long strike that year.

In a way, it was easy for me to transfer some of this against rowing's venerated institutions: Henley regatta, its hallowed 'Pink Palace', Leander club and the ARA, all became objects of scorn or derision; some for a 'good' reason, others for things that now seem rather petty. Maybe it was rather small-minded, that I felt particularly resentful of the Boat Race. But in 1985, I saw this pointless and boring race between two crews of students attracting huge sponsorship, while Olympic gold medalists like me, training for the 'real' races, like the World Rowing Championships, got nothing.

You won't be surprised to learn that I wasn't the only one to feel resentful against this venerable institution. But maybe you might think a little strange that in the summer of '85, I met a rower who, perhaps more than any other, has been deeply scarred by his experiences of that event.

Chris Clark was then a tall blond-haired student who was spare-man to the US coxless pair. I noticed them because they had a guy coaching them who was clearly into alternative methods in a big way. His pre-race preparation seemed to consist of holding his hands above their solar-plexus for several minutes, while telling them that he was energising their bodies for the race ahead. Then I thought all this stuff no better than mumbo-jumbo – now, I'm not so sure – and it certainly didn't seem to do the US boat any good. They didn't make the final, but through an illness to one of the pair, Chris Clark got his first chance to race in the World Championships, subbing in to win the 'small final' with his buddy Dan Lyons.

Two years later the two of them would be embroiled in the biggest controversy ever to hit the Boat Race. The events of that year completely changed the course of Clark's life. If I thought I had a monopoly on feeling resentful in 1985, it was nothing compared to the bitter feelings that the whole incident stirred up in Clark. His resentment at the treatment – most of it unjust – that he suffered then, and in the years that followed, still runs deep. Even now, years later, it is a significant force in his life.

But when we both prepared for the 1985 World Championships, rowing was a sport with which Clark could still feel comfortable. For me, though, the lack of any recognition in the New Year's Honours list was just a prelude to what would happen later that year.

Six months had passed since our gold medal but there was no pot of gold at the end of the rainbow. To put it bluntly, I wasn't going to make any money out of winning an Olympic gold. The notions that car companies would be falling over themselves to lend, or give me, their latest super-fast coupes had soon disappeared. The four of us did visit the Motor Show in Birmingham that autumn to publicise a new truck. We were paid £100 each for our troubles. It was all I ever got paid as a 'celebrity'. Grounds enough for resentment? Perhaps you might be thinking that I was a little greedy? Well, I could live with not being a sporting millionaire. What was difficult to accept was having to make large contributions towards the cost of my own rowing in the next season. My SAF grant was as generous than ever. But it was soon swallowed up by the expenses of training camps and regattas.

Soon, news leaked out that there was insufficient money to cover an adequate training or racing programme. That situation might have been alleviated if the ARA had managed to procure a sponsor for the team. You might think that as the sport had just won an Olympic gold then this might be a mere formality. Far from it. Although finding sponsorship is never easy, the association didn't seem to be up to the task. The day after our triumph, the ARA proved unable to deal with requests for information. They simply

Hampton, 1986: David Lewis's cartoon for the front cover of Hampton School's magazine *The Lion*, gives an idea how at least one of my pupils viewed his history teacher. The rowers in the background belong to Jonny Searle's crew.

hadn't planned ahead. Rumours abounded that potential sponsors' interest had simply not been followed up by the office at Hammersmith.

For someone who had spent the previous year fighting ARA officials by trying to set up the International Rowers and Scullers Club, it wasn't exactly hard to feel resentful towards them at this point. They had done a bloody good job in mobilising their forces to stop the IRSC in its tracks. But when it came to doing something useful, they were lost.

I knew that many of the ARA 'heavies' were giving up their time to run the sport for nothing. But that made no difference to me then. They were the Establishment; essentially the same lot who supported Thatcher and her government. Like Ken Livingstone with the GLC and Arthur Scargill with the miners, I would try to wage a guerrilla war against the Establishment, although without any real hope of winning. Still, the resentment of the self-righteous is a powerful armour

It even carried over into my working life. I mean in effect, I was part of the Establishment, particularly working at an independent school (these days under Tony Blair it's a lot easier on the conscience of a Labour supporter than it was then). It was the days of the teachers' dispute and the cerebral Sir Keith Joseph, then Minister of Education, had been invited to present prizes. It was seen (by what was a fairly radical staff), as a provocation. A group of the more 'bolshie' ones among the common room objected and planned to boycott the ceremony. Then the IRA exploded the Brighton bomb. Joseph was injured in the blast. Gavin Alexander, the headmaster insisted that we go; to do otherwise would look bad. Some staff changed their mind. Thirteen of us stayed away. To his credit, Joseph granted us a meeting with him at the Department of Education. We hardly changed the direction of Tory education policy. But in a way, it was a small victory against the Establishment.

They were pretty few and far between that year. Penny Chuter, the chief national coach whom I saw as part of the Establishment, was still ordering me around, making me do what I didn't want to do. From our four, Budgett and Holmes had stopped. Redgrave was once more in the single. That left only me rowing. Penny wanted to find me a partner. In the end, she came up with Adam Clift, the man with whom I'd rowed in the quadruple scull two years earlier.

There couldn't have been someone less from rowing's establishment than Adam. He learnt his rowing in Rochdale because his dad was desperate for something to 'keep him off the streets'. He'd hitch-hiked down to Henley for his first set of junior trials, sleeping in a doorway near Luton and then in a tent next to the river. Really, he was like a breath of fresh air to a bunch of stuck-up southerners. But his thick Lancashire brogue and his uncomplicated philosophy on life did make him the butt of many jokes. I respected him but I didn't want to row with him.

At that time he was at agricultural college in Chester. Adam had always wanted to be a farmer and was prepared to live in a damp caravan to afford the course. Penny, to keep him in the team, agreed to pay his rail fare to London for the weekends. We used to train at weekends. He'd come up to London and we'd thump this pair up and down the river, going nowhere fast. Usually, we'd argue. He'd tell me that I was too brutal and had no 'feel'. Rather helpfully, I usually told him to 'get lost and find somebody else to row with'.

On the occasions when we were communicating, Adam would tell me of the latest thing he'd learnt at college. His descriptions were always particularly graphic. Castrating bulls was a case in point: he had all the actions and noises down to a tee, particularly the 'gadoompf' as a special instrument macheted its way through the bull's gonads. At times like this, I used to think I was rowing with a person from another planet. Why and how we stayed together, I'll never know. I'm glad we did because I was to learn more about human nature and my own shortcomings from Adam than any other person I've rowed with. In later years we were best man at each other's wedding, but then that closeness lay in the future.

Of course, staying together had something to do with the speed of our boat picking up. By the summer, we'd gone to Amsterdam and comfortably beaten our main challengers for selection in a very fast time. We, or rather I, had decided not to race at Henley in order to be better prepared for the Lucerne regatta a week later. I knew that the result there would be crucial for selection. So much for the rowing reasons. My resentment against the Royal Regatta ran much deeper than that.

Peter Coni, the chairman of Henley, had some years earlier been instrumental in a decision to dismiss Amanda's dad, Pat, from his post as bar steward of the London Rowing Club. I organised a petition and pleaded before the committee, but all to no avail. The Brennans were given notice. I felt powerless and excluded from a decision-making process which had clearly already been made by the club's hierarchy, of which Peter Coni was a key part. I felt deeply wounded and lashed out, boycotting the presentation of my crew to the Duke of Edinburgh as part of the club's 125th anniversary celebrations, and later resigning from the club.

That was hard enough to deal with – but not as hard as the incident that

Henley, 1983: My first Grand medal. Despite the smile, inside I was furious that my dad (well dressed complete with blazer and tie) had been refused entry to the Stewards' Enclosure and therefore missed this presentation.

127

occurred when I won the premier rowing event at Henley for the first time. Receiving the Grand Challenge Cup is a proud day in any rower's life and certainly one which my parents wanted to share as they cheered me on from among the crowds in the general enclosure. They chose not to watch from the exclusivity of the stewards' enclosure. It is there, though, that the prize giving takes place. Traditionally, the carefully guarded gates of the hallowed turf are thrown open to the general public who are then able to watch the ceremony.

On that day the security men seemed to have different instructions. While my mother and sisters had ghosted through unassailed, my dad had been stopped by a security guard and told that he couldn't enter without a badge. I was informed of this just as the prize giving was about to start and rushed to the gate to bring him in. Dad looked smart, dressed in a blazer and tie, and I explained to the security guard the urgency but he would not budge. In desperation we went to the secretary's tent, where a similar response was received. I was furious.

This was my sport, my river, my regatta, at which I had just won the premier event – and they wouldn't let my dad in to watch me receive my medal! I immediately felt excluded and humiliated, all of which I began to cover up with a growing sense of anger. I wanted to boycott the ceremony but the wise counsel of my dad prevailed and I took my place on the rostrum. But from that moment on, I felt alienated from the Royal Regatta and the people who ran it. How could they do that to my dad? What kind of regatta excluded parents from a prize giving ceremony where their son had just won a major event?

In reality that was why, in 1985, I wasn't racing at Henley. I couldn't let go of that resentment, even though I recognised that it had probably all been a silly mistake. Henley just got lumped into my whole anti-Establishment feeling. In fact the only pair left to challenge us for selection that year were racing at Henley. Riches and Pearson had won the Goblets the previous year, beating the selected Olympic pair. They wanted to do the same to us, win selection that way on what they regarded as their stomping ground.

It won't surprise you that I assumed that when Pearson and Riches rowed past the enclosures, the 'blazerati' in the stewards' would be shouting for them, rather than us. Both of them seemed to fit the image of an Establishment crew. Riches was an intense person. Very much a product of a boarding school education with a touch of arrogance, although at the same time he was a bit of a cold fish. I never really felt comfortable in his company. Ewan Pearson was a Cambridge Blue; a fine oarsman too. But I didn't let such niceties get in the way of a healthy resentment of all things Boat Race. A couple of years earlier, Pearson was rowing at bow in the Blue Boat as they made ready for their last important training piece before the Boat Race.

The Oxbridge crews seemed to take over the tideway for two weeks and the flotilla of ridiculously large coaching launches that accompanied them made the water unrowable whenever they passed by. The Cambridge flotilla imperiously swept up-river from the Putney boathouses. That was why we were so eager to gatecrash Cambridge's big day. I was in a mischievous national squad four. We scented the chance for a little sport at the expense of the Light Blues. Casually we paddled off, allowing the two eights and the armada of following launches (complete with a BBC television camera crew filming for the Boat Race preview programme) to bear down on us at full speed. John Beattie, who was steering (somewhat arrogantly I thought), positioned our boat right in the middle of the Blue Boat and the Goldie reserves. It felt threatening because we could not easily drop out of the 'race' as the two eights began to bear down on us.

By now Graeme Hall, the Cambridge coach, was shouting for us to get out of the way but instead, when their bows were practically touching our stern, we took of at full speed. The chase was on. Initially we moved away by a length, but after a minute or so it was all we could do to hold off the two eights. Our presence was clearly unsettling their coxes and as they were jockeyed for position under Hammersmith Bridge, the boats collided and lost half a length on us. It was exhilarating, not least because by placing us in between the two eights, rather than on one side, it was not possible for us to pull out of the race. By Harrods, though, Hall was fuming. He risked washing his own racing crews down, pulling alongside us and threatening to ram us if we didn't stop. It was sport enough and by sprinting ahead, we just managed to extricate ourselves from the two boats.

As sportsmanlike behaviour goes, it was a red card offence and worthy of a lengthy ban. But we got off scot free. We even received a mention in some of the next day's newspapers reporting the race. The following week we made a guest appearance on *Grandstand*, in the background as the Cambridge crew was profiled. It was a memorable jape. But it was born out of the resentment that we, as national squad rowers, felt over the Boat Race.

As such, I didn't really rate Riches and Pearson as worth bothering about. It was sheer arrogance; they were a better crew than my big-headed nature suggested. That they duly won at Henley for the second time proved that. But in effect, their success there was made meaningless by our result at the Lucerne regatta. We came a good second, beating the previous year's Olympic silver medalists in the process. In soccer terms, they'd just won the League Cup, while we'd made the European Cup Final. It was clear that we were a class act. I knew that selection would be assured.

But before that decision was finally made, we still had to race at the National Championships. There we would meet Pearson and Riches. It was a contest that everyone was salivating over, especially the heavies from the rowing Press. The portly pair of Richard Burnell of the *Sunday Times* and Geoffrey Page of the *Daily Telegraph* were both former Oxford Blues; real Establishment men. I had no reason to think that they wanted to see an upset at Nottingham, although they were none too keen that we had not raced at Henley. When we withdrew from the race, though, they scented blood. At a hastily-called conference, Chuter had to make excuses in front of a pack of press who suspected foul play.

In fact, Adam had been complaining of feeling unwell in the run-up to the championships, with a sore throat. The only reason that we hadn't withdrawn earlier was that in a belated gesture to recognise our achievement in winning the Olympic gold, Princess Anne had been invited to Nottingham to present the four with our racing blades, which had been specially painted. Even then, we considered racing. We went out for a trial bust on the River Trent. As we wound the rate up, Adam started to cough. I immediately stopped and said, 'That's it! We're pulling out.' Adam tried to argue the point. But I stuck to my guns. It was pointless racing with an illness in the crew. That night we went out to a carvery in Nottingham for a meal. It was my 28th birthday. As luck would have it, the press were sitting opposite us.

Our meal made the Sunday papers. Geoffrey Page used all his medical training (he was an art teacher) to diagnose from a distance that Clift 'did not look very ill'. He wrote as much in the *Telegraph* the next day The inference was clear: we were playing chicken. To say that it left a bad taste was an understatement. It made our result in the World Championships that year all the more sweet.

The final is a race that those who saw it still talk about. The Russian pair of the Pimenov brothers were the strong favourites and had beaten us by a mile to win at Lucerne. I didn't really believe that we could beat them in the final, although Jim Clark, then coaching an Italian crew, thought we had a chance. Conditions for the race were very fast and exceptionally rough. True to form, the Pimenovs shot off and were out of sight by 500 metres. We were going well in second place, although I had 'missed' a couple of strokes in the rough conditions. By the time we moved through 1,000 metres, we had reeled the Pimenovs in. They were only half a length in front of us. I felt good – then I thought about the water. The race was crying out for a big push to put them under pressure. It would have won the race. But I lost my bottle, thinking that it would be sensible to keep 'cool' in the conditions. In effect, I was so 'cool' that I actually froze in the third 500 metres. The Pimenovs disappeared again; the Spanish and Italians moved up level. I wasn't even making calls. Adam started screaming, 'Go!' at the top of his voice. Then something clicked; I woke from my suspended animation and went mad.

On the line, nobody knew what happened. Adam lay back and thought he was world champion. Nickolai Pimenov collapsed, while his brother Yuri mouthed expletives. I thought, 'My God, we've won a medal!' The photo finish showed we'd failed to overhaul the Soviet pair by 8/100s of a second. Being a natural pessimist, during the wait I'd never really allowed myself to think that we might have won. Thinking the worst seemed safer, rather like assuming that West Ham were going to get relegated at the start of each season and then pretending to be pleasantly surprised when they stayed up.

At least the medal ceremony was fun. Nickolai Pimenov had to be carted off to hospital, so it almost felt like we had won. In a way, I suppose that I thought I had. I rationalised that if I could do well in a pair (the most technically demanding of the rowing boats), then I'd really won my spurs. In addition, it showed that I could win (well almost) without Redgrave. He'd struggled in his single scull, finishing at the back of the 'small final' that year. For once, I felt I was the King of British Rowing.

No doubt, after his result in the 'small final' that same year, Chris Clark must have thought that he had arrived too. I never really registered his presence until two years later during that fateful year of 1987. Then, the Boat Race had attracted a mammoth amount of publicity, causing me to feel even more resentful than usual. The fact that it was because the Establishment, in the guise of Oxford University Boat Club, had decided to drop a stroppy international rower named Chris Clark made it all the more so.

That day, it must have been a blue moon. The Boat Race was on the same day as the Tideway Head of the River Race. The BBC was to televise the event for the first time. Unfortunately, the organisers of the Head treat commercial opportunities with the same suspicion that French shoppers reserve for British beef. It's why the Head will never give the sport the showcase it deserves. Nevertheless, my national squad eight was determined to enjoy the day. After a loosening paddle early that morning, my crew

Hazelwinkel, 1985: Adam Clift and I charge past the Pimenov brothers in the final of the World Championships. Unfortunately, the 'Cross Factor' appeared a fraction too late. On the line, we were 8/100s of a second down.

crowded round a small television set in the headquarters of the ARA at Hammersmith to watch what we regarded as the warm-up for the main event. We knew that it would not be much of a race. Despite the presence of Tom Cadoux-Hudson, this Oxford crew was known as 'crap' around the rowing world. Bookies were offering odds of 1-5 for Cambridge.

In fact, the University Boat Race of Saturday, 28 March 1987 was a memorable one. The events played out on a turbulent, angry Thames that morning have long since become the stuff of rowing legend. A bunch of 'no-hopers' from Oxford University, stripped of their American stars, beat the overwhelming pre-race favourites from Cambridge to win the Boat Race. The sensational press coverage spun the story to perfection as they told of upstart colonials attempting to usurp a hallowed British institution. In a world where Britain had gotten used to being the tail wagged by the American dog, it was a comforting reminder of the values that had once 'made us great'. Two years later the Oxford coach, Daniel Topolski, triumphantly pitched another curved ball with the publication of *True Blue*.

In one of the most entertaining (if not wholly accurate) sports books ever written, Dan set about demonising one of the American mutineers, Chris Clark, while practically sanctifying the then Oxford president Donald Macdonald. Chris comes over as a spoilt rich kid, prone to laziness. A sun-drenched surfer from Newport Beach who wasted the natural talents with which he was gifted. Worse still, he is portrayed as a child among men, whose word cannot be trusted. As character assassinations go, it is ruthless. Macdonald, on the other hand, is an honourable man. Hard work and determination in the face of adversity earned him first a place at Oxford and then a seat in the Blue Boat. From his first appearance in the bleakness of a Stockton-on-Tees winter to the plucky defence of Boat Race tradition among Oxford's ancient spires, the man is a hero, a true Spartan, fighting and winning against all odds.

Dutch director Ferdinand Fairfax captured Macdonald's struggle forever on celluloid. Released in 1997, the film, despite being chosen for a Royal Command Performance, never achieved the same plaudits as the book. At the time of writing it had yet to be released in the USA. Nevertheless, the same characters of Clark and Macdonald glower at each other from the screen as they face their 'High Noon' on the Thames. In the tradition of Hollywood 'goodie versus baddie' westerns, Macdonald cuts a fine Gary Cooper, standing alone in defence of traditional values to Clark's outlaw, together with his unsavoury cronies.

Just before that race, two of our crew, John Maxey and John Garrett, had placed over £1,000 on the 'sure-fire' winners Cambridge, hoping to clear their overdrafts. By Chiswick Eyot, they were looking green as their money disappeared into Cambridge's ineffectual puddles. It was a body blow for them. Not least because sympathy from their crewmates was in surprisingly short supply.

Chris Clark

Chris Clark must have had similar emotions when he heard the result. Dan reports him as saying, 'It was just another slap in the face.' That 'slap' must have turned into a punch in the mouth and a knee in the groin as first *True Blue* was published, then was made into a film. For Chris, the whole experience was a nightmare. After 1987 he never rowed internationally again. Dan mentions this in his book as if validating his decision to exclude Clark from the crew. He even implies that, in later years, a top Oxford college crew lost in the first round of a lowly Henley event because they were coached by Chris Clark. The image of a broken man, full of resentment, springs from Dan's pen.

Even ten years later Chris was still vilified by some people when he returned to Britain, although it was clear, from talking to the coaches on the US team, that Chris Clark was anything but the demon portrayed in *True Blue*. One described him thus: 'A sensitive, bright guy, he doesn't make wars, He's just a surfer from California.'

As I tried to understand my own way of dealing with resentment caused by rowing, there seemed no more obvious person to turn to than the demon of *True Blue*. Through a mutual friend, I had approached Chris to ask if he would talk about his experiences. Understandably he is reluctant to speak at all about events in 1987; indeed, he has refused all requests for interviews since then. So I felt particularly privileged when we met at the World Championships in Cologne during September 1998.

As fate would have it, just as we were introduced outside the boathouse, Dan Topolski wandered over, trying to tempt some US college rowers to his college scheme. It was a tense moment for all concerned, not least because I counted myself as a friend of Dan. I was to learn later that although Chris knew Topolski was 'not a bad guy', Dan must have lived in ignorance of the effect that he's had on Chris's life. So as Dan tried to play the old rowing buddy, Chris blanked him, saying afterwards to me, 'He wants to be friends now, to talk to me and think it's all right, but he's making a ass-hole out of me.'

As we talked, it became clear that Chris, now a top American rowing coach, did see the events of 1987 as *the* fulcrum of his life. If they had never have happened, then Chris would have gone on to make his fortune on Wall Street, like many of his contemporaries have done. But now this man was making much less money as a rowing coach at the University of Wisconsin. What was he doing in a sport which had given him so much heartache and grief?

In 1987 he left Oxford a shattered man who had no desire to row again. Against his better judgement, he rowed with his fellow 'mutineer' and closest friend Dan Lyons in a coxless pair in the US national team trials of that year. They never made the final. Chris threw his blade away, not wanting to touch another oar again 'ever'. It was hardly surprising for underneath the brash, arrogant student portrayed in *True Blue*, there lurked a completely different man; one that Dan had never even scratched the surface of.

In reality Chris had little confidence in his own ability as a rower. Sure, he was big and naturally athletic and these talents had seen him do well in sports like baseball at high school. But until he found rowing, he saw himself as a 'quitter'. The memory of him feigning sickness rather than face the pressure of being the starting pitcher in the all-star team of his Little League baseball competition still hurts.

In rowing, Chris found a sport with a unique camaraderie that he had not before experienced. He revelled in the fact that he was an important member of the crew, but did not have to take the limelight and be its leader. In fact, all Chris ever really wanted to do was to show exactly what a good subordinate he could really be. Once the right leader showed up, he could repay the trust placed in him with hard work and dedication. The so-called 'lazy' member of the Boat Race and self-proclaimed 'quitter' threw himself into this new sport with a vengeance. Much of his training then was done on the prototype of the concept ergometer, a machine being tested in Seattle in the autumn of 1981. Since that year he has regularly clocked up three million metres each year, or about 250 hours on the machine each year.

His persistence paid off when he was chosen as the spare man for the 1985 World Championships team. When Dan Lyons' partner went sick before the final, he jumped in at stroke to take seventh place in the 'small final' of the coxless pairs. As Dan admitted, 'It was an impressive effort.' The Oxford coach was clearly looking forward to working with the CAL student as he came to Oxford for a post-graduate degree. Indeed, Chris and his fellow American, George Livingstone, took on a crucial significance to the 1986 Dark Blue boat. As far as Dan was concerned they were 'the biggest men and the most experienced racers that we had'.

Chris was given a heavy burden of responsibility in the key '6' seat but, despite outward appearances, he was ill-suited for the role of crew 'leader'. Perhaps with his experiences as an international rower, the whole 'Boat Race' thing had gone to his head; he had forgotten how much he had still to learn about the sport. Chris describes himself as 'out of control' that first year at Oxford. Neither Dan nor Mike Spracklen, who took the final weeks, were impressed with Chris's performance in the 1986 Boat Race.

Oxford lost by a crushing seven lengths. There is little doubt that Chris had allowed the weakness of the Oxford crew to act as an excuse for him to opt out of what was a lost race after the first mile (shades of the Little League again). In reality, though, his boat had little chance against the Light Blues, half of whom were accomplished international

rowers. Chris wishes that he had taken a more 'responsible' role that year but felt that Dan's leadership of the crew then was not conducive to bringing out the best in him.

Worst of all, from Chris's point of view, he had probably lost confidence in himself and his own abilities as well as in the Oxford chief coach. The seeds of the resentment that was to destroy the relationship between coach and crew in 1987 had already been well and truly sown.

But Chris still had international ambitions. He was due to stroke a four with Lyons, Riley and Swinford, but developed a stress fracture in a rib. The crew got another stroke and went on to become world champions in Nottingham. It was clearly not Chris's year.

The advent of the 1987 season at Oxford saw Chris return with three outstanding American internationals. Chris Penny, an Olympic silver medalist, Dan Lyons, a newly-crowned world champion, and Chris Huntingdon, with two World Championship bronze medals to his name. For Dan (who has spent much of his time trying to recruit foreign rowers for Oxford), it must have seemed like the Dream Team had descended from on high and landed on the Isis.

In such company Chris would be happy to play the role of subordinate in the middle of the boat, although his rib injuries had meant that he was not at the peak of his physical condition. It was this problem which was at the root of his struggle to secure one of the last seats in the boat as the selection decisions were made.

At the start, though, clashes over training programmes soured the winter air. After the debacle of 1986, Dan was keen to reassert his authority. He wanted to do this by increasing the volume of training significantly. But the American contingent were keen on the short hard sessions they were used to, rather than grinding out thousands of kilometres in distance work. Matters got so fraught that in November, Dan resigned as coach when the crew refused to go on the water for a technical session after a particularly hard workout. In *True Blue*, Chris Clark is portrayed as being the villain of the piece, despite the relatively higher profile of rowers like Lyons and Penny. Dan makes no secret of his view that, during this infighting, Chris was the weaker character compared to that of the other Americans.

But it is hard to see how a 'weak' character could have had such a

The Tideway, 1986: 'Quasimodo', rowing at '6' while training for the Head. My bent inside wrist is hardly out of a rowing textbook.

harmful effect on a whole squad. Dan records Chris's missed training sessions, his petulance (even on some occasions to the annoyance of his American friends). In short, Chris could be seen as a spoiled brat, who didn't want to do any training and who made boats go slow.

In reality, though, Dan did not have the grip on his crew that he would have wished. The famous magic that the little man weaved from ten years between 1976 and 1985 had gone. For a few short, crucial weeks, or months, Dan had lost an effective grip on his squad. In his efforts to re-establish his own control, he somehow seemed for the first time vulnerable as an Oxford coach. In these circumstances, the strong leadership, combined with sensitivity, that Chris needed to bring out the best in him as a rower was sadly lacking.

That Chris was under pressure is in no doubt. In addition to the stress fractures to his ribs in 1986, he had volunteered to switch sides from stroke to bow in order to correct an imbalance in the crew. Each rower usually has a favourite side that they prefer to race on. But when Chris was not producing the results in the boat against rowers like Macdonald, whom he must have considered lesser in ability to himself, it was clear that his place was in jeopardy. Chris's future was on the line.

But by the New Year he had reacted by throwing himself into the training with gusto and by putting himself back on to his favoured stroke side. His tactics were successful. Chris's standing improved enough by the end of January to beat the president, Donald Macdonald, in a crucial seat race at Henley. With every indication that his improvement would continue over the next few weeks, at last Chris stood ready to claim the last seat on strokeside.

It is in response to these events that the infamous 'Mutiny' began. If Chris Clark already felt a burning resentment against Dan, it would be nothing to the pain he would feel in the future. In Dan's mind the president, Macdonald, had done more than enough to prove his place in the crew. Perhaps more importantly, Donald had been a crucial supporter of Dan throughout all the winter's arguments. To lose him from the crew would have seriously weakened Dan's position.

But it was clear that Dan could not ignore Chris's return to form. The answer was to put Chris in the crew but on his apparently weaker side: 'bowside'. This meant that Donald would remain in the boat on 'strokeside', while Clark would displace Tony Ward. This would be the second year running that Ward had lost his seat at the 11th hour. Given the previous problems between them and Dan over the winter, it seemed that the Oxford coach was over-reaching himself. It seemed clear to the crew, that Clark should row in the boat in place of Donald, not Ward.

This was when the mutiny occurred. When Chris and I spoke, he did not wish to go into his role in these events. But I don't think that it was he who was not the prime-mover behind the crew's decision to close ranks and simply inform Donald that he was deselected and that Chris was rowing in his seat. In this order, they even organised their own training sessions, rowing at Marlow under Mike Spracklen for a brief three days. In Mike's estimation this crew was one of the strongest Boat Race crews he had ever seen. But, despite this, the in-form Chris Clark knew that he was living on borrowed time and confided as much to his friend Dan Lyons.

The Establishment is often slow to respond to a threat, but once threatened gains an unstoppable momentum. Donald Macdonald and Dan, aided by the Dark Blue stalwarts, marshalled their forces impressively. With the benefit of hindsight, it's easy to see that both the American contingent, as well as the other British rowers in the crew, had not appreciated the weight of the Establishment they were taking on.

By then, the increasingly fatalistic Chris Clark was not playing a key role; rather just 'sitting back and watching it happen'. But there was no question that his friends were intent on fighting his cause against that of Macdonald and his ally, Dan. The 'end' that Chris had predicted, was never really much in doubt, despite the drama of *True Blue*, once Donald Macdonald had determined not to resign and to tough it out instead. Chris Clark offered to 'withdraw from the crew' when he realised that his American friends were prepared to miss the Boat Race rather than row with Macdonald. It was an offer that was never taken up: The president went on to achieve his own immortality by winning the Boat Race.

So far, for Clark, the events seemed like a never-ending nightmare. His rowing at Oxford was finished for ever; the Establishment had won. Around Oxford, apart from the press, which he was drawn to read with a morbid fascination, he had begun to receive hate mail and even became the object of graffiti in Oxford toilets. This provided enough fuel to ignite a lifetime's resentment.

But there was more: Chris took up rowing because of the strong relationships and loyalty that he was able to forge and experience. Now, from his standpoint, he had let his friends down. They could have rowed in the Boat Race. He told them not to withdraw on his account and to carry on and row with Donald Macdonald but his efforts were to no avail. To this day, Chris still feels that he owes his friends a deep debt of loyalty. He even tortures himself wondering if he'd have had the 'strength' to do the same thing. There was the vilification of his friends as disloyal American rebels.

On top of this Chris had lost all confidence in his ability to row. The words of support he had been offered from such sages as Mike Spracklen were drowned out by the chorus of Establishment denigration that was heaped on his character. If he did not wonder then, he must have done so later, that maybe Dan and Donald had been right all along about his worth in a boat. This interpretation can only have been strengthened when the Oxford Boat proved that it did not need the American champions to beat Cambridge.

Chris had to face this in the country that was his self-proclaimed 'second home'. On the face of it, it seemed to be a country that had turned against him. He returned to America to lick his wounds and rebuild his life. But it was not easy. The resentment still ran deep. It would not allow him to get on with his life. He hung out at Huntingdon's New York apartment, then moved to California, working in a retail store for a couple of months. Unsettled there, he went up to the solitude of Alaska to fish with his brother. But by April 1988 he was back in Huntingdon's apartment. Unfortunately for the man who was finished with the sport of rowing, it was a hive of Olympic gossip. Huntingdon and Lyons were off to the Seoul Olympics. Chris felt uncomfortable in the thick of it.

That summer, for the first time, he returned to England to visit his friends at Oriel College. He ended up helping Mark Machin coach the Oriel first eight for a few sessions as they trained for Henley regatta. The eight lost in the first round, although that could hardly be blamed on Chris. Yet the rumour mills started again. Perhaps the American loser had spread his 'hex' on another Oxford crew. Dan suggests as much in his epilogue to *True Blue*. To escape, Chris returned to the States and drove his VW camper van down to Florida by himself, although every sports report on the radio (the Olympics were then in full swing), seemed to rub further salt in his wounds.

By the fall of that year, he thought that he had found his new métier, as far away from the sport of rowing as one could get. He saw the movie *Cocktail* and went to bartending school. In the following years, he was to cut a fine Tom Cruise around the bars of New York, even ending up owning a part share of a night club. He was good at his job and the confidence he had lost began to return, so much so that for the first time since those fateful days in 1987, he once again picked up an oar. The 'Power 10' were a high-powered drinking club of ex-Olympic rowers, who mostly worked on Wall Street. They had a boat up in Columbia, Manhattan, and needed another stroke side for their thrice-weekly training jaunts. Chris was persuaded. It was fun rowing; no pressure and he enjoyed it. As a target to aim for, the crew wanted to put an entry in the Ladies Plate at Henley Royal Regatta.

It was a big decision and a brave one at that, perhaps in retrospect one of the bravest things he ever did: to return to race in the home of the very Establishment that had ruined him as a rower. Chris loved England. His relationship with this country was like an amazing love affair that went badly wrong but was so very passionate and so romantic that he became nostalgic about it. He could not stay away. He returned in the full knowledge that Dan's account of the 1987 Boat Race was about to be published.

If Chris thought that things couldn't get worse, he was in for a shock. The book contained one of the most comprehensive character assassinations that you could wish to find on a sportsman. While Chris was at Henley, there were articles in the press about him, or the book, almost every day. Again, he read the press articles with a kind of strange fascination, buttressed up by the support of his crew and his friends from Oxford and Cambridge, Tony Ward and Mark Machin from Oxford and Steve Peel, the defeated Cambridge president from that 1987 Boat Race.

The only word Chris could find to describe his experience that summer was 'brutal'. His appearance at the Fawley Bar would set the tongues of the 'blazerati' wagging, as if to say, 'How dare he walk in here.' If he had begun to find ways of rewriting his life story and dealing with his resentment, he could tear up the book and start again. It was as if wherever he went in England, people would know of him. His wife thought that he was being paranoid. But while on vacation near Tintagel in Cornwall, in 1995 (post-book and pre-film), Chris's wife heard the family next to them whisper, 'That's Chris Clark, that's Chris Clark, the man who ruined the Boat Race,' as her husband went up to the bar to get a beer. In his life now, people who know nothing about rowing will be aware of the events of the Oxford mutiny, although perhaps less so in America, where the film version of the book has yet to appear.

Through it all, though, he still stuck to rowing, in between his bartending. But more and more, Chris began to feel dissatisfied with his life. He began to feel that he didn't really belong in an industry where money seemed to talk. He began to notice the low life more, drunks and drug addicts and some of the worst characteristics that the human race had to offer. More and more, he kept contrasting them with the guys that he knew in rowing. They were 'people who would back you up all the time'. After a spell of hitchhiking with his friend Dan Lyons in the summer of 1992, he was persuaded to come back into the world of rowing but this time as a coach. He went to help Dan Lyons as a freshman coach at Navy.

As a coach, he was immediately successful (although this fact was missing from later editions of *True Blue*). For the first time in 20 years, Navy beat Harvard. Two years later, he was poached for a top job in the rowing programme of the University of Wisconsin. Rather amusingly, (Chris tells the story with a smile on his face), he was asked to call the university while he was in England, watching Henley regatta that summer. In clipped English tones, the voice on the public address boomed out, 'Will Mr Chris Clark please report to the secretary's tent.' Clark, not knowing why anybody should page him at that moment, remembers a flush of adrenalin and thinking, 'Jeez, what I do now? I'm in trouble again.'

In coaching, though, it was as if he could do no wrong. His success with Wisconsin was recognised by the US national coach, who put him in charge of the pre-elite rowers (one level before international). His crew went to the Nations Cup and won a gold medal. They did the same the following year. Lyons, the world champion rower, told his buddy, 'You know, you never really had any breaks as a rower, not one. But in coaching it's the opposite, you get all the breaks.'

But as a coach it was not as if he was coming back into the sport without any baggage (being honest, most of us have suitcases-full anyway). But it seems that for Chris, every single thing that he does in coaching is a reaction to what happened to him at Oxford. As he put it to me, with passionate commitment, 'Oxford was the fulcrum upon which my life turned, it completely affected my outlook on everything, everything.'

In some ways, he is clearly a hard taskmaster. How could it be otherwise when he feels that every single thing that he does as a coach is the exact opposite of what he felt that he got as a rower. It is crucial for him that he teaches his rowers to react to adversity in a better way than he did. No matter how difficult the situation they must push forward and not complain because to complain is to find an excuse. It's hypocritical because it's totally different to what he was as a rower. Everything that made him weak – he coaches the opposite of that. Of course, it's a hard burden to bear but he still has something strong, driving him along.

In his mind there still lay the resentment that he felt from the treatment he received at the hands of Dan and Kris Korzenowski, the former US coach, and it was clearly, in part, driving him on. The lack of understanding that he received from the former while at Oxford was a heavier burden to bear than anything that Dan subsequently published. Chris shows no arrogance. About his own coaching abilities, he can't believe how lucky he's been. But he does rate himself as better than either of those two coaches. Not because 'he's great' but because he 'understands people and what rowers need, better than them'. His family background – his father was a college teacher, his mother a principal – had clearly given him a sense of how one should – and, crucially, how one should not – relate to students.

It is a background of which he is fiercely proud. In *True Blue* he is portrayed as a spoilt rich American. But his background is far from that. Both his parents were from poor backgrounds. His dad came from a blue-collar family who had to live in a 'basement house' as there was no money to build the upper stories. Although he could mix with the society people at Oxford, he always identified more with the menial workers, the janitors. In that sense, he was less a 'blue blood than a blue collar'. In some ways it was that background which gave him such a sense of injustice when the 'upper classes' of the Establishment shunned him. Chris was denied the pleasures of being an arriviste and, as I had done, took his treatment to heart. In that sense, like me, he is a man with a mission.

To me, it seemed that after many years of introspection, Chris had laid his own psyche bare. Because of what he had been through at Oxford, there was nothing that he didn't know about his own character strengths and weaknesses. He had come to coaching as a man with no illusions about himself but with a mission. Through it, he was to find a way to deal with the deep resentment that he felt for his treatment in the past. For him, coaching rowing was to be his 'repechage', a chance to be in the sport which he had lost. Now, to coach well was his lifetime's goal.

As a rower Chris thinks that he wasted his whole career, along with any talent, because he had no confidence in himself and lacked wisdom to take up any advice that was offered. Just as he saw himself as 'misunderstood' by those who coached him, he wanted desperately to show his own rowers that he understood them.

As we talked, Chris was keen to tell me that he never leaves any of his squad's questions unanswered because he 'had a million and no one answered them'. In doing this, he feels that he is helping his rowers to avoid the bitterness and regrets that he once felt. He told me, 'I want them to love rowing.' When I heard this I was immediately drawn to ask him if he'd ever coached rowers whose personality in some way resembled his own. He looked at me hard and it was a while before he started to respond. 'Guys that are difficult to deal with but really, really, really want to work hard and can't deal with...' But then his Californian voice trailed off and we both shared a quiet moment. It was only after that I wondered if he had been thinking just how fairly, as coach of a Boat Race crew, he would have treated himself.

But one thing is clear. Chris Clark once more has an ambition. It seemed a dirty word to him after all that happened at Oxford. It meant greedy, pushy and terrible. But now he has learnt that it means his desire in his field to be as good as he can be. That field is coaching and 'as good as it can be' means the Olympics. Something that he missed out on in 1988. He has a strong desire to coach at a future Games But if he doesn't make it, or even if he does, some day there will be a fast crew from Wisconsin, or from the US team, coached by Chris Clark that races and wins at Henley in style. Perhaps then he will be able to lay to rest the resentment that has been driving his life since that Boat Race back in 1987. Maybe then, he will be finally accepted as a True Blue.

Seoul Mates

"I DON'T want this wedding to get in the way of his Olympic training.' David Tanner's demand to my fiancée, on a spring evening six months before the Seoul Olympics began, stunned her into a painful silence. Chris had never had to face, so blatantly, the implications of my immersion in the world of international rowing. Until then she had chosen not to attach any significance to marriage in an Olympic Year. Now there was no escaping it. For the moment she chose to bury her outrage, questioning whether the man with whom she had chosen to make a lifetime commitment was not already promised elsewhere.

Freezing dark winter tideway mornings, cold blistered hands that never quite warmed up, and the pain of working right on your anaerobic threshold were all signs of our sacrifice and dedication – absolutely essential to win an Olympic medal. It was to a large extent sustained by the fact that we all shared those burdens equally. A crew's pschye is a powerful engine, able to drive a boat to achieve more than the sum of its individual parts. But at the same time it is fragile entity. When one member questions the goal, the whole boat suffers. In the past I had profited from the almost mystical sense of shared vision. Indeed, I often craved it, taking my strength from the fact that my crew were soul mates and I – I imagined – was theirs. Now, in finding another, I was weakening that unity which bound my boat together. Throughout the season the very process of this was disquieting enough to raise fundamental issues in my mind that would lead me to look at my relationships with others in the team, and in particular Steven Redgrave.

As chance would have it, wedding bells and a honeymoon in the West Indies would also disrupt the Olympic preparations of Steven that year, although the date in February – unlike mine in June – was several months away from the Games. I couldn't have imagined that Steven's crewmate, Andy Holmes, would have been too bothered by the interruption either. With a new baby at home, he was glad of the chance to have a more relaxed regime for a few days. In fact he was probably glad of the break for another reason; it was well known that neither he nor Steve were particularly close. In fact sometimes they were downright uncomfortable in each other's company. If you'd have suggested to me then that the two of them were in any way 'Soul Mates', I'd have laughed. Now, though, I see their

Whitton, 1987: Chris during her air hostess days.

relationship differently. It is often said that our true soul mates are not those with whom we are perfectly matched but those who are sent to teach us something fundamental about ourselves. Those lessons are often painful, take many years to sink in but are always enlightening. Perhaps, as I tell the story of their relationship as I saw it during those years, you'll see what I mean. But as I prepared to deal with my own fiancée's feelings that spring of 1988, Steve and Andy's relationship was the last thing on my mind.

For me, the purpose of that surprise 'friendly' visit from my coach – I was on training camp in Switzerland – was all too clear. My total commitment to the four was now brought into question by the fact that I could even contemplate marriage in the year of the Seoul Olympics, and worse still in July 1988, only three months before the Games.

Even now the audacity of David's demand seems breathtaking. At the time I said nothing in response. I had already had an argument with my crewmates over this issue earlier in the year – of which I had told Chris nothing. I told them that my marriage was more important to me than rowing and that if they didn't like it, they could find another stroke man. I felt justified but then threatened, so while I was annoyed at my coach's words, I did nothing about it. I saw that David was reacting to my crew's concerns as well as to his own fear of losing control of the crew's destiny.

As far as he and my crewmates were concerned, a wheel had just fallen off their stroke man's wagon, and another was distinctly shaky because unlike them – who were virtually full-time rowers – I was holding down a permanent teaching job at Hampton School at the same time. Just as the early prospectors were consumed by a single-minded, all-excluding desire for gold, so it was meant to be with us. We had only to look to the one-track mind of Britain's 'greatest' rowers, professional oarsmen and medal machines – Steve Redgrave and Andy Holmes – for the example of how to behave.

Andy's determination and focus towards training were legendary. He would often would cycle the 35 miles over the gently rolling hills from Guildford to Marlow, train intensively for over three hours with Steven in the pair and then cycle home. It was the type of training that even a top triathlete would baulk at. While even Steven could not match that, the past four years had seen him undertake a training programme the volume of which I could never hope to match. My greatest asset in previous years – or so I told myself – had been the level of training that I could endure relative to other rowers. Now with ever-increasing responsibility at work and eager for the commitment and security of marriage, I was going to endure it all and be a teacher, husband, international sportsman, you name it! I could take it all in my stride. Let the Olympics come and I would show the world. In my narcissistic way, I therefore imagined that I was once again enduring more than any other rower and my Olympic triumph would be all the sweeter for it.

The reality, if I'd cared to look below the surface, was very different. I was feeling increasingly insecure and adrift in a world of younger, full-time rowers, three of whom were in my crew. To avoid the feelings of guilt that I was desperately suppressing, I clung to my life raft – the 'Cross Factor': my ability to pull results out of the bag at the end of a race when all seemed lost. It was something that I owned. It had saved me in the past and would, I rationalised, do so again. In the past it had been the unassailable shield that I'd sheltered behind, strengthened by my view that I was a better racer than any of the rowers in the British squad. But now, I looked to one person and wondered.

I had long counted Steven as a friend. Not an inseparable companion, although our relationship had been forged by two years as crewmates and a further two as training partners, sharing the same coach. The ribald humour which Steven and I had shared, often aimed at other crewmates

Knightsbridge, 1987: With some of my closest friends the night before the Serpentine International. We swapped rowing stories, talked politics and drank the Pimenov's vodka until late. Left to right: Nick Pimenov, Alf Hansen, Valerie Dosenko, Yuri Pimenov, me, John Maxey, John Garret and Rolf Thorsen.

like Adam Clift, was, at its most extreme, a form of male bonding. Endless hours spent in each other's company in the boat on the swirling grey waters of the Thames from Marlow to Cookham, added to easy chat during mealtimes, had made for a familiarity, while the camaraderie born of joint goals achieved, and burdens shared, had been tempered in the heat of many a hard race.

I had got to know Steven's family well. Their Marlow Bottom house was a second home for Steven's crewmates in between training sessions. Geoff and Sheila, Steven's parents, were great friends with my mum and dad – how could they be anything else when they had shared the tension and joy during that epic Olympic final of 1984? To me it was important that I was friends with the men with whom I rowed and, as such, Steven's friendship was meaningful to me.

But by 1988 the easy flow of the relationship was submerging under a deluge of my own insecurities about my abilities compared with Steven's. In reality the competitive tension between us had always lurked just below the surface, bursting out periodically, often during competitive training pieces with or against each other.

Most of all, before July 1984, I was the athlete in the boat with world and Olympic medals, while Steven hadn't then won any. I felt he resented my feeling of satisfaction with 'just' a bronze medal in the Olympics of 1980. It was as though he thought that my crew could have won a better medal, if I had adopted an approach similar to his. At a deeper level – on the few occasions that I bothered to really connect with myself – I saw insecurities about Steven's own inability to achieve success in the single scull being projected on to me as a resentment against my own contentment. That resentment was a powerful force to his own training.

However, those insights were few and far between. For the majority of the time, I allowed my jealousy of Steven's success on the water to threaten the belief that I had in my own abilities. By 1988, he had already added to his Olympic gold in 1984 by winning the coxed pairs World Championships of 1986. Together with Andy Holmes, in an unforgettable race, they rowed through the East Germans in the last few hundred metres. In the same year, Steven was awarded the MBE after winning three golds in the Commonwealth Games regatta.

One of those golds was in 'my' event of coxless pairs. Adam and I had raced Steven and Andy earlier in the year for the privilege of representing England. I had wanted to concede the honour without racing but was goaded into racing by Adam. The ten-second verdict merely confirmed that I had lost the race in my mind before the starting line as so many other of Steven's opponents seem to do. The image of Steven as some kind of unbeatable Titan was further enhanced the following year when he and Andy decided to try to win not just one World Championship event but two.

The World Championships in 1987 were held on Lake Bagesverd, tucked in among the pine-clad hills a few minutes away from Copenhagen's suburbs. Here, even the elements seemed to favour Steven against me. By then, I was rowing with Adam in a coxed four. Our world record-breaking performance in the heats was swept away when our semi-final result saw us given the unsheltered lane five for the final. In the most unfair day of racing ever held at a World Championships, everyone in lane five finished fifth and those in lane six, last. On the calmer, sheltered side, in lanes one and two, the less talented crews, protected from the wind by a high bank, won medals.

Initially, I had felt more secure when Steven and Andy's superhuman attempt at doubling up in coxed and coxless pairs seemed to be coming unstuck. In their semi-final they had trailed in an unconvincing third. The draw for the final could have placed them either in the worst lane – six – or on the other side of the course in the calm, sheltered water of lane one. As

Copenhagen, 1987: This photograph of my four racing in Copenhagen was chosen for the cover of the first issue of *Regatta Magazine*. The choice was made, as a consolation for our bad luck with the lanes. But the editor also wanted a change from yet another 'Redgrave shot'.

luck would have it, they drew lane one and won by miles. I have never felt more of a sense of powerlessness and of being cheated in the whole of my life than I did on that Saturday. On Sunday, Steven and Andy 'only' managed to win a bronze in the coxed pairs.

But the fact that Steven was doubling up in both events at the same regatta only added to the apparent gulf in achievement that I was allowing to separate my abilities from his. As a refuge, I hid behind my 'Cross Factor' shield and tried to remember the times when my sprinting ability had won races against all the odds. This worked best when I remembered the times that I had raced without Steven.

Perhaps you'll forgive me one brief recollection now? One thousand metres gone – halfway – in the final of the 1986 coxless pairs at Lucerne regatta. Across the Rotsee's placid waters there was a yawning gap between the bows of our wooden Stämpfli shell, trailing in lane one, and the carbon and kevlar sterns of the first three crews surging ahead in front of us. Seven seconds adrift of the leading crew – a lost cause, even to my bow man Adam, who knew my tendency to sprint at the end. What happened at that moment I still don't really know. but I suddenly began to feel the surge of the boat in my legs as I was driving them against the stretcher. As I realised that I could add to this sensation, our boat begun to increase in speed. The increasing turbulence of the American's shell in the next lane told me that we were gaining.

We rowed the second 1,000 faster than the first and beat the East Germans by clear water. Our victory was so unexpected that the television director had not caught us in his cameras until the final ten strokes – the 'Cross Factor' had dramatically triumphed. I was king of Lucerne… at least until Steven and Andy come down the track in the coxed pairs and made our time look 'ordinary'.

You see, even in recalling what I think was my best ever performance, something that I created and fashioned, I slipped back into type and allowed something I had achieved to be judged by Steven's results.

At least then, in my relationships I thought I was secure. Looking back on it, God knows why. My partner in 1986, Ann Callaway, had been waiting over a year for me to make a real commitment to our relationship, but I felt unwilling, or unable, to do so. I knew it then, even more than I can see it now. In reality I had been carrying a torch for Amanda. The trauma of my break with her, while I was seeing Ann during the 1984 Olympic campaign, had shattered the image I had of myself as a 'loyal and honest' partner. So rather than make a clean break, I tried to convince myself that I still had some vestiges of loyalty to a relationship with Amanda. Withholding my love for Ann was, in part, my way of kidding myself that I had not lost those qualities. After 18 months Ann tired of saying that she loved me; she got fed up of waiting for a response and stopped asking. Her eyes turned elsewhere: to Steven.

Looking back, the signs were obvious but I was content not to probe too far into painful territory. In Nottingham during the 1986 World Championships, I had wandered into Steven and Andy's room to borrow a razor. Ann was there. They both went red and their looks of embarrassment made me feel like an interloper. I sheepishly withdrew. After all, Ann had told me just a few weeks before not to worry if I saw her spending time with Steven because 'he needed help' after the break-up of his long-term relationship with Belinda Holmes.

The truth did not even dawn when on the day after the championships, on our return to London and the flat we shared, she told me that she wanted to talk about our relationship. In the hazy sunshine of Hyde Park she told me that she thought it best if we had a 'trial separation'. I ranted and raved and moved all my possessions out of her Fulham penthouse back into my small Hampton flat.

The next day my flat burnt to a cinder. Everything I possessed went up in smoke. To this day I don't know why it happened, then of all days. God sometimes acts with impeccable timing. Adam, who had left all his possessions there, lost everything too, including £250 stored in his brown briefcase! But Adam, never one to let the significance of the deeper things in life pass him by, declared the next day, as we woke up in my mother's front room, 'I feel like a new man.' Indeed, it was therapy of a sort, shovelling the remnants of my Olympic blazers and prized East German racing singlet out the window. In desperation I realised what a fool I'd been for the last two years and looked for Ann. 'It would be different now... give me another chance.'

Of course, that 'chance' had long gone and her life was now inextricably linked with Steven's. Jim Clark, who I always turned to for advice, confided in me that a rower had heard Steven say to Ann after he had won his medal, that just seeing her standing in front of the medal rostrum while he was receiving a medal meant more to him than anything he had won.

Still I refused to accept it, until one Sunday afternoon four weeks later when Adam and I turned up for a scull at Molesey Boat Club. Steven was there with Ann, taking her boat away from the rack that I'd arranged that it could be kept on. We crossed paths on the forecourt and looked into each other's eyes. I saw an uneasy guilt. He spoke no words. Perhaps it was my fear of losing his friendship, or just recognition that it was not he who had made the running in starting his new relationship.

But God works in mysterious ways. As I moved back to live in my parents' house, a British Airways trainee stewardess took up lodgings. Like me, she was 29 and a Cancerian. Similarly, she too was suffering from the after-effects of the break-up of her first marriage. The release of being able to share my true feelings with my soul mate was heavenly. I asked Chris to marry me six months later, on Valentine's Day 1987. The marriage was to be in July 1988 – as soon as the annulment and decree nisi permitted.

Our wedding was held in the afternoon at St Theodore's RC Church in Hampton on 25 June – the morning had been devoted to an intensive sprint training session of 400 strokes of fartlek. Chris and I asked for no presents or speeches, although Adam, my best man, was not to be denied. David Tanner had been 'gracious' enough to allow me two days off training for our honeymoon, so in theory disruption to training could be kept to a minimum before the big pre-Olympic regatta in Lucerne.

If my crew were worried about me losing form because of the wedding, their fears seemed justified. Our coxed four failed to make the final at Lucerne regatta, finishing in a distant tenth place. David Tanner's worst nightmare came true: he lost control of the crew. It was not to my wife, though, but to Mike Spracklen, then the men's chief coach. Mike knew that we had not been following his heavy training programme. He saw the chance to make a point. In any rate, as chief coach he had a responsibility to deliver results from his crews. The opportunity was there for him to help us at the same time as allowing him to feel how great a coach he really was by turning around this 'crew of rebels'.

From then on, David sat next to Mike in the launch for our outings. You could cut the tension between them with a knife. Of course, it translated to the crew, I wanted to resent Mike's interference but we needed him, and his coaching wisdom and acumen began to bear fruit. We picked up speed during August. So I buried my feelings and waited.

Mine was not the only crew coached by Spracklen to suffer a loss of form in the same year as a wedding. Steven and Ann were married in the spring of 1988 in the Chapel at St Paul's Cathedral reserved for the Weddings and Baptisms of Members of the British Empire. It was a

St Theodore's Church, Hampton, 1988: Chris and I process under the traditional arch of oars, towards a reception and a two-day honeymoon.

sumptuous affair, to which both I and Chris were invited. Another guest was Andy, although he was not one of the ushers, nor did he hold one of the oars forming an arch through which newly-married rowers walk at the conclusion of ceremonies. It was not meant as a slight, although it was certainly a talking point among those at the service. It merely confirmed that outside rowing the two had little or nothing in common and neither had any desire to alter that.

For better or worse the wedding ushered in a difficult period for the pair. Steven's transatlantic honeymoon necessitated ten days out of training. When combined with their understandable but risky decision to race in the San Diego Crew Classic – one of the few 'jollies' available to top European rowers – a few weeks later, the resulting jet lag and a dose of the runs knocked the pair's Olympic preparations right back.

Mike continued to push Steven and Andy hard during the squad's Easter training camp on the long, tranquil lagoon in Sabaudia, just south of Rome, frustrated by the amount of time out of training. The result was a disastrous performance at the first regatta of the season on the crowded and rough waters of the Baldeneysee outside of Essen. They trailed in third in the coxless pairs on Saturday and just scraped a win behind an undistinguished field in the coxed pairs on Sunday.

Their already terse relationship was further tested. Andy suspected that Steven had settled for a less than good performance at Essen. Uncomfortable training rows, in what turned out to be a twisted boat, led to further arguments. Although the manufacturers solved the problem by building a new and stronger hull, Mike was reported as saying in *The Times*, that the pair were unhappy '80 per cent of the time'. Perhaps it was the amount of time that Andy had spent on the punishing ergometer – the third session of the day on Spracklen's programme. Maybe it was the incessant demands on his lean frame made by mile after mile, showing Steven that he could pull as least as hard as the bulky Marlow man. Whatever, Andy sprung a rib just before Henley. Crestfallen, the pair had to miss both Henley and Lucerne and watch the Rumanian boat that had trounced them at Essen set a new Rotsee record in the process.

Although I could not see it at the time, Andy's injury had laid the foundations for a renaissance of the blistering speed that had eluded them over the last year. Ultimately, it depended far more on the delicate psychological balance between the two men than on almost any other factor. For months that balance had been shifting too far in favour of Andy, chiefly at Steven's expense.

Like Andy, I and others in the team had been blaming Steven for the pair's poor form and scrappy technique. Britain's most talented rower was struggling to perform under a burden of self-doubt. But now at a stoke that load was lifted and the balance shifted. It was Steven who now had to ease Andy back to fitness, paddling at half pressure, while Andy fitted in behind him. In these weeks Steven's confidence visibly grew. It was Andy who now

Chun Cheon, Korea, 1988: A cox's eye view of David Tanner, coaching my four at the pre-Olympic training camp. By then David was back in control of the crew. In the foreground, Adam Clift's blade has just entered the water.

had to make amends. The effects of this change begun to show on the water in the final pieces before the team left for South Korea. The pair began to set their fastest-ever training times and give the bigger boats – including our four – a run for their money over shorter distances.

The Han River rowing basin, site of the Olympic regatta of 1988, was only a 20-minute drive from the Olympic Village. It nestled alongside the broad sweeping bends of Seoul's main artery. As a course it was like any other man-made rowing lake. As you stood on the pontoons of the boating area by the grandstands and finish tower (as rowers always do when they arrive at a new course), your eye would be drawn inexorably along a line of buoys stretching ramrod straight to the barely visible starting tower over 2,000 metres away. Paddling on it felt like any of the European basins, Nottingham or Roundnice, gently sloping banks set in the flat landscape of some alluvial plane or other. Even the crews had the same faces that you would expect to see at any World Championships.

But it was the sense of expectation that everybody carried in them that created a radically different atmosphere. The media attention and hype surrounding any Olympics was bound to generate this, as was the expectation and excitement of living in the village alongside some of the most famous athletes in the world. One evening, in our village apartment set in a maze of Korean high-rise tower blocks, we watched the television replays of the famous American diver Greg Louganis smashing the back of his head on the concrete of the ten-metre board. It was a major item on all the world's news that day. A few minutes later there was a knock at our door and Louganis stood there, a large bandage on his head, kitbag slung casually over his shoulder, asking for John Maxey who he had met the previous day in the dining hall. It was surreal but that was – is – the Olympic experience and the chances are that it will make competing at your best all the more challenging.

Perhaps it was this pressure that made our opening race such a disaster. Unlike Steven and Andy's confident showing, we had a disastrous heat, trailing in a distant sixth and last behind the East German world champions, who broke our championship record in the process. This meant an unusually tough repechage. That we won showed just how much we had improved since Mike had taken us on. The semi-final was altogether another challenge.

The night before the race was one of the worst experiences of my life. The pain of the race and the doubt of its outcome was all-consuming. Beneath it lay a deep fear that I was not good enough; an Olympic champion defending his title, who would be laid bare as a fraud, not even making the final. Our form in the repechage, or the fact that the race would soon be over and life would go on, counted for nothing. The relaxation techniques that I had so painstakingly learnt from the team 'shrink' were of no avail. Even the blissful but temporary release of a few moments sleep never came.

By the morning I was in no condition to race but felt the inevitability of the whole process – it was happening to me but I was not part of it – drag me through the warm-up routines. Worse still, the course, was unfair, a cross-headwind from the far bank gave the high-numbered lanes a clear advantage: we were in lane one. I went out for the warm-up paddle, writing my sporting obituary.

With a few moments to go, the reprieve came. Racing was postponed until the afternoon. David Tanner had relentlessly harried the officials, demanding that the lessons learnt from the unfairness in Copenhagen were acted upon. The release was glorious and the previous night faded into oblivion as I grabbed two hours' sleep in the village and faced the afternoon's semi in perfect conditions with a clear, relaxed and confident mind.

I was still in that mood with 1,500 metres gone. Our boat was moving well. The problem was that we were in last place, five seconds down on the leaders and four seconds off the third qualifying place with only 500 metres to go. A hopeless position. Coxed fours don't make up that much time in less than 90 seconds of racing. But then it happened.It was like deja vu, a feeling through my legs of the boat surging and the faintest glimmer of a target; the Russian stern far lay ahead over my right shoulder. The chase was on, the 'Cross Factor' engaged, I scented blood and went for the kill. With a glorious abandon the crew responded as one, the rating moving effortlessly up to 43 strokes per minute. A risky glance with 250 metres to go and the yellow and black stern of the Russian Empacher was there. There was a blanket finish. All six crews crossed the line within a second of each other. We had won the race and were safe in the final. In the small hours of the morning Dan Topolski waxed lyrical back in London on Channel 4 television.

The 'Cross Factor' did not make an appearance for the final. Again we moved the fastest in the last 500 metres but this time our spurt lacked the verve it had shown in the semi. We finished fourth. It was the first Games in which I had missed out on a medal. I never felt that bothered about it (no, honestly), except that I wondered if relying on my finishing talent was

Seoul, 1988: The most incredible sprint finish of my career, after which 'The Cross Factor' became well known. I am rowing in the crew nearest the camera, wearing a cap. We won after being five seconds down with just 500 metres to go.

perhaps an excuse for going off too soft in the first place. Again, I had only to look to Steve and Andy to see how races 'should' be won. They won their coxless semi-final imperiously and qualified with ease in the coxed pairs race, despite having only 50 minutes in between the two races following a nasty head-on collision between two of their opponents.

Steven and Andy's second consecutive Olympic title was secured the same day as Ben Johnson won the 100 metres final. It did not make as much news but it was history in the making. They led the Rumanian pair from the start. Steven's revolved around to shake Andy's' hand in a celebration of joy that gave no clue to the tension between them. Both of them expected to add to their titles the following day. Most of the British press stayed away, preferring to see how Linford Christie fared. Anyway, the newshounds expected another gold in the coxed event on Sunday – then there would be a story. That it never materialised and they had to settle for 'only' a bronze medal therefore seemed like an anticlimax. There was no celebratory hand-shake and Andy left the village early to be with his family back in England.

It was the last time that the two men would ever compete together. No plans were made for the next season. But then they never were. Andy didn't know it but Steven had had enough of the tension of their relationship. He longed for a partner with whom he could be friends and still go just as fast. He and Spracklen chose Simon Berrisford, the tall, talented, rather loud-mouthed powerhouse from the coxless four, whose pair in training had been pushing Steven and Andy hard. If Steven could make a pair work with new partner then it could be seen who was the real boat mover and Andy's contribution put in its proper place.

Andy's initial reaction was to come out fighting for the following season. Unable to find a full-time pairs partner, he raced in a fast coxless four which won at Duisburg regatta early in the next season. But his heart was not in it and he dropped out. After a brief six-month flirtation with the marketing side of the sport, promoting French rowing, he disappeared from rowing. It was like he had never existed.

Steven did not stand on the winners' rostrum for another three years and then it was in the bow seat behind Matthew Pinsent. If Andy knew how to get the best out of Steven, then he seemed to be keeping it to himself. I knew that if I wanted to understand my own relationship with Steven, I had to find Andy and hear his side of the story.

I was not sure if he would agree to talk. It was just over a year earlier that he had point-blank refused to appear on a *This is Your Life* special on

Chun Cheon, Korea, 1988: Fun during a training session for the Seoul Games. John Maxey is nearest the camera, then John Garrett with me in the stroke seat. Adam at bow is taking the shot. Of all the crews I rowed in, this four meets the most regularly. Our Christmas dinners together have become an annual event.

Steven. The researchers had tried in vain to tempt him to appear – the long-lost crewmate arriving at the end of the show would have made for a great finale. In desperation they asked myself and Richard Budgett – both from the LA four – to try to persuade him to appear.

I was too nervous to ask Andy. But he told 'Budge' that for him, rowing was 'dead and buried' and he had no wish to resurrect any part of it. But as Andy and I talked on the phone to arrange a meeting, it seemed that he was more than happy to exorcise his past: that part of his life which he had buried for nine years. In doing so he wanted to face his resentments against Steven, the cause of so much of his silent suffering over the past.

I was initially surprised at how different he looked from my last recollection of him. At 30, his face had seemed bold, noble and finely chiselled; his lean features and incredible physique mirrored the awesome toughness that marked him out from any oarsman I ever knew. Now it was far fuller; not quite bloated but not Andy. His black hair, normally cut short, was now long and tied back in a bunch, like a 19th-century Jack tar. Yet at 39, only a few wisps of grey showed through and then the similarities; the slightly incongruous John Lennon spectacles, the inevitable jeans and denim jacket covering a musculature that, while not as finely-honed, was still enormously strong, fed by the sheer physicality of the building and removal work that he had made his living.

I had never been close to Andy. Admiration and respect were always there but he was never someone that allowed you that near. But now I felt as if I was greeting a long-lost brother. The sense of our comradeship from the campaigns of the mid-1980s was almost overpowering and I realised then that it was something I had completely lost when Andy began to row with Steven. We were two old veterans, talking over past campaigns and the scars of battle that were left. One of those scars we had in common was the effect of rowing with Steven. For Andy, the sense of anger, frustration and bitterness still ran deep, although I sensed that that for him the process of telling his story would be cathartic, a necessary step in letting go of the resentment that he felt was just beginning.

He started as he must, when the two 'Seoul Mates' split in October 1988. There had never been a phone call, from either Mike or Steven, to tell Andy that partnership was over – perhaps they imagined that it would have been too painful? He learnt of the split during a meeting with DAF Trucks at the Motor Show in Birmingham. Pat Sweeney, their cox, recalls that when the conversation moved on to the next four years, Steven said that he did

Seoul, 1988: Guiseppe Abbagnale throws his arm aloft in triumph after taking his second Olympic gold. Part of his elation was due to his defeat of Redgrave and Holmes (centre), who finished a distant third.

not want to row the pair with Andy. Andy looked at Steven in disbelief (as did Pat), and stormed out of the room. Pat and Steven travelled back to London in the same car. Not a word was spoken until Pat got out in London. As he closed the door he said, 'Steve, I think you're making a mistake.' Pat left more bemused than angry. But with Andy it was a different story.

His anger was all the more so because that he felt that Steven's new partnership with Simon Berrisford would be a complete waste of time. Berrisford could not extract the performance levels out of Steven in the same way that Andy had.

Although he never said so, it seemed to me that Andy may have been secretly yearning for the call that never came, or the chance to make Steven, or Mike, work for his continued commitment. What made it worse was that Andy felt that as a double gold medalist he should by now be living in 'a mansion, raking it in', especially after his years of hard labour. Of course, the uncertainty of his and Steven's relationship did nothing to help Andy find sponsorship or promotional work. Furthermore, as the months wore on, Steven looked set to reap the benefits of a partnership. To Andy it seemed once more that things had fallen into Steven's lap without him really trying. This simply confirmed Andy's view of himself next to Steven.

Andy was the youngest of three brothers, 'the runt of the litter', and as such he always struggled to drag himself up on to the pedestal that he had placed his brothers. Rowing was his escape from mediocrity and the ladder to filial recognition. His physique became an obsession and to develop it further, he chose to do hod-carrying based on price work. He used an over-sized hod and ran up and down ladders all day long carrying huge loads of bricks – in between training sessions.

Steven, he felt, was in contrast, someone who had never had to work for anything in his life. His physique was God-given and the cosy, sheltered existence he led in Marlow, where he was nurtured, first by his parents then by his coach Mike Spracklen, was far from the Darwinistic ideal that marked out Andy's perception of a true Olympian.

His experience, both of racing with Steven and seeing his partner perform in a single scull, further strengthened this view.

In 1986 Steven was the overwhelming pre-race favourite to win the diamond sculls at Henley. His opponent in the final was a Danish lightweight sculler, Bjarn Eltang, who was eminently beatable – if Steven was able to transfer the power and skill of his rowing into a single. Down the course, Steven held a narrow lead, then Eltang, who had figured that Steven would be vulnerable in the second part of the race, began to apply pressure. Slowly his bow edged closer to that of Steven's. It was too much for Steven. In a dramatic moment he stopped racing and sat there, while Eltang moved into the lead.

Pete Spurrier, the photographer who was on the following umpires' launch, remembers the gasps of incredulity as the Henley roar died to a whisper. The launch driver had to throttle his vessel back to avoid hitting Steven. In the silence around him, Spurrier heard the agonised voice of Steven suddenly exclaim, 'What have I done?' A few moments later he began to race again: a beaten man. Andy remembers the looks of incredulity on the faces of Steven's family, as he came into the landing stage.

There was no doubting Andy's satisfaction with the result. A few hours later Steven would race again, this time in the final of the Goblets, with Andy behind him. The result had confirmed Andy's view that Steven had a soft centre, and that when he was on his own in a sculling boat, his physique was not enough to see him through. But with Andy behind him in the bows of a pair, Steven would feel his tough, unrelenting presence and push through his own fear of performing flat out.

It was not the only time that year that Andy experienced this side of Steven's character. After they had won the coxed pairs title at the World Rowing Championships in Nottingham, they met in a pub for a drink. They were talking with cox Pat Sweeney, about the race and their plans for the following year. During that race Andy had rowed himself into the ground trying to get through the East German pair of Greiner and Forster. The Germans had led all the way until, with just 200 metres to go, they blew wide apart, letting the British boat through to win. In the last ten strokes, to hold off the fast-finishing Abbagnale brothers, Steven had put in a massive effort, so great that Andy could not respond, nor Sweeney compensate for it by using the rudder, and the boat was pulled across the lane on to the buoys under Andy's rigger. 'Where the fuck did that come from?' thought Andy, 'He should have died trying to get through the East Germans.'

In the pub he thought he had found the answer. Steven said, 'I looked across [at Greiner and Forster] at 1,650 [metres gone] and thought, it's silver.' At that moment Andy glanced across at Pat and 'their jaws hit the floor'. He suddenly thought that, under pressure, his partner had displayed the characteristics of a loser. As if to underline the point to me, Andy went on to describe Steven's physiological abilities: 'He's so outstanding that he can row half-cock and still win.'

This tale was not new to me. What was striking was the vehemence with which Andy was relating it over a decade after the event and with another two Olympic gold medals in Steven's trophy box. I said to him, 'Come on Andy, how could the greatest oarsman the world has ever seen possibly be a loser?' But Andy went on, 'There was only one time, one time, when I was hanging on to him and that was in 1987 when Mike made us do a 2,000-metre piece at race pace in Amsterdam, before the World Championships.'

I remembered the day and the place well. The Bosbaan rowing canal, ringed with tall trees, is set in a park under the flight path of Schipol airport. That day the grey water was flecked with streaks of foam whipped up by the warm easterly breeze. Their boat had not so much skimmed over as ploughed through the unsettled water. Their time had drawn a gasp of disbelief from the assembled oarsman. Six minutes and 24 seconds was 11 seconds inside the current world's best. It was not an idle fantasy to speak about it in the same breath as Beaman's leap in Mexico City.

Andy's narrative became at once questioning and bitter. 'It was the only time… all the championships that we rowed in were nothing to that. Why, why… what was it on that day that motivated him? Nobody else knows, only Steve and I were in that boat. Maybe Steve doesn't even know, maybe he

Nottingham, 1986: The last few strokes of a dramatic coxed pairs final. Olaf Foerster stroke of the GDR crew (centre) has 'blown', letting Redgrave and Holmes (furthest away) through. The Abbagnales (foreground) charge for the silver.

thinks that he's a winner, or above anyone else who's rowed with him. I knew what Steven's strength was, physically he's just awesome, but beneath it...'

It was a deeply-held conviction and spoke volumes about Andy's perception of his toughness relative to Steven. Whatever the truth about their performance in 1986, Andy was convinced that Steven's apparent weakness in the single had surfaced in the pair. This belief was to determine the relationship between the two, not only for the remainder of their partnership but on into the present. When mixed with the resentments following the media's attention to single out Steven and 'ignore' Andy, it made for a bitter brew.

The inherent stupidity and in-built bias of the British system of recognising achievement injected further poison. In the New Year's Honours list of 1987, Steven received an MBE – and Andy nothing. It was a travesty, although certainly not Steven's doing. He had been in Australia when notification arrived and his parents accepted on his behalf. But the whole incident led to a bitter and public row between the two men at a party to celebrate Steven's success; it was a running sore that would not heal easily. Steven's answer in October 1988 was to break the partnership. For Andy, it was not that simple.

To provide the answers he first looked to the sport he knew. Andy flirted with the idea of sculling. No matter if it took another four years, and he could only reach the final, it would be worth it; sixth place was higher than Steven had ever achieved in his best-ever finish in the single in 1985. Andy even bought a house to renovate in Banyolas, Spain, site of the 1992 Olympic regatta, reasoning that if he was to try sculling it would have to be in a place where he felt comfortable and in the sun. But ultimately, the lack of a sponsor forced him to reconsider.

Again he looked to rowing and the offer of a four-year consultancy post in French rowing as an 'advisor' seemed attractive. He loved France, spoke good French and when he had set his family up in a Parisian apartment he was sure that 'it was going to be a great life'. After six months of frustration when he was cold-shouldered by the coaching staff, who saw him as no more than a motivational figurehead (and probably a threat to their jobs), he realised that he could take no more and returned home.

But the world had changed. The properties that he had bought with the money that his father had left him slumped in value as interest rates became crippling. He started racking up massive debts. The one type of work that he could always rely on to bring in the money – hod carrying – was not available as the building industry collapsed. It was the lowest point in his life and he turned his back completely, for ever, on rowing. Although he had read the Sunday newspapers to see Steven's results in the first year of his new combinations, first a silver with Berrisford and then a 'lowly' bronze with Matthew Pinsent – Andy felt a certain amount of satisfaction at Steven's failure to win without him – he now attempted to avoid all rowing coverage.

His Olympic medals, photographs and other trophies went into a big suitcase in the attic. He spat the words out with contempt: 'There was nothing, nothing, in the house that would suggest that I had anything to do with rowing.'

At once I was struck by the contrast with Steven. His Olympic medals – three of them won with Andy – were on proud and regular display on the lunch and dinner circuit, set in a beautifully inlaid wooden box; Andy's proud and hard-won possessions, the highest sporting honours in the world, sat in a gloomy loft gathering dust.

A journalist 'found' him on holiday in his Banyolas house during the 1992 Olympics, completely oblivious to the team and Steven's performance. At the time I found this hard to believe. But when Andy asked me what Steven was doing now – 'Who's he pairing with?' – from his genuine surprise that Steven was now in a four, it was apparent that his self-imposed isolation was genuine. But it was not so easy to hide from other people's attention. They would come up to him and say, 'You're that rower aren't you?' And he would vehemently deny it, only for them to say, 'I thought I saw you in a boat with that Steven Redgrave... and you've got the same name.' Again Andy would refute the connection. Then there was, 'But you're built like a rower.' Perhaps, unlike St Peter, Andy never heard the cock crow, but for him the denial was just as painful.

To recover his self esteem he took to his first love, music, and bought a drum kit. He got himself a good tutor, like a rowing coach, and set himself training routines, just like he had done on the water. 'Two hours on fingers in the morning, half an hour on feet in the afternoon.'

Within two or three years he was very good. So good that he played in a group, together with his brother and an anarchist guitarist from the States. They sometimes did anarchist gigs and busloads came from Holland to Brixton to hear them. I had this wonderful image of this long-haired, sweat-covered man beating the hell out of his drum kit to get the short thumpy sound out in a smoke-filled hall in South London, full of people plotting the end of capitalism.

Rowing was never that far away, though. He would have dreams: he was rowing along, nowhere in particular, and discover that he was just about to race in the World Championships and then suddenly remembering that he hadn't rowed for four years. It was an anxiety dream, which spoke volumes about the way he had suppressed a large part of his life. Outwardly, it didn't make sense. In three years Andy had won every honour the sport had to offer. But deep down, he knew that if he was to move on, the suitcase had to come down.

It had happened about three months before we met. His daughter Amy, had seen a picture of him in a Penguin book of the Olympics and recognised that she had a famous daddy. He'd long had an antique Edwardian vitrine sitting in his garage. Sensing Amy's pride at her father's achievements, and seeing his own chance to come to terms with his past, he took it to a cabinet maker and got it polished up. He took his medals out of the suitcase and put them on display, with a picture of our Olympic four from 1984 on top of the cabinet. He had come to terms with being able to say that he, Andy, was a double Olympic champion and what went on before, after or during that didn't matter. A great rower had come home.

But while Andy could now embrace and celebrate his own achievements, it was clearly going to take some more work before he could accept Steven's. As we talked about Steven and his rowing achievements since 1988, we inevitably lighted on Matthew Pinsent, Steven's inseparable partner since 1990 and – unlike Andy – his close friend. Andy saw Pinsent's racing toughness as in a similar mould to his own. But there was more and it was clear that in every way, Andy's last tale was the supreme irony.

In 1989, just before Andy had stopped rowing, he tried one last time to find a winning combination. The coxless four in which he rowed up until May, although fast enough to challenge for bronze, or silver, to him seemed to lack the real 'killer instinct' which would convert their speed into a gold medal. But he remembered the trials that spring, when his crew had been racing against other squad boats.

He had always prided himself on being able to tell who was moving a boat: 'Call it arrogance.' In the very next lane there was one crew of youngsters who his four was struggling to beat. In the middle of an effort to move away, he looked across to see who it was in this boat that was making them move stroke for stroke with his more experienced combination. 'And there it was. It was him… I saw the look in his eyes… we were sort of staring at each other, into each other's eyes. I could see the determination that said you aren't going to beat me, you bastard, or I'm going to get you, you fucker.' The rower was none other than 18-year-old Matthew Pinsent.

Andy said goodbye to his four and, as one last parting shot, telephoned Mike Spracklen, still men's chief coach. He asked to try a pair with 'that youngster who had been pulling that four along'. Mike was non-committal, saying that it was too late in the season to make such a change. Perhaps he did not want competition for his pair of Redgrave and Berrisford. Andy was not to be put off and got hold of Pinsent's telephone number, which happened to be his parents' house in Portsmouth. He left messages but to this day does not know whether Pinsent ever received them.

But for years, whenever Andy had heard of Redgrave and Pinsent's latest crop of Olympic titles, he had been engaged in 'virtual' rowing, tormented by what might have been. 'Holmes and Pinsent': was it a whisker away from reality? At first, Steven's attempt to stroke another winning combination floundered; Redgrave and Berrisford could finish only second in 1989. In 1990, with Steven in the key stroke seat, he and Pinsent struggled to a bronze medal. But in 1991, Steven was able to switch comfortably into the less demanding bow seat of the pair – the one Andy had rowed in – and profit from the bull-like physique and absolute determination of Pinsent. They have won gold medals ever since.

Of course, history does not deal in what nearly happened. The reality is, and will be for some time, that Steven Redgrave is the world's greatest rower. He has one of the shrewdest and sharpest minds ever to read a rowing race. He is not the toughest, the fittest, the strongest, even the best technician in the world – but he is still 'the greatest'. For the simple reason that he is still there and has been there at the top of one of the world's most demanding sports for the last 15 years. Even Andy admires him for that.

Steven would dearly love to stand and face Andy on equal terms, although I suspect that their reconciliation will have to wait until they meet in that great regatta enclosure in the sky – a sort of rowers' Valhalla.

Perhaps this is somewhat fanciful but I can imagine them meeting under some leafy tree. And with a firm handshake and a knowing gaze into each other's eyes, they would each understand why they were each other's soul mates. Steven would explain how Andy's relentless drive to prove he was the toughest rower in the world was like an arrow that winged its way straight to the centre of what Steven perceived was his own weakness: that at the heart of the world's greatest rower, there was a soft centre.

Steven would talk of many things that he had never had the chance to

Indianapolis, 1994: Mum, my number-one supporter and only member of the family who watched me pair with Steven in the 1994 World Championships.

say to Andy: his fear of pushing himself to the limit and the costs of the stress-induced diseases that have long plagued him; the way that part of his defence against a 'soft centre' was for him to build up an image of a great invincible athlete, for whom losing was unthinkable and Olympic titles were second nature; he would explain how that constant pressure and the tension which existed between them were too much for him to take and how he realised that to carry on he had to find a different partner.

Andy would tell Steven of how his seemingly God-given strength, physique and sporting talent were a constant reminder to him of things which he never had; how he had pushed himself up to and beyond all normal limits to develop those qualities so that as an Olympic champion he could look at himself in the mirror each morning and feel comfortable with what he saw. Andy would explain how whenever he felt Steven had given less than 100 per cent effort, it had the effect of undermining the very foundations of his own relentless struggle. He would tell of his feelings of resentment and discomfort with the idea that somebody could be as good as him, and win, without a superhuman effort.

Perhaps all the above are just the wistful imaginings of someone who prefers reconciliation to conflict. No doubt you will have your own ideas on that subject. If not, perhaps the following tale might prompt a few thoughts.

The year 1994 marked my last championships. It was the year that Steven and Matthew Pinsent won their fourth and toughest coxless pairs title in a tremendous race during Saturday's finals. I was rowing in a coxed pair and my partner had been feeling unwell all week. Consequently we had failed to reach the final. My last race ever in the World Championships, on that final Sunday of racing, would be the small final, for places 7-12, hardly a race to look forward to. Jonny Singfield had struggled on all week but was too ill to race. I was by myself, without a partner, or a race. Then Steven, shattered from the efforts of his victory, offered his help for the next day.

The competitors in the small final could hardly believe their eyes as the massive bulk of the world's greatest rower lined up on the start. It was a great race and a wonderful curtain-call to leave the World Championship stage. We led off the start, fell behind, struggled to hold on, then moved imperiously through in the last 300 metres to win the race – shades of the 'Cross Factor'.

As soon as we crossed the line, Steven turned around with a look of sheer joy and exhilaration on his face, a look which was mirrored in my own, and offered me his hand. I took it warmly and gratefully. The gesture was not missed by the rowing cognoscenti watching in the grandstand. As Dan Topolski said, 'There was a lot in that handshake.'

The Singles Game

THE dull glow of a portable television lit up our bedroom in the middle of an October night. Chris and I were watching the closing ceremony of the Seoul Games. In between gulps of hot tea, I listened to Samaranch invite the youth of the world to assemble four years hence in Barcelona. I wanted to be there, although it felt like I'd had it with rowing for a while. Adam was stopping and most of the others were going to spend the winter rowing at the Leander club. I felt about as welcome at the Pink Palace as Ben Johnson might have been at an IOC drugs convention.

In retrospect, it might have been a good time to call it a day. At 31, I'd done most things in the sport. Now marriage and family beckoned. Sporting retirements were in the air: Seb Coe turned to politics, while in tennis Chris Evert was fed up at being beaten by teenage prodigies. It wasn't right for me then, however. That night, as the Olympic flame begun to flicker out in Seoul, the germ of an idea crossed my mind. In 1989 I would try the singles game.

I wouldn't be the first oarsman, or the last, to try my luck in a single scull. Given the choice, it's the boat that most rowers would want to do well in. That year I wasn't the only rower to dream about success in the singles. The 17-year-old Greg Searle was then in his last year at Hampton School. He was the younger (by three years) and the physically bigger of the two Searle brothers. Even then he cut a dashing figure. Later, his 6ft 5ins frame with broad shoulders and fresh matinee idol looks would see him into *Company Magazine's* 50 most eligible bachelors.

He already had 'star quality' written all over him. That season would see him win the first of his two junior gold medals. But Greg had his eyes set on greater things. Some time in the future he wanted to make it as a single sculler. In October 1988 he was featured preparing for his first race in a single scull on Channel 4 television. The programme touted him as the next Steve Redgrave. It was a challenge to which Greg was prepared to rise, although to do so he knew that he'd have to achieve what Redgrave had failed to do: make it in the single.

In years to come, when Greg became one of the world's top single scullers, I remembered his promise to me at school: 'I'll be the best ever

British rower, better even than Redgrave.' Confidence was never a quality that Greg lacked. Perhaps it was this, as much as anything, that drew me towards him. Confidence was a quality that I imagined all the top scullers possessed. Yet when I contemplated racing in the single, it seemed in short supply. Back in 1988, the reasons why this was so were so completely ingrained in my psyche as to be unchangeable.

The single is much narrower and shorter than any rowing boat. With only 20 centimetres of hull supporting my weight at its widest point, just keeping it balanced was much harder than balancing a rowing boat. Of course, holding two blades, rather than one, made the whole action more difficult. Mistakes were even more costly in the slower-travelling single as it had less momentum than a rowing boat, so a blade scuffed along the surface of the water on the recovery would make a real difference in speed. Most of all, in rough or swelly water sculling a single was like riding a bucking bronco. Bigger boats could plough the waves but the single often seemed to be at their mercy. It was like crossing the Channel in the relative comfort of one of those monster roll-on-roll-off car ferries, ploughing imperiously through stormy seas, while watching an apparently helpless fishing smack being tossed and thrown from crest to trough.

Perhaps because the best scullers had learnt to handle these conditions, they became the hardened seafarers with a mystique attached to their art, looking rather contemptuously on the ferry passengers in their relative security. The old professional scullers who used to race for huge purses in the 19th century were cases in point. That year, perhaps hoping that their magic would rub off on me, I began to collect some prints of the old scullers

Thomas Eakins painted many of them. He left his studies at the Ecole de Beaux Arts in 1870, just before Haussmann's new boulevards would ring to the sound of Prussian siege cannon. In the quieter surrounds of his native Philadelphia, the man destined to become one of America's greatest painters spent the next four years working on a series of rowing paintings. Mostly they featured the single scullers who raced each other in front of the large crowds that lined the banks of the Schuylkill River for purses of thousands of dollars. These rugged individualists, like Max Schmitt and John Biglin, were friends and heroes of Eakins, himself a rower. As a sportsman he knew that he could not hope to equal their feats. But as an artist he knew well their distinctive qualities of self-discipline and an ability to be alone with themselves in the midst of a challenging task. In his art, as he stood in front of an easel, engrossed and focused, sometimes basking in his solitude of his métier, on other occasions cursing it, Eakins was to be metaphorically a single sculler all his life.

His painting *John Biglin in a Single Scull* brilliantly captures those qualities. Eakins fills the foreground with the image of the champion sculler, his blades just ready to lock into the waters of the Delaware River. Bright sunlight dances off the water and Biglin's eyes are like narrow slits, set in a swarthy face, made to seem almost piratical by a red bandanna wound around the top of his head (those were the days before Oakleys and baseball caps). From his barrel chest, two pale, sinewy arms protrude, arms that would do justice to Popeye; they mirror the powerful musculature of his calves. Yet the presence of the bows of another sculling boat, just two-thirds of a length behind Biglow's boat, belies the fact that this man is racing and at once we know the quality in those eyes is a focussed determination. There can be no doubt of the outcome of this contest. Eakins sets a minuscule eight against the distant New Jersey shoreline. They are dwarfed by the intense presence of the sculler – they are, quite simply, out of his league.

I suppose I felt a bit like that too. The images of those old professional scullers and the presence of their modern counterparts, like Karpinnen,

River Delaware, 1873: *John Biglin in a Single Scull* by Thomas Eakins.

Kolbe, or Lange, were pretty intimidating. So as I tried to decide what boat I would aim for after the 1988 Olympics, the single was for me an enticing but daunting prospect. Enticing because with a demanding job and new marriage, the flexibility that training in a single would offer could save me no end of pressure trying to fit my life around other people's schedules. Daunting because I suspected in my heart of hearts that I was really a crew man.

I was a gregarious animal. To thrive, I needed people around me. When I had turned to sculling for one season in 1982, it had been with three others scullers in a quadruple. It was still a challenge but of an altogether lesser nature than the single. My inner demons told me that I could not face the anxiety of being beaten by others in the single; of becoming an also-ran in the selection process. It was a fear of failure. And lurking behind that, the fear of all extroverts, that of the solitude that I knew I would have to face if I committed to the single scull.

So I prevaricated; it wouldn't do for me to face up to those painful 'truths'. For the winter of 1988-89 I trained in my single but without a real commitment to give me a kick-start. At the least I needed a coach, and probably some training partners too. In fact it was too convenient for me to train by myself at Molesey. Not least because as a newly-wed it would be great to spend some time with Chris. Earlier that year we had enjoyed all of two nights away in Kent for our honeymoon. Without ties to any training group, it was easy to contemplate taking a 'real' honeymoon in Kenya.

The three weeks we spent there provided me with my longest break from training since I was 15 (if you don't count a half-hearted run part-way round the red earthen shores of Lake Baringo). I told myself that this break would in some way 'make up' to Chris for the two months I had spent away in South Korea during the Olympics, which had in part dissipated the spell of our romance.

The magic of Africa was overwhelming. Even at the end of the 20th century, it was easy to relate to the romantic idyll of Karen Blixen's colonial Kenya, or to Hemingway's fatalistic visions of man against beast. We were overwhelmed, as they were. From the vast African sky merging into the endless plains of the Serengeti, to the shimmering sands of that languid laid-back island in the Indian Ocean, Lamu, it was easy and fun to live the life of the 'big white hunter' in luxury lodges like Kichwa Tembo, or Governor's Camp. In our own Suzuki jeep I could feel that we were better in some way than our fellow rich American guests who were herded into crowded vans for their game drives.

Nottingham, 1986: A classic singles duel: Bjarn Eltang (foreground) fights for a third lightweight title, but, with metres to go, Peter Antonie's glance helped him to find something extra. The little Australian went on to take a sculling gold in Barcelona.

In truth, we probably missed more than we should and usually ended up in the same places as the vans, but on the occasions that we hired a Masai tracker and went our own way, we usually were repaid. As Christmas Day turned into twilight on Fig Tree Plain we saw the ghastly but compulsive spectacle of a solitary wild dog tracking and goring a young wildebeest, grabbing what flesh it could before a lion, alerted by the beast's bellows, chased off the dog and settled down to a 'free' meal. We, too, dined on the strength of that tale that evening, as we regaled fascinated American tourists and revelled in sounding like experienced game trackers. Not for the first time that holiday, I enjoyed playing Robert Redford opposite Chris's Meryl Streep, as we drunk deeply 'Out of Africa'.

A day or so later, as night fell on the other side of the Mara near the great wall of Olo Olo Ridge, the 'great white hunter' missed a path in the gloom and got hopelessly lost – so much for compass work in the Boy Scouts! We ended up by the crocodile-infested Mara River. There was nothing for it but to pitch our tiny tent and brave the hippos, hyenas and buffalo that wandered out of the river, or down to its banks searching for food in the night. As it turned out we were the victims of human predators that night.

Two Masai lads must have seen our lights and charmingly but firmly demanded a healthy sum to protect us from the numerous wild animals that they assured us always frequented this particular part of the river bank. Unfortunately they hadn't yet got themselves equipped to take Visa (although the way Kenya is going I'm sure they'll have got themselves registered by now), so I parted with my last Kenyan shillings and, still feeling none too protected, zipped up the tent door. It absolutely poured down all night but our Masai 'bodyguards' had taken the sensible option and slept safe and soundly in our jeep. In the morning, right outside our tent's door, was a steaming mass of elephant dung. I could see 'sucker' printed all over my forehead as the two Masai went off to invest in a couple of extra cows for their night's work.

The Africans that we came into contact with were, by and large, lovely, warm and gentle people. But the political instability that dogs Kenyan life was never far from the surface. On our way up to Lake Baringo, we were literally driven off the road and pelted with rocks by the motorcade escorting President Moi back to Nairobi. Apparently motorists are expected to get out of their cars and stand respectfully by the roadside. In an instant I felt exposed and vulnerable. Like that night in the Mara, the cheerful image of Kenya – 'Jambo Bwana, hakuna matata!' – that had been so

Kenya, 1988: Chris and I, on the plains of the Masai Mara, during our 'real' honeymoon, which had to wait until the Seoul Olympics were over.

implanted in my brain seemed a long way from reality: At that moment, I was a Mzungu, who felt like he didn't belong.

It was a similar feeling that Easter when I walked through the hallowed portals of the Pink Palace at Henley for the first time to compete in the national squad trials. The Leander club was as exclusive as any Kenyan game lodge with its membership of Old Blues, Establishment types, fronted up by some of the top oarsmen in the national squad. Given the lack of a 2,000 metre-rowing course in the south, the Henley reach was the next best thing and Leander's earning potential as a prime site for sponsorship during the Henley Royal Regatta had been put to good use in attracting the best young talent. Subsidies towards meeting the costs of racing abroad were combined with the talents of the top coaches. Hence Mike Spracklen, together with his protégé Steven Redgrave, had been lured away from their beloved Marlow Rowing Club.

Having got this far, perhaps it won't surprise you that such inducements only acted to strengthen my loyalty to Thames Tradesmen's Rowing Club. It suited my anti-Establishment bias, belonging to what used to be a work-ingmen's club. Long ago tradesmen had been barred from racing at Henley. The great Jack Kelly, father of Princess Grace and the world's fastest single sculler of his day, was banned from racing at the Royal Regatta because he worked with his hands. Leander's membership was, I imagined, full of Tories and as such to be avoided, especially by the secretary of Hampton Labour Party. By now you may have spotted the contradictions inherent in my life, especially as someone who worked in an independent school.

I'm sure I was acutely aware of them then, although I didn't like to look too deeply. If I'd cared to scratch the surface I would have seen my allegiance to Tradesmen's as little more than a convenient badge, dressed up by the sentimental allegiance I still felt from my schooldays. In fact, the membership of the club was now far more yuppie than the carpenters, fitters or builders who rowed there in my youth. In reality it was for me, too, a flag of convenience. I visited the club's Chiswick base only once a year, instead training in my single out of Hampton School's Molesey base.

So, to the Leander-based chief coach Mike Spracklen (who wanted all squad members to train together out of the Henley club), I was in effect opting out. He knew me as a nuisance from the previous year, when my four had stayed out of his system and opted out of his Olympic training programme. To him I was a troublemaker who, at 31, could anyway be replaced by younger and more willing talent. As far as Mike was concerned,

I was best left to my own devices in a sculling boat, outside of the Spracklen squad system.

So I tried the singles game. Trouble was, it didn't seem to be going that well. Now maybe in my heart I knew that I wasn't fast enough, or perhaps I just fancied rowing with someone after being by myself for so long in the single. Whatever, that Easter I decided to try out for the squad in a pair with Saleih Hassan, veteran of the last two Olympics.

On paper the squad system seemed fairly open. It was worked out between Mike and his boss, Penny Chuter, the principal national coach. All the top rowers (excluding Redgrave and his new partner, Berrisford) were to be raced against each other in a pairs' matrix on the Saturday. Based on the results of this there would be fours trials on the Sunday, and crews formed for the first international regattas. I was pleased enough with my results at the end of the first day in pairs, which by my reckoning put me firmly in one of the fours to be tried on the Sunday.

But Mike, presumably with Penny's blessing, had a surprise in store. The crews posted in Leander club that Sunday morning were already set. There were to be no trials and I, along with the other national squad 'thirty-something', Richard Stanhope, were excluded. Stanhope had done even better than I had in the pairs races. It was a gross miscarriage of justice by any standards.

What made it worse for me, was that the other rowers said nothing. It was more comfortable for them to look in the other direction. I can understand it now; they were in and I was out. Even John Garrett, my crewmate for the last two years, could not find any words of comfort. In previous years, most notably 1984, I had stood up for my friends who I thought had fallen foul of poor selection decisions. Perhaps I was expecting too much of the other rowers. At any rate, my behaviour then had in part led to Mike's decision to drop me; he could do without another season from a stroppy and 'over the top' rower.

It was then, more than at any other time in my rowing career, that I should have had the strength to 'show them' and turn to the single scull. The standard of British single sculling was pretty low at that time and I had had a whole winter of practice. But I didn't have the bottle to go for it. I never once gave it a thought. I was dropped for the first time in my life. It served to confirm my fears throughout my solitary winter's training that I was past it, not good enough and too old. I felt threatened and vulnerable. This was no basis to turn to the solitude of the single. Instead, I looked for comradeship and support from Richard Stanhope.

Richard, tall, handsome and photogenic, was a much better sculler, or athlete, than me, with a great feel for the boat. He was blessed with an incredible endurance-based physiology and a tough, driving competitive instinct. The latter often got the better of the former in triathlons or marathons when he sprinted off, only to die of exhaustion within sight of the finishing line. But in the boat these qualities were allied to a smooth and seamless rhythm that was a joy to follow. He stroked the British eight to silver medals in Olympics and World Championships and positively dominated the longer distance events, such as the Chester Head, which he has won on ten occasions.

But despite all this ability, he lacked the self-confidence and power to be a top-class international sculler over 2,000 metres. Furthermore, Richard was not someone that you would choose to lift you out of a depression. Unless that is, you were sitting behind him in a boat. Like me, Richard was a rowing junkie. His job fitted round his rowing, as did the rest of his life. Retirement was not an option (he was still winning Henley at the age of 42), so there was no chance of him seeing any of Spracklen's ten-foot-high writing on the wall. Thus the two of us fell together, almost on auto pilot because we didn't know anything else. Rowing was his life as it was mine.

Both of us looked to sculling to carry us through this patch and proceeded to try the double scull. The rowing options seemed closed off and there was just a chance that the boat might work for us. I have to say that this was a misplaced optimism; it didn't work. By mid-season we were back in a pair. It was like being free again and our times were substantially quicker.

We decided to switch to the pair and race it in Duisburg. Despite performing well, Richard, in one of his bouts of melancholy introspection, felt that it was pointless to continue in a boat class that Steven Redgrave dominated. Moreover, he saw no way back into Mike's rowing group. He decided to return to his single.

I was alone again, but on this occasion I had found my fighting spirit and was determined to use it on two fronts. The first was political: like the history of the Russian Revolution which I was then teaching at school, I saw myself a Bolshevik in the midst of an autocratic selection regime that I perceived had not only over-reached itself but was about to tear itself apart.

It was an open secret that Penny Chuter did not see eye-to-eye with her chief men's coach, Mike Spracklen. The latter did not much care for Penny's well-meaning but often bombastic managerial style. In effect, because of the level of personal control and coaching that that Mike exercised over the men's rowing crews, Penny had been effectively frozen out of directing this area. She was vulnerable and it was this that I wanted to exploit.

In cancelling the fours trials at the Easter trials weekend, Mike had over-reached himself. Fours races, based on the results of the pairs trials, were a key part of the clearly set out selection document and, as such, any appeal from an athlete complaining against the selection procedures was bound to succeed. In addition, it would give Penny the chance to assert her authority over Mike.

So I let it be known that I would appeal against the result of the selection decision, and in response Penny told me that he did 'not have a leg to stand on' and would be ordering a new set of men's trials for the following weekend. She had thrown down the gauntlet to Mike but it was difficult to envisage the ferocity with which it was picked up and flung back.

In an unprecedented gesture Mike led a Leander club mutiny against the national squad. He had no intention of allowing Penny to disrupt his planning. He was satisfied with the results that his crews had obtained and, feeling sure of the loyalty of his oarsmen, determined that he would not attend the trials. Mike took with him all his rowers bar two, Hassan and Garrett, who diplomatically chose to do a pair. In doing so, they avoided the bans that the other rowers faced (Redgrave, already selected in the pair with Berrisford, was also not affected).

Mike hoped that by packing all his remaining athletes together in a 'big eight' he would beat the rest of the world's eights at the Henley and Lucerne regattas and hence make his own and his athletes' position unassailable. Penny's stance would then be untenable. It was like the famous mutiny on the *Bounty*: Mike was playing Fletcher Christian to Penny's Captain Bligh. No doubt Bligh's loyal crew members, who chose to remain with their captain in a small boat, questioned their wisdom as the *Bounty's* sails sunk under the South Pacific horizon.

Now that I was on board Penny's boat, perhaps I should have felt more secure. But unfortunately I was one of those metaphorically cast adrift with her in a small open boat, facing thousands of miles of lonely ocean. I had won the right to have new trials but had no one to row with. There was nothing for it but to return to the solitude of my single for the series of races at the London Docks the following weekend.

Molesey, 1993: Training in a single. Since John Shore found this shot of me, more than one coach has paid me the compliment of saying that, at first glance, they thought it was of a 'proper sculler'.

That much led me to attack on my second front: I was doing the single for the first time because there wasn't anything else left. Now I was in the boat from a position of determination, rather than resignation (how else could Bligh's crew have made one of history's most epic small-boat voyages?). On the day of the trials, Richard Stanhope noticed the 'new Cross' when he remarked on the fact that for the first time in my life I had turned up two hours early for the trial races, thus being the only one of the singles to have the luxury of a warm-up paddle.

So this was what it was like to race in a single. I was aware of being in unknown territory the whole time. It felt like being at stroke in a crew without anyone to back me up, Nowhere was this more apparent than off the start and in the first 500 metres, where my lack of sculling technique and finesse lost me valuable lengths on the other scullers. I found myself rehearsing reasons as to why it wouldn't matter if I performed badly. But in the middle of the race, as I craned my neck round to see the sterns of the other boats, it was clear they had stopped moving away. Although it was hurting and there was nobody to share the burden, it began to feel more like the rowing I was used to. I sculled through the field in the last 500 metres, beating Richard and also Anton Obholzer, the talented under-23 sculler. I finished second, just behind the experienced sculler Rory Henderson. It was a gutsy 'Cross Factor' performance.

It showed me that if I'd made a real effort to do the single early on, I could have at least achieved selection in the boat that year. Instead, I ended up sculling but in a crew boat: a quadruple scull – a reprise of 1982 except now the sculling world had moved on. We were good enough as a unit, although youth was not our strong point. The press called us 'Granddad's Army'. From the way we performed at the Lucerne regatta they probably thought that we'd suit a couple of walking sticks better than a pair of sculls. We were selected for the World Championships, but only just. In fact, in the racing there we were eliminated, finishing in the slowest time.

Maybe that result should have killed off any pretensions that I had of being a sculler. But the sculling bug didn't leave me; it never really has. I've raced a few times in a single since, on the whole without any distinction. Much of it was because, as I got older, it was easier to fit in outings on the river at my own convenience in a single rather than wait around train in a crew. But there was something else too: a feeling that I could somehow crack what I saw as the secret of being a top-class single sculler.

I think I partly saw it as something of a mystique and secret – apart from the world of rowing skills that I knew – because the only top-class scullers that I knew seemed rather remote, even aloof. Britain had always been short on top-quality scullers. In the last resort, rowing always lured promising athletes away from the single. But in 1997, that changed when Greg Searle switched from rowing to sculling. Straightaway I was intrigued. Here was someone that I thought I really knew. In some way I felt that by picking Greg's brain, as he learnt to scull, I might learn the 'secret' myself.

As you might guess, in the end the things that I actually learnt were far removed from what I thought I might at the outset. But perhaps that much will become clear as I explain something of the relationship between Greg and me.

As with his older brother, it began in Hampton School. We got on well in the classroom where, among other things, I was responsible for his 'moral' education: sex, drugs and rock 'n' roll was how it was termed. In front me and his contemporaries, for a 15-year-old he was pretty open – far more than I imagined I might have been – about his experiences. Underpinning this was a large measure of confidence. Maybe that much wasn't surprising when you considered his success in rowing.

In the Junior World Championships, gold medal followed gold medal, while in an unprecedented move he got a senior call while still only 18. By any standards it was an electric performance, every bit as stunning as Michael Owen's introduction in the 1998 World Cup. The fact that Greg was rowing just in front of his brother sealed his future – at least until the Atlanta Games.

Perhaps the fact that Greg had a brother, who I knew pretty well, was another element that drew me towards him. I'd sometimes wondered how I might have turned out if I'd had a brother. Also, maybe it revealed something of the reason why Greg decided to turn to sculling in the first place.

Jon's influence on Greg (as I guess is the case with most brothers) is enormous. Much that Greg did in his early life was following in the footsteps of his academically-gifted elder brother. Greg hated playing Dungeons and Dragons but he felt he should play it because his brother did.

Once at Hampton it was but a short step for Greg from participation in the role-play fantasy games of Jonny's primary school days to his brother's new game, rowing. Although Greg soon became the star of Hampton's rugby team, at 13 he switched to rowing. The promise of a glittering career in a sport that he loved, or the pleading of Steve Timbs, Hampton's rugby coach, could not outweigh the entreaties and enthusiasm of his brother, Jonny, urging Greg to try 'his' sport.

When the two of them rowed together, Greg always sat just ahead of Jonny, who would call the race and decide tactics. Greg would play the dutiful younger brother and, listening intently, send down 'a few big ones' whenever his brother called for an effort. It was a great partnership, although it reached its apogee early on.

Nothing that Greg has done since that race has come close to the feeling of ecstasy he experienced in winning his Barcelona gold. What made it so (more than the manner of their triumph), was the fact that he was standing on the same medal rostrum with his brother. At only 20, Greg had achieved the ultimate sporting accolade. More important, though, he had helped Jonny realise his own fantasy: winning the Olympics with his kid brother.

Not surprisingly, that victory was to indelibly shape Greg's future. A measure of financial security was assured, although that was secondary to the tremendous sense of security it gave him. On the one hand, almost anything seemed within his grasp. On the other hand, in his more introspective moments he wondered if he could ever feel so intense about anything again.

The year after Barcelona they again won the World Championships. It was only FISA's reprehensible decision to abolish their event from the Olympics (making way for a new class of lightweight categories) that stopped them adding another gold in the Atlanta Games. It meant that they turned to a new combination, this time a four, although the 'Searle Magic' didn't seem as powerful. For three years a gold medal eluded them.

In effect Greg's long partnership with his brother ended when they lost the 1996 Olympics to Australia's 'Oarsome Foursome'. A fast-finishing French crew surprisingly took the silver. To both Searles the bronze 'seemed like nothing'. It was not the note upon which either had hoped to finish their partnership.

But in the aftermath of Atlanta, for the first time in his life, Greg felt free; if he wasn't going to row with his brother, there was no one that he wanted to row with – not even Redgrave, or Pinsent. At last, Greg felt able to 'play his own game': he chose to scull. It was at this point that I began to watch his progress with a special interest.

Part of my pleasure in this was that whenever we seemed to talk, I felt a willingness on his part to speak openly about his feelings. I sensed much of this was the trust that had developed between us over the years. But part of his openness also seemed to be that, in articulating his thoughts, Greg was learning about himself. Sometimes, as we spoke, it was almost as if I could see the wheels of his mind ticking over, evaluating the implications of what he had just said.

It was clear that in the single he felt the freedom from all sorts of pressures that had lain below the surface while he was in a rowing boat. Like playing the peacemaker in arguments between his brother and other crew members. As a self-professed 'control freak', Greg felt that he could be his own boss. He relished simple things like landing the boat after an outing. In the single he always glided into the stage, right next to his shoes, whereas in the four he had resented the sloppy way they often came into the bank.

So being in the single was about being free of his older brother's influence; he had paid a debt to him and now was striking out on his own. The one thing he did not yet know was how he would perform without his brother behind him. Secretly, Greg wondered if some vital spark that had powered him to the finish in Barcelona had been missing since that day. Sculling was Greg's attempt to try to recapture the intensity of that moment.

Apart from trying to understand the psychology, I watched with interest as Greg set about learning the mechanics of sculling. In his four-year plan to win a gold in the single sculls in Sydney, he enlisted the help of Harry Mahon. It was another break from the patterns established by his brother. For five years, Greg had been coached by Steve Gunn, who had always seemed closer to Jonny, particularly as a mentor and role model. So having Harry coach him gave Greg a fresh start as well as another outlook on how to move a sculling boat.

If you've read the chapter 'Harry's Game', you'll probably be familiar with the ways in which Harry tried to develop Greg's style. Rather than getting him to slam his legs down as quickly as he could in a rowing boat (as Steve Gunn had once coached), Harry emphasised that Greg needed to move more sympathetically with the pace of the boat.

It was all about taking more time, to feel connected, and learning how to use his back as a lever, pulling with his lateral muscles rather than wrenching with his shoulders or arms.

I loved all this. Especially when I saw Harry tell him to pull less hard. Often Greg would see his electronic pace coach register an increase in the speed of his boat for apparently less effort on his part. This was what I wanted. So after watching Harry coach Greg, I would jump into my sculling boat and try the same thing out myself. But for all my efforts, I didn't seem to be moving any more quickly. Perhaps I didn't have that certain 'magic', which I felt all top scullers possessed.

I'd been steeped in the mysticism of the old professional scullers. Serving a long apprenticeship while learning the wiles of a sculler's craft seemed to be essential. Not just in terms of the tricks that were needed to handle their singles on the demanding tidal reaches of the Thames, but also in the little psychological ploys that scullers feel are so important in establishing their superiority in the unique 'one-on-one' rivalry during a sculling race.

But to Greg, the 'really good' single scullers, like Porter, Koven and himself, were just exceptional athletes who happened to be in the single. Sometimes he kidded himself that he could feel some kind of mystical symbiosis between himself, the boat and the water. But in reality, he knew that he got more feedback from his pace coach.

So unlike me, Greg had little time, or inclination, to study or cultivate the aura and mystique of the great single scullers of the past, or indeed the present. I remember the surprise that I felt when he told me that he didn't even enjoy watching single sculling races. In fact I was shocked when he said that he found watching races boring (perhaps now you're thinking Greg's more 'normal', than most of the other rowers in this book?). There's no doubt that he's more at home in the packed stands at Twickenham singing *Swing Low Sweet Chariot* at the top of his voice cheering on England, than on the bank at Henley, or the World Championships, watching his opponents battle out their races in the single sculls.

In his first year, despite poor early-season results, his confidence was high. He knew that his physiology was the best in the British team. His strength endurance was second to none. That much was clear once he had broken the world record for two kilometres on the ergometer. All that was needed was a little bit of time to groove in the sculling movement and races would start going his way. So he was able to ride out his indifferent early-season form of 1997. Besides, there was nothing unusual about Greg losing races early on in the season. Given his tally of World Championship and Olympic medals, it's incredible that he's yet to win a medal at the Lucerne regatta. In fact, after his failure to make the final at Lucerne in 1997, it seemed to me that he would have to spend his time at the Aiguebelette World Championships fighting for places in the small final and come out fighting in 1998.

But in the weeks between Lucerne and the World Championships, something clicked with him. Greg deliberately avoided travelling with the

Tampere, 1995: A jubilant Iztok Cop, surrounded by fellow countrymen, celebrates his win in the single sculls at the World Rowing Championships. Due to the heavy rain and poor light, it was one of the most difficult photographs that Pete Spurrier has ever taken. The details for those of you who know: a Nikon with a 600m lens and a 1.4 converter. Pete used 400 ASA film pushed 2 stops.

men's team. He and Harry chose to train with the women's boats in France. By the time they got to the World Championships, Greg was moving beautifully; completely at one with the boat, unhurried, connected and fast. His wins in the heat and semi-final seemed to suggest that a medal was possible, although with 500 metres to go in the final it looked unlikely. He then produced a spurt, reminiscent of his 'Barcelona burn', leaving Chalupa and the world champion Cop for dead. Another stroke and he would have surely caught the German for silver. But bronze was a pretty incredible achievement after only a year of sculling.

It was then that I expected Greg to bask in the warm glow of satisfaction and perhaps drink some beers in the company of some of his opposition. I was particularly struck with Greg's friendship with Jamie Koven of the United States, the winner of the gold medal. The similarities between the two men were striking: they had both rowed in crews with their older brother and both had become world champions in rowing. Now they had discovered the way to play the singles game in their first year, winning World Championship medals ahead of much more experienced scullers in the process.

So the night after the World Championships, I wasn't surprised to see them both drunk together in the square of Aix-les-Bains, carousing together into the night. I saw it as proof of a special kind of camaraderie that I thought existed between scullers. Maybe it does, but when I later asked Greg about this I was rudely surprised by his reply.

With a kind of ruthlessness that I had not often seen in him, Greg told me that there was no special relationship between the two men. In fact, Greg thought that Koven was the one who 'needed to talk to me' rather than the other way round. 'He's the one with the problem. I can be nice and pretend that we're good buddies but at the end of the day I can live very happily and not talk to the guy.' Greg went on to tell me that that he himself was one of the most hard and selfish people that he knew; a person who was 'superficially nice' but in reality 'quite cold'.

This image did not accord with the Greg that I thought knew; someone to whom friendship and camaraderie were important. I'd always marked Greg down as an extremely nice, personable, friendly sort of guy – probably similar in temperament to me. Was there something of the Jekyll and Hyde about him? The fact that Greg was telling this was, I suppose, indicative of the implicit trust in our relationship. But I was still surprised: there was much more under his surface than I had thought. Perhaps these qualities were what marked him out as someone who was able to scull at the top level?

It was when I looked at Greg's racing that I began to understand his (and my) dark side more clearly. We all like to keep our fears and anxieties buried deep inside us, but sometimes they can be a powerful force, often emerging to dictate our behaviour during moments of stress and tension, such as in the middle of an important race. The chance for Greg to release the tension between his 'Jekyll and Hyde' came in the last 500 metres of a race. This was the time that he could come out of himself and be really hard and unpleasant. He admitted to me, 'Something almost animal emerges.' Then the easy-going, personable character that I knew so well would disappear and be replaced by something much more savage.

Perhaps it was to feed this instinct that he couldn't allow himself to profess to being friendly with his opponents? He had an amazing coolness about his opponents. As we talked about his opposition, he referred to 'the German guy'. This man, to whom Greg had never said more than two words, was none other than Andre Wilms, the 1994 world sculling champion. He'd beaten Searle to the silver medal in Aiguebelette. I sensed the omission of his name was deliberate. It matched Steven Redgrave's famous 'gaffe' on *A Question of Sport*, following the Atlanta Olympics, when he did not know the names of his two Australian opponents who took the silver medal only a few metres behind him in the coxless pair. When I mentioned this to Greg, he saw it as evidence of how 'hard' and 'focused' Redgrave was compared to him. In other words, that was a quality that Greg wanted more of. So, despite the fact that Redgrave had been an 'also ran' when he tried the single, Greg still wanted his qualities.

Just why is easy to see when you understand something of Greg's lifestyle. Because, just as in his racing, there is something of the inner turmoil there too. Greg has to reconcile his admiration for the hard, selfish athlete (like Redgrave), who lives for nothing except rowing, blocking out his opponents and approaching each race with the same professional attitude, with the type of athlete he is around others: gregarious, strong on people skills. In short, being more than 'just a rower'. There has always been tension implicit in Greg's life as he has tried to develop the people friendly side of his character.

After his degree, he secured a job as a management trainer for Adrian Moorhouse's company, Lane 4. At first it was to do the sort of motivational type of work for company executives that Olympic champions are being increasingly called to provide. But very soon he found himself wanting to develop his own skills as a trainer. The problem was (and still is) that his work had to be fitted around the demands of a very tough training schedule. Naturally, when he was away for a couple of days working with a company, the training could suffer.

But in 1997 it seemed like Greg had it all: success in his personal life, his work and his sport. He was far from being just 'another boring rower'. To him and me, he was well on the way to win the singles gold in Sydney. But of course, life is never that simple. Greg's own belief that he could always raise his game at the very last race of the season – *ie* the World Championships or Olympics – allowed him to find an excuse for his relatively poor speed and disappointing performances during the first part of the year. These could probably have been 'turned round' if Greg had given his life over to rowing. But living the daily grind of Redgrave, Pinsent and company up at Leander would have curtailed Greg's freedom. So both he and those who knew him got in the habit of excusing second best because, when it mattered, he had always delivered.

So the 1998 and '99 seasons had a familiar ring about them: poor results early on and improvements at the World Championships. The problem was that as the Olympics got closer, the really classy scullers had begun to raise their game beyond the point to which Greg could respond. Xeno Muller, the Atlanta Olympic champion, got faster and faster, as did the Slovenian champion from 1995, Iztok Cop. Meanwhile, a new sculling phenomenon emerged, Rob Waddell of New Zealand. Anyone who saw the emphatic manner of Waddell's win, at the 'worlds' of '98 and '99 (not least the way in which his huge frame could move the fragile shell of a single scull) had no doubt that the event was being moved on to another plane. To be fair to Greg, his attempt to respond was hindered by injury and by Harry Mahon's illness. By August 1999, Greg's plight was such that even his selection for the World Championships was in doubt. In a frank session with chief coach Jurgen Grobler, Greg asked for his help, so that year Jurgen took him up to train at altitude while Mahon stayed at home with the eight and quad.

There were some improvements evident in Greg's speed. But in truth, Greg never felt confident with Jurgen's more cautious approach to key races. The German coach's instructions to just try to qualify, rather than concentrate on winning a race, may have been the logical approach but they did not satisfy the 'Mr Hyde' side of Greg's character. Jurgen might as well have asked Greg to give back his Barcelona gold medal.

So Greg ended 1999 without even finishing high enough to win an automatic qualifying place to the Sydney Games. In a supreme irony, it was Jamie Koven and he who had an ignominious scrap for the final qualifying place at the bottom end of the small final. It was a complete come-down from when I was sure that Greg and Jamie were the brightest prospects for the Sydney title. Now the gold almost had Waddell's name already engraved on it

The Kiwi took the Olympic title in Sydney and there must have been more than a wistful glance in his direction from Greg, who raced in the Olympics with Ed Coode in a coxless pair. Although their early-season form had been poor, they had looked imperious during the Olympic regatta and looked set for gold until the last 750 metres of the race, when Jean-Christophe Rolland, stroke of the French pair, produced a stunning turn of pace to row through the British pair and take gold. It was a similar burst of inspiration that had won Searle the gold with his brother in Barcelona some eight years previously. Now he could only watch and wonder as the Americans and Australians edged him and Coode out of the medals.

In one of the most heart-rendering 'hot interviews' ever filmed, a devastated Searle and Coode paddled over almost straight away to talk to

Cologne, 1998: Greg Searle, playing the Singles Game, moves off the start in a heat of the World Championships.

Steve Rider for BBC television's *Olympic Grandstand*. Coode's tears mingled with the sweat dripping off his body, as Searle tried to come to terms with the fact that he had missed out on an Olympic medal for the first time. It made for great television.

Just out of shot, Jonny, Greg's elder brother, loomed. His face was downcast too. As the interview ended and Jonny went to embrace Greg, the medal ceremony was taking place. Just eight years before, the two of them had been together on a similar Olympic rostrum in Barcelona. Then that feeling of elation had been the best moment of Greg's life – standing on the medal rostrum after winning the pairs event. Not just because it was a gold medal but because it was with his brother.

Whatever Greg does in the future, the chances are that he will always be remembered for what he achieved with his brother in Barcelona, rather than in the singles game. So it was with John Biglin in Eakins' portrait of the single scull. For although he was to be immortalised in oils as the ultimate competitor, at the time he was better recognised for prowess in a pair with his brother. That single sculler was really a rower at heart.

So what had I learnt about the singles game? I knew it was not for me. I was a crew-boat man, somebody who needed the motivation of others around him to perform. But on the other hand, the 'what ifs' have become tantalising. I'm sure that if I had found the right coach when I was in my prime, I could have at least played the game respectably. You may ask why I still bother to wonder? The answer partly lies in the emotions displayed when Iztok Cop won his first world title in the single.

It wasn't just that the race that Cop won was probably the greatest sculling duel the world has ever seen, or because with his slight bulk and strength he had no right to be a champion. It was also because Slovenia was a 'new' country, looking for an identity. With Cop's brilliant success they discovered part of it. His delirious supporters braved the freezing water and teaming rain to swim out to the elated sculler, their national flags raised above their heads. The message was clear. That one man embodied the hope and spirit of a nation. What's more, he had done it in a boat on his own, with no one else to help him.

It is *that* feeling which draws me to wonder, even now. I suspect it may still have the same effect on Greg Searle. Whether he rows or sculls in the years after Sydney, one thing is sure: for him they will provide more questions than answers.

R & P - Rowing Perfection

AS YEARS go, the 12 months from November 1989 was pretty epoch-making. Life just threw up a whole bunch of surprises. Some of them sucked me in, churned me up and threw me out the other side, others I watched with awe from a distance. As millions of Berliners danced in front of the garishly-painted concrete of the Berlin Wall, the sounds of hammers and pickaxes ringing out above the ecstatic multitudes, it seemed to me like the world would never be the same again. The Cold War would soon be over. East Germany would be a thing of the past. The nation whose athletes I'd battled against would be no more. They would bow out with a bronze medal in the men's eights during the Tasmania World Championships just 12 months after that heady night in Berlin.

As the East Germans were taking their curtain calls with a bronze medal, another crew were making their debut with a medal of a similar colour. Redgrave and Pinsent's first World Championship finish was hardly the stuff of history. Yet it was the start of the most successful and prolific partnership that the world of rowing has ever seen. A decade later they were still together, unbeaten in Olympic or World Championship competition. Back in the autumn months of 1989, I could never have guessed that anything I did would have a direct bearing on the event that brought them together. Come to think of it, if you'd have told me that I'd be rowing in one of the world's fastest boats, based at the Leander club, I probably wouldn't have believed you.

Of course, the lure of rowing with Matthew Pinsent (a true Leander man, down to his pink socks) was too great – even for me – to ignore. The ability to deliver a win, or snatch an unexpected medal in a tight race, is one that few people possess. Matthew has it in abundance. Little did I know then that I would be rowing behind him in a crew as fast as the wind and set for World Championship glory, only to have it plucked out of my grasp by Steven Redgrave as he searched for a new pairs partner who could deliver

Henley, 1990: The four in which I almost got the chance to make history, during a heat of the Stewards Challenge Cup. From left to right: me, Pete, Matt and Tim.

the perfect race, like the one at Lucerne in 1994 where they obliterated the world record in the race of a lifetime.

But all that lay in the future. As far as I was concerned, the fall of the Berlin Wall was not the most important event that happened in my life late in 1989, although as Chris and I entered West Middlesex Hospital on the night of 23 November, nothing could have possibly prepared me for the roller coaster ride that we were about to undergo. I knew that childbirth was an emotionally high, adrenaline-charged experience. Although, like the tensions and drama that I had experienced in a race, I imagined that I would be able to take it in my stride. But the arrival of Natasha, our first child, blew my mind apart in a way that no race ever has.

It had not been a particularly easy pregnancy for Chris, but all seemed to be going well enough when we arrived at the West Middlesex Hospital on that Thursday evening. With a bit of luck, I thought, our child would arrive in time for me to race in the Tiffin Head on Saturday with Shane O'Brien, the New Zealander with whom I'd been pairing. With a studied nonchalance, on the way in I stopped to buy some fish and chips which I scoffed in the labour room while Chris suffered the pain of contractions. It wouldn't do to go hungry whilst in training. But after 19 hours of labour, things were not going to plan.

To control the pain, Chris was mainly relying on good old gas and air and some focused breathing exercises. Helping her to focus on her breathing

Berlin, 1990: I'm trying to demolish a part of the Berlin Wall. It was remarkably tough to hack off even a small piece. But as a teacher who'd taught the Cold War for 12 years, I relished the chance to be a small part of 'history'.

at least made me feel more than just a spectator and provided a bond between us, but after those 19 hours, those methods of pain relief were clearly not enough; Chris was clearly in distress. I began to wonder about her and my ability to cope without some extra help. She made the decision to ask for an epidural.

But at the point where the anaesthetist sat her up, Chris suddenly began to shake and fell back on the bed unconscious.

The doctors in the room could not revive her and a crash call went out for emergency help. I was convinced that she had suffered a heart attack and was possibly dead, or dying. In fact, Chris had undergone an eclamptic fit – a highly dangerous event which is fatal during pregnancy for one in ten women. I could not stay in the room to watch as they fought to save her life, but went out into the empty green corridors, clasping my hands together in a traumatised state saying, 'God, please don't let her die,' over and over again. Chris's parents, who by this time were waiting outside the room, could see that something was seriously wrong. But I could not face them. After what seemed like an eternity – but was little more than ten minutes – I was called back into the room. Chris had recovered but was barely conscious. She was to be rushed into theatre for an emergency Caesarean.

I was in a state of shock, my senses in a state of overload. When Natasha, wrapped tightly in a hospital blanket, was placed in my arms, I felt nothing. But duties had to be done. I suppose it was a way of coping. It was in this state that in a monotone, flat and emotionless voice I phoned family and friends to announce the news. To all of them it sounded as if I was announcing a bereavement, not a birth. Within an hour, while holding Natasha, my feelings recovered enough for me to be able to experience the first wonders of parenthood.

In truth, it was a long while before the trauma of those events passed. I was left with a feeling of guilt over my inability to cope when Chris had her fit. Initially, I wasn't the least bothered about not rowing, although it didn't take long for that urge to return. Since I'd come back from Bled, I'd hardly been out of a rowing boat. In October I'd raced in the Serpentine Sprint regatta. A week later I'd travelled to the States to row with Tideway Scullers in the Head of the Charles at Boston. Driving me on was a poster I had seen three years earlier of the deeply wooded ravine in Tasmania where the World Championships were to be held the next season.

The image of that wild, remote lake on the other side of the world was at once beguiling and seductive. As soon as I had looked at the blue-green

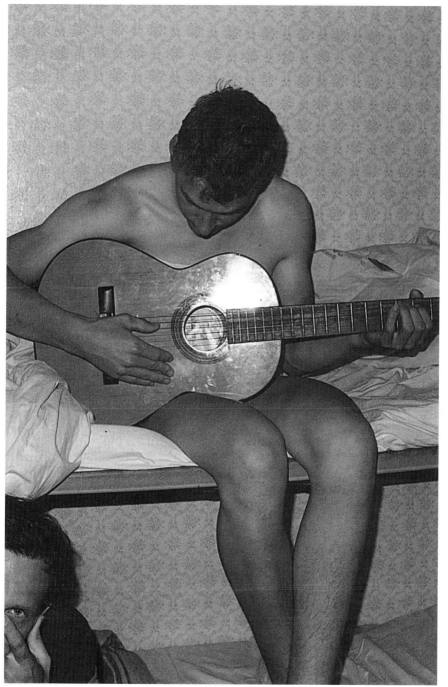

East Germany, 1990: A naked Matt Pinsent tries to play a chord on my guitar just before lights out. The bunks were typical of the low-grade accommodation rowers then endured.

hue of Lake Barrington, I imagined myself rowing down it. In some ways, my mind went back to the last time the 'worlds' were in the Southern Hemisphere. Then, in Karapiro, I'd had the time of my life. As I visualised that poster through the dark winter months, it was more through the eyes of a carefree 21-year-old than a thirty-something parent. The mortgage, Chris's need to return to work, Natasha's unwillingness to sleep through the night – none of it seemed to matter much compared to the need I had to be out on that lake. I desperately wanted to feel the excitement of a race again; to be up there in the hunt, adrenaline charged up, fighting with the best rather than lurking at the back with the also-rans. It wasn't long before my wish came true.

Luck played a part in it, I suppose. David Tanner, my old coach and family friend, was in charge of the men's squad. When he'd asked me who I wanted to pair with in the spring trials, I had no hesitation in replying with the name of Tim Foster. He was Matthew's partner in the coxless pair that won a junior gold two years earlier. More than that, I'd raced once with him in a trial earlier in the season. I knew he was sensational in a small boat. Rowing in a crew with him would be my passport to Tasmania. As luck, or fate, would have it, at the spring trials Tanner paired me up with the 20-year-old Foster, my first-choice partner. Would I have got the chance otherwise? Probably not. But there was a logic to it, much in the same way as in the Ryder Cup where the experience of players like Mark O'Meara blends with the youthful zest of Tiger Woods.

That spring, if Tim and I were not the top pairing, we were pretty close to it. Steven Redgrave and Simon Berrisford had nothing like the invulnerability that Redgrave and Holmes had once shown. That much was clear from their disappointing performance in the Bled championships. Simon, who everybody called 'Frankie', was very much the junior partner in Steven's pair. Although he had to wear the look of frustration at his silver with Steven, there was the suspicion that he was really pleased at what was his first medal. When Simon got to pair with Steven, it was as if Jimmy Saville had fixed it for him. Unlike Andy Holmes, Simon did not have the authority to bring the best out of Redgrave. Nevertheless, that season they were still the combination to beat.

Vying with Tim and me to challenge Steven's boat were Matthew and Pete Mulkerrins, another of Tanner's blends of youth and experience. Pete was a tall, spindly beanpole of a man with short, jet-black hair. His raw Bedfordshire brogue was forever laced with a kind of proletarian wisdom on the subjects of women, cars and racing. Pete's background was markedly different from almost all the rowing team – with the exception of Steven. It was unusual then, and I suspect unheard of now, to see a HGV mechanic rushing to clean his grimy hands with Swarfega before driving the 140-mile round trip between Bedford and Henley to train two or three times a day. He was the nearest incarnation to Alf Tupper, the working class comic strip hero who dined on fish and chips wrapped in newspaper by night, while beating all-comers on the track during the day.

They don't make 'em like anymore and I was glad I got the chance to race with him. Tanner, trusting his instincts, put us together in a four. Tim and Matthew were in the stern, with Pete just ahead of me in the bows. It felt like Christmas had come early. Stuart Pearce couldn't have felt better when Keegan rejuvenated his England career at the age of 37. I was pleased enough to be with Tim and Pete, but Matthew was dynamite. The last time I felt the same power and brutality in a boat was when Steven had stepped into our four for the first time at Mannheim in 1984. To have rowed with one such talent during the course of a rowing career was fortunate, to have it happen again was bloody amazing.

It was that feeling of excitement which made me determined to row in

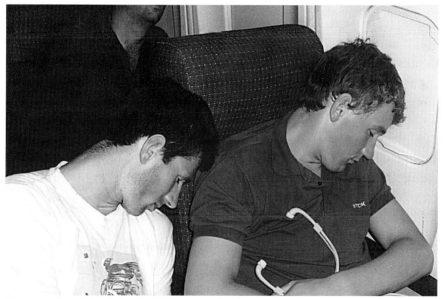

30,000ft above the Atlantic, 1990: Returning from Seattle. Pete Mulkerrins (left) and Matt Pinsent (right), who had been inseparable throughout the season, were never to be so close again. The day after the flight, Matt went off to pair with Steven Redgrave.

that crew come what may, despite the fact that it was based at Leander. Naturally, that brought with it a whole host of problems, not only because of the demands that a new baby makes on her parents but also with my job at Hampton. I usually trained in a pair with Tim before school or at lunch time in London and then disappeared off to Leander to fit in an evening session. Weekends were generally spent at Henley. And although I felt guilt about my absence from home, I knew it was going to be a special year.

Rotterdam was the venue for my first international of the season. Traffic on the Rhine was stopped for the first time ever while ten eights lined up to race upstream in the swelly waters of Europe's main artery. We behaved outrageously, drinking too much beer and partying till late. But everything seemed to go right. Our main opposition from East Germany ended up racing in a twisted shell, which took them ages to set up, while we used our own boat. The East must have thought it couldn't get any worse for them – that was until the officials drew out our lane for the race: lane one; it was the draw everyone wanted.

Pete, who was stroking the boat, knew that there would be no false starts in the chaotic conditions that existed on the Rhine just before our start. I heard him turn round and tell us, 'Watch my blade. We're going early 'cos there ain't gonna be any false starts in this race.' We went before the 'go' and were never headed. The East Germans were sick; it didn't look like it was their year. We rubbed it in by parading the $6,000 cheque by the windows of their coach. It was not really malice, more like making hay while the sun shone. That night was one long party for the crew, which returned to the hotel the next morning at 6am.

But the form we'd shown in the eight was no fluke. Our first race in the four was at Essen regatta. It was there that I first truly experienced the awesome power of Matthew Pinsent in a racing situation. We enjoyed a fairly good start and were leading by 250 metres. But when I called for an 'effort' on the minute and again at the 1,000 metres mark, there was an incredible surge in the boat. Matthew exploded and the effect on the boat was dramatic. The race was over and the characteristic late charge of the Dutch four seemed almost irrelevant.

It was much the same story in East Germany for our next regatta.

Crossing Checkpoint Charlie then was so far removed from my previous experiences there. The border was now an irrelevance and, indeed, would eventually become simply a tourist attraction and museum. We travelled through the Berlin Wall on the last day that they were stamping visas in East

Henley, 1990: Chris, Natasha and me with the Stewards Challenge Cup.

Germany. With the images of that heady November night in Berlin still strong in my mind, I was anxious to grab a chunk of history. Then at the crossing point you could rent a hammer for 10DM. I struck 'Die Mauer' and it took a few hefty blows before it yielded up a small piece of reinforced concrete for a souvenir. On two previous visits, I had gazed in awe at the sandy 'killing strip' between the wall and East Germany, I now strolled along it, the demoralised border guards not caring to stop me. It was an unbelievable experience for a child of the Cold War. Now those experiences have become a regular part of my lessons to GCSE students.

Tim and I lost narrowly to Matthew and Pete on the first day of competition, while on the Sunday we beat the home team, world and Olympic champions, with some ease. As far as I was concerned, it was roll-on Lucerne regatta where we would face the new Australian coxless four. Before then, though, there was the small matter of Henley regatta to negotiate. It was then that Tanner's grip on the squad began to fail.

Pete wanted to beat the West German world champion eight, entered in the Grand. He was fed up that the German crew could turn up at Henley and walk off with the Grand with seeming impunity. As far as he was concerned they were 'shitting on our patch'. But Tanner, mindful of the young British eight in training for the Henley Royal Regatta, was adamant that he would not let two British eights go 'head to head' in the Grand.

Henley, 1990: 500 metres to go in the final of the Silver Goblets. Tim (second right) and me, take a narrow lead on the Austrian pair. Unfortunately the Sorcerer's magic deserted us on the last stroke and we lost by a couple of inches.

Pete was livid. With Matthew's support he decided to race in a pair at Henley, against Steven and Simon. It was posturing of the first degree; there was clearly little point to it. It had already been agreed that the Rotterdam eight would race just after Henley, at Lucerne, in order to warm-up for the rowing events of the Goodwill Games, which were to be held immediately after Lucerne in Seattle. What was more, it did nothing for the crew spirit in the four, which I had assumed was to be the first-choice boat for the World Championships. In the end, Tim and I decided to race in the Goblets too, ending up on the other side of draw and scheduled to race Steven and Simon in the semi-final.

It was an encounter that was never to happen. In an event that was to have profound implications for the future of British rowing, Simon withdrew from the regatta after the first heat. His chronic back injury had become acute. He was out for the season. Our semi-final became a row-over. Ironically, Pete and Matthew lost theirs to a fast Austrian combination. So that year, I ended up in the final of the Goblets with Tim. It was an epic race, which we lost by twelve inches. The Goblets had eluded me again, although we still had the consolation of an easy win in the Stewards, the event for coxless fours. I hoped that the bitterness that preceded the regatta would not jeopardise our four's chances of World Championship selection. But, of course, there was now a much greater menace lurking on the bank.

Steven Redgrave did not have long to wait before he was in action again. An injury to Anton Obholzer meant that he would have a ready-made seat in the eight that was to race in Lucerne and the Goodwill Games following it. It was the first time I had raced with him in a regatta since the Commonwealth Games in 1986, although we had raced together in sprint races on the Serpentine. The thought flashed through my mind that he might somehow displace me in the four (that way, Tim, Matthew and Steven could have ended up rowing with each other seven years before they finally got together in 1997). But Steven's brain was still tuned to units of two. Simon's injury was a godsend for Steven. If they had stayed together, Steven would not now be looking at Olympic immortality. We all knew that Matthew would be top of Steven's shopping list. But I was not going to let go without a fight.

The chance to show what I was made of came with two gut-busting races. At Lucerne we faced Mike Spracklen's new Canadian eight, with a host of future Olympic champions including Derek Porter, a future world sculling champion, and Darren Barber, a pairs opponent of Steven and Pinsent's four years later. I was 'riding shotgun' up in the bow seat; not a seat for the faint-hearted. It was a roller-coaster ride, especially when we moving off the start at over 50 strokes per minute. Storming off the start in a coxless four was pretty frenetic. But the eight was altogether another experience.

There was never much in the first three positions all the way down the course. But we had the lead all the way down. In the very last few strokes, the Canadians charged and briefly headed us at the medal pontoon, which is only 15 strokes from the finish. 'Remember Henley,' I called to Tim who was sitting ahead of me and, forgetting any technique, slammed in the last few strokes as hard as I could. Unlike the previous week, we held out. It was a glorious triumph. I jigged and hugged on the medal rostrum, being the first on and the last to leave. My parents photographed eight-month old Natasha with the medal around her neck. I was back at the top of the sport, although Steven's shadow was beginning to lengthen over the future of the four.

Our four was due to race in the Goodwill Games, although even that was in doubt because following post-race celebrations in Lucerne and a long transatlantic flight, Tim was badly dehydrated and needed to be hospitalised just 48 hours before the race. He should never had rowed, but in the middle

of the race it seemed that he had made the right decision. We had begun to row down the strong East and West German crews. With 400 metres to go, we briefly held the lead. But Tim began to go dizzy, he lost control of the steering and we scrambled across the line in third place. Tim keeled over in the boat and had to return to hospital, complete with hundreds of ice cubes packed around him to keep him cool.

Matthew was absolutely livid. Like me, he expected to win the race and felt that Tim's sudden collapse had snatched the victory from him. I had felt a little uneasy with Matthew that year. Given that at the outset I had felt myself a little fortunate to be in the four, perhaps it was not surprising. Even at 20, Matthew was an overpowering character. Confidence and self-assurance seemed to flood out of every pore; it was not just his strength and endurance that made Steven want to row with him. On the plane home from Seattle, it was clear that Steven would get the chance to row with Matthew in a pair for a few days. If it was fast enough, they would stay together.

The two of them came together like two great stags, fighting to be 'monarch of the glen'. On their very first outing, they practised some racing starts. Matthew, at bow, was determined to show Steven who was the strongest. He pulled him round for the first few strokes. It was Matthew's way of saying that their relationship was going to be one of equals. Someone of his character was not going to play second fiddle to Steven (a role into which Simon had fallen all too comfortably). The ritualistic sparring seemed to work. By the Nottingham trials, Steven was 'best mates' with Matthew, tossing him the keys to his brand-new sponsored Saab, that he wouldn't let anyone else near.

The two of them drove up in the Saab together, almost as if their partnership was a fait accompli. Almost as soon as we had arrived, Tanner called a meeting between Tim, Pete, myself and Steven. The atmosphere was intense. Already it felt like our four, which had practically carried all before it, was now a three. Steven explained how the pair with Matthew was by far the most exciting thing that he'd rowed in since his days with Andy Holmes. But Tanner could see the other side of the argument. It would be wrong to split up our four without a race. It fell to me to pick up the gauntlet and race Redgrave and Pinsent.

Leander, 1993: At arm's length – the relationship between medal and man captured in Pete Spurrier's study of Matt Pinsent's first Olympic gold seemed to symbolise the way I used to feel about my medal.

With Tim still under doctor's orders, it was Pete who was to be my partner. I'd hardly paired with him before (there were no Henley warm-ups for us) but we had a real chance. Furthermore, there was no doubt who the national squad rowers, watching the race from their cars and motorbikes, wanted to win. Neither Steven nor Matthew were exactly popular among their contemporaries then. To a man they were cheering for us. It looked pretty bleak after 500 metres when Steven and Matthew led by two lengths (those practice starts at Henley had come in handy). But during the middle of the race, we rowed them back to almost level. The crowd, scenting a kill, went wild. But it was not to be. In the last 200 metres Steven and Matthew edged out to almost a length. Hardly an impressive verdict for the first race of the world's greatest-ever pair, but then it was enough. They would move on to kill bigger fish than us.

To accommodate them Tanner played musical chairs with all the other boats. The big quiet Irishman Gavin Stewart (stroke of the famous 1987 Oxford Boat Race win) was moved from the coxed four to take Matthew's place. Without Matthew, the sparkle had gone, although by the final race in Tasmania we were moving really well. In fact, with only 200 metres to go the silver seemed ours. But the Dutch and the East Germans squeezed through us. The race was won by the 'Oarsome Foursome' of Australia, who went on to win Olympic golds in 1992 and 1996. After a fantastic season it was a desperate disappointment. Tanner's decision to put Steven and Matthew together seemed to have backfired too. They took only a bronze, despite the wacky approach to overcome jet lag, which involved training in the middle of the night at Henley for ten days to adjust to Australian time. In the wake of the lack of medals, a rowers' revolt led by Jonny Searle unseated Tanner and left the way clear for Leander's new East German coach, Jurgen Grobler, to step into the void.

He would take 'R & P' on to new heights. If Matthew had stayed in the four, or Simon had not been injured, I suspect that we would have given the 'Oarsome Foursome' more than a run for their money in Tasmania. At the very least it would have been one of the great races in history. But holding on to Matthew was as futile as Aston Villa trying to convince Dwight Yorke that he could achieve more with them than with Manchester United, or Benetton trying to hold on to Michael Schumacher when the prospect of immortality with Ferrari beckoned. Matthew was the perfect complement to Steven, who at the age of 28 was looking for a partner to bring the best out of him, as Andy Holmes had done two years earlier. It was a rowing marriage made in heaven, in the words of Alan Green after their second Olympic gold: 'R & P, rowing perfection.'

Perhaps Green was a tad over the top with his 'perfection' label. For all their training and expertise, Steven and Matthew are not the best rowers in the world. Certainly Matthew's technique, with his slightly crooked arm draw, would never feature as a model for teaching young people how to row. It's true that, over the years, they have learnt to row the pair (and latterly the four) with more of a sympathetic feel. But their chief weapons have always remained Matthew's bull-like strength and zest for the race, combined with Steven's limitless endurance and unparalleled racing savvy. So, while the boat did not move as smoothly as their opposition between strokes, it always moved further when it really mattered. Their own imperious attitude psyched out potential opponents before they ever got to the start line. They were in every sense the true professionals.

Of course, it's a relationship that has captured the imagination of the media too. Their apparent closeness, both in and out of the boat, seemed hard to understand when one looked at the difference between Steven's solitary CSE and Matthew's Oxbridge degree. What's more, despite his personality Matthew seems prepared to play a supporting role behind Steven's lead. Of course, things are rarely as they seem on the surface. Often the key to understanding relationships and the personalities within them comes at moments of pressure. It's then that the bonds which hold the partnership together are often revealed. Every time Steven and Matthew raced, they put themselves on the line. But illness apart, nobody ever got close enough to put them under real pressure – apart from one race in July 1994.

I met Matthew to talk about the race on his home territory in Henley during the spring of 1999. We'd always exchanged pleasantries in the past. Certainly, Matthew knew me well enough to 'take the piss' out of me ruthlessly when I mishandled the tape recorder at an interview. But despite the fact we'd been crewmates for a season and teammates for five more, there had never been any sense of real connection between us. So I felt a sense of trepidation as I walked into meet him. It was to disappear in no time as both of us warmed to the talk of what Matthew regarded as his hardest-ever race, in the year after what had become a personal disaster for him.

As president of Oxford, Matthew was responsible for putting together the personnel for the Boat Race crew. In 1993, he had assembled the most talented squad of rowers that Oxford had ever seen, including two

The Tideway, 1994: Leander weren't the only crew to clash with Cambridge. Above, Richard Stanhope (third right) lashes out at Thorsten Strepplehoff, while Gavin Stewart (right) looks on. Below, Thorsten (left) retaliates. Richard still has the cox's cap as a trophy.

Olympic champions. What's more, none other than Mike Spracklen was to coach it.

But a slick Cambridge, coached by Harry Mahon, won comfortably against Pinsent's rough Oxford crew. It was like seeing a slick passing continental soccer team take apart a rough and ready English side. For Matthew it was a bitter personal blow. He has no hesitation in admitting that he messed up and it remains his biggest regret in the sport.

It still ran deep early in 1994 when he and Steven, rowing in a powerful but none too smooth Leander eight, took on the Cambridge crew over a shortened Boat Race course. The whole affair was ill-tempered and marred by clashes of blades as the coxes fought to keep the best water. Facing Matthew in the Light Blues that year were two Germans, the sight of whom he was soon to be heartily sick of. Fresh from their world champion eight, Peter Hoeltzenbein and Thorsten Streppelhoff were to complete their studies with a year's research at Cambridge. For them it was a chance, not only to experience the tradition of the Boat Race, but also to develop their own potential as pair rowers. Hoeltzenbein had finished second behind Steven and Matthew in the Barcelona Games. With Strepplehoff, who occupied the key 'six' seat in the German eight, he reckoned he had a boat that could challenge the British pair's dominance.

Pete and Thorsten had signalled their intent of racing in the pair early on. Normally the fastest German pairs went into the eight. But on this occasion they chose to stay in the pair. Matthew had read an article that came out from Cambridge around February about 'these two blokes who were saying that they were going to win the Boat Race and then get into a pair and then beat me and Steven'. It was not the 'lay down and die' respect that Olympic champions usually received from their opposition.

So it was hardly surprising that the Cambridge–Leander encounter had added spice that year. But Thorsten Strepplehoff was surprised that it was Redgrave, rather than Pinsent, who seemed to be the most rattled by the clashes. But neither of them could have been left in any doubt as to the strength of the challenge laid down by the Germans, as Cambridge emerged clear victors. There was no doubt that 'round one' had gone to Strepplehoff and Hoeltzenbein.

But if that encounter had any effect on Steven's or Matthew's racing psyche, it didnt show, although in the early-season races, as usual the opposition didn't seem to be up to much.

In Piedilucco they raced the top Italian and French pairs, who they dispatched clinically. After 'jaunts' against low standard opposition in Mannheim and Henley, Matthew turned up in Lucerne, where he knew they would face the German pair for the first time, feeling confident, despite the fact that other pairs with the similar intention of knocking Steven and Matthew off their perch were there.

Darren Barber and Phil Graham were already Olympic champions from the Canadian eight; now they too wanted the British pair's scalp. On the night before the final Matthew met Barber on the front at Lucerne while he

Lucerne, 1995: Steve and Matt in motion an instant after the 'Go'. The bend on Matt's blade is an indication of his phenomenal power. The boats are still being held by the 'stakeboat girls'.

was having a coffee with his Canadian girlfriend (another Olympic champion) Marnie McBean. Matthew said he hoped that the Canadians would do really well against the Germans in the following day's race 'because then they might return to the eight'.

It might have seemed an innocuous comment – nothing more than rowers' chat – but to Barber and McBean the message was clear. Matthew had seemingly written off the Canadian pair's chances against them with a perfectly straight face. Barber was incensed at what he saw as Matthew's arrogance and walked off. McBean, herself a double Olympic champion, looked at Matthew and said, 'I can't believe that you just said that.' But Matthew was in race mode and unapologetic. McBean went on, 'The thought of losing just doesn't enter your head does it?'

Matthew said that it did 'but not to the Canadians'. In truth, Barber had allowed himself to be out-psyched by Matthew, who was not really trying. It had the same effect as Alex Ferguson's masterstroke against Kevin Keegan, when Newcastle and Manchester United were both running for the title and Keegan appeared to 'lose it' during a television interview. Barber and Matthew have never spoken since. The incident added more than a little spice to a race that already had an explosive mix.

As Matthew sat on the start, though, he was blissfully unaware of the events that would unfold over the next six minutes. Sure it was a good field, probably the strongest that they had ever raced, with the French and Italian boats in contention for the medals. But Grobler's talk before the race had not prepared them for what was to follow: 'Watch the Germans, they will be in the picture; the Canadians too, and maybe the improving French and Italians.' But to Matthew it was like any other race. Perhaps the tail breeze blowing down the Rotsee should have given them more of an indication of the competition to come. In a headwind Steven's and Pinsent's enormous power generally proved impossible to overcome. But in the faster moving conditions of a tailwind – where quick, smooth economical movements were at a premium – the less powerful boats knew that they might have a chance.

Matthew never expected to lead a race in the first 500 metres, it was just what happened if they rowed well. As the crews sped away from the start line, though, it was clear that good rowing would not be enough to secure an early lead for the British. The Canadians – Darren Barber with a glint of revenge in his eye – had blasted away from the start pontoons at a speed which caught even the fast German pair by surprise. As the crews settled into their race rhythm after the first minute, the Canadians led out the German pair followed by a chasing pack. Matthew hadn't looked up much in the first 500 metres. But coming up to the mark he remembers Steven calling that they were lying in second place. In fact, they were in third. The Canadians, who were busting every gut, led through the 500 metres in a very quick time. Everybody knew that Barber and Graham were a very powerful pair but it was clear from seeing them paddle in training that they didn't seem to have the finesse to hold a blistering pace such as this. It was rather like watching a pacemaker go out ridiculously fast and gradually be reeled in. Except that on this occasion this was the last thing on the Canadians' mind.

Matthew was still confident. His boat was moving well and Steven's calls showed little or no anxiety. At 500 metres, Matthew turned a little to look at the position of the Germans who were in the lane next to them. He had to move his head more than he expected as they were already nearly a length clear. By this time the Canadians had run out of steam and were moving back to the pack. Barber might have done well to remember the advice that 'revenge is a dish best served cold'. Matthew hardly noticed them, stuck as he was in a chasing pack for the first time in ages. The thought flashed through his mind, 'What the hell's going on here?' But at no time was there any attempt by the British to get back on terms with the

Germans. For the next 500 metres, Matthew rowed along in the pack, just concentrating on the basics, kept cool by the normality of Steven's calls which assured him that the boat was moving all right. In retrospect, though, they recognised that they were far from 'all right'. They had settled to, what was for them, the mediocre level of the pace of the pack.

Meanwhile, approaching 1,000 metres, the Germans were flying. Thorsten and Peter were nearly three lengths of clear water ahead. They had managed to combine the attacking style of the German eight with the fluency of Harry Mahon's technique. It was a potent combination. Looking back on the field, through the 1,000 metres Strepplehoff thought that they would win the race. Nobody had ever taken that much out of the British pair before. They had blitzed the field and still felt good. The crowd sensed a huge upset.

It was at that point when I got my first sight of the race, while listening to my 'psyche-up' talk for the final of the coxed pairs, due on the water later. I was in awe of the amount of water that the Germans had put between themselves and the field. Even from a distance I could see that they were moving effortlessly and fluidly. Part of me felt pleased. I knew and liked Thorsten and Peter. Thorsten had visited my house during the winter, while at Cambridge. He was an articulate and genuine guy. Although we were not particularly close friends, two years previously, he had taken the trouble to give me a nod of good luck as we were going out to race each other in the Olympics. That expression of camaraderie among opponents was something that I valued. Peter was a little more cocky by nature, although it was more the brashness of youth than arrogance. It was he who was driving the German minibus to the World Championships in 1993 when it left the road, nearly killing the whole eight in the process (although they recovered and went on to win). He had an impish face and generally dressed down for most occasions. What was more, from my point of view he was always approachable and easy to talk to.

I suppose that, in part, what was also behind the pleasure of seeing the gap was the expectation that Matthew and Steven would finally get beaten in open competition. It is part of the British malaise that we seem more comfortable with winners that seem to triumph against all the odds. The Manchester Uniteds of this world have always been willed to fall by the neutrals. For me, Steven's and Matthew's relentless professionalism and clinical efficiency made them fall into this category of champions there to be knocked. To some extent I had been there myself in 1983, in '87 and again in '89, written off as a has-been. Now I was a former poacher turned gamekeeper, salivating over the seeming inevitability of their come-uppance.

In the boat, though, Matthew had other ideas, although when he looked round at 1,000 metres and could hardly see the stern of the German boat, he recognised for the first time the enormity of the task which faced him. Through the 1,000 metres, Steven called a push, for 100 metres, or 15 strokes. Matthew pushed in the rhythm, determined not to panic and raise the rate. It was enough to take them away from the pack but made little or no impact on the Germans, who had already had their own effort.

At that point on the Rotsee, the bank edges out to meet the course. Rowers are always aware of reaching this point, which comes up just before the 750 metres-to-go mark; not least because of the shouts from crewmates and coaches watching the race from the boating area. Matthew looked around to see the effects of his effort. It didn't look as though they were much closer than they'd been at 1,000 metres. The thought went through his head that they had already been trying 'pretty hard'. As if to justify this, he heard Steven's commentary as they came up to the 750-metres mark, now sounding a touch more urgent. 'We haven't made much impact there; we're going to have to go now... next stroke – go!'

Matthew knew that the position was now serious. They were going to have to move out of their race plan for the first time in the race and launch a superhuman effort to surge for the finish line at least a minute before they would have intended.

It was at this point in our conversation that Matthew broke off his narrative. It was as if the memory of that point in the race had stirred some deeper emotion about his relationship with Steven. I knew that the issue of race tactics and call, particularly in a pair, was a sensitive issue. Generally, like two batsmen there was only room for one person to make the call, or else confusion could result. On this occasion Matthew accepted Steven's call without question. It had not always been the case.

I asked him when things hadn't been like that. He hesitated, almost as if wondering whether or not to reveal any past discord between them. Like one partner in a marriage might hesitate about revealing details of their quarrels to an outsider. He refused to call it a 'power struggle' between them, but to me that's exactly what it seemed like. It was at its height during their second season together, in 1991. As I suspected, the decision to be made was who was leading the crew. In most boats the stroke man is the acknowledged leader. Setting the tempo and rhythm dictates that much.

But in a pair it is the bow man who generally makes the calls, decides the race strategy. That, too, is a position of power. With Steven and Matthew the question was: 'Who is in control?' Both in the pair with Pete, and initially with Redgrave, Matthew, rowing at bow, had made the calls and decided the race strategy. But when Grobler moved Matthew to stroke, things changed.

Steven could now call the race as he wanted. Matthew felt like he was a puppet and Steven the puppet master, pulling all the strings, making all the moves. His response was to ignore Steven's calls during races. It was more out of 'pig headedness' than malice but behind it lay a real fear of being dominated by Steven. Sometimes he felt that Steven would goad him just by calling 'annoying things'. I was amazed when Matthew told me that in the middle of their 1991 World Championship final he had simply ignored many of Steven's calls. The thought of them going down the course like a push-me-pull-you horse sounded ridiculous. At the finish Matthew flung his arms in the air. It was his first gold medal. But his partner was not happy. It was only after that, deep down, that Matthew recognised that picking and choosing a race plan was 'no way to run a pair'.

But logic was only part of what was driving Matthew to change his tactics. There were strong emotions at stake too. Matthew's imperious exterior hid a welter of emotions, one of which was the fear of losing a race. He often coped with this by deciding to follow Steven's calls completely. He told me that before races, he'd say to himself, 'All you've got to do is do what he says – and if we lose, then he can't blame that on you.' It was the first time that I had ever really seen Matthew's own vulnerability. That their relationship meant a great deal to him was clear because of his worry that by not following Steven's calls he may be 'letting him down'.

But behind Pinsent's own emotions there was also an empathic response to what Steven was feeling. Matthew knew that there was also a fear behind Steven's supposed 'dominance' in the bow seat. Although the bow man seems to have control, in fact under the surface the real power lies with the stroke man. It is not for nothing that the old rower's motto runs, 'They all rowed hard but none so hard as stroke.' Steven had always been the 'glamour boy' in the stroke seat. Now he had to find a way of not being overshadowed by the brilliance of his young partner. Thus, calls were a way of Steven asserting, staking out his own 'territory' in the pair.

So Matthew's growing maturity led him to give Steven some leeway by accepting 'some bad calls' without it ruining the race or the outing.

Whatever the level of anger during the outing, the two of them were almost always able to put the boat on the rack and express their feelings and frustrations with each other. It was an ability which would prove indispensable after their Lucerne race. For Matthew this was the reason why they were still rowing together. I could see this level of openness and empathy was important to him and I reflected his thoughts, 'That's quite a gift to have.'

Matthew's eyes softened as he briefly reflected on this relationship. Then he said softly, 'Yeah, yeah, it was.'

I almost felt like an interloper as I dragged him back to the race. 'So you're at 750 to go and you've responded to this call?'

His eyes grew steely again as he relived the moment. 'Yeah, the rating moved up from its cruising level of 36½ strokes per minute up to 38 and it began to really hurt. But at least our boat was now moving.'

To cope with the pain, Matthew ignored the distance to the finish line and just concentrated on doing 15 or 20 strokes at a time. After each, he would have a look round to register if his efforts had achieved any effect. Then his head went down for the next few strokes. Meanwhile, he had Steven's progress reports that for the first time in the race indicated that they were beginning to pull back on the Germans. The big question remained: was there enough time?

Certainly, the 15,000 spectators massed around the grandstands at the finish had no doubt it was possible. They had already seen plenty of crews get rowed down on the line. Those who could interpret the split-times knew that something special was happening and that this was no ordinary race. But the gap was still there and for all Matthew's pushes it was closing only very slowly. From the outside, Thorsten and Peter looked as if they were beginning to hurt. And it would be surprising if they weren't after the speed in which they had covered the first 1,500 metres. But they were still rowing well and moving quickly. With 500 metres remaining they were still just over a length ahead of the British pair. Both crews were light years ahead of the chasing pack. It was a race to the death.

It was just as they moved into the last 500 that Matthew, who could see the Germans' stern for the first time, felt sure that he would emerge victorious. He stuck in another 20 and looked around, to see a gain of just half a canvas. The calls were coming thick and fast now and space was running out. Another 20 still saw them over half a length down. Suddenly, victory began to slip away from Matthew's grasp. He had long since lost control of his ability to increase the tempo and had resorted to some primeval urge to win and compete, that seemed to provide the energy just to sustain the incredible tempo that he had set himself.

His narrative was becoming more urgent and frenetic. But I briefly halted him. 'Where does that "drive" come from?'

'I don't know… it's something that you practice in training. You know, when I'm out there on the river doing 20k with Steve, I probably spend half an hour visualising race situations. If we're doing race pieces in the pair, I'm always thinking ahead to the race next weekend. It's what I do… you know.' To Matthew, it was clear that this race had already been rowed a thousand times in training on the Henley reach. The problem was that it wasn't going according to the script.

As the noise of the crowds reached deafening proportions, he began to feel that he was 'dragging himself along'. It was then that he looked out of the boat once more and saw the look of agony on the German pair's faces. With only ten strokes to go, Steven called, 'We're level!' All Matthew could think of was just two more strokes, then they'll stop and we can paddle over the line in front. It was something that he had seen happen often enough in sculling races, where the leading sculler realises that he is beaten and stops, like a wounded stag, retiring to leave the territory to the stronger animal.

But the Germans didn't stop, or blow, or give up. Matthew had reconciled himself to just two or three more strokes, yet although the British pair were now just in front, there was no let-up in Matthew's torture. He had expected them to stop, and was expecting the race would end before the line. Now it hadn't he had to somehow 'get himself going again'. It was with that thought that he crossed the line. They had beaten the Germans by just half a canvas. But for Matthew there was no joy, or relief, just an intense pain compounded by a ringing sensation in his ears. He threw-up over the side of the boat. It was all he could do to hold himself together for the medal ceremony. Back at the boat trailer he just lay down in the shade for over half an hour, unable to move.

I remember the scene as the two of them came back. Steven had recovered quicker and had the presence to tell me not to break his course record in the coxed pair – some chance! In fact their time of 6.18.37 was nothing short of astounding. It broke their own world record by a full three seconds. At the time of writing it still stands unchallenged. I was in awe of their performance.

But this was not how Matthew viewed the race. When he had time to recover, he felt nothing but disappointment. In the thick of all the

Lucerne, 1994: Steven looks round for the finish line at the end of their epic encounter with the German pair, who are just out of picture.

plaudits from the team at the airport on the way home, he turned and said to Steven, 'It feels like we've lost.' He felt that they had rowed the most dangerous race of their careers. He always wanted to win races with at least one card up his sleeve, so that the opposition would never know their limits. 'But in that final 250 we were on our last legs and they had seen everything that we had got.'

So for Matthew that race was a 'defeat'. They used it as such to goad them on over the next six weeks of training before the Indianapolis World Championships. Although they had a great altitude camp, it was not always easy. The water at the training camp in the States was very swelly. Miriam Batten, then rowing in the women's eight, remembers, 'Steve wasn't talking to Matt during the training camp.' Matthew's recollection, however, is of a 'really good preparation camp'.

Whether the tension of racing the Germans again, combined with Matthew's notorious lackadaisical attitude to paddling in the poor water, was causing the problem is not clear. But in the first heat they drew the Germans again – headwind this time – and blew them away. The same happened in the semi-final, again a headwind. The British thought that they had effectively laid to rest the ghost of Lucerne, even though the wind turned round to a tail breeze for the final. That was until they made an uncharacteristic false start.

Their plan for the final had been to anticipate the same German tactics as at Lucerne and move out quickly. But the nerves of the false start put paid to that. Matthew had to wait for the 'Go'. The Germans took the advantage and piled off like bats out of hell. But this time there was no reprise of Lucerne. Even though Thorsten and Peter thought they had enough of a lead at 1,000 metres, there was always that lingering sense of deja vu. In addition, Matthew and Steven were rowing better than they did at Lucerne, especially through the second 500. They won in another quick time, the Germans struggling to hold off the fast finish of the Australians to take the silver.

Thorsten and Peter had had enough of the pair. From then on they would go back in the German eight. Matthew saw that win at Lucerne as absolutely crucial to this. He had no doubt that even if he and Steven had won at the world's that year, losing at Lucerne would have given the incentive to stay in the pair for the Olympics. That would have presented 'R & P' with a much more formidable challenge to the one which they actually faced from the Australian pair that took silver behind them in Atlanta.

Matthew has never been tested to those limits since. During 1999 there was a brief moment when Matthew's four was headed by the Norwegians with less than 300 to go; a great race was in prospect. With 25 strokes to go there was a dramatic surge from the British boat. They crossed the line comfortably clear. I knew where that strength in the finish had come from. As they crossed the line I said on BBC television, 'That was Matthew's race.'

If Steven Redgrave is the greatest oarsman that the world has ever seen, then Matthew Pinsent cannot be far behind. Already in Sydney he proudly carried the Union Flag aloft as the British team marched into the stadium for the opening ceremony. It is difficult to see anyone challenging Steven's Olympic record, although Matthew would surprise nobody if he added a fourth gold to his collection in the 2004 Games in Athens. He alone has the potential to emulate his partner's achievements. Perhaps when he is feeling the strain – he'll be 34 in Athens – he'll be fortunate enough to find a young, racing machine with a bull-like physique to carry him through to his international rowing dotage in the same way that he once did for Steven.

But whether he finds anyone or not, in all the years that Matthew rows, he will probably never row as hard as he did that day in Lucerne. It was a race the like of which happens perhaps once for each generation of rowers. For me, talking through that race gave me the chance, at last, to understand an old crewmate, a man with whom I nearly got the chance to make history.

The Sorcerer and his Apprentice

AS THE 1991 season dawned, Tim Foster and I were an article; inseparable on the water and, seemingly, in our habits off it. Pete Mulkerrins coined the phrase 'the Sorcerer and his Apprentice' to describe us. I was the wily old magician, teaching the young Tim the tricks and the lore of racing and rowing. He was the up-and-coming star, anxious to learn all he could; he wanted to wear the sorcerer's hat himself. Eight years later, with an Olympic gold medal, that hat was firmly planted on Tim's head. He was the star of BBC television's *Gold Fever*. *Big Brother* came in to the world of rowing and the viewers watched enthralled as Tim poured out his heart to a video camera while he fought to recover from a serious back operation and tried unsuccessfully to regain his place from sub Ed Coode in Britain's 'Fab Four'. Later that year, when the bows of the British eight forged into the lead with just 500 metres to go in the final of the World Championships, there was no doubt that it was the presence of Tim in the boat that had inspired them to believe in themselves. In short, Tim is the most talented, controversial and talked-about rower in the country.

As I reported the story throughout 1999 for BBC radio and television, it was hard for me to keep the network's customary balanced approach. As the eight crossed the finish line in St Catherine's, I blurted out, 'Who's to say now that Tim shouldn't be rowing in the coxless four at the Sydney Olympics?' I knew Ed was rowing bloody well in the four. I had my binoculars trained on just him during their semi-final at Lucerne. I had to agree with James Cracknell's post-race evaluation that the sub's performance was 'just awesome'. Yet I was sure it was something more than just friendship that made me feel in my bones that Tim was the best man for the three seat in the 'Fab Four'. Perhaps, though, it was as much about my fascination with a rower who refuses to be categorised.

It's clear that the media's fascination with him is as much about trying to fathom the mystery that lies behind his enigmatic smile and long golden locks as it is with his achievements. In 1998, word leaked out slowly that Tim's hand injury, which forced him to miss much of that season, was not just some unfortunate incident but the result of a late-night drunken revelry. Rowers who train three times a day are not supposed to spend their evenings drinking and partying like England soccer internationals. The newspapers scented blood. But if the press thought that they had found rowing's answer to Paul Gascoigne – a great natural talent ruined on the rocks of alcohol and socialising – they had got it wrong. Tim is made of much sterner stuff than 'Gazza'.

It was the reason I wanted to pair with him in the first place. By 1991, our partnership had breathed new life into my faltering international career. Years later, I pondered the choices and doubts facing Tim as he headed for the Sydney Olympics. Would he regain his place in the four? Should he stick with the silver medal eight? Or would his fragile spine, already scarred twice by the surgeon's knife, hold out that long? I found my mind reaching back to the start of that 1991 season, leading towards the World Championships in Vienna. Perhaps that would provide me with some of the answers as I tried to unravel the enigma, not only of Tim but of our relationship.

But if Tim and I were still an item after Tasmania, as usual with British rowing it was all-change after Tasmania; new coaches, different crews and a fresh chief coach. Tanner was out, unseated in an athlete-led coup led by Jonny Searle. For months there was chaos. The ARA didn't have a clue about how to run international rowing. First, Bruce Grainger, an outstanding junior coach, was appointed; he was gone after a few months. In the senior world he seemed as unable to act, like a rabbit caught in a car's headlights. His replacement was a Leander man, John Pilgrim-Morris; nice enough but completely unsuited to the task. His most memorable contribution that year was to select just three people to row in a four. However, the real influence on British rowing was Jurgen Grobler, the Leander club's newly-appointed East German coach.

Jurgen was one of hundreds of East German coaches out of a job following reunification. Thick-set, with a ruddy complexion and deep voice, he spoke with the same quiet sense of authority as Arsenal's studious French manager, Arsène Wenger. His effect on British rowing was to be no less significant than the Frenchman's presence at Highbury. I respected him, more than liked him. Jurgen was not a man to inspire you to greater efforts on the water, unlike the charismatic Bob Janousek, of whom his athletes said, 'We would have stood on our pricks if he'd asked us to.' Nevertheless, Jurgen brought with him an understanding of physiology that was second to none and a shrewd ability to handle the personalities of any crew he was coaching, most notably Redgrave and Pinsent. But his greatest problem came in adapting from a rigid, authoritarian system where there was only one way to achieve success, to a flexible, Darwinistic and frankly argumentative squad. Janousek had drawn from both traditions to succeed. For Jurgen, there was only one way.

Those at Leander quickly had to fall into an East German training regime and low intensity work on the water for long distances became the norm. For a rower who loved to train competitively it was like receiving a life sentence of drudgery. After a few weeks of it you'd either have to develop a very thick skin, or go crazy. In addition, Jurgen was far more reliant on physiological tests for selecting the personnel for a crew than their performance in boats on the water. His favourite tool was the ergometer. A static machine which simulated the rowing movement, it favoured tall, heavy rowers for whom sheer power mattered more than timing. Most of the 'lighter' rowers disliked the 'erg'. In a boat, the racing nouse and athletic co-ordination of the 'three Jons' – Searle, Hulls and Singfield – regularly saw them post faster times than the bigger men. On the 'erg', they had no chance. Using it exclusively for selection was like selecting the Ryder Cup team from those who could hit the ball furthest on the driving range.

In time, Jurgen would learn. But for that season a rebel enclave developed away from the Pink Palace at Leander, setting up camp at the Purple Portals of the University of London boathouse with Marty Aitken. You could not have imagined a greater contrast with Jurgen than the diminutive Australian. For a start, he never stopped talking. By the time the session finished, you generally knew exactly what he had been doing for most of that day, or indeed (if you happened to have forgotten) the previous week. He was a great coach, though. If he hadn't left Melbourne, he would have been coaching the 'Oarsome Foursome' (or so he told us). But it may not all have been Aussie bullshit because he coached Xeno Muller to an Olympic gold in the Atlanta single sculls. Aitken's training programme was a sensible mixture of long distance and shorter, more competitive pieces designed around students who had to travel to lectures or tutorials. It was no surprise that under him the University of London had its halcyon days, attracting most of the fresh talent, including Tim, who was starting the first year of an economics degree course at UL.

Although Tim came to UL after two gap years, he was determined to compensate for any extra maturity that he might have picked up behind the fish counter of Safeways in Bedford. He fell into student life, or more accurately its social side, with a vengeance. He began to look less and less like a rower and more like the lead singer from one of the psychedelic bands that nobody seemed to have heard of except him. His hair grew and grew and was often laced with a purple dye. No doubt, if he'd had to do any work, his rowing might have suffered. Luckily, though, Tim had his priorities right. He'd go through the day in a daze, missing lectures and tutorials, but always turn up to outings after a furious pedal from Central London to Chiswick on his Peugeot mountain bike. That summer, he forgot to turn up to one of his exam papers. It was no surprise that he had to retake his first year.

Sometimes Aitken despaired of him and asked me, as the older statesman, to point him in the right direction. The trouble was that I was hardly 'Mr Responsible' on the time-keeping or organisational fronts. In addition, I knew (and so did Aitken) that Tim was a rare talent. It wasn't as if he was some kind of Gazza or Georgie Best, missing training sessions. I loved the idea of rowing with someone who could live life to the full and still beat the shit out of the opposition. On one pre-Olympic training camp in Seville, Tim famously partied the night away before creeping back to his room five minutes before he was due to get up and race three times 2,000 metres against another crew. Needless to say, Tim's crew won all three races.

Both of us wanted more to life than rowing. For Tim, rowing was a path away from his fear of 'normality' in a humdrum nine-to-five office life. Although all he ever wanted to be was a rower, perversely, he has a horror of being labelled as 'just a rower'. As Tim looked at me, in my mid-30s struggling to make two outings a day in between teaching, rushing off home to catch a few minutes with my kids, or standing as a Labour Party candidate in local elections, he saw someone whose life was about as 'abnormal' as one could get. Off the water we would frequently work as a double act; flirting with any girl around became a game. I would bullshit on about star signs and compatibility, while introducing Tim as the grandson of a gypsy fortune teller. Fortunately – for the object of our attentions – he had inherited his grandmother's mystic powers of palmistry (Tim even bought a book to make our act more realistic).

It was not surprising, then, that Pete Mulkerrins called us 'the Sorcerer and his Apprentice'. Both on the water and off it, we made a great combination, playing off each other's strengths to cover our weaknesses. Tim, the introvert whose feelings and emotions lay deeply hidden beneath his enigmatic smile, and me, the extrovert who wore his heart on his sleeve and whose feelings were an open book.

As you might expect, rowing with Tim was never boring. On our Easter training camp in Sarnen, on an afternoon off I went out for a drive, only to discover my partner with his foot in plaster on my return. He had broken his ankle while playing football against some local lads. It was the first in a long line of injuries that was to dog Tim's career. He was out of the boat for over a month. Not surprisingly, I was anxious to paddle in the pair as soon as possible. We went out for our first row in five weeks on the day of a team 'erg' test at Leander. The priorities were clear in my mind. I reasoned that getting Tim back in the boat was more important than arriving on time for a test. When I eventually arrived at Leander, two hours late, I was subjected to a kangaroo court by Jurgen Grobler, Pilgrim-Morris and Brian Armstrong, the administrative director of BIRO.

There I was hemmed in a corner seat in the bar at Leander, feeling about as comfortable as a Celtic fan stuck in a pub full of Rangers supporters. Tim's recuperation was an irrelevance. When I pointed out that they should be more concerned about one of the most talented rowers in the country, Jurgen begged to differ. 'But he's got two junior gold medals and a senior bronze already.' I argued.

'Junior gold medalists are ten a penny in East Germany.' Jurgen snapped back. In 1997, when he invited Tim to row in his four, he'd clearly changed his mind.

I did the bloody 'erg' test that afternoon, posting a respectable score. But I was clearly out of favour with the selectors. That much was clear at the trials the following month. Although Tim was clearly still recovering from injury, our performance was not considered good enough to gain selection in either the coxed or coxless four. The latter was put together by the 'driving range' technique of taking the four biggest 'erg' pullers and putting them together in a boat. Compatibility did seem not matter. On paper it looked great, four John Daley's together. On the water it bombed, as anyone with a bit of savvy might have guessed.

For the first international regatta, Tim and I were left to fend for ourselves in a pair. We made the final but were beaten by Redgrave and Pinsent. Still, with Tim on the comeback trail it was a good result. Outside the pair and the two fours, there was a definite feeling of being the dregs of the squad. On the Saturday there was even no place in a boat for Jonny Searle, Olympic champion a year later. He was left doing an ergometer on the bank. In effect it left me, Searle and the rest with a tremendous chip on all our shoulders. We were all shoved together in what was only the fourth boat in the team. Marty Aitken was given the job of smoothing off the rough edges and making us into a workable eight.

Given the time we had together, I didn't give much for our chances. Neither at that time did anyone else. The crews at the Leander club thought so little of us that, for a while, they toyed with doubling up to race the Grand. Even worse was the verdict of the press. One newspaper's verdict was that we would be 'humiliated' by the Canadians. But I underestimated the powerful effect that being 'written off' has on a group of talented performers. Aitken played the 'hard done by' card well enough, although even he couldn't do anything about the opposition in our first race in the Grand at Henley. Although we were given a bye to the final, in the other half of the draw lurked Spracklen's Canadians. I left before they raced on semi-finals day, against a rather mediocre Russian eight. My expectations of victory were so low that I did not even bother to bring the obligatory blazer and tie for the prize giving.

On the morning of the final, Aitken was giving us a chat before our warm-up outing. I was a bit distracted but thought that he had made the mistake of referring to us racing the Russian crew that afternoon. Sensing the opportunity for a wind-up, I chimed up, 'Marty, this is the final of the Grand. The least you can do is get our opposition right; you mean the Canadians.'

Quick as a flash, his nasal Melbourne drawl laced with sarcasm, Aitken replied, 'First with all the news for a change Crossy. Don't you read anything? The Canadians got beat yesterday; you're racing the Russians.' I looked round my crewmates, searching for confirmation. Surely he couldn't be right? In support, a programme was produced. The Canadians had incredibly bombed out. I reacted with the same gleeful inappropriateness that Basil Fawlty showed when he realised that the guest he'd delivered breakfast to had been dead for hours and not killed by the out-of-date kipper that he'd just served. Then, as the crew gave me strange looks, I remembered we still had to race the Russians.

That afternoon we beat them by nearly two lengths. As we crossed the line the occupants of the press box were on their feet, applauding. It can't have been too often that the winning crew has responded by calling them 'a bunch of fucking wankers'. The intensity of emotion displayed on the finish,

Henley, 1991: Raw emotion after an unexpected victory in the Grand. The press (watching in their box out of picture, left), who had rubbished our chances, had just been given a double-barrelled blast of expletives by most of the crew. James is fourth left.

especially by James Cracknell, still surprises me to this day. Maybe that's because it was for James, as it was for me, an unlikely Henley win.

I collected my medal wearing Tanner's ill-fitting jacket and trousers. Lucerne was a different story, though. We finished out of the medals but the continued failure of the coxless four meant that Aitken was able to 'rescue' Greg Searle from the 'big erg' four. He took the place of a distraught James Cracknell in the eight. James and Greg had won junior golds in the same four. But Greg always seemed to just pip him at everything that he did. As the Sydney season started, James was still worried that Greg might 'steal' his place in the four. Of course, in the wake of Sydney it is James who is the 'star'. But in 1991 James felt so frustrated that he gave up the possibility to row in the Olympics to play rugby.

So it was a different crew that left to train, somewhat reluctantly, on an isolated lake on top of an Austrian mountain. In the sunshine it was a paradise; in the rain, a nightmare. Jurgen had taken the East German women to Silvrettasee every summer for altitude training just before the World Championships. Now, despite a half-hearted attempt to mutiny, before we left, it was our turn. We lived in wooden huts just below the dam wall. When the tourists left in their big coaches, we were alone save for a few wild horses. Comparisons with life as a wartime PoW were hard to avoid. In fact one year up there, to while away the hours in between sessions, we made a video in homage to the old war movies. The Escape Committee was arguing over the length of an escape tunnel. Jurgen, played by a deadpan John Garrett, argued for a 20 kilometre-long tunnel, dug very slowly; only that would be good enough to escape. Needless to say, he was out-voted by the London contingent who preferred a much shorter escape route, dug at speed.

Behind the humour was a very real sense of motivation for our eight. We developed our own identity to distinguish us from the rest of the squad. We were the 'SMF', a group of football hooligans portrayed in a television drama. We aped their language and yobbish mannerisms. We all knew it was juvenile and rebellious; the point was, that was how we felt in relation to the 'serious' rowers of the Leander contingent.

Our eight was hardly out of the textbook of East German rowing. For a start, we were too light. Only Greg Searle and Anton Obholzer were over 90 kilos. Marty put Jon Singfield, the lightest in the crew, in the 'six' seat. That was like asking Jeremy Guscott to play in the front row. Tim, in the stroke seat, was not much better. Any self-respecting sparrow would have had more muscle on his legs than Tim's 'pipe-cleaners'. Jon Searle and Richard Phelps were hardly the powerhouses you'd expect to find in the middle of a boat, while Richard Stanhope and me, the grizzled old veterans up in the bows, could be seen (and frequently were) as 'past it'.

Even our cox was wet behind the ears. Garry Herbert was another product of the Vaughan. He had started rowing when he was inspired by the picture of my 1984 Olympic crew which the headmaster had placed in the lobby. Now one of his ambitions, of coxing me, was coming true. The other, of winning his own gold, wouldn't have long to wait. Garry could bullshit for England and the majority would probably have believed him! As a barrister he found the ideal outlet for his talents. Sometimes he left a lot to be desired in a cox; after an outing it was rare that he could manage to guide the boat deftly next to the stage. But he had a magical talent for switching on to the mood of his crew. His voice could convey not just the essence of his own dreams, but also that of the crews. In a race he was sensational. He was one of the few coxes who have made a real difference to the result of a crew.

The result we were looking for that year in Vienna was a medal. It was a delightful city for a championships, particularly if you were a cappuccino

Cardinal Vaughan School, 1988: This portrait of my LA triumph (hung in the Vaughan's lobby), inspired at least one more student of my old school to take up rowing. Here my dad (for the benefit of the readers of a local newspaper) is pointing out to Garry where I rowed.

addict and a history teacher. Strolling almost anywhere was a treat, down spacious, traffic-free boulevards with posh shops with their baroque façades, beautiful marble sculptures, some as fountains with water cascading down them. We often went out as a crew. I even thought I'd managed to hold their attention with my eulogy on neo-baroque drainpipes, until Singfield (a big breasts man) shouted, 'Look at the tits on that one.' It confirmed to me that their appreciation of 19th-century architecture would take some time to develop. Although they preferred breasts to baroque, I found the atmosphere haunting, particularly the crypt of Capuchins. There for 30 years, at the end of the 18th century, the Empress Maria Theresa had heard Mass next to the body of her husband lying in the huge, ornate bronze sarchopagus in which she was herself to be buried. At its feet, on the cold stone slabs, lay a small, plain bronze coffin. It was the resting place for their son, the great Emperor Joseph II. Even in death he was capable of making the most powerful statement imaginable.

It was impossible to escape from history in Vienna. We stayed in a hostel, just across from the rebuilt Karl Marx Hoff, the innovative inter-war workers' housing project which was the flagship of Austria's Socialist Government. During a brief but bloody civil war in 1934, it had been the bastion of Socialist defence against Fascist forces. That week it looked as though the championships might be overshadowed by another coup, with far more important implications.

On Monday, 19 August we heard news that Gorbachev had been overthrown in a putsch organised by the KGB and the military. After living through the springtime of peoples, it looked as though the freeze of the Cold War might be returning.

My mates the Pimenov brothers looked particularly miserable. The Soviet team was in little huddles all over the course. Apart from the Pimenovs, most of the boats were made up of combinations of different nationalities. The Estonians and Ukrainians in the Soviet quad had no idea of what might happen to their nascent nationalism. Even the Russian Pimenovs told me that they would go and buy some guns to use in Moscow on their return. The mood was sombre and it was against that background that we raced our heat.

Expectations were high but the reality was crushing; it was an ordinary row and we got 'dumped' by the Rumanians, and a new Chinese crew too. It left us with a mountain to climb in the repechage the next day, against the Canadians, now moving far quicker than at Henley, and the Americans. Aitken was worth his weight in gold the morning of the repechage. He set us up to do two extra-special 20-stroke bursts the morning before the race and wound us up big time just before. Each stroke had to have aggression and hatred. As he put it, 'I want cunt on the end of everyone's blade.' To mix metaphors, it was Aitken's way of saying, 'Pull your balls off.' They were two of the most exhilarating bursts I have ever done. It was the first time all eight of us really gave 100 per cent.

In the 'rep' we were a different crew to the one that rowed the heat. We rowed the States down in the last 250, finishing less than a second behind the Canadians.

The night before the final, Brian Miller, the BOA psychologist, told us a story about Sho Fujimoto, a Japanese gymnast from the 1976 Olympics. He broke his ankle in the vault. But in order for the Japanese team to win gold, he would have to complete the last exercise, the high rings. His willingness to endure agony for the team saw him complete his routine before spotting his double-backed dismount. A second later he collapsed in agony but the team won gold. There was more emotion just before the race. Aitken, who usually displayed as much warmth and affection towards his crews as the archetypal lager-swilling Aussie might show towards his

Vienna, 1991: The SMF (for the unititiated, Sad Men's Fim) in exuberant form just after winning a bronze medal in the eights. The photograph was taken by the BOA psychologist, Brian Millar and arrived in the post with the caption, 'This one's for Sho Fuji Moto'.

girlfriend, said he was proud of us. I could see from the emotion in his eyes that he meant it too.

On the start Herbert said, 'This one's for Sho Fujimoto.' It was our best and hardest start. I thought we would win after 30 strokes. But reality set in when the Germans, Canadians and Rumanians all disappeared from view after the 1,000. Somewhere, I think at 1,250, I called, 'Let's go now.' In the middle of the boat Jonny Searle took it up. We were up at 40 and steaming for the finish. Herbert was going down the boat, tailoring his calls individually to each one of us, cajoling the most out of us that he could. It was incredibly motivating. With 400 to go, he called for 'the mother of all burns'. We were fired up and took off. The last 250 was a blur. Just before the line, Herbert called, 'I'm level with their stroke.' We'd won a bronze. It was my first medal for six years.

The medal ceremony and that night's party were riotous. After midnight I ended up at the Russian hotel, miles from anywhere, with the Pimenovs. Although they hadn't won a medal, they were celebrating because Yeltsin had overthrown the coup. The two Russians were particularly close friends of mine. Nickolai was a fine artist, while Yuri, unusually for a member of the Russian team, spoke good English. That night I got drunk on the finest

Russian vodka and, I think, smoked my first cigarettes (the Pimenovs always had a packet handy).

At the airport the next morning, Jurgen came over to congratulate me. His handshake was firm and sincere as he said in his deep Germanic voice, 'I have a lot to learn about British rowing.' It was a lesson that Jurgen must have taken to heart because in 1997 he offered Tim a seat in his four, with Redgrave and Pinsent. It was the boat that was going to take Redgrave to his fifth gold at the Sydney Olympics. It was recognition by Jurgen that although Tim was a mere 86 kilos (both Redgrave and Pinsent weighed in at 100 kilos, while Cracknell was not far behind) he was something special.

But Tim's road to a seat in the four was never easy. Not least because of his own doubts as to whether his body is strong enough. All three of his new crewmates were built like 'brick shithouses' with seemingly invulnerable physiques that could take whatever was thrown at them. Even Cracknell – who, according to Tim, thinks of himself as 'small' beside Pinsent and Redgrave – dwarfs Tim's frame. In training and racing, Tim has more than once looked at their bodies with a longing or jealous eye. In his mind is the picture that their bodies would not let them down, as Tim's own has disappointed him.

As we talked, it was not hard for me to guess the most traumatic year of his life. It came two years after that Vienna race, in 1993. By then he was in a fast four preparing for the World Championships but was in constant back pain caused by a bulging disc at the base of his spine. Tim prided himself on his ability to block out pain. But it was not the kind of discomfort that he could shut off by pushing harder as he had done so many times before in training and racing. His nightmare scenario happened and his body let him down. He was pulled out of the crew at the last minute. I remembered him walking around the World Championships, the ever-present smile on his face hiding a welter of conflicting emotions. At that time, he still didn't know if he could ever row again.

Before the 'worlds' he'd had a back operation to correct a 'bulging disc'. It was extremely painful, not least because he had to learn to walk again. In fact, he was in pain for some time afterwards. Slowly his back grew stronger and he was able to start rowing again. With a new stretching regime, he gradually began to feel confident about his body again. It was a belief that was shared by the Searle brothers and their coach Steve Gunn, who invited him and Rupert Obholzer to train in a four for the Atlanta Games. Exactly a year to the day after his operation, Tim was stroking the four to a bronze medal in the World Championships. He felt that he had closed a chapter in his life and was ready to turn a new page.

Within two years he had established himself as the best rower in the squad behind Redgrave and Pinsent, his pair with Obholzer finishing a close second to them in the trial races. A silver medal for the four in the year before the Olympics seemed to confirm their progress. By the time of the Atlanta final, Tim's crew were marginal favourites for a gold medal in what was an exceptionally tight field. But once again Tim's body was to let him down. In the heats, they'd always started slowly but rowed through in the middle 1,000.

But the pace in the final was much hotter. By halfway they were still only in fifth place and the 'Oarsome Foursome' were moving like a train. Tim's dream of an Olympic gold was slipping away from him. He chose to sprint for the finish with 750 still left. It was an impossible target really, but achievement in sport – and life in general – is often about suspending rational belief and facing the prospect of losing control. For someone who rationalises everything before races, that is quite a step to take.

Prior to this race, as before all the others, Tim had been waging a constant mental battle with himself. While to all outward appearances he seemed the least nervous of the crew, wandering affably around the boat-park with a Cheshire Cat smile, in reality he was already 'within himself', analysing and rationalising everything that he was going to do from within. The man who saw himself as 'capable of pushing myself harder than any other rower' told himself that he was 'soft'. But the very nature of that thought brought with it an immediate denial and a determination to expunge its memory by some heroics in the race ahead. It was a mind game that always occurred in his races, as it did that day. Tim couldn't remember a race during which, at some point, he has not thought of stopping, only to purge himself of that notion by pushing himself absurdly hard.

He started to sprint for the finish. Sure enough, the crew moved back into the race but with 500 metres to go, Tim realised that he had passed his threshold. His body was telling him that he couldn't sprint twice – his legs and lungs were telling him to stop – but he knew that he would have to go again. It was new territory for him and it was frightening. At that instant he had a realisation of the mountain that it was necessary to climb to win an Olympic gold medal. With the summit of Everest so close, Tim went for it. With 250 metres to go they were in second place, challenging the Australians. But then, with the summit tantalisingly within reach, the

blizzard closed around him. In the last ten strokes the intense pain merged into a whole body cramp. His mind was willing him forward to become Olympic champion, but his body had stopped working. In the final few strokes the French crew inched past them to steal the silver. Tim would have to wait four years before mounting another expedition to the summit.

Tim thought the pain of failure might be dulled by a sojourn in the Blue Boat. He swapped the purple of UL for the dark blue of Oxford and again fell into student life with a vengeance, although he will be remembered more for his late-night partying than for his academic excellence. It was not surprising that Tim did not make an early start with his winter's training. He was already a dead cert for the Blue Boat. Moreover, the style of coaching was not conducive to hard, competitive training. Rene Mijnders, coach of the classy Dutch eight who destroyed the world's best to take gold in Atlanta, was the Oxford coach that year.

Tim relished his methods and mindset. Mijnders was a sexy coach, who talked in Tim's sensual language; about the feelings and sensations that it was important to be aware of in the boat. The Dutchman schooled his crew in the gentle art of foreplay. Athletes had to be like sensual lovers, gently caressing the boat, working with its innate rhythm and flow. Mijnders had no time for the 'Wham, bam, thank you maam' school of rowing so beloved of previous Oxford crews.

But if Tim thought that the Atlanta final was to be his hardest-ever race, he was mistaken. In the closest Boat Race for years, two crews tussled for the lead well into the second half of the four-mile course. Oxford lost. Tim had been in physical agony since Chiswick Steps, although his mental anguish was worse. He had allowed his Dark Blues to get pushed all over the river by the Cambridge cox. As the leader of the boat, in the stroke seat – the only man who can communicate with the cox – he knew that he had let the crew down in that moment.

Despite that defeat, Tim was the only choice for a bow side rower in Redgrave's new four. With typical nonchalance, he proclaimed that it would have been harder for him stay out of the crew than it was to take up his seat. The athlete who had with me, six years earlier, shunned Jurgen's training programmes as dull and boring, would now subject himself to an even more demanding regime. The first thing that Tim found

Hampton, 1991: I felt proud, as I displayed the Minet trophy, which I won for being 'Rower of the Year' for 1991.

out was that Jurgen was a much better coach than he had given him credit for. No doubt the German welcomed the new challenge that having Tim in the crew implied. It wasn't as if Tim exactly threw himself with enthusiasm into the mind-numbing high mileage, low intensity workouts that are the basis of Redgrave and Pinsent's training.

For Jurgen, the crews that won were those that went fastest in the middle of the race. And that meant building up their aerobic capacity by doing endless miles of low intensity. It wasn't that Jurgen shunned the competition, but for him too much racing in training built up high lactate levels, which by creating tiredness hampered the recovery for the next outing. That meant the overall volume would have to be cut, meaning less aerobic training. In the end, logic followed that the middle of the race had to suffer. Tim tolerated it but not without some changes. He was unhappy that Steven and Matthew seemed to measure their training in terms of kilometres; just 'doing the distance' rather than achieving certain technical objectives.

Tim pressed Jurgen to introduce a pace coach into the boat. This was a device that measured the boat's speed each stroke. Before Jurgen's crews had stuck rigidly to the heart rates they had been set; if the heart rates had been reached, then the targets had been met. However, rather than wait for Jurgen to tell them their '500' speeds, Tim wanted to have the immediate feedback of the boat's speed. If they were rowing better and the heart rate dropped but the speed stayed the same, or increased in pace, then there must have been an improvement in the technique. It was Tim's ability to caress the boat along which proved such an asset to the four. It had become more refined than when we paired together. Now, when things were going well, he felt as if his every movement was determined by the flow of the boat. It was as if the boat was his partner and he was its sensual lover, responding to her every need. Moreover, he was determined that others in the crew needed to become more responsive too.

Of course, each of the crew saw things differently; that was part of their strength. Matthew seemed to be most concerned about the balance of the boat, while Steven would talk about the level of effort that the crew was putting in. James would generally agree with Redgrave, while adding his own comments about the quality of the training.

It was not just Tim who upset Steven and Matthew's established routines. James's desire to be seen to train harder than anyone else in the crew sometimes led to friction with Steven. Often, James would fit in 'extra bits' after the sessions were finished. Steven, who was famed for doing more sessions than anyone else (famously training on Christmas Day) now just wanted do the set work and get off home. On the other hand, he did not want to be seen as doing less than anyone else, especially James. It was a situation which often led to Steven expressing his annoyance at his younger crewmate. In fact, the competition that this implies has spilled over both off and on the water. Tim can't compete with any of his crewmates on the 'erg', although his score is still better than most of the other rowers in the squad. However, in a sculling boat he is unbeatable by any of the crew.

His first gold medal came in the 1997 'worlds' with an imperious win, although it was not without Tim's traditional doubts. In the heat they had established a length's lead by 1,250 metres when Steven called to lower the rate, to relax and let the foot off the pedal; he knew that a win was in the bag. Tim suddenly thought, 'Am I going to stop?' Immediately, he battled with himself for thinking the unthinkable, and used it as an incentive to work harder in the new rhythm.

But during the next season the 'unthinkable' happened. It came as a result of Tim's desire to be more than 'just a rower'. Although he was in the top crew in the world – where he wanted to be – he was clearly now a professional rower. It was not how he wanted to see himself. He tried to circumvent this label by remaining firmly in the circle of student life that he had established at Oxford. Tim was by then something of a star in the firmament of the Oxford University social scene. He made a deliberate choice to ignore the quiet backwaters of Marlow and Henley, where his crewmates lived the lifestyle of professional rowers, and keep his keep feet firmly planted in Oxford student life.

The two lifestyles, although necessary for Tim's own peace of mind, were, not surprisingly, incompatible. Although for a long while he lead a charmed life, staying up late at student parties, drinking more than he should while at the same time holding his own in the fastest four in the world. It was only an exceptional person who could have kept up the lifestyle for so long. However, it was bound to end in tears.

In April 1998 there was a party in the old Oxford University boathouse where Tim still lived, despite no longer being a student at the university. James, Tim's room mate (on trips away), was there along with many of the Oxford Boat Race crew. James left before midnight, mindful of the crew's outing at Henley the next morning. He was more than a little concerned that, as usual, Tim was the life and soul of the party. not least because James would have liked to party himself but felt the weight of his conscience. To

James, when he left, the party was heading into the small hours, but then he reasoned that Tim seemed to operate under different rules to everyone else.

His luck run out in the small hours of the morning when he lost his balance and fell on to a plate-glass window. He severed tendons in his little finger, cut deep into his ring finger and sliced his thumb down to the bone. An artery was severed. Early-morning revellers standing nearby were sprayed with Tim's oxygen-enriched blood. The bleeding was staunched and he was taken to hospital. His long blond locks, dyed a garish red for the party, seemed to mirror the blood all over his clothes. None of the doctors attending him could believe that this ghoulish sight was a world champion rower. Of course, that was what Tim would have wished.

But for him to be out of the boat for six weeks was not in anyone's plans. The normally meticulous preparations of Steven and Matthew, and their coach Jurgen Grobler, had been shattered by Tim's seeming irresponsibility. For him, it was a nightmare. The introvert who had thrived on being in control of his two separate lives had seen them collide with explosive force – as of course they were bound to do. For a while his world was out of control. He retreated inside his shell, too embarrassed by the consequences of his actions. He felt unable to contact his crewmates and apologise outright, which he knew he must do.

The resentment, particularly from James, who prided himself on his approach to training, was understandable, as was the crew's determination to proceed without Tim as if it was business as usual. Luka Grubor, an Oxford colleague of Tim's, was chosen to replace him for the first World Cup regatta of the season in Munich. Perhaps Tim was irreplaceable, or perhaps the crew just had a bad weekend. Whatever the cause, Steven and Matthew went down to their first defeat in over six years, finishing an ignominious fourth behind a strong Rumanian crew. At the airport James was still bitter, determined not to have Tim back in the crew. But within a week Tim was back in the boat. Still unable to hold a pen, he could hook his fingers in a claw-like shape around the blade. They missed the next round of the World Cup in Brussels and returned to impressive wins at Henley against Australia's 'Oarsome Foursome', and in Lucerne against the Rumanians. Tim's second World Championship gold came that year in Cologne. It was not as comfortable as at Aiguebelette, but it was still impressive.

Tim's luck had returned. But then those who knew him well knew that it was not luck, much more the ability of an outstanding athlete and competitor, which shone through in the end. Rowing in the key 'three' seat of the four, his natural length, rhythmical flow and innate sense of balance acted as a link between the aggressive, attacking style of Matthew at stroke and Steven's relentless power behind him at 'two'. James, in the bow seat, felt that with Tim back in the boat he was able to work flat out in the race for every stroke, without worrying about it lurching from side to side.

Nevertheless, it had been at some cost to Tim. He'd had to undergo some painful behind-closed-doors sessions with his crew and coach where no holds were barred. It was clear that he was back, although there were conditions. He would not be able to allow his need to be different to become the victim of the apparent invulnerability of his youth. In future he would have to search for different ways to express his own unique nature. As part of this process he began to put down roots; a house in Oxford seemed to be a symbol of his new outlook. Just as he was seeming to settle, his body seemed to let him down again.

It was his back once more; a similar problem with a bulging disc, except this time a second operation was less likely to succeed. Ultimately, there was a limit to the number of operations that Tim's back could take. Indeed, it was suggested to him that he should stop rowing then and allow his back to recover naturally. That would mean his dream of winning the Olympics would disappear. It became clear that the only way Tim could row in Sydney was to submit to the surgeon's knife again.

I telephoned him on Christmas Day, just after his operation. He seemed cheerful enough on the telephone, although I knew that movement was difficult and his future uncertain. I asked him what presents he'd received. Among them, he told me, was a jigsaw. I asked him what the picture was. 'No,' he said laughing, 'it's a saw to cut wood with. I'll need it for jobs around my house.' I thought it was ironic that just as Tim was settling down to a life of domesticity, his future as a rower was in doubt.

Jurgen decided to take no chances. He fitted Ed Coode into Tim's place in the boat. The tall Cornishman had emerged as the strongest rower in the national eight. More important, his relative youth and temperament were perfect for Jurgen to develop further. At that stage there was no suggestion that he was doing anything else but keeping Tim's seat warm. Memories of the problems that the four had with Tim's last substitute in Munich were still fresh.

However, the longer Tim's back took to recover, the more Ed became a fixture in the crew. Ed's first appearance came during a warm-up

Barcelona, 1992: The Sorcerer and his Apprentice during the opening ceremony of the Games.

competition in Seville at the end of February. The crew had clearly found someone who could do more than just 'fit in'. After Seville, James thought that the boat was moving better than it had ever gone. The implication was clear. Tim would have to fight to regain his place.

By the first World Cup regatta, in Belgium at the end of May, Tim had been back in a boat for three weeks. His back was not strong enough for the twisting motion of a rowing boat, although he could race in a scull. His first races in the single were hugely impressive, particularly for someone who had missed a whole winter's training. He just missed the finals but recorded a time fast enough to suggest that he could slip back into the four and it would be business as usual. But the four were performing just as well without him. Although there were timing discrepancies between Ed and Steven, from their commanding performance it was clear that the four might win a gold medal without Tim. When I interviewed Ed for BBC Radio 5 Live after the race, we had a good conversation about his place in the crew. He was bullish about his prospects of keeping his seat.

After the day's racing, I gave Tim a lift back to the team hotel in Antwerp. As we talked it was clear that he had no idea what might happen.

He felt able to row, but his big fear was that he would be 'sidelined' in the eight which had been well beaten by the Rumanians. It seemed to me that he would have to make clear to Jurgen that he would only accept a seat back in the four; the eight would not do. That night at the hotel, while Tim and I were having a beer, Jurgen came over and asked me to step outside the hotel and talk in confidence. I was, to say the least, intrigued. I wondered if he might have objected to me talking with Tim. In fact, Jurgen wanted to know what Ed had said to me in his interview earlier that day. Tim's performance had clearly impressed Jurgen, who was now getting all the information that he could before making a decision: the 'Foster versus Coode' battle was on.

For the next round of the World Cup, Jurgen managed to convince Tim that he should ease his way back into a rowing boat by stepping into the eight, rather than take on the full responsibility of racing in the four. It was probably the key moment of the season. If Tim had stood out for a seat in the four, or if Jurgen had given Tim a chance, then Ed would have been relegated back to the eight. As it was, Jurgen kept the issue open. The four won again in Vienna and, more important, the eight seemed to have picked up a bit of extra speed. We all wondered if the Tim magic was working again.

By Lucerne it was clear that it was. The eight's performance seemed nothing short of miraculous, taking a silver behind the Russian eight. Tim had clearly proved his exceptional quality. Without him there was little chance that the eight's form would have been so inspirational. But by helping the eight to a silver, Tim had been caught in 'Catch 22'. To win his seat back in the four he had to do something exceptional, but now the eight was a contender for a medal, Jurgen dare not move him.

The rowers in the four had their own preferences. Steven was probably neutral, Matthew favoured Ed, while James thought that Tim deserved his seat back. In the end, Jurgen asked none of them. The decision was his alone. Ed had been rowing like a dream in Lucerne, although there was no question in my mind that in a close race, Tim would have made the four quicker. The media hype before the selection announcement was just that. The conservative Jurgen was never going to play musical chairs at that stage of the season.

Whether he would after the four's win at the 1999 World Championships was open to question. I thought Matthew's preference was clear when he announced that their performance in winning was their best-ever in a World Championship final. It was hard to argue with that, although Jurgen said that as far as he was concerned, the 'Fab Four' was now a 'Fantastic Five'. All places would be open. It was music to Tim's ears.

His place in the crew for the Sydney Games was sealed with a convincing win in April's pair trials. Stroking a boat with James behind him, the two made the other boats look ordinary; Steven and Matthew were left in their wake. During the season, Tim slipped back into the crew with the same ease as one would sink into a favourite armchair. But it was not just with a blade that he was able to hold his own. Writing for the *Daily Telegraph*, on the crew's progress through the season, Tim proved that he could wield a pen with equal aplomb.

It was not until Lucerne that the first question-mark hung over his performance, when his crew were beaten twice in two days. With a demanding Henley behind them, questions about Tim's endurance came to mind. He was the lightest in the boat. Perhaps the schedule had proved too much for his slight frame. Whatever the truth behind that result, Tim was determined that the crew learn valuable lessons from the defeat. He had always took immense pride from his own power-to-weight ratio. Although his was the lowest 'ergo' score in the boat, if one took his weight into account there was no doubt as to who was the most efficient. Tim looked at the massive bulks of Steven and Matthew, each weighing in at over 100 kilos, and persuaded coach Jurgen that for the boat to improve between Lucerne and Sydney, the two should lose five kilos each. It was a radical suggestion and one which would not have been considered but for that defeat. But it was followed through, nevertheless. It was a leaner and more efficient machine that took to the water at Sydney.

The crew's progress through the regatta looked imperious, as indeed it was. But during the semi-final, Tim's own gremlins returned to haunt him. He felt a twinge from his back. Nothing out of the ordinary for most rowers, but from someone who has had two back operations it was a signal that stood out as brightly as aircraft's warning lights. Surely his back would not break down again? In the event, physio Mark Edgar managed to stabilise the injury and Tim rowed on to glory.

He has returned to fame and not much fortune. The demand for his commercial appearances was not as great as the other three, though in June 2001 he featured as a nude centrefold for *Cosmo* magazine. That apart, he has not forgotten his roots, taking an unpaid job as assistant coach to the University of London Boat Club. There remains a problem, though. Tim

Sydney, 2000: The British coxless four, with Tim (wearing a cap) move off the start.

would dearly love to row on for another four years but he knows that his back would not stand another operation. As he savoured his Olympic triumph, he was waiting for the results of a back scan to determine if his spine could face another gruelling four years. I secretly hoped that the results would give Tim an excuse to turn his considerable talents to other areas. Although in my heart, I knew that he should not really need the results of a scan to give his battle-scarred body a chance to recover. Whatever Tim's decision, there is no doubt that the Sorcerer's Apprentice has become the Wizard of Oz.

Tales of Eight

THE last event of any championships is always the eight. For sheer spectacle there is nothing to beat it. The sense of explosive power and boat speed that eight men can generate is phenomenal, both to experience from within the boat and to watch from the bank. There is no finer sight in rowing than six matched boats fighting each other down the course: 48 massive rowers sprinting like hell from the 'Go', each rower fighting their own battle to push harder while locked into rhythm of their crewmates. The icing on the cake comes from the six diminutive coxes screaming instructions at the tops of their voices. I was hooked from my experience in Vienna; apart from anything, sentimentality told me that the eight was the boat to be in for what I knew would be my last Olympic regatta.

But as much as anything my views about the eight were influenced by Mike Teti. I'd known Mike since '84, although we had both been in international teams for seven years before that. So we went back a long way. Chances were that the first thing either of us would do at any regatta was look for the other to catch up on some gossip, watch the crews training or just hang out together, sitting on two boat stools watching the world go by. Maybe it was because he was American that Mike loved the eight so much.

The eight is practically made for the land where the speed and power of its jocks are the stuff of legends. Until then, American eights had won 11 out of the 21 Olympic titles. The tales behind those triumphs had become part of Mike's dreams.

So maybe you won't find it surprising that Mike often used to tell me, 'Martin, you just gotta row the eight one year, just one before you stop.' It somehow seemed right that the two of us would face each other that year in Barcelona for our last Olympics, both 'riding shotgun' up in the bows. If I could have gazed into the future then, it wouldn't have surprised me at all to see that, eight years later, for the Sydney Games, Mike's life was still inextricably linked with the eight; this time as a latter-day alchemist attempting to bring an Olympic eights gold back to the USA for the first time since 1964.

In 2000, it seemed to me that everyone in world rowing was asking the same question: has Michael Teti got what it takes to bring the 'big one' back to the States? Perhaps it was because I felt so close to Mike that I wished that the answer would be 'yes'. Maybe it had something to do with the fascination that I had for his tales about the eight he was coaching. I was in awe not so much how he coached (Mike was no Harry Mahon) but of how he could mould the minds of eight very different men towards accepting one purpose.

When I look back on my time in the eight for Barcelona, I sometimes find myself wishing that I'd had a guy like Mike coaching us then. Perhaps if I tell you my own 'Tales of Eight' from that year, you might understand why.

The eight that won a bronze in Vienna would not race again. Anton Obholzer's back was permanently damaged (by rights, he should not have raced at all). Greg and Jonny Searle were dreaming of fraternal Olympic glory in a pair, not an eight which they thought would have little or no chance of winning a gold. From early on they were single-minded in thinking only of winning the Easter pairs trials. To motivate himself through the winter Jon Searle stuck a particularly ugly picture of Redgrave and Pinsent on his fridge, rather as someone on a diet might use an unflattering photograph to stop them eating too much. Maybe Tim and I could and should have been as single-minded and aimed higher. But then we thought that we had little to fear from the Searles. Our aim was to finish in the first three of the pairs. We felt sure this would land us in the top boat for the Games.

It was the job of Mark Lees, the ARA's principal coach, to decide which oarsmen rowed where and, more important, who was to coach them. It was a role for which he seemed well suited. As a crew coach, first at Nottingham, then at UL and latterly at Cambridge, his boats had been distinguished by a fluid, effortless and easy style. It was why, five years earlier, Clift and I had asked him to coach our pair. I liked Mark and was pleased that it was he who was doing that demanding job.

But by the spring of 1992, Mark was not his usual healthy self. Always obsessive about his weight, even he looked rather thin and drawn. That spring he was admitted to the Chelsea and Westminster Hospital with a lung infection. It seemed to clear up after a couple of weeks. None of us knew then that Mark was HIV-positive. Still less that his illness was the start of full-blown AIDS. The chances were that Mark's first Olympics would be his last. It was a heavy burden for him to carry.

Nottingham, 1987: Mark Lees (left with Steel), contemplates the implications of our ignominious defeat by Redgrave and Holmes in the April trials. It was the last time he coached Adam and me in the pair.

Mark's illness, though, did not stop him trying to live life to the full. Perhaps when he looked at me that year, trying to gain Olympic selection while cramming three or four lives into one, he felt some sympathy. It was another complication for me that 1992 was a General Election year and as secretary of the local Labour Party there was much for me to do.

Since 1986 I had been organising monthly meetings, car boot sales or weekend stalls for the comrades of Hampton. There were about 70 or so members out there but whatever I did it was always the same five or six people who turned up. Not that some of our meetings weren't interesting, especially those at Peter's Costello's house. Peter was then running Social Services in Hounslow. With a large house in Hampton and a little pied a terre in Morocco he was quite a colourful character, who seemed to have some even more colourful friends. On these occasions one of these friends (we assumed he lived there) took to wandering in and out of our meeting room – usually stark naked – muttering under his breath, 'Fuck the Labour Party.' Mind you, if you had sat through some of our meetings, you'd have probably thought that he was the sanest one there.

Perhaps it was the lure of becoming a Labour MP that made my sanity temporarily desert me, leading me to stand as a candidate for all manner of local elections. I always ended up losing but was still convinced that Labour would win the 1992 General Election and, despite my Olympic training, I wanted to be part of that triumph.

So I canvassed in Feltham, turned up at all manner of Labour functions touting my status as an Olympic gold medalist, and was even filmed in my sculling boat for a Labour Party political broadcast. I remember feeling sure that the electorate couldn't forget Thatcher's poll tax fiasco and vote for the Tories. But the vibes I'd had picked up on the doorstep were that people felt uneasy about the idea of Neil Kinnock as a Prime Minister.

On election day the *Sun* brilliantly played on the floating voters' unease with a cartoon of the Labour leader as a light bulb accompanied by the caption, 'Will the last person left in Britain turn the lights out.' It didn't work in Feltham, where Alan Keen won back the seat. But it did in Basildon and most of the other Labour target seats.

I went to bed in the small hours with no Labour victory in sight, but the prospect of a hung parliament. When I woke early, even that had gone. I felt so miserable; how could the Tories be in power for another five years, 18 years in all? It was much worse than Labour's defeat in 1987, not least because now I'd put so much work into the campaign. I remember feeling bitter at Kinnock and carried a huge resentment against all those smug Tories, who wore their smiles for months afterwards.

So four days after the election, when I turned up at the Olympic selection trials in Nottingham, I wasn't in the best of moods. Marty Aitken, who was then coaching me and Tim, realising my distress, told the team, 'Whatever you do, don't mention *anything* about the election to Crossy.'

Needless to say, it had the opposite effect; there were lots of sly asides about the Basildon declaration, or questions like, 'Just how much time did you spend canvassing, Crossy?' In fact racing came as a welcome relief.

Tim and I finished third overall behind the Searles and the Redgrave-Pinsent combination. Mark Lees left those two pairs alone and put us into what, on paper at least, looked like a powerful eight. As with all big boats, the different styles of the rowers needed careful blending. I felt excited about its prospects, particularly as Marty Aitken was to coach it.

But that excitement soon faded as we seemed off the pace for the early-season regattas. Marty, who was actually paid to coach the students of the University of London, never really spent enough time with the crew to synchronise the different styles. It started badly enough at the first regatta in Essen. On the first day we rowed well enough but lost to the German world champions by a length. The second day saw us in a tough heat with Rumania and a second German crew put together from their fours. We came third and didn't make the final. Marty asked Mark Lees to make two changes for the next regatta at Cologne, but for some reason Mark refused.

Worse was to follow. At the Cologne regatta, Marty was staying with his University of London charges. Their hotel was miles from where we were staying with the national squad. In effect it meant that he saw us only once before our first final on Saturday, a ludicrous situation for the Olympic eight designate to have to tolerate. That day we lost to the Germans and, disappointingly, to a new Danish crew coached by Jim Clark.

Marty never saw us between our defeat then and our final on Sunday. As the oldest in the crew I slipped into the role of player-manager, giving the crew a pre-race motivational talk together with a completely different set of race tactics to that which we'd had the previous day. At least we beat the Danes, but the Germans were still in front. It was clear that neither Marty nor us were going anywhere like this and Mark broke up the eight. The Olympic team was in chaos. Presumably Mark was waiting for a miracle to happen at Lucerne.

It didn't come. No one from the British team won any medals. There was no British eight racing either. Mark had decided to split most of the squad into fours. Before the regatta my crew had shown real pace. I'd even began to dream of a medal. But a back injury to Tim and my misreading of the start time for a crucial race (which we missed), put paid to any chances of glory. Despite a whole season's racing, there was practically no form to go on to select the Olympic crews. It was a poor show and I blamed the coaches and especially Mark.

He clearly felt under pressure. His health was just about holding up but the mental strain was telling. On the way home from Lucerne, he had lost his cool and screamed abuse at John Pilgrim-Morris, the coach of the quadruple scull. Brian Armstrong, the Director of International Rowing, clearly thought that Mark was cracking up and took steps to ensure that he would be kept away from the team during our pre-Olympic training camps – once the crucial selection decisions were out of the way.

So Mark made key selection decisions under extreme pressure. To his eternal credit, he resisted all pressure to bring the Searle brothers back into one of the bigger crew boats and allowed them to stay in the coxed pair. As Redgrave seemed to be recovering from colitis, his selection was not in doubt. As for the rest of us, it seemed like Mark formed the Olympic crews by playing lucky dip. New combinations were thrown together. There seemed no logic. Tim and I were kept together and ended up in the eight (at least I would row in the Olympic Games in the boat of my choice). But if crew selections were poor, coaching decisions were disastrous.

To coach the eight (the boat that needed the most experienced coach) Mark chose the inexperienced Dave Lister while Aitken was given the coxed four. It was a tall order to come into the Olympic Games with no previous experience, but Lister's profession as a philatelist meant that he had even less time to coach us than Marty and we soon discovered that he could not make the first ten days of our altitude camp in Silvretta.

We were a new crew who effectively would be 'uncoached' at the most crucial time of the year. In desperation we looked to Mark Lees, himself an experienced eights coach, to help us, all the time blissfully unaware that he had been banned from contact with the Olympic team. The first I first heard of it was from Mark himself, who told me that he'd like to coach us at altitude but had been barred from the team.

It was the last straw. By then I'd had enough, and so had the rest of my crew. With me as shop steward (at last all that politicking with the Labour Party had taught me something) I read the riot act to International Rowing's management. I told Brian Armstrong bluntly that unless Mark was reinstated, the British Olympic eight would declare UDI: we would not fly out to altitude training with the team, we would have our own camp in Chester with Mark. If Brian wanted to deselect us, then he could.

Within an hour of issuing my ultimatum, I got an answer. Mark was reinstated. For a while it seemed a great victory. But perhaps you're reading this now, thinking as I am, what on earth was going on? Was a crew really expected to perform under those conditions. Well if you are, wait until you read about the farce that was our pre-Olympic camp.

Maybe I could have guessed that the wind and snow at altitude wouldn't suit Mark, who had already had one bout of pneumonia. After four days, just when the crew was beginning to 'move on', Mark developed a cold. Worried for his health, he quietly left our remote mountain lake for London. He would not return.

Yet again, we had no coach. As if that wasn't enough, in the cold of altitude most of the crew's old injuries returned to haunt us. On the day of our most important training pieces, we had three substitutes in the boat: Richard Manners, the spare man; Cal MacLennan, who had been flown out the day before to cope with the injury crises; and, wait for it... Derek

Drinkwater, the trailer driver who was a complete novice! In fact, the only time the whole crew rowed together was the last day of the camp, when a blinding blizzard forced us to come in early. As Olympic preparation went, this camp was a disaster.

Despite these setbacks, we raced bravely in Barcelona. I fantasised about a medal but in my heart of hearts I knew that we were not as fast as the big eights from Germany, Canada or the USA. You won't be surprised to read that I felt it was achievement enough just to make the final. Mark Lees was well enough to be in Barcelona and bask in the triumph of the two pairs. In my heart, I can't now find it in me to blame him for my result; perhaps I grew to like him too much.

In the year or two that he lived after the Games, I felt closer to Mark than I had ever done before. Perhaps it was seeing how brave he was in the face of so much suffering. Despite his illness, he worked hard to leave a legacy: the Mark Lees Foundation which supports young rowers is still a testament to Mark's love for the sport.

Perhaps it was serendipity that the boat from which we scattered his ashes on the Thames was an eight. It was packed with world and Olympic champions. For Mark, the end came in June 1994 after he made the decision to stop taking the noxious cocktail of drugs which kept his body going. We scattered his ashes about a mile from the start of the Boat Race course. When my turn came, I thrust my hand into the urn, felt the fine ash dig under my fingernails as I grabbed a handful and watched the wind spread all that was left of Mark in a billowing cloud over the grey Tideway waters. I still find it hard to find the words that adequately describe how I felt at that moment.

During that same summer, Mike Teti was starting out as a coach. In some ways, he and Mark shared some similar characteristics. Both could be generous, warm-hearted and both had a wicked sense of humour. But the similarities stopped there. Mike projected a far more confident air than Mark. One sensed that there was always a certain fragility to Mark, which it was hard find in Mike.

When Mike was on the US team he was everybody's favourite rower, a talisman; the guy everyone wanted to pair with, indispensable for his smooth, fluid movements and aggressive determination to win. Mike was champion of the seat race in the land where seat racing was king. Perhaps Mike was so popular because he was a good listener, although it was as a raconteur of a seemingly inexhaustible supply of tales about his life in the sport that he excelled.

Seoul, 1988: Mike Teti and me, surrounded by women from the Canadian rowing team during the opening ceremony of the Seoul Games. Mike, has his arm around Kay Worthington, his girlfriend since 1994. Their marriage will take place (eventually) in June 2001.

I loved to listen to Mike's tales. Sometimes I feel so much a part of his story that the effect is almost hypnotic. Reproducing some of them here may not have the same effect on you. But perhaps in the telling, you may learn why sports psychology is second nature to this man.

One of the tales he loves to tell is of the night before the finals of the Atlanta Olympics. Mike was not yet coaching the eight, rather a lightweight four which I thought had only an outside chance of a medal. As his crew edged their way out on to the course to begin their session, they had to pass the medal rostrum. Mike stood on the medal pontoon and as they rowed past, beckoned them to come over.

When their boat was nestling against the landing stage, Mike paused for effect then began to speak. 'The reason I asked you guys in here is that tomorrow, in the final there's all this confusion, the crowd shouting, the emotion, television and all that shit, and you're gonna cross the finish line and you're not gonna know where to go in all that confusion and I just wanna make sure that you know what to do. This is where you gotta go. I don't want to confuse you, 'cos right there, that's where second place will land and right there, that's where third place will land. But you guys are gonna land right here.' Teti pointed to the spot where the gold medalists would land. '...OK? Clear? Does anyone have any questions about where *you're* gonna land tomorrow?'

He went to shove them off the stage to continue their outing and then added as an afterthought, 'Do you *really* need to row tonight? I don't care, but do you really *need* to row?' The crew as a man said no, as Teti knew they would. As he told me the story (which I've heard on more than one occasion) I felt there was no room for doubt that his crew were as entranced listening to him as I was after the event. Mike recounts all his stories with the same freshness on the day that the words first left his lips. It is as though he wants me to feel the same emotions as his crew did. The effect of the story is made by the fact that on the next day, his crew won an unexpected bronze medal.

Listening to that story, I sensed that it was a pretty emotional moment for Mike too, as he stood on the stage. He's a passionate guy. Perhaps it runs in his Italian genes? Rather than stick to any plans, Mike is always prepared to trust his feelings and coach by intuition. It's something he's learnt from his earliest days.

Mike was born in South Philadelphia – 'on the wrong side of the tracks' – and grew up in a family of ten children. They lived in a small home, with one toilet, one fridge and one telephone. It certainly wasn't the wealthy Ivy League background that most American international rowers seemed to enjoy. As you might expect, Mike's background has long since passed into folklore among his crews. Every one of his athletes could recite, chapter and verse, what Mike's upbringing taught him (they get the story a few times each season). Self-reliance, communication and the importance of a structure figure pretty high. Mike claims that his family home was the coaching academy which taught him all the inter-personal skills that he would ever need to run an eight.

His mother was the matriarch that kept the home and family together. Every morning, each of the ten children would have newly-washed and ironed clothes to wear for school. Their sports kit would be spotless and ten lunch boxes were lined up alongside each other. As well as looking after the family and holding down a job, Mike's mother, a devout Catholic, managed to hear Mass every day. If you had to pick one hero in his life, it would probably be his mother. Her influence on him extends even into the team talks that he gives his crews before races.

Before the eights final during the 1999 World Championships in Canada, Mike was motivating his crew to give their all during the three big efforts that he'd planned for the race. Pete Cippoloni, the cox, was to yell

Casitas, 1984: 'That push is for your mother.' Mum and I embrace after the medal ceremony, with my sister Catherine (first left) and dad (second left), looking on.

out the focus for each push. For a key burst at 1,000 metres, Mike told his crew to think about their families that had travelled up to St Catherine's to watch them, and in particular their mothers (Mike's own mother was watching too).

'You wouldn't want your mothers to be upset after coming here all the way to watch you win would you? So let me tell you something. When you go at 1,250... that push is for your mothers.'

It's hard to imagine Jurgen Grobler, Harry Mahon, or any other coach in the world invoking their mothers at a key point in a World Championship final. But that is Mike's way; it has become part of the magic.

Family is incredibly important to him. You only have to hear the way he talks about his kid brother Paul, who he now coaches as part of the lightweight squad. There is genuine tenderness in the relationship. But the passionate Italian is never far away. After Paul's crew under-performed during one regatta, Mike visited his brother's room to find out why. Half an hour later, as Mike left the room, I heard Paul say to his room mate, 'I just had a visit from the Don.'

Mike is ideally suited to play the role of the Don Corleone of US rowing. There are many 'offers' that he has made to his rowers, most of which 'they couldn't refuse'. Almost always, this occurs when he feels that the unity of his group is threatened. For one thing that Mike learnt was that petulance and dissent in a large family is a dangerous thing; it is crystal clear to his athletes that he will not tolerate this. One of his top rowers, Porter Collins, fell foul of this rule during a training outing at Princeton. It is another story that Mike relishes telling.

During crew selection on Princeton's Lake Carnegie, Mike had two even eights racing against each other. All the athletes knew that the results of these contests mattered. What was more, they knew that Mike had them under intense scrutiny. That day, Porter Collins was in the slower crew. Before he began the story, Mike was at pains to point out to me that Collins was 'a really nice and a really good guy.' But that wasn't going to save him from Mike's wrath.

When the boats stopped for a breather at the top of the lake, Mike heard Collins say something to the rower in front of him. I sensed that Mike knew exactly what Collins had said before he asked. In fact that was why he chose to make an example of him.

Mike moved his launch closer to the crew. 'Hey Porter, what d'ya say?'
'Nothing.'

That response guaranteed that Collins was about to be made his 'offer'.

'Yeah, you did say something.' Mike turned the engine off. 'I got all fucking day. What did you say? What *exactly* did you say?' Pointing to the rower in front of Collins (when telling the story, Mike makes a similar gesture with his hand): 'Don't make me ask *him* tell me what you said.'

Collins, now wishing a whirlpool would appear and swallow him up, replied sheepishly, 'I said let's go, or something. Let's get a little more aggressive, you know. Let's get fired up.'

It was all Mike wanted. He was going to make a crucial point about individual responsibility at the expense of Collins. Mike responded. 'Who? Who...the guys in your boat? Chris Ahrens is not pulling *hard* enough for you? Bob Khaler is not putting enough in there? He doesn't want to win as much? Porter, listen. You're allowed to get away with that shit at Brown [University]. But I am not going to tolerate it here.'

As I listened to Teti, I already felt guilty for all the times I had moaned in a boat. But as he moved his head closer to mine to continue the story, I began to feel a certain menace.

'So let's make a little rule here [Porter]. Next time you open your fucking mouth to say one thing in the boat, like you might say... I love you... *anything* you say in the boat from now on and you're fucking done!'

There was a pause and he looked me in the eyes as if it was me who had made the comment and with that look said: 'I don't need you!'

In the silence that followed I thought, 'Shit, he really means that.' No doubt in the silence that followed on Lake Carnegie you could hear the drops fall from the looms of the blades to splash on the surface of the water. As he began to explain his reasons for acting that way, the smile returned to his face, The point was: if he let Collins get away with it, then the rest of the group would think there was one rule for the superstars and another for the rest.

Mike is similarly blunt when it comes to the distribution of the performance grants to which athletes are entitled if they 'medal' at World Championships. Mike sees arguments over cash as a potential source of disruption to the squad. In reality, the best grants are supposed to go to the rowers who finish highest in the World Championships. But Mike feels that, because so many in his squad are close to being in a medal boat, it would be unfair not to share the money around the whole group, including those who didn't 'medal'.

Furthermore, because he has been responsible for finding most of them employment, he has a fair idea of what they earn. His whole squad were told that if he received one criticism about the distribution of money, the athlete would be thrown out of the squad forever. 'If you receive a cheque, you keep your mouths shut. If you don't get a cheque then you say nothing.' Mike's logic – which drives a coach and horses through the principle of rewarding performance – is that over a four-year programme 'things will even out'. It's a different and even refreshing view on sporting rewards in the country that has more sporting millionaires than any other.

The image of a father laying down the law to his children is inescapable. Indeed, it was the role that Mike's own father fulfilled in their home where it was clear that things like racism or sexism would not be tolerated. But being one of ten meant that each child had to develop a certain independence to survive. It is a quality which he insists his athletes attain. The kind of professionalism that is the norm elsewhere in the world is almost anathema to Mike. As far as he is concerned, that kills the freedom of spirit and, ultimately, the will to win that he is trying to foster.

Nowhere is this more clear than in the lifestyle he insists his athletes adopt. Mike's firm belief (somewhat refreshing in this age of the professional sports person) is that it is possible, even necessary, to win the

World Championships while holding down a responsible job at the same time. Much of his time is spent finding employment for his squad members, usually in blue chip companies through contacts in the wealthy network of rowing alumni on the east coast of the USA. Mike never asks for charity though, far from it. He insists that his athletes work in nine-to-five jobs and structures his training programme round this ethic. This ensures that he has the best athletes in his group. Normally, few of the highly-qualified Ivy league graduates who row successful varsity crews would want to stay in the sport once they had left college. For them the lure of Wall Street is much greater than the prospect of international rowing.

In an age where full-time training is the norm, it is somewhat perverse that Mike schedules his work-outs around his athletes' jobs. Often, his squad rows only six mornings a week with training in the evening left to each rower to complete on an ergometer, after they have finished work. This type of approach is in complete contrast to most other top nation's rowing programmes and represented a complete volte-face from the system Mike inherited after the Atlanta Games.

Its success was undoubted. Mike's eight won three straight gold medals at the World Championships between 1997 and 1999. As they prepared for the Sydney Games, there was no doubt that it was the Americans who ruled the waves. Part of Mike's success lay in attracting athletes back into the sport who had given up: rowers like Jeff Klepacki.

Klepacki had quit rowing for a job after the 1996 Olympics. He had been on the team since 1989 and rowed with Teti in the Barcelona eight. He had won several medals, most notably when he famously stroked the American eight in 1994. His father had died just before the race and Klepacki stormed down the course with his dad's business card tucked inside his sock. They just held off the Dutch in a last-gasp finish. But he failed to make the Olympic eight and finished a disillusioned and lowly 11th in the coxless fours. Then, Klepacki had been a full-time rower in San Diego. After Atlanta, he decided that he needed to 'join the real world' and so took up a job with a blue chip company on the west coast.

But in November 1997, after seeing the success that Mike's coaching methods were having, Klepacki was getting restless. He called up Mike, telling him that he wanted to row again. Behind this logic was the expectation that he would be transferred to Princeton to run the mid-Atlantic division of his company during the following April. Most coaches would have said that April was far too late in the season to let anybody into their squad, but not Mike who leapt at the chance: 'Gee, that would be great Jeff,' he responded on the telephone.

Mike's philosophy becomes clear at his response to Klepacki's demand for a training programme that he could follow until April.

Mike paused: 'Jeff, you rowed in two Olympics, you have three medals, do I really have to send you a *training programme?*' (I remember thinking that he spoke the words 'training programme' as if they were some kind of infectious disease).

'Do you *really* have no clue what to do?' On the end of the telephone there was a silence. Klepacki wasn't used to a coach talking to him in this way.

So Mike continued. 'Jeff, really, don't insult me by asking me. You've rowed in all these national teams. You don't have to be in Olympic shape when you show up here in April. Just do a work-out every day.'

Klepacki showed up in the April of 1998. That summer Teti put him in the key 'six' seat, the engine room of the boat. Since then Klepacki has won gold medals in two eights.

Before Mike finished telling that story I already realised that, for him, routine in the training programme is the enemy. That was why he told Klepacki to invent his own work-outs. Even when they are in the squad there is no 'set' programme. Most of the time Mike's rowers won't know what work they are going to do until they have finished their warm-up at the top of Lake Carnegie. Likewise, when they turn up to the World Championships his athletes don't have a schedule for the week. Mike likes to ask them when they feel like rowing each day; they must be the judges of when is the best time to eat, or for how long they should sleep. His rationale is twofold: first, it is the way that he himself used to like to race; second, he feels it discourages reliance on him. Thus, when his crews are on the start line they are used to being alone and making decisions by themselves.

It is why Mike is so reliant on the ergometer for training. He has devised a whole talent identification around the machine and receives scores from all over the country. As he talked about the 'erg', his eyes lit up. 'Those people who say they can perform on the water but not on the "erg" are talking bullshit. On that machine, you are naked. Those numbers are real.'

As Mike 'poured it on', I began to feel guilty for ever having doubted the 'erg's' efficiency for selecting crews.

'If you're a psychological mess on that machine, you're a psychological mess in the boat; period!' While his athletes are on the machine, Teti always watches them intently.

Vienna, 1991: The final strokes of the eights final at the World Championships. The British eight is in the foreground, trailing Canada and the German crews. At bow, I'm keeping a careful eye on the Rumanian boat, with whom we duelling for the bronze medal.

Mike and I sometimes row the ergometer together these days, at World Championships, and check each other's scores to see just how much fitness we've managed to hold on to despite our age. Sometimes these sessions become rather too competitive. Just as I was going up to do a half-hour on the machine, by myself, Mike, caught my eye.

'Goin on the "erg" Martin? What ya gonna do today – 8,500 metres?'

I nodded.

With a smile on his face, he added gently, 'Just try for eight six, OK?'

To row that much in half an hour would have been too hard for the type of session that I wanted to do. But as I sat on the machine I thought only of achieving the target that Mike had set. I made it – just – and fell off the machine, calling Mike all sorts of names under my breath, although with the intense satisfaction of knowing that I'd just pulled a total that would have been beyond me but for Mike's cajoling. He knows me too well.

But Teti is also adept at taking pressure off his athletes. One of his new college rowers was awkward, although he could pull a big 'erg' score. But he seemed to look unhappy in the boat. Mike knew that his poor technique was bothering him, so it wasn't a surprise when he asked Mike for some technical guidance in the middle of an outing.

Mike gently guided the launch towards the eight and switched off the engine. 'Kurt, do you know that when I took you in this crew, my 'phone never stopped ringing? All these old coaches of yours were ringing me up, telling me, "Yeah he's a great athlete, so powerful... if only you could teach him how to row." Do you think I put you in this boat for your *rowing* ability? Let me tell you now, I couldn't give a shit about how you row. I want you for your power. OK, I am giving you licence to pull the fucking side off this boat from now on and for every fucking stroke you ever row. Is that clear?'

By now you may have worked out that Mike did care about the way that his new recruit rowed. But Mike reckoned that the guy's worries about his technique were restricting his natural flair for racing. That summer the raw recruit won a gold medal in Mike's eight.

For Mike, the eight is all about power. He reckoned that if he could just get eight big strong 'erg' pullers comfortable in a boat, then they could blast down the course and nobody would be able to catch them. It was a totally different philosophy to that of Mark Lees, or Rene Mijnders, coach of the Dutch eight which won the Atlanta title by a length. Mijnders's oarsmen were all brilliant technicians (mostly successful scullers) who made a virtue of timing the catch with lightning fast, easy and precise movements. In football terms they were like the great Dutch soccer side with Cruyff and Rep in the 1974 World Cup: for Total Football read Total Rowing. If most coaches had to pick the best eight ever, the Dutch crew would be top of most lists. But Teti draws his philosophy not from the beauty and flow of soccer but from the power and guts of the Super Bowl. His crews were going to blast away the opposition, like the offensive line of an American football team, battering a hole through their opponents' defence.

The contrast in approach was apparent when Teti met up with his old coach and rowing guru, Kris Korzenowski. As a technical purist Korzenowski dislikes the aggressive style of Teti's crews, considering it too wasteful. When Korzenowski was looking at a Rumanian eight doing a burst while Mike was standing alongside him, Korzenowski bemoaned their brutal, aggressive style of rowing, which for him was not using the athletes' natural power in the best way.

Yet the Rumanian eight were one of the fastest in the world and by implication Teti felt that his philosophy on rowing was being criticised too.

He was stung into the reply, 'Chris, you know, I used to be a Catholic... but I changed my religion. Now this is what I worship... Nielson-Kellerman man." As he said this, Mike shoved his stopwatch (most rowing coaches use a type made by Nielson- Kellerman) in front of Korzenowski's face. The implication was that if Mike's crews (or the Rumanians for that matter) were going fast enough to win, who cared about the way they rowed?

But Mike does care deeply about the way his crews row. In St Catherine's, his eight looked awesome. He also cares deeply about his athletes. It is for that reason that he is so short with them. He knows that sometimes he goes over the top. But in a way those occasions are part of the Teti legend and generally find their way into the team's revue at the end of the year. They are part of the folklore that the US rowers pass down about a coach they love.

At heart, Mike's rowers know that first and foremost he still sees himself as an athlete. He still trains with his squad regularly on the 'ergo', pulling scores that would put him into most international teams. During the day, when the early morning session has finished, he is always to be found on the water in his black millennium single, a gift from his friend the boatmaker, Mike Vespoli. At Princeton, Mike is living his fantasy life. When he's not coaching or training, he's often to be found 'slobbing out' in front of the television, eating pizza, watching the latest ball game, or court case.

It's a lifestyle that doesn't fit well with the notion of raising a family – something his partner of 12 years, Kay Worthington, knows all too well. Every year people used to ask her the same question: 'When are you and Mike going to get married?' Three engagements, in 1987, 1990 and 2000, and at least the same number of break-ups later, they will finally tie the knot in Princetown on 9 June 2001. Why so long? Kay wanted a family but Mike was worried that the responsibility would change his idyllic existence. In any case, Mike already had a family: his squad of rowers.

They are his children. On his shelves at home in Princeton he has a copy of a musical, written as a PhD thesis by a Princeton student who rowed in one of his college crews. Mike was surprised when this student offered the carefully-bound volume to him, and even more surprised when he opened it and saw it was dedicated to the student's parents and 'Mike Teti, who never gave up on me when others did'. Mike remembers 'shouting at the kid a few times, to encourage him', but nothing out of the ordinary.

The fact that Mike takes his rowers when they are novices with potential, and spends all his time coaching and training them, makes all the difference. Mike gets emotional about it too. When he shoved his eight off for the final in the Cologne World Championships, he was close to tears: 'It was like I was sending these little kids out there into the lion's den and what made it worse was that I knew that this was going to be the last time that

Sydney, 2000: Mike Teti's boys during an Olympic heat in Sydney. Chris Ahrens is rowing at stroke (in front of the cox), Jeff Klepacki is rowing at '6' (sixth left) behind him, while Porter Collins is at '3' (third left).

they rowed together.' In fact, despite his predictions, the same crew emerged again in 1999. For all Mike's protestations about open competition, he still remains incredibly protective about his eight.

Nowhere is this type of relationship more apparent than with his protégé Chris Ahrens. Ahrens has stroked all of Mike's crews, from the time when he first arrived as a freshman rower. When Mike talks about Ahrens rowing it is with a different tone of voice from that which he uses for anyone else. It is almost reverential. Their relationship has been one of the key reasons behind the American eights' recent success.

But when Ahrens's Princeton crew failed to win the men's eights at the Eastern Sprints because of an unfair crosswind, Mike saw their relationship in a different light. Mike watched his young protégé, who had always delivered everything he had ever asked of him, congratulate the winning Harvard crew, exchange shirts, then sit on the bus, a solitary figure with his head in his hands. He was devastated. As he saw Ahrens there, Mike felt a huge sense of guilt welling up in him.

As he told me his last story, it was with the voice of a father who has made his son a man but forgotten that he was still a boy at heart. Mike decided to call Ahrens the next day and ask for a meeting at his house. It was so important to Mike that he had spent all day thinking what he might say. There are not many national coaches in any sport that open themselves up so transparently with their top athletes. For a man who spends his time working on his gut instinct, it was not an easy conversation.

Sydney, 2000: It was the Great Britain eight not Teti's crew who saluted the crowd after their gold medal performance. In rowing there is often more jubilation when the crew link hands for the first time, than the moment when the medals are awarded.

The words, awkward at first, poured out. 'Chris, you know, I feel like... really awful. You had so much pressure on you. Everyone sees you as the stroke of the US gold medal eight; a big super star – everyone talks about you.'

His voice oozed guilt and contrition as he switched the angle to himself.

'In addition... I'm a really controversial guy and there's a lot of people out there who hate me. All's I ever do is talk about how great *you* are and that makes them hate you. Your picture's probably up on every boathouse wall and they're throwing darts at it. But I always forget, because I look at you as this man. And I really forget that you're a 20-year-old kid. So, I wanted to apologise to you because... it's like I've created this and you can't have any fun any more because everybody's out to get you.'

When he had finished, Mike turned away from me and shrugged, as if recalling the awkwardness of the moment. As he did this, one of Mike's favourite sayings about life in a large family flashed through my mind: 'You never got too much love because being one of ten, my parents had to ration it.'

Maybe I was reading too much into it, but for me it was almost as if Mike, in mourning the passage of Ahrens's youth, was remembering the times he wanted some love and understanding as a child but didn't receive it. For Mike, who tries to spread himself over all the squad, spending time coaching every oarsman, it must have been like his parents trying to spread their love around such a large family. The problem is that this 'strength' can also be a weakness; in trying to help such a large number of people, creating one big happy family, his eight sometimes suffers.

Until the Sydney Olympics, he got away with it. But when his crew appeared for the first time on the Penrith course, it was clear that all was not well. The personnel were largely the same, as was the fact that this was their first major race of the season. In training, they had been flying, so much so that on that form, they might have won the Olympic title by clear water. Their second place behind that season's dark horses, Croatia, in the opening heat, was by no means a disaster, nor was their repechage win, which qualified them for the final. However, Mike knew that something had happened to rob his crew of their speed; he knew they were just not fast enough to win, let alone challenge for a medal.

But there was still a trick or two he could play. He chose to move Chris Ahrens out of the stroke seat and replace him with Jeff Klepacki. When I saw the crew change, I knew then that his eight were not going to win. Mike knew that too. In fact the triple World champions came trailing in a lowly fifth place.

Mike, the dreamer, weaned on tales of the USA's gold medal-winning eights of 1956 and 1964, had come up against a cold dose of reality. Both his and America's rowing dreams were seemingly shattered. If his crew had won, then his place as an alchemist – the man who turned the raw base metal of college kids into the golden gleam of Olympic champions – would have been assured.

But for Mike, there was something more important. What mattered more to him was his own and the crew's integrity; that, after the race, rather than go away and sulk, they could congratulate the medalists with a warm, heartfelt handshake. More than anything, for a crew that had conquered all before it over the last three years, Mike wanted them to retain their integrity in defeat. He was not to be disappointed. It was to be the last act of a crew whose young members would turn away from their oars towards the lure of Wall Street. They will watch from afar, as their coach sets off on another journey, when over the next four years, the alchemist plots how to bring back that elusive Olympic gold medal for eights to America.

Shoot Me!

THE sun had already made the flagstones baking hot by the time I left the Olympic village. I was alone. There was no one to bid me farewell as I struggled out through accreditation with my heavy luggage; no messages either for me on the internal e-mail which I checked for the last time, more in hope than anticipation. Most of the athletes were in bed from all-night frolics in the pool. I'd felt too melancholic to join in. They were staying for the parties in Barcelona during the second week I was going. In the bus, the air-conditioning burst into life, cool air playing down on my hot face. I took one last glance back and I knew that I was leaving for the last time as an Olympic athlete. As the bus began to pick its way through the narrow Banyolas streets, thoughts of retirement began to cross my mind. They were slightly less public circumstances in which to contemplate leaving the sport than those chosen by Steven Redgrave four years later.

What do you say to a guy who's just won his fourth Olympic gold on the trot? A simple 'well done' hardly seemed to suffice as a response to one of the greatest moments in Olympic history. As the victorious pair spun round and guided the fragile shell alongside the 'hot' interview raft, nestling at the end of Atlanta's giant floating grandstand, I ran down from my commentary position trying to find the words to congratulate Pinsent and Redgrave. The world's greatest rower was exhausted and sweaty; a haze of steam seemed to rise up from his skin. Twelve years earlier I had seen his bulk from inside the boat as he had stroked us to his first Olympic gold. Now it seemed vaguely appropriate that a former crewmate would be the first person to congratulate the 'old bastard', just after he had won his fourth. Their muscles felt hard and unyielding as I slapped first Pinsent, then Redgrave on the back. 'Well done Steve... well done Matt.'

'Cheers Crossy.'

'Thanks Mart.'

The cameras and microphones were there to record his immediate feelings for posterity. I stepped back as Dan Topolski moved swiftly in to interview Redgrave for BBC television. Almost at once I was struck by the bitterness in his voice: 'If anybody ever sees me near a boat again, you've my permission to shoot me!' As resignation statements go, it sounded pretty final; with one sentence he had wrenched himself free of the pain, torment and stress that he had put himself through for over 20 years. 'Good,' I thought smugly, 'he won't be breaking my record for most appearances in a GB vest.' But then it occurred to me that his invective, while understandable, was ever so faintly unconvincing. From bitter experience I knew that for him to let go of the sport he lived for would be much easier said than done. I somehow knew then that before long yet another rowing milestone would be his.

Steven's resolve to end his record-breaking career lasted no more than a few days. After a family holiday in Disneyland, the itch to get back in a boat again was unavoidable. It was to be some months before he would announce his intention to search his holy grail of a fifth gold in Sydney, or even step into a boat again (thus inviting the possible attention of all manner of sharpshooters). I found out during a Leander dinner, held as a thank-you to all those who had helped him.

When I quizzed him as to his rowing plans, he asked, 'What would you do Mart?'

The answer came almost immediately – it was what I'd done after Barcelona.

'Take things a year at a time. I wouldn't stop now… I mean you're only 34. I'd row on but no commitments beyond a year.'

Lake Lanier, 1996: A weary Steven Redgrave goes through yet another round of press interviews after his opening heat of the Atlanta. My dad, in the forground, shows a look of almost childlike excitement.

Nottingham, 1986: Although Steven was usually the focus of the world's media, even in his pair with Matt, it just takes a glimpse of Andy's unrelenting gaze to understand why their pair went so fast.

He smiled, his decision already made.

'No, if you're going to carry on, it's no good just doing it for one year, it's got to be for four... hasn't it Mart?'

The question was rhetorical. 'Mr Olympics' had spoken. Some people, most people, take each year as it comes; Steven has been planning in four-yearly cycles since 1980. When he announced his intention to the guests that evening, there were a few gasps, although nobody who knew him was in the least bit surprised.

In deference to the private nature of the occasion, the media heavyweights there, like Michael Calvin from the *Telegraph* and Alan Green from BBC Radio 5 Live, held back while Steven planned his announcement to achieve maximum publicity. On the day of the press conference, the Radio Four *Today* programme brought their interview van (parked rather ostentatiously outside the headmaster's office) to Hampton School for my comments as to what Steven's decision might be.

I played the game, pretending that I didn't know what his decision would be. John Humphreys was nothing if not persistent. I thought, 'I'm not a bloody government minister.' But he continued, 'If he did continue, how could he find the motivation to carry on for so long?'

I wanted to say, 'Because he's scared at what he might do if he stops.'

But I baulked at introducing something so personal into the interview, so I waffled on about his *raison d'être* being to break Olympic records. Anyway, what right did I have to think that it would be the same for Steven as it was for me when I wondered if I should retire after the Barcelona Games?

At 35, Atlanta, four years ahead, seemed too distant a prospect. I knew I'd probably be there, but only in my capacity as the athletes' representative for FISA. In reality my performance had peaked physically the previous year. In the run-up to Barcelona, my ergometer scores had stopped improving, but more significantly, younger athletes were pushing for my place in the team and the chance to row with Foster, my pairs partner. It was unsaid but we both knew that he would need a new and younger pairs partner to develop his potential to the full.

For three years we had been fitting training sessions around the demands of my job. Morning and evening sessions were the least demanding but often, to complete two sessions, it was necessary to train at midday. Then, I had to rush away from a class a few minutes early to make a lunch-time session at the University of London boathouse in Chiswick, some seven miles away. I had an hour and a half for lunch. with the drive taking 20 minutes, that meant only a 50-minute outing. Then, I had to rush back to school, arriving on two wheels (usually five minutes late) to teach Arab-Israeli history to a group of GCSE students. Having had no time to change, I would be wearing my rowing suit, smelling and dripping with sweat. It could not have been a more inappropriate way to try to explain the nuances of the Middle East conflict. The boys were remarkably tolerant – God knows what the staff thought! It was no way to teach, let alone train for the national team.

Even if I was mad enough to continue, the sport was changing around me. Before 1992 it had still been possible for me to compete at the highest levels, fitting in two sessions around a full-time job. Already, though, Redgrave and Pinsent had blazed the trail of professional athletes. Now with the promise of more state funding available and more extensive training programmes, others would follow, putting their careers on hold for life as an international rower. It was a path I could not follow. I knew I was an endangered species.

Then there was my family. I had pretensions to being a good father and husband but I suppose after a summer away, my wife might have had a different perspective. Our second child, Lara, was due in December. Whereas Chris could just about cope with with Natasha during my absences at weekends or training camps, a younger baby would bring all sorts of different pressures. After Barcelona, it was clear that Chris had just about had enough. When I travelled back from the Olympics to spend a few weeks' holiday at our French house, communication between us was fraught. I still had my mind wrapped up in the Olympics, while all Chris wanted to do was settle down to a life of normality.

Trouble was, that was the sort of life I hated, even feared. Being an Olympic rower made me feel special. I wanted to be on holiday with the family (I hadn't seen them for a month) but I also wanted to be in the Olympic village with the other athletes, having a great time. So, both Chris and I settled into a stony silence in our French house, one resentful against the other. It was a mood broken only by an extraordinary incident which finally wrenched my mind away from the Olympics.

We arrived home from a day out to be greeted by an agitated Frenchman, gesturing for me to go with him in his car as quickly as possible. Our English neighbour, who lived about a mile down the road, was apparently distraught after hearing the news that the helicopter in which her son had been travelling had crashed in England. Two were dead and her son was on life support and not expected to live. Hanson Air had offered to land a helicopter next to her house in France and fly her to London to be at her son's bedside. Too scared to fly on her own, she had asked for me to go back with her. I did not want to go but really had no choice. The whirring rotors and throaty roar of the exhaust shattered the rural peace of the Suisse Normandie as the helicopter landed.

Within no time at all we were in the middle of London, racing through the traffic to get to the hospital. I felt sure that her son would be dead by the time we arrived, but in trying to keep her calm kept telling her the opposite. Mercifully, when we arrived at the London hospital she was told that her son would probably live. The next morning Hanson Air flew me back to Normandy. The whole thing was a completely traumatic experience, but it had dragged me back to reality. As the aircraft disappeared and I was left standing alone in a French field again, my longing to be part of the Olympic jamboree had disappeared. At least we could now enjoy our holiday.

We had bought our French house in 1991, with the intention that the idyllic lure of a rural retreat would help soften the blow when I had to quit rowing. In fact the location of the house, just a kilometre or so from a 1,500 metres lake, probably had more of an impact in prolonging my competitive

Normandy, 1995: The garden of our French house, pictured in the morning sunlight.

career than anything else. Every school holiday I would load up our car with a 10-metres long pair strapped to the roof, hoping that the French customs or gendarmes would not stop our ridiculously overloaded vehicle leaving the port.

The locals, who had never seen a rowing boat, looked upon us with incredulity. '*Ils sont fons, les Anglais,*' we would hear them muttering under their breaths as we as we fought our way to the remote lakeside through muddy fields full of cowpats. In a way, I suppose I was mad. Chris must have thought she was too, in agreeing to spend her holiday with a rowing-mad husband, together with Foster (who usually brought his girlfriend) and a two metre overhang each end of the car.

At least there was some humour in daily life there. We attended Mass regularly at our French church. This was a hazardous occupation. The curé (who looked more like an orthodox monk than a priest) often acted like a kind of French Michael Barrymore. He insisted that everybody took a turn at something during his Mass. Since the congregations numbered only about 30 or so (not hard to work out why) it meant that more often than not, Chris and I would be called up to do something. We had to listen very carefully to Père Roussière's unintelligible French for the phrase, *Les Anglais parmi nous.* That was the sign.

One Sunday, Chris, who arrived late, was horrified to see me in the pulpit about to give the sermon to the congregation. There was a visiting Irish priest who was concelebrating the Mass. By then I understood enough of Père Roussière's French to know that Father O'Boyle couldn't speak any French. He went on '...*Heureusement nous avons parmi nous* [my heart stopped beating], *Monsieur Cross qui peut traduire les mots de notre prête Irlandaise.*'

By some mysterious power, I found myself involuntarily walking towards the altar, fondly imagining that the stone covering the crypt might open up and swallow me.

'Oh great, you speak French then?' said Father O'Boyle, in his broad Dublin accent, as I approached him.

'Er, not really,' I said. His face fell.

'But what'll we do?'

For some reason, instead of walking away, I found myself saying, 'We'll busk it, Father.'

It must have been Père Roussière's mystical powers that gave me such confidence – it certainly wasn't my non-existent French.

What Father O'Boyle wanted to talk about were the similarities of rural Ireland to Normandy. The most obvious, apart from *Les champs, les vaches et la pluie* (which even I could remember from school), was unemployment. Fortunately, this was a subject which our neighbour Mr Carville – whose interpretation of the news often made the grim reaper seem like a cheery soul – always seemed to be discussing. *Le problème du chòmage* cropped up (and still does) in just about in every conversation we ever had. So my response, in view of my horrendous understanding of French, was to at least try to sound as if I really understood him. So there was always a knowledgeable *Mais oui* or I would shrug my shoulders in what I took to be a Gallic-type gesture and let out a knowing exhalation of breath, which sounded something like 'Fwoof.'

This much experience at least made me prepared to bluster my way through the sermon. I guess the small congregation wondered why this Irish priest kept going on so much about unemployment? Of course he didn't; there was plenty about the delights of living in rural Ireland, or the difficulties of administering to a flock in such areas. But I couldn't face translating all these. The funny thing was that after I mentioned *le chômage* for the third or fourth time, I could have sworn that the locals started to give Father O'Boyle knowing looks with an ever so slight shrug of their shoulders. At least he was striking a chord with his audience.

Unemployment was the least of my worries when I returned home from France that summer. I was given new responsibilities at work, which would mean spending more hours at school each day. In addition, it was a demanding time for me being athletes' representative on both FISA and the British Olympic Association. With FISA, the big controversy was the question: should lightweight rowers be admitted to the Olympic programme? It was controversial enough anyway. Sometimes there is not much love lost between heavyweight and lightweight rowers. What made it worse, though, was that this could only be done by dropping three of the open category classes including coxed fours, the event I'd won in Los Angeles and the coxed pairs that the Searles had just won in Barcelona.

Passions ran extremely high within the sport, with lightweights desperate to get their own events in the Games. Most open weight rowers (almost all of whom looked down on lightweight events as second class) were determined to keep them out. I put myself in the latter category. Jonny Searle and I organised a petition to Samaranch from 50 out of the 52 Barcelona Olympic gold medalists, indicating their opposition to the proposal. It led to huge controversy in the sport. Denis Oswald, the FISA president and IOC member, was behind the push to admit lightweight events. He was furious that Samaranch had been approached behind his back and threatened to ban Jonny from racing. On the other hand, John Boultbee, the Australian secretary-general of FISA, was directly opposed to Oswald. It all made for dramatic and controversial meetings in both Lausanne and Budapest during that winter.

As if that wasn't enough, I also ran the British Olympic Association's Athlete Council. We had initiated a major survey of all the athletes in the Britain's Olympic team, not just to provide evidence that British athletes were desperately disadvantaged compared to those of other nations but to recommend ways forward. The collation of material, let alone the process of securing the BOA's agreement on some of the report's more controversial ideas (like using Government money to pay international athletes a salary), took up countless hours. Ultimately, the whole process was very productive. Its ideas form the basis of the current funding of successful athletes through the National Lottery. All in all, I needed someone to shoot me (probably my wife would volunteer) if I dared to set foot in a boat again after Barcelona.

But I wasn't about to go 'cold turkey' just yet. Like all addicts who are supposed to be kicking the habit, I found myself working out how I could sneak a drag here, or a dram there without being seen. I wanted to break the news gently to Chris. I suppose in part this meant being 'economical with the actualite'. But the more I thought about the prospect of stopping rowing, the more desperate I became to carry on. To all intents and purposes this meant that my training over the winter would become part of a 'general fitness programme'. Peter Mandelson, the spin doctor par excellence, couldn't have put better spin on the purpose behind my workouts.

It's well known that athletes who've trained for long periods of time needed to acclimatise their bodies to inactivity by gradually relaxing the training load. Chris was well aware of this fact, mainly because, I'd kept bringing up 'casually' in conversation. Although I don't suppose that my 'I'm just popping out for a row mate' fooled her in the least. So along with a new baby, as well as a demanding job, Chris had to cope with a husband who was working full-time, sitting on several demanding committees and being an international rower on the quiet!

By Easter, with the pairs trials for national team places being held in Belgium, it was no longer possible to keep my intentions secret. During our holiday in France it would have been hard to hide the presence of my new pairs partner, Matt Parish, his girlfriend Zoe, together with boat blades, coaching launch and coach. By then, though, Chris had become resigned to my intentions, although things became more difficult to bear that summer. By then I'd just scraped into the bows of a young national eight, after a fairly inauspicious season. After the selection announcement, I felt pleasure, yet it was tinged with a great element of relief. I had secured my 17th consecutive international vest but the writing was so clearly on the wall. Nothing made that more clear than the faintly ludicrous events of that summer, when we moved house.

With a larger family, we wanted to move to have more space. House hunting after training was hard enough. But the exchange of contracts was to prove fraught. At the most crucial time for the sale, neither of us were at home. Chris was spending the summer at our house in Normandy. At the same time I was on training camp with the eight in Chester. To complicate matters further, neither the French house, or our training base in Chester, had a telephone. So it was not possible for estate agents, solicitors and vendors to contact anybody else involved in the sale. In fact we couldn't even contact each other! All the intricacies of offers, last-minute hitches and exchange of contracts had to be conducted using pay phones and the odd letter. It was a situation that could have provided material for any number of farces. But we were in the middle of it.

Even at the championships, held in Czechoslovakia, I was constantly on call, attending the FISA Congress or trying to drum up support for the athletes meeting. That our eight made the final in these circumstances was, I suppose, a small miracle. But the result and its effects seemed to give me some form of temporary amnesia about all the difficulties of that season. I was in the final again. To me that meant that I could still produce 'it' when it mattered. Once again sixth place would secure me a healthy Sports Aid grant for the forthcoming season – if I cared to carry on. If I needed any encouragement, I had only to listen to all my international buddies, who buttressed my ego with comments that generally ran, 'How old are you? God, I think its fantastic that you're still there competing.' It was comments like that which convinced me that it was indeed 'fantastic', rather than ludicrous. So, as I travelled back home from Prague, I found myself scheming as to how I might carry on for the next season.

If I had thought the 1993 season demanding, it was to have seemed like a doddle compared to the following year. Chris was determined to develop some of her own interests. That autumn she was chosen to be Twickenham's Constituency delegate for the Labour Party Conference. When I joined her for the eve-of-conference social, the major topic was whether John Smith's plan to modernise the party by introducing One Member One Vote would attract enough votes. Chris had been delegated to support the motion. But she didn't feel well enough to really get involved in the conference debates that week. On the morning of the 'OMOV' vote, she found out why: she was expecting our third child.

Frank was born at almost exactly the same time as John Smith died of a heart attack, on 12 May 1994. If the rest of the family read anything into fate, they might have expected Frank to develop into a socialist rower. As the news about the Labour leader's death was relayed to us during Frank's delivery, it interrupted a conversation about rowing. The surgeon had studied with Budgett when he won his Olympic gold, the anaesthetist trained regularly at the UL boathouse, while the nurse had just taken up the sport. As coincidences go, it was a pretty big one. At the time even Chris saw the funny side of it, although the realities of bringing up three children with their father in the middle of his 18th season of international rowing would soon wipe the smile off her face, As anybody with more than two children will know, the biggest jump in the demands and responsibilities of the parents comes from two to three children. Almost everything from feeding, to baby-sitting, to going out seems infinitely more challenging. In addition to this, the week after Frank's birth my father was taken ill, necessitating a lengthy stay in hospital. The portents were clearly telling me to stop rowing but I chose to ignore them.

By now, I was on the fringes of the squad. To race at the international regatta in Paris, I had to enter in my single. I wasn't last, but it was a close-run thing. I was almost half a minute behind the top competitors. In desperation, I looked at the coxed pair, itself a doomed boat. The talented Jonny Singfield had been overlooked by Jurgen Grobler in selection for any of the other boats. I suggested that we try a coxed pair for Lucerne. It was only three weeks away and it seemed pretty much like a last shot for selection. We were coached by my 'old' pairs partner Adam Clift. The boat flew and at the Lucerne regatta we won a silver medal in a time that was faster than anything that I had ever rowed in pairs. I had never expected to stand on the medal rostrum at Lucerne again, but here I was. It was proof of my indestructibility. Stuart Pearce had nothing on me. With that time, Grobler had no choice but to select us for the World Championships in Indianapolis.

With the summer holidays just beginning I began to wonder how I could divide myself into two people, the rower and the husband. Rather than travel with the rest of the team to an American camp, I settled for a plan where I would train by myself in France for a week, then Jonny would join us for a few days and we would row the pair. A few days after Jonny's return, I would travel back to Bedford to row in a pair there, return to France and so on. I felt guilt everywhere – guilt at not spending enough time with my family as well as remorse that I wasn't committed enough to training. The surreal nature of events was compounded by the situation of our new cox, Hayden Bass. He had to get down from a healthy 61 kilos to just 50 kilos; he simply smoked and drank black coffee for four weeks. Of course, sometimes the dehydration he induced caused him to 'lose it' on occasions. The same happened to me that summer when I returned to France after a few days training in Bedford.

I was travelling with my mother (my father still being in hospital). But due to a mix-up over ferry schedules we had travelled to Le Harve, not Caen. When we arrived late at night, Chris was not there to meet us. Eventually a message got through to her to make the two-hour journey to pick us up. When she arrived some time after 1am she was frustrated and annoyed, having had to leave Frank and bottle with her sister-in-law. I was tired and angry too. It was a volatile mix and an incorrect word or intonation could be the spark to set off a blazing row. My mother and Chris' brother saw us flare up in the road on the roundabout just outside the entrance to the port. The experience shook us both. It was clear to me then that the blame could be fairly and squarely laid at my door for deciding to carry on international rowing.

Yet even though the result in Indianapolis was a disappointing seventh place, it did not stop me scheming to find a place in the team for the next season. Mercifully, a serious back injury intervened in February. Up until then, I had been training 11 sessions a week. But it was not all over yet. I stepped back into a boat for the first time that summer, the week before selection trials for the coxed pair. My back injury made me feel stiff and upright but I was determined to chance selection for the 19th time. My then partner, Richard Manners, had a similar injury. We creaked and buckled our way up the Henley course, with dreams of a summer in France and World Championship glory in our minds. When the times were announced, Grobler said we were too slow to go. It was my last attempt to row in the World Championships. My age, lifestyle and health had finally caught up with me. In the end, rather than my own good sense, it was Grobler's stopwatch that delivered the coup de grace.

You could be forgiven for thinking that at the grand old age of 38, Steven Redgrave had put himself in the same unenviable position. For all his incredible achievements, as he prepared for the Sydney Olympics he was still at the mercy of Grobler's stopwatch: everything he does is measured, timed, in some way.

The first thing that Grobler did when he arrived at the Leander club was to measure out each 250 metres on the Henley reach precisely. He knows precisely the level of Steven's performance and was aware, more than anybody else, of the toll that advancing years had taken on his ability to beat the best in the world.

But I suppose in a way all that is history now. 'Sir Steven' has achieved the impossible. The iconography of his struggles against his opponents, whether they be foreign oarsmen, diabetes or even a difficult spell in his marriage has long passed into British sporting legend. Perhaps it is the nature of what he has achieved, despite his problems, that has made him such an accessible hero for ordinary folk: seven million people can't be wrong, as they thrillingly found out when they tuned in to watch him win a fifth gold in Sydney. These were unprecedented viewing figures for rowing.

More remarkable than this was the crowd that turned out to watch Steven's 'last race' during his own super sprint event, held at Dorney Lake in October 2000. There were 15,000 people there; the queues stretched back miles, even on to the M4 motorway. But what was remarkable was the kind of people that they were; just ordinary folk, the type that you would never expect to see turn up to watch a rowing event during a hot summer's day, let alone a cold autumn afternoon.

They were there to pay homage; to catch a glimpse of the man himself, maybe even to grab one of the hundreds of autographs that he signed on that day. Since then the legend has grown: Sports Personality of the Year, a knighthood. There are even plans afoot for a feature film on his life. So you might think that it is a little grandiose of me to compare my own experiences with those of Steven's. Perhaps you're right, although at least the story of his journey to Sydney is worth hearing once more. It is a tale which at the time stirred things in me, whether I was looking on from afar or a part of the events themselves. Much of that was to do with the stress that I knew lurked beneath the impassive exterior of the model Olympian, the ideal racer, the world's greatest rower.

It was in Atlanta, during the 1996 Games, that the pressure boiled over for all to see. He knew that he had let himself in for most of it. Since 1992, both he and Pinsent had been promising the world that they would deliver another gold in Atlanta. The pressure of racing other crews was bad enough, but it turned into a nightmare when the full glare of the media spotlight turned on him in Atlanta.

At the press conference after the first heat he'd expected to meet 20 to 30 journalists – there were over 200. Steven was shocked. It was a very public reminder that people had been listening to his promises of the last four years. In that moment the thought that had lurked in his at the back of his mind for four years surfaced. If he did not deliver on his promise, his whole public image, the one that he'd been so careful to cultivate, would be destroyed.

Once outside the conference, his anxiety increased markedly. I'd seen him in the boat park that week. He was moody and tetchy, arguing with Pinsent and Grobler about the pitch on his boat. Earlier, between outings, he had walked around the back of the grandstand, hoping to get some solace from the pressure that he felt under. Instead, he felt more pressure as fear gripped him. He found himself saying, 'You physically can't do this, you're going to blow this.' He was near to tears and he coped the only way he knew how, by putting a picture in his mind of his chief opposition, the Australians. Then the confidence slowly began to return, blotting out his fear as he saw himself as the world's greatest rower once more.

However, the fear was never far away and it surfaced most dramatically with his famous 'Shoot me!' comment. The first thing that crossed his mind after the line, when he had beaten the Australians, was that he never wanted to put himself under such pressure again. Of course, the lure of Sydney and a fifth gold, or the fear of stopping   which was it? – proved too great. Hadn't he proved to himself that he had the resources to deal with stress?

It wasn't always the case. For much of that time, like me, Steven thought that he existed in a relatively stress-free environment: a nice bit of exercise in the morning in a calm environment, finishing in the afternoon to maybe play some golf. After all, he was doing what he loved – wasn't he?

These days, though, with two episodes of colitis, not to say his discovery of diabetes, behind him he can see the reality. When we had trained and sculled together back in '82, under Mike Spracklen's tutelage, stomach problems had been the sign for stress. I remembered that Spracklen started to think that Steven was putting it on to miss training. To both of them now, it is clear that these were the first physical signs of stress.

If you talk to him about it now, the chances are that he will talk about this reaction as his weak link. So in one sense the perfect racing machine has at last come to terms with his own physical frailties.

That Achilles heel was first thrust into the spotlight in the run-up to the Barcelona Olympics. The previously invincible pair of Redgrave and Pinsent began to look vulnerable. They lost the national trials to the Searles and although Steven won in Cologne three weeks later, he later lost to the fast Slovenians in Essen.

By then, Steven had already started shitting some seven or eight times a day. He rationalised that it was the effects of a mild form of salmonella which he had contracted during a South African training camp earlier that spring. But it still couldn't explain why he was struggling on almost anything he did. He felt powerless when he couldn't even hold '1.50' splits on steady state 'ergo' sessions. He had become just an 'ordinary' rower. Neither he, nor anybody else, knew why.

So the fear of the unknown, which had always floated around unacknowledged at the back of his mind, started to gnaw at him – although it did not stop him trying to complete as much of his enormous training load as he could. Resting achieved little, while training even at 80 per cent capacity would at least give him something to do.

In fact, as much as anything it was the level of sessions that he was doing that persuaded the specialists who examined him initially to exclude the possibility of ulcerative colitis. Clearly a patient with such a disease could not be training 15 times a week. Perhaps in the end they had to rewrite the medical textbooks because eventually the truth had to emerge. Redgrave's colon was badly inflamed.

Reassuringly, the effect of the medication was almost immediate. What's more, Steven now had a condition that could explain away all his poor form. Nevertheless, his ability to perform at the level that he knew was required to win the Games left a huge question-mark in his mind.

The effect of that doubt on him is clear when you talk to Steven about his best performances. It was in the opening heat of the Barcelona Olympics. He and Pinsent demolishing their main rivals, Slovenia. In that moment, Steven knew that he had overcome his illness and would surely win another Olympic gold. As he paddled back from the finish he felt the goose pimples rise up on the back of his neck. To this day, it still ranks in his mind as one of the pair's best-ever rows and remains, for him, a more fulfilling moment than crossing the line to win his third Olympic gold, which he did in the final a week later.

Between Barcelona and Atlanta, his illness must have seemed like just a coda in his career as Steven demolished both world and Olympic records. After Atlanta, perhaps it was easier for him to write off his impulsive 'Shoot me!' comment as a momentary aberration, rather than the inner plea of a tortured body demanding a rest, a plea that was somehow wrenched up from his gut and broke free in a moment of unguarded weakness. But then so much of Steven's life has been about facing his weaknesses, or at least those things which he thinks are his weaknesses.

After Atlanta at least (surprisingly for a triple Olympic champion) for the first time in his career he no longer had to worry about being overdrawn at the bank. A lucrative sponsorship deal with a financial services company, Lombard, brokered over a round of 18 holes with BBC television's sports anchorman Steve Rider, ensured as much. For four months Steven took every speaking engagement on offer. Sometimes he was present at two functions a day, at a going rate of around £4,000. He was at last reaping the fruits of his labours.

It also made him rowing's first recognisable celebrity. He was surprised by Michael Aspel (in front of a live television audience of 11 million) whilst starting Saturday's National Lottery draw. The subsequent *This Is Your Life* biopic was televised the following week.

It was just one factor in a changing lifestyle for him. Steven was now being regularly recognised in the supermarket or, on the occasions that he and Ann were able to get out to a meal, in a restaurant. All too often, though, the reality is that a 'quiet night out together' turned out to be a charity dinner where the two of them had to sit next to others and Steven had the pressure, not only of making a speech but also of being in bed early enough for training the next morning.

Public speaking produced its own pressure for a very private man. Steven is an introvert who has been thrust – somewhat unwillingly – into the full glare of the world's media spotlight. His sometimes cumbersome manner of expressing himself ensured that he had no chance of winning the possibly inappropriately named BBC Television Sports Personality of the Year award after Atlanta. Did it really take five golds before he proved his worth for the award?.

At least these days the introvert has learnt to become adept at presentations. Steven doesn't use notes but draws on his own feelings and rowing experiences and, in some ways, public speaking is something that he has grown to enjoy. But in reality, it is all part of the 'job', where charity work, promotion and motivational speaking have become an extension of

Hampton, 2000: Steve and Ann Redgrave perform a joint opening ceremony of Hampton School's new boathouse. Post-Sydney, Ann was happy to bask in the light of her husband's achievement, knowing that her support had been a crucial factor in his success.

every top sports star's career. To those who see him speak, he seems completely at home. Often, though, the opposite is the case. When he gets the chance, Steven will always shun media attention. When the press came to talk to the crew as a whole, he would try and stand back, letting others speak.

This man's favourite place is at home where he loves to 'slob out', his feet adorned in his favourite pair of slippers in front of the television, with his family around him. But a family creates pressures of its own. Sitting in front of the television is just not possible when his children have been waiting for him to come in and take them out. Steven wanted to relax, yet he also wanted to spend time with his children. These pressures have increased since his daughters began school. When Zak, their third child, arrived in 1997 the pressures multiplied. In addition, with so many absences through foreign training camps, Redgrave has reluctantly had catch much of their childhood over the phone.

There were pressures on his marriage too. These started to emerge just after the birth of Sophie, their second child. Ann was fed up that their life seemed to be completely dominated by Steven's sport. She had her own medical practice near Marlow to run, as well as the responsibilities of being the team doctor. No doubt the demands of another baby exacerbated this situation. She felt that they could never catch up on old friends, or just pop away for the weekend because Steven always had to be at the Leander club – every morning – and if he wasn't, then he was most likely out of the country on training camp, leaving Ann to fend for herself.

The situation began to polarise as resentments and blame hung in the air. Ann saw her demands for a more 'normal' life as reasonable, while Steven thought that he needed – and probably deserved – unquestioning support for what he had always regarded as his job. Frustrations increased as Steven retreated more into his shell on the occasions when Ann would try to raise matters.

That much has been pretty much public knowledge in the tabloids since Sydney. So, too, was their decision to attend joint counselling sessions. What isn't so clear are the circumstances that led up to that. I can only guess that Ann may have presented Steven with some kind of warning as to what may happen if they did not agree to work on their relationship with somebody. It can't have been an easy thing for Steven to have to do. Talking about his feelings for his wife in front of somebody else may have been his worst kind of nightmare. But in the end it proved to be the step that, more than anything, may have helped him achieve his aim of a fifth gold.

That much was to become clear in the months after the World Championships in Aiguebelette when Steven in his new coxless four seemed as invincible as his pair had once been. Together with Foster, Cracknell and Pinsent, he won the World Championships with room to spare. The September break afterwards gave him a chance to take his first holiday with Ann since his children had been born. Two weeks in the Bahamas would give him a chance to recharge his batteries for the forthcoming season. Little did he know that his problems were only just beginning.

Diabetes came first. He came home to a weekend full of engagements, followed by his first training session at Leander on the Monday. He felt shattered but put it down to jet lag. That afternoon, though, he began to feel very thirsty and started to drink lots of fluid. It was when he was on his fourth pint of blackcurrant juice that he started to think that things weren't quite right. Instinctively, he tested his urine with some dipsticks that Ann had at home. It showed that he had sugar in his blood. His wife told him to see the GP. That afternoon, he was in hospital, by the evening he was injecting himself with his first shots of insulin.

Steven did not have time to contemplate the fact that his rowing career might now be over. In the car on the way to hospital he thought, 'Well, I've had a good innings.' But within a few hours, the specialist was telling him what he wanted to hear; there was no need to stop rowing although his new condition would take some managing. When he heard this, Steven breathed a sigh of relief and thought, 'Business as usual.'

Of course, it was not that simple. It was crucial that Steven could learn to regulate his sugar and insulin intake sufficiently accurately enough to ensure that his body could perform at its peak, both during the demands of the low intensity, long distance work and the shorter high intensity loads during racing. Finding the different levels would take time, but once he got to know his body's needs the rest would be simple. That was the theory – the practice was very different.

In November 1998, Steven was on training camp in South Africa. Back home rumours circulated that he was under-performing compared to every- one else. It seemed like time was catching up with the 'old man'. Nowhere was the difference more marked than on the bike rides. He would often come in over half an hour behind the rest of the squad. But he would complete every session; for him, it was a matter of intense pride. He thought his under per- formance was just a matter of getting his blood sugar levels right. Things got worse on his return. His test at the British Olympic Medical Centre showed he had about the level of a member of the women's team. He didn't seem to be so bad on the lower intensity work, but when the final steps came he just folded. There was no option but to return hospital for some intensive tests.

As Christmas approached, colitis reared its head yet again. But this time it was worse. The disease can often be the precursor of a much more serious illness. When he was tested this time, he knew that the doctors were much more concerned about his health than in 1992. Then they had taken four samples from his intestines, now they wanted to take 12. As Britain's greatest athlete lay in the operating theatre with a tube being inserted up his anus, it seemed like his Olympic battles were over.

Instead of facing the Rumanians, or Australians, he thought that he might have to deal with Crohn's disease, or possibly even cancer. On the journey back from Charing Cross Hospital to Marlow, the effects of the operation, combined with the realisation that his decision to continue after Atlanta might have hastened him on to the operating table, made him feel sick. Ann had to stop their car while he puked-up over the barriers on the side of the M4.

Maybe then, his post-Atlanta invitation to 'shoot me' can't have been far from his mind. He was within a whisker of calling it a day without even waiting for the results of the tests. Things got no better when he returned home; he started shitting blood for three or four days. For the first time in his life he played hooky from training – not even telling Grobler what he was doing or where he was going. The man who had always made a virtue of training on Christmas Day, because he was sure that all his rivals were taking it easy then, left the country for a ski resort. As he walked up the aircraft steps, he had no idea whether he would ever again walk into the Leander club and pick up his boat and blades in anger.

He left with his family and Eric Sims, one of his long-standing proletarian mates, who had sculled with Redgrave in the early years. As he relaxed with his family and friend, the pressures of the training programme, media appearances and celebrity recognition disappeared. Now, at least, with his family and Sims around him, he could relax and be himself. Despite his physical symptoms, he began to feel better. It was during that first week that he felt able to ring up Charing Cross Hospital for the results of the tests. As anyone who has ever done it knows, waiting for the results of tests for a possible serious illness creates a challenge all of its own. But for Redgrave it was something that he did together with his wife.

His marriage has clearly been the rock upon which much of his success has been founded. Now, more than ever, when his health was in doubt, Ann's attitude was to prove crucial. It was well known that Ann did not want her husband to continue after Atlanta. Her concerns were as much about his long-term health and well-being as they were of the family's needs, or indeed the imperative for him to develop a life after rowing.

Thus when Steven fell ill, he expected at the least his wife to tell him to call it a day; at worst there would be (with some justification) and 'I told you so'. Instead, there was nothing but partnership and support for his Sydney ambitions. As far as she was concerned, willingly or not, she had agreed to support him in his goal. That meant finding a way, if it were possible, to beat his latest illness.

It must have been of great significance to their relationship that the two of them had been able to listen to each other's cares and concerns within a supportive counselling environment. Goodness knows that Ann already knew how important rowing was in Steven's life. But now that Steven had shared and understood her worries, she felt able to respond by backing him all the way. So Steven's illness, rather than becoming another cause of stress or an obstacle, became a means of bringing the two of them together.

Now Ann could be really involved in Steven's response to the illness. The emphasis, rather than being, 'You don't need to let this thing beat you,' became 'We don't need to let this thing beat us.' It seems crazy to think that diabetes and colitis could have actually helped Steven towards his fifth gold. But through the revitalisation of their relationship, this was just what happened.

As Steven and Ann listened together on the telephone, for the results of the tests, the news was comparatively good – that is if you call the re-emergence of colitis 'good'. There was no sign of Crohn's disease. So it was back on the same medication that he had taken in 1992. He started the course immediately and his condition began to improve quickly. So much so that a week after he returned from skiing, he was able to participate in a series of pairs races. To his delight, despite being the slowest of his four, he more than held his own against other squad members. Up until then, Grobler had said nothing to him about his unscheduled break from training. On his return, Redgrave was expecting 'a real bollocking' from his coach. It never came. The holiday had represented a real psychological turning point for him. However, he was not out of the woods yet. Yet another problem manifested itself.

Hampton 2000: There is much in this book about fathers and sons. Perhaps that's why I was struck by this shot of Zak Redgrave, the weight of his dad's medal slung nonchalently over his shoulders.

His medication for colitis had a dramatic effect on the levels of insulin which were needed to control his diabetes. It was almost the last type of medicine a diabetic trying to control his levels would want to take. Frequently, his blood sugar levels would go haywire. He knew what was wrong with him and what to take to control it; he just couldn't balance the quantities out to achieve a world-class performance. In training he was constantly having to settle for second best. Exasperated, it seemed to him that he was now spending most of his time battling with other things rather than trying to develop himself as an athlete. In addition to this, he began to sense an increasing isolation from the crew (more marked now in the four than the pair). It was him, rather than they, that had to cope with his illness.

Sometimes this feeling was to do with the age difference between him and the rest of the crew. The discussion of the previous afternoon's television programmes among Cracknell and the others (which Steven never felt he had time to watch) would sometimes leave him reflecting on how much older he felt. But after engaging in a bit of youthful sporting banter, the feeling of camaraderie kicked in to reassure him. At these moments Steven felt he was still in his youth: of course, this was a powerful draw for him not only to continue but a motivation to stick with the training.

So through the spring of 1998, he struggled on, although gradually getting on top of his levels. It was a constant game of 'catch up' but during his return to racing, Steven – and the crew – did not exactly cover himself with glory: minus Foster, the four went down to a seven-second defeat at the hands of Rumania. They withdrew to lick their wounds and give Foster time to recuperate. It gave Steven the time he needed.

Wins against the Australian 'Oarsome Foursome' and Danish lightweights at Henley prefaced a crushing defeat of the Rumanians at Lucerne that year. Any trace of the same man whose head was hung over the barrier of the M4 had disappeared. Steven was back to his imperious best, in control of the crew.

That summer I interviewed Steven and the crew after their Lucerne win for BBC *Grandstand*. I knew that for him the Lucerne regatta was a major psychological milestone in charting the extent of his recovery. Before the race I'd noticed that he seemed even more 'psyched' than normal, so my first question struck a chord with him: 'How nervous were you before that race Steven?' He paused for a moment, thinking of his pre-race nerves. His lips parted into a wry smile and he answered, 'Thanks Mart,' as if to say, 'Well you spotted that one.'

After the medal ceremony came a special moment for me; thinking about it now makes me feel slightly embarrassed at my eagerness to sub in at bow for James Cracknell for their wind-down paddle. Cracknell had to rush from the medal rostrum in time to hitch a lift to Denmark. So I got to row in the four'. I enjoyed every second of it.

Lucerne, 1998: The day I subbed in 'Redgrave's Four' during the Lucerne regatta. I relished the occasion. Turn back to the photograph on page 194 and you'll see why everyone was smiling: I'd just told them that Steve could seat race Mulkerrins for his place in our four.

As I rowed back in the bow seat, sitting behind Redgrave's broad bulk, I fantasised about rowing in the crew at bow during the World Championships. When I offered my services to Redgrave – should Cracknell fail to return – as they were de-rigging the boat, he hardly looked up as he threw me a spanner and said, 'Shut up Mart and take a rigger off.' I'd had my dreams a few years back. Steven was still living his.

Later that year he won his 12th gold medal at the Cologne World Championships. With the year that he had just faced, it must surely rank as one of his greatest triumphs.

It was deja vu the following winter, though. He was constantly plagued with illness and his insulin levels were haywire again. Although he produced a respectable performance on the ergometer that November, he did not race in any domestic trials. In February 1999 he missed a fortnight's altitude camp in Spain, with what was described as a bout of 'flu. The cognoscenti suspected that it was as much occasioned by yet another psychological low point from which he needed a break to escape. So once again he faced rumours about his fitness to be in the boat. At one stage the injured Foster was even being touted as Steven's replacement. But the old man held on yet again. With Coode his crew notched up three World Cup wins, defeating the

Danish lightweights again at Henley and taking the world title yet again in St Catherine's with consummate control.

During that series of races he struck me as being more relaxed and carefree than I had seen him for a long time. After the Vienna round of the World Cup, in May, I interviewed him again for *Grandstand*. It went like a dream. Steven was enjoying their victory over a fast Norwegian crew. When we talked, the chemistry felt great, like two old pros, both on top of their work. He candidly revealed that Grobler had told him that he would have no say in the selection battle between Coode and Foster.

It was as surprising to me as it must have been to the audience watching. But Steven preferred to be left out of it, knowing that in a few months time, when Jurgen Grobler considered whether Steven deserved a place in the British four for the Sydney Games, it will be no different; it would be entirely Grobler's call.

Throughout his preparation for Sydney, Steven expected no favours from the German. Viewers who watched BBC television's fly-on-the-wall documentary *Gold Fever* in the weeks before the Sydney Games might have been aware of the unspoken tension in the crew, starting the Olympic season as a 'five'. In effect, Coode, Foster and Redgrave were challenging for just two seats on bowside.

Steven knew that a 37-year-old diabetic, with a history of chronic colitis, could not expect to hold all-corners at bay for much longer.

Of course, in the end we all know that Steven won his place and his fifth Olympic gold. But when I spoke to him at the start of the season, it was clear that the pressure was on. As we talked of the possible scenario of a seat race between him and either Foster or Coode to settle the selection issue, his eyes drew into a furrow. 'Seat racing is something that I've never believed in all my life. My place in a boat is won through the hard graft of a year's training and the fact that I always produce my best performance in the championships at the end of the season.'

What the old gladiator, champion of so many contests in the Olympic arena, was saying was something profound. He had decided that he would not face either Foster or Coode in a sudden-death duel on the Henley reach at dawn, rather he would throw down his blades and walk away. As we talked, his face remained serious. It had the same look of determination which has subdued countless opponents, even before the race had started. After a moment's pause, as if to underline the point, he forcefully said, 'I'm not going to end my career on a seat race.'

'Wow,' I thought, 'he really means it, doesn't he?' Despite the fact that both of us knew that Grobler did not favour seat-racing as a method of selecting crews. This was not a conversation that Steven would have had when he was in his prime, when he was fearless to all-comers.

It was recognition that Steven's age – let alone his health – does not enable him to perform at his peak throughout the whole season. In fact he and Pinsent could only finish a poor third in the Olympic pairs trials. But he'd done enough to suggest that, come the summer, he would be ready for the big occasion. Even that must have looked in doubt after the four suffered two defeats at the Lucerne regatta, just a few weeks before the Sydney Games. After the racing, Steven came round to the press area for interviews. He talked in hushed tones and looked shell-shocked. It was a point that I put to him for the television cameras. He did not deny the shock but refused to believe that the gleam of that fifth gold was any less bright. Ultimately, Steven knew that his greatest strength was his consistency.

Earlier that month we'd watched Pete Sampras chalk up yet another win at Wimbledon. He's a favourite of Steven's. Like him, Sampras has an understated personality: he does not thirst for the limelight, nor does he have a flamboyant style of play. But he has held his own at the top of the sport against all-comers. His consistency may be boring to watch but it is what Steven so admires.

Racing for him is not about reproducing his best performance every time he competes. Steven loves to perform in the comfort zone during races and hates having to perform constantly at the limits of his performance (Grobler's low-intensity training programme has been a major factor in allowing him to continue for as long as he did). Most of the time his opponents are not fast enough to put Steven under the relentless pressure during the middle of a race that he fears.

As Sampras slammed ace number 15 past a bewildered opponent, I remembered Steven saying, 'You know Mart, anybody can produce an outstanding performance once but being a great athlete is not about that. It's about being able to perform close to that level all the time.' At the end of the Lucerne interview, I remembered that comment and thought, 'They'll still win in Sydney.'

On the face of it, it was that 'win' which took Steven into the hearts of the British public in a way that few sportsmen have achieved. However, there is something deeper at work than that. The fireworks and brilliance of an Agassi will always endear him more to the crowd than the 'boringly' consistent Sampras. It is not Steven's ability to win that has earned him that affection but rather his ability to triumph, not just in the face of physical, but also psychological adversity.

Depression is no stranger to Steven. I knew that much when he once unselfishly offered me his help when I was feeling very down. Yet it is what he has been through that has made him a more complete person. So his decision to stop after Sydney came as no surprise to me, or I suspect anyone else. But I suspect that the experience of the four years between Atlanta and Sydney may have prepared him better than ever to face a life without rowing.

Rowing has given Redgrave his life. Everything that has happened to him since Sydney has followed from his decision to pursue his talent to the limits. Of course, to some people that may seem an obsession: after four medals he had nothing more to prove; he may have been damaging his health in the long term; or just not have been willing to face the prospect of a life without the sport that is his métier.

Perhaps his decision in those four years was born out of an obsession. But I suppose that if I had been in his position after Atlanta, my decision might have been no different to his. Now he has chosen to walk away from the sport. All of us know that it will not be an easy path for him to follow. But as the last four years have taught him, it is never that easy to lose an Olympic obsession.

Crises

THE narrow Georgian bridge over the Thames at Henley is always difficult to pass during regatta week and the regatta of July 1996 was no exception. The absence of most of the world's top crews, in preparation for the Atlanta Olympics, had made no difference to the endless flow of bodies on the bridge. Stopping to take a look down the course is always difficult; a shout from a policeman generally follows quickly. But if you found a moment to pause, you would see quite a scene.

Downstream, the grassed lawns and huge tented village hugged the river bank. Further on, the white piles of the regatta course stretch into the distance. About them play the wakes of countless cruisers, punts and pleasure craft of all description. Upstream, nestling just under the bridge, lies the Angel pub, full and noisy. From its beer garden by the river, children sometimes toss crumbs to the flocks of geese and swans that congregate on that side of the bridge to avoid the traffic during regatta week. At night it is full of rowdy rowers, drowning their sorrows at races lost, or celebrating a coveted Stewards' medal won on the Sunday after the regatta. I don't suppose that either myself or Adrian Cassidy thought that this illustrious setting would be where our crises would begin but, looking back on it now, it seemed fated.

On 2 July 1996, a careful onlooker might have seen two coxless pairs slip out from the concrete pontoons and head up the regatta course for the quarter-final stage of the Silver Goblets Cup. Ahead of me in my boat sat Richard Stanhope, my old crewmate and sparring partner. Although neither of us would care to admit it, we were both at the end of our top-class rowing careers. In the other craft sat two much younger men, both former pairs partners of mine: Singfield at bow, while in front of him was Cassidy.

As a junior, Adrian showed real star quality. A natural athlete with a wonderful sense of speed and movement, he became a world junior champion in 1989, despite his relatively small frame. With a drive and determination to succeed at anything he put his hand to, further success in the sport seemed assured. He was on the fringes of the '92 Olympic team but never quite made it. The next year, I rowed behind him as he stroked the British eight to a final place in the World Championships.

The Angel pub at Henley, where Adrian Cassidy suffered a terrible accident.

To him, I was the 'father of the crew, guiding us youngsters along'. But in reality, it was Adrian who had organised and coached the crew, filling the void created by the absence of a proper coach for much of the year. It was in tribute to his leadership skills that his nickname was 'Captain Sensible'. The next winter, I followed him into a pair and rowed on into the next spring. We rowed well but were never quite quick enough to challenge for a seat in the eight, which was what Adrian really wanted. That summer he chose not to go for the coxed pair, the last boat in the team, and we parted amicably. Now, like me, he was pot-hunting at Henley. Both Cassidy and Singfield had been unjustly passed over for Olympic selection that year. The Goblets was meant to be their consolation. That day they did better than us. Ironically, they went on to lose the final to the Austrians, who were the only Olympic boat still in Europe.

Adrian's 'crisis' was not to begin that week. But suddenly and dramatically in the river, down by the Angel pub one evening in November. For me there was no suddenness or drama. In reality it was a much slower and more insidious process. But there was no doubt that its seeds were nurtured that day at Henley, as Stanhope and I went out to face the Swiss lightweights in the Goblets. I'd had a very sore throat all week. In addition, I'd been staying up very late to finish writing the comments on the sixth form reports. Later, I could do it in a quarter of the time; then, it was a nightmare. My spelling had never been great, yet here was I having to check all my colleagues' comments before they went out to parents, as well as

Henley, 1996: Adrian Cassidy, right, with Jon Singfield racing down the Henley during what was a fateful year for Adrian.

Henley, 1996: Two old war-horses charge for the line. Richard Stanhope and I just fail to catch the Swiss pair. The look of agonised desperation on my face depicts the personal crises which was looming in my life.

finding something useful to say. The pressure got to me, more than the time. But by Henley, I was drained.

Outwardly, there seemed no cause for alarm. My glands weren't up. It wasn't the first time that I had experienced these symptoms, raced and got away with it. Of course, I was younger then. Maybe it wasn't the cleverest thing in the world to race with them at Henley and, of course, I knew better. God knows I'd given enough people the same advice. But I thought that we had a genuine chance of winning the event. When you're 38 and have never won the Goblets before, that's a pretty strong reason. It rode roughshod over all the good intentions that I had of pulling out on health grounds.

We lost heroically by one foot. We even woke up the enclosures who roared us on. It even made the newpapers the next day: 'The old war horses Cross and Stanhope...' A close race always left me drained; with a virus it knocked me out. In a way I was grateful for the defeat because at least I didn't have to fight with the 'good intentions' of my conscience. School had finished and I had an all-expenses paid trip to the Atlanta Olympics as a BBC Radio 5 Live reporter. After that, it was off to our French house for the rest of the summer. I was sure that then my tired body could recover. But it was not to be.

It didn't help that I was just a spectator in Atlanta. I had raced most of the oarsmen on Lake Lanier and I wanted to be out there in a boat. It was worse that I was also there as the athletes' representative. My credibility in that post had, in part, rested on being active in the British team. But that was over two years ago. To establish my credentials in front of the rowers, I was desperate to get out on the water and check out the already perfect course installations. Failing that, I would hang out in the ergometer room with my buddies like the US coach Mike Teti. There, it was easy to get drawn into a little session on the 'erg'. But even then I began to worry that the little training I was doing wasn't a great idea. Being there with all these top-class athletes was infectious in its self; despite feeling tired, I wanted, even needed, to train. More often than not I would start a gentle session only to stop, feeling vulnerable and stupid.

On top of that I was fully stretched between two jobs. Race commentary was fun but demanding. With rowing's early start it generally meant working flat out from 7am to midday. The positions were great. But they were on the wrong side of the course to the rowers. So I had to spend the rest of the day on the other side of the course, fulfilling my responsibilities as chairman of the Athletes' Commission. There was no shortage of controversial issues. With the number of rowers strictly controlled by the IOC for the first time, there was no accreditation for each team's spare rowers. They'd been living with the team for a couple of months in training camp, only to be dumped by their officials at Atlanta Airport, without accreditation or often even Olympic kit. It was a scandal and nobody in the IOC much seemed to care, which left the FISA Athletes' Commission as their only forum.

It wasn't surprising that I left the Olympics feeling more tired than when I had arrived. Even a month's summer break at Le Presbrytère in Normandy didn't improve matters. I returned home to start a new term at school, feeling low and worried about losing my voice. With hindsight the signals that I was depressed were crystal clear. The viral symptoms were my body's way of telling me to slow down and rest more. But I never took the time to listen to them. Rationally, I knew that I had to stop trying to be an international rower sometime; that it was a crazy lifestyle for someone with my commitments.

But it was emotion that drove me on. Whenever I got in a boat, it was like popping Viagra. Not that it did much for my sex life, but without it I felt impotent. Without rowing, life felt 'ordinary', dull and drab. When I had raced that season, beating the Australians, or the Dutch, I'd got such a buzz through my system. Even at my age, I could still perform and beat people. Now, as it looked like the sport was slipping away from me, all the adolescent insecurities that my success at rowing had masked returned to bug me. I'd been on a drug; without the sport I was going cold turkey and paying the consequences. The longer my symptoms went on, the more anxious I became. I was desperate to have an identifiable illness to call my own. That September, I gave my old roommate from the 1984 Olympics, Richard Budgett, a ring.

He'd seen all this before. As the doctor in charge of Olympic medicine, he'd helped plenty of over-trained athletes. It was to him that I turned to then. Little did I know that he was to play a central role as my depression deepened that winter. He didn't look much like a doctor. Come to think of it, he never looked like much of a rower either. Co-ordination was never his strong point. The Cambridge coaches passed him over for a seat in the Blue Boat. But they never saw the heart of a lion within his 6ft 7ins frame. No matter how tired he was, you could always ask him for an extra effort and he would respond. Perhaps his strengths were masked by the great tooth-filled smile he kept almost permanently on his face, or the inane guffaw to match. Nevertheless, the Olympic gold was the making of him. He used his 'celebrity status' among his fellow physicians to build a niche for himself as a sports doctor.

It was in the dull grey buildings of Northwick Park Hospital in Harrow, headquarters of the BOMC, that we met. In between the back-slapping 'old buddies bit' he proceeded to look like he'd heard it all before from so many other athletes. What I had was post-viral syndrome – or even better from my point of view – over-training syndrome. He gave me some charts to keep track of my symptoms, a blood test (nothing wrong, of course) and a very light training programme. I could exercise for ten minutes a day, six days a week, and gradually build up to 20 minutes if nothing had deteriorated. I had to keep my pulse down below 130 but I felt ecstatic. At last I seemed to have a real disease that I could own. I felt much better, when I told people who asked what was wrong with me, that I had 'over-training syndrome'. What's more, 'Budge' had given me a path to health and fitness. I did not know then how torturous that path was about to become.

September rolled into October and on into November. Nothing seemed to change. Well why would it? These things take months, some times years. But I didn't have that long. There were things to do, especially at school where I was in line for promotion. That precluded me taking any time off work, so I struggled on. My psyche made it easy for me to adopt the role of a wounded soldier who struggles on through the campaign, bearing his heavy pack heroically. Being me, though, I didn't exactly keep it to myself. Everybody knew that I was suffering. Not least Chris at home, who was sympathetic at first but starting to lose patience, particularly as when I arrived home I generally flopped into a chair and did little to help around the house.

And towards the end of November, for the first time I began to worry that I might have something seriously wrong with me. I noticed a swelling on the left side of my neck. Something there was ballooning out when I swallowed. But what concerned me most were the twinges I was starting to feel on the left side of my body. I felt guilty going to see 'Budge' about this problem, so I went to my GP. It was the first time that the 'C' word – cancer – was spoken aloud. She sent me for a chest X-ray – 'Just to reassure you Mr Cross'. It was negative, of course. But the worries had taken root. At the back of my mind I was already fighting a heroic battle with myself. The only thing that would stop me from rowing until I dropped would be the 'king of diseases' – cancer. A fitting end to an apparently endless career.

So my mind began to twist reality. The whole thing took on an element of fate. Others could see what was happening, but not me. That much was clear over the New Year when the annual reunion of my 1988 Olympic four took place. Although they were all younger than me, they had stopped international rowing long before I had. They knew of the frustration of 'letting go' and could see that I was still maniacally refusing to do so. My tenacity was a quality that they all knew and had seen put to good use in many a race or training session; now it was working against me. One of the crew, John Maxey, now a Jersey GP, assured me time and time again that my symptoms were not caused by cancer, that it would have shown up in the blood tests. Quite rightly, he pointed to stress as the likely cause of my ill health. I heard but I didn't want to listen.

One piece of advice I did heed was to try to get some more tests done, to try to find out what the problem really was. So in January, worried at the continuing twinges on my left flank, I returned to Budgett at the BOMC. He listened reassuringly and again, to allay my worries, sent me for an abdominal X-ray. When the image came back it seemed as if something was blocking my large intestine. He assured me that it was almost certainly not cancer, particularly for someone of my age (although I could think of plenty of young people who had died from the disease). Just to 'reassure me', though, he arranged for me to see a consultant gastro-entorologist. I left feeling happy that things were on the move. But by the time I got home, I was a bag of nerves.

From that night on, I didn't sleep. My anxieties now began to run riot through my life and in a much more public way than hitherto, particularly as my symptoms seemed to multiply: mysterious twinges appeared, pins and needles came and went and still I had the same sore throat and tiredness. I became an assiduous reader of the medical textbooks in the school library (or indeed of medical columns in all manner of journals). Each day, I found some new (and usually serious) disease that was causing my symptoms. In the very short term the process of looking offered some relief. But, of course, a few minutes later the anxieties only piled up further. How I managed to do my job I don't know, although the fact that many colleagues were prepared to spend some time giving me a shoulder to cry on was invaluable.

One of them was my therapist. Maurice Xiberras had just turned 60. He was a natural athlete with looks to match. You might have easily have mistaken him for a forty-something, particularly when you saw him nutmeg a boy while playing for the staff soccer team. In the classroom, he was a brilliant if unconventional and sometimes forgetful history teacher.

His experiences outside stretched from being deputy leader of Gibraltar's legislature in the 1970s to (rather incongruously, for a socialist) being a reserve major in the army. Following the breakup of his marriage he had in desperation turned to therapy and later qualified as a body analytical psychotherapist. It was pretty weird going to deep therapy with a friend, particularly someone of whom I was nominally 'in charge'. But his understanding and compassion kept me going, although in truth, during those first few months the sessions served as little more than momentary relief from my anxiety.

The whole thing was made to seem even more strange because the two of us were also joint facilitators of a kind of 90-minute therapy session with groups of 17-year-old students. There would be 25 of us, sitting in a big circle, and the atmosphere would often be charged. Life Skills was a unique course, more encounter than therapy, where the boys spoke of their worries at home, pressures in school and difficulties in relationships and family life. It was challenging enough anyway, but with thoughts of cancer tests drifting in and out of my mind, each week became a real test.

At home I was struggling too. We were having an extension built to our kitchen and living room. I wasn't sure if we could really afford it (who ever does?) but it was going ahead anyway. Demolition of internal walls, with hordes of builders tramping through a house asking for cups of tea, causes tensions at the best of times. They must have wondered what planet I was on as I wandered about the house like a zombie in the mornings. Perhaps all their clients were as miserable as me? They seemed a happy enough bunch with (I fondly imagined) apparently simple, uncomplicated lives. At times I fantasised that if I'd been a builder with an 'uncomplicated' life, none of this would have happened. But then I found out that one of them was still on Prozac to help his depression.

I hadn't yet started on anti-depressants myself. I'd tried sleeping tablets but they seemed to make no difference to me, so I stopped taking them. As my symptoms seemed to worsen, I took to any number of measures that seemed to offer relief. Ringing cancer help lines during free lessons was a favourite. It was sound advice and help I received, but any relief was purely transient. The same was true of the alternative medicine that I tried. Reflexology was a wonderful respite, but as my anxieties multiplied it became impossible to really benefit. Despite spending £30 on Chinese herbal medicine, I only stuck that treatment out for two days. I had, however, been assiduous with my anti-allergy diet. That my symptoms were caused by some allergic reaction was another of my hopes. I cut out red meats, dairy produce, wheat, caffeine, eggs, potatoes – you name it – from my diet. It did not 'cure' me, the most obvious effect being that I began to lose weight.

I hadn't weighed myself until I stepped on to Mr Jaycena's scales in his room at the Northwick Park Hospital in late January. I realised, to my horror, that I was the lightest that I'd been since I was a schoolboy. Of course, this was a clear sign that I had cancer. For some reason the thought that sleepless nights and a radical diet had caused me to lose three or four kilos never entered my head. Jaycena told me that I had IBS (irritable bowel syndrome), itself caused by stress. In fact, just to reassure me he decided to perform a colonoscopy a week later. Instead of feeling reassured, I became even more anxious.

I was so certain of the result of my colonoscopy, that the unpleasantness of having a metal tube with a camera on the end of it shoved up my rectum didn't bother me. I had even thought through how I would react, seeing the bloody mass inside of me in glorious Technicolour there on the video screen in front of me as I lay in the operating theatre. I was genuinely surprised, when the camera showed that I had a perfect colon. My blood tests were absolutely normal. Although (as I had unhelpfully learnt from the medical books) that was not necessarily a guarantee of anything. Still, for a few hours I was happy. I even went out for a celebratory scull. It was then that I began to feel briefly free and unencumbered by illness – like I could start training for a fresh season again. But then I realised that I couldn't. I still had the same symptoms and 20 minutes exercise was my maximum. It was then, on the river, just in front of St Mary's Church at Hampton, that I remembered that I still had a lump in my throat. That was it; I obviously didn't have bowel cancer. It was something else instead.

I had long since forgotten what a night's sleep felt like. I'd become accustomed to listening to the noises of the middle of the night, waiting for that distant sound of the first train to clatter its way to Waterloo, signalling that the long night was almost over. I tried Temazapan but it had little effect. I stopped taking it after a week, concerned that I might get addicted. I suppose this was a sign that, underneath it all, I knew I'd be all right. But to all intents and purposes I was convinced that I wasn't going to last the year out. So I did without sleep as I rolled on to see the next specialist. This time it was a consultant ENT surgeon, who looked at the swelling in my throat and said, 'What swelling? There's nothing there.' What he meant was that from his point of view, there was nothing to worry about. He seemed not to take me seriously but offered me a CT scan 'just for reassurance'. When I thought about the anxiety of my last wait for a test, I 'bottled' and said no.

So, the medical profession did not think that there was anything seriously wrong with me. But what did they know? At any rate, my crisis deepened as my anxiety served up another symptom, drastic heartburn. None of the drugs, herbal or otherwise, seemed to do anything for it. My potential list of diseases began to increase exponentially. At first it was angina, but when my GP practically laughed me out of his surgery, telling me to get my head sorted out, I found a much better explanation: stomach cancer! It all made sense. The lump in my neck was a 'secondary' lymph gland, swelling up in response. Not content with finding just one 'secondary', I began to develop the remarkable facility of finding foreboding lumps, bumps and spots all over my body.

Not surprisingly, Chris began to despair of me. My behaviour was bringing a whole new meaning to the commitment 'in sickness and in health'. In desperation she now phoned up 'Budge'. He had never really seen this side of me. Whenever I'd seen him, I'd always put on the old 'rowing mate' face. Chris now told him how things really were at home. We went to see him in the cramped bustle of his Acton surgery. When he realised that my problems were psychological, he gave me short shrift, telling me that none of my 'lumps' were anything of the sort, although he did say that the swelling in my neck was worth another look and referred me to another specialist.

But both Chris and 'Budge' knew that my real need was to see a psychiatrist. My father had experienced a breakdown before. Now perhaps the same thing was happening to me. Budge made the necessary appointment for a week hence. To me that route was an irrelevance but I agreed, not least because Budgett had also agreed to refer me to a blood specialist. It was another trek up to Northwick Park with my long-suffering and, by now increasingly despairing, wife. I left school early on Thursday to drive up through the bustle of the afternoon's traffic, through Greenford past Harrow and in to Northwick Park Hospital. I was convinced that I would not be coming home, that the specialist would discover the 'real' cause of my heartburn, which was now intense, and admit me. When she said that levels were fine and that the chest X-ray showed nothing, it did nothing to lift my gloom. Even the offer of an ultrasound scan on my throat in a few days 'just for reassurance' meant little.

The weekend that followed was unbearable. By then I had not slept for weeks. And I had stopped eating. My anxiety was worse than ever. What's more, I was in great discomfort from the acid swilling around my body, giving me acute heartburn. That Sunday, I was now convinced that I hadn't long to go. Chris had pretty much given up listening to my contention that I was seriously ill, with not long to live. With the interests of our children and her own sanity at heart, she'd begun to distance herself from me. I determined that on Monday morning, rather than go the see the psychiatrist, I'd present myself at a hospital casualty unit. They would admit me and that's where I'd stay. That night, all Chris wanted was to get some sleep before the important training contract that she had to begin the next day. All I wanted to do was write my goodbye letters. They were of little literary value.

As Monday morning broke, I was in the very midst of my crisis. But the chores of life still went on. Chris made me drop her at the railway station in the morning and left me to take the kids to child-minders. She tried to get me to promise that I'd keep my appointment with the psychiatrist. But my mind was made up. Still, the normality of life went on around me. Monday morning commuters sat in cars, struggling through the traffic to work, oblivious to my problems. I felt like the condemned man smoking his last cigarette, while all around me nobody cared.

Out of gratitude to 'Budge', I graciously decided to absolve him from the onerous responsibility of not spotting that I had developed stomach cancer. So after I had dropped the kids off, I phoned him up. Remarkably, I got through the first time. I told him that I 'forgave him' and was about to go to a casualty department. He pleaded with me to keep the appointment with the psychiatrist and begged me not to go to casualty, where, he said, I would get short shrift.

Something in his voice made me think again. I don't know why, but I agreed to keep the appointment. Before I left home, I called my close friend David Tanner, who had been highly supportive of me throughout. I knew that he took Mondays 'off' from his job as executive director of British International Rowing. I asked him if he could take me up to the hospital and thankfully he agreed. Tanner always treated my woes with a healthy scepticism and somehow, when he turned up, I at least felt able to cope. We drove up to a private psychiatric hospital in Harrow on the Hill. I still thought this was a completely pointless exercise. I was dressed in scruffy rowing kit, unshaven, hollow-eyed and about as low as a person could get.

I perched on the edge of one of the psychiatrist's comfortable chairs and in a deadpan, matter-of-fact voice, told him my story. I showed him what I thought was the shrunken muscle bulk on my once-proud forearms and told him what I thought was wrong with me. Nothing seemed to startle him, apart from my contention that I'd had no sleep at all for the last three weeks. 'What, no sleep?' he said. The tone of surprise in his voice made me feel almost proud for an instant. Not surprisingly he diagnosed me as clinically depressed. He was willing to admit me to the private psychiatric hospital then and there, so I could rub shoulders with the minor showbiz celebrities that checked in, looking for cures to their depression. Unlike them, I didn't have over £2,000 a week to pay for the privilege, so instead he referred me to an NHS hospital, although they couldn't see me until the evening. I left with a prescription for a hefty dose of anti-depressants and tranquilizers, and feeling completely desolate and wondering where to spend the rest of the day.

By some coincidence, which looking back now seems remarkable, I remembered that weeks earlier I'd booked an appointment see 'Budge' that very morning at the Olympic Medical Centre. Northwick Park Hospital was just a short drive away. So, once again, it was back to 'Budge' as I waited to keep my appointment at the psychiatric department of Roehampton Hospital. As I sat in the corner of his surgery, images of Budgett and me taking on and beating the world in the Olympics flashed through my mind. I wondered what he must he must think of me now, this once fine athlete and friend of his brought so low?

He was desperate to assure me that there was nothing wrong with my stomach and that my best course was to seek a cure for my depression. I would have none of it, so with a decisive move, characteristic of his pushes in the rowing boat, he picked up the telephone and arranged for an immediate endoscopy, an examination of my stomach by a video camera passed down my throat. Although it was only a couple of hours' wait, they were the two most stressful hours that I'd ever spent. I was convinced that the operation would discover cancer. As I sat in the waiting room, with David Tanner being as supportive as he could be, my blood pressure was sky high. On the operating table I swallowed the metal and plastic tube of the video camera and looked up at the video screen in front of me. In a few seconds, it was clear that my insides were as clean as a whistle.

I was reprieved. From that moment on, I lost all the sensations of heartburn, and my mood swung from one extreme to another. Almost immediately, I felt relaxed, even laid back. A member of the human race again. My mood lightened and for the first time in ages, I had a smile on my face. I could sense the relief in David's face too. It had been a hell of an ordeal for him to go through.

But I still had that appointment at Roehampton Hospital to keep. There, the young doctor on casualty was genuinely incredulous that a person who had been diagnosed as so profoundly depressed a few hours ago by a consultant psychiatrist could now be so lucid, phlegmatic and even humorous. Thankfully, she found no reason for me to stay in the hospital. So instead, I drove home with Chris for a meal in Blubeckers by Hampton Court. It was almost a Jekyll and Hyde transformation. That night I slept for the first time in months. Two days later, I was buying a surprised 'Budge' a drink as I somewhat unexpectedly turned up at old rowers reunion.

But of course, Jekyll and Hyde it wasn't. To make it sound that everything was completely all right from then would be disingenuous. I still suffered from a feeling of anxiety for some time – although nothing like that which I'd been through. Gradually the tension did lessen, although the one or two panic attacks that I experienced that spring were particularly unpleasant. I've no doubt that they were necessary; like the aftershocks from an earthquake that must rumble on for a few weeks or months afterwards, in reaction to the initial shock. It was great to be back with the rest of humanity, although it was from the perspective of a different person. Gradually, I began to dabble again in rowing, doing gentle sculls or short jogs, but it would never be with the same intensity and sense of need as before. My 'crisis' seemed to enable me to finally let go of international rowing, recognising that it would not be the end of the world.

Of course, it was, to say the least, inconvenient that the only way I could deal with the reality of stopping life after so long as an international rower was by experiencing an apparently life-threatening crisis. But spending 20 years maniacally pursuing a career as an international athlete has to have some consequences. The anxiety that I felt, when I was ill was very similar in kind to the pressures that I had felt while waiting for big races – except then I knew it would stop once the race was over.

In the worst moments of my depression, I could not see my mental torment ceasing. No doubt there was something of that same manic quality that pushed me on during races, particularly in the last few hundred metres.

Maybe I was mad to carry on rowing as long as I did. But then as George III replied to the Duke of Cumberland, who protested to him about the intensity of the young General Wolfe, 'Mad is he? Then I wish he'd bite a few of my other generals.'

When I look at many of the other rowers that I raced who were much taller, stronger or had better physiology than me, there must have been some reason why I was able to beat them. If it was because of the same passion and intensity as Wolfe had, then so be it – my 'crisis' was something I had to go through. I have learnt a lot from it, though, not least how to better deal with similar pressures that will come my way. But one of the most enlightening aspects of dealing with a crisis is encountering people who in reality have to deal with something far worse than you yourself do.

One of those people was Adrian Cassidy, although as he breezed into the Angel pub in November 1996, surrounded by his friends, he had his mind full of the joys of a stag night. He had no idea of the crisis that was about to engulf him.

He had every right to expect that the last few months of 1996 would see his luck turn in what had been (in rowing terms), a rotten year for him.

Desperate to make the Olympic team, he had pushed his body over reasonable limits, with the result that he fell victim to the dreaded over-training syndrome during a winter camp in Seville. It debilitated him for some weeks and he never got the chance to show his true worth. He was cruelly dropped from the Olympic squad early in 1996, rather curiously as he remembers it, in the High Street of Henley-on-Thames.

Sean Bowden, his coach, was more interested in rowing brawn than in what Adrian's racing brain had to offer. After a few very depressing weeks, he began to look into the future; there was always the Sydney Olympics, by which time he could develop more strength. With a course at Cambridge planned for the autumn, it seemed as good a year as any for him to marry his fiancée, Siobhan. He proposed that Easter. The marriage was to be in December.

His stag night was on 9 November. It started in London and the party moved out to Henley later in the evening. The natural location was the Angel pub, just by the bridge. It was an unusually warm evening for the time of year and with a few beers inside them it seemed an appropriate occasion to go skinny-dipping in the Thames. A few of the lads beat him to to the water and there was much laughing and shouting as they all trod water, watching the naked Adrian do his graceful, flashy swan dive into the dark waters of the Thames.

Of course, it was bad luck that he chose the exact spot where a plank was fixed under the water. Even worse luck that he did not see it. At first he thought that he had just hit his head awkwardly on the water, the way you do when you execute a high dive. But his friends, Dave Gillard and Damian Rimmer, could see the blood on his head.

What they couldn't see was what had happened inside his neck. The impact had broken the two postulate vertebrae at C6 and C7 in his neck. At C6, the spinal process snapped off. At C7 the vertebrae just burst open. The trauma severed half of his spinal column, which immediately ballooned up. Adrian's neck was broken. His 'crisis' was about to begin.

The first time that he realised he was paralysed was when he tried to kick his legs up to get out of the water. He couldn't move them and his friends had to drag him out. They laid him on a bench in the pub. Dave Gillard punched his leg as hard as he could, shouting with anxiety, 'Can you feel that?' But Gillard's blows were in vain. Adrian felt nothing, his leg was completely dead. His mates dressed him, which with hindsight was stupid. But Rimmer sensibly held his head secure as they waited for the ambulance.

That night, as he lay in the geriatric ward of Reading Hospital, with patients shouting and wailing, Adrian felt like he was in Bedlam. But rather than panic, he coolly thought through his options. He could still move his arms. Could still have kids? That was if Siobhan still wanted to marry him in this condition. Even with that 'worse case' scenario, life was still worth living, he reckoned. In the middle of the night his fierce determination – that would have served any Olympic eight proud – did not desert him as he tried for two hours to move the big toe of his right foot. He convinced himself that he saw an infinitesimal move and called out for the nurse, who thought he was 'a bit mental' or something. But being positive was something that Adrian had learnt the hard way.

He was very close to his mother, who had had died of cancer in the middle of his finals. He remembers the day well. It was the day of the qualifying rounds for Henley regatta. One might almost be tempted to say that the fact it happened in that place was fate. Certainly it seemed to be stretching a coincidence too far. Perhaps it was serendipity. Whatever, Adrian learnt much from the way that his mother dealt with her illness. He believed that she never fully believed that she was healed. While in remission, she would have dreams of running away from these grey cancer cells. When she fell ill again, as a devout Catholic she put her faith in Padre Pio. Adrian felt that was handing over responsibility so that she didn't have to take it herself. From then on he decided that if he got ill, he would take responsibility for getting better. He believed in the healing power of the mind and positive thinking.

But when he was meeting his fiancée for the first time in hospital, he took the strength of character of his mother, who could keep a brave face no matter how bad things were. He had not heard of Stoke Mandeville Hospital before but it was to be his home for the next few months. He was to be married there too. It must have been difficult for Siobhan to think of marrying a man paralysed from the chest down, who was held rigidly in traction, who could only drink through a straw and whose bed moved from side to side every few hours to avoid him getting bed sores. But she stuck by him.

They got married in the seminar room above his ward. Adrian's uncle brought in a shirt, cut the back out of it and dressed him in it, complete with a flower. He was wheeled to the lift and taken upstairs, looking at his bride and guests around him out of the corner of his eye, or from the mirror above his bed.

Perhaps at this point in Adrian's story, you're wondering how he felt during the ceremony. Looking back now, it seems a superfluous question. But as he told me his story, I felt drawn to ask him how he felt when he spoke the words '...in sickness and in health'. At that moment Adrian's eyes began to well up. I felt mine water too, just as the eyes of the 'congregation' had done on that day.

He is still in wonder of the 'awesome nature' of the commitment that his new bride made on that day. He thought that if the two of them could go through this thing now, then they could face anything. His brother David gave a short best man's speech. As Adrian repeated it to me, tears ran down his face. At the risk of over-sentimentalising events, a small part of it bears repeating here: 'Ever since Adrian has been in hospital it's been grey, cold and murky... but today the sun's come out.' It was too much for those assembled, many of whom wept openly. Then it was champagne in plastic cups. Adrian couldn't drink too much because he was on Warfarin which prevented his blood from clotting. Their honeymoon was a night on the ward, with two beds pushed together, curtains drawn around them and balloons floating from the headboards. It was the first chance that they'd had to be alone together. But it wasn't to last.

Visitors flooded in to see Adrian. Of course, like his mum when she was

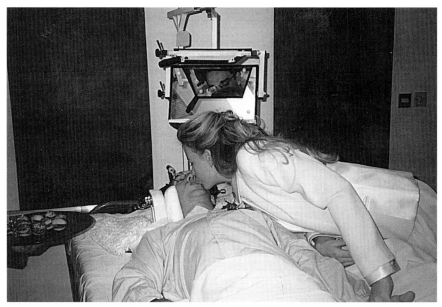

Stoke Mandeville Hospital, 1996: Adrian and Siobhan Cassidy's wedding reception.
Two bolts, screwed into Adrian's scull, secure his head to the bed.

ill, he felt that he had to talk and chat – put a face on. Often he became little more than a table for his mates' take-aways which they brought round after work to eat off his bed and talk over him. Over New Year he was on emotional over-load and reacted to it the only way he knew how, by withdrawing into a kind of numbness, a world where emotions ceased to exist. He even told Siobhan that he didn't love her. It felt tearful but he didn't cry. He'd only cried twice before anyway. Once on the day that his mum died. But he'd felt that he'd dealt with that then. He'd shaved his head and wore black as he hacked his way down the course at Henley in the qualifiers for the Diamond Sculls. He thought he'd exorcised all his demons that day but the tears came back later, when he saw his brother win the Boat Race and realised that his mother wasn't there to see it.

But dealing with his condition was harder for another reason. For the first few days in hospital he had been given Temazapan to help him sleep and had hallucinated wildly. He felt the sensation of being locked inside his brain and not being able to get out. Images of Christopher Reeve flashed through his mind. The former star of *Superman* had broken his neck in a riding accident and was a quadriplegic. Adrian became animated when he talked of his amazement that Reeve was still carrying on his life. He felt that if he had been as badly injured as Reeve, then he would have killed himself.

In effect, though, after the first few days in hospital Adrian came to realise that his 'end-game', the extent of his final injuries, was not clear. It became clear that he could move his right toe just a fraction. This did not mean that he would be able to walk again, though. He thought it was easier for the guy in the bed next to him, who had fallen off a fork-lift truck and broken his back. He was in traction for eight weeks, then out in a wheel chair, dealing with the rest of his life. The doctors knew that his was a complete fracture.

But Adrian was in no-man's land. He could gradually move more of the muscles in his legs but nobody could tell him if he was ever going to be able to walk again. The healing process of broken backs is more akin to witchcraft than science. Nobody knows why things happen the way they do. He was told that it was his neurology that was the real key to his healing. He thought that maybe all the intricate linking of nerve movements down his spinal column could in some way be re-routed. Perhaps by the positive power of his mind.

Bit by bit he continued to make progress. The physiotherapist tried out a new method on him called Bobath. It relies on the fact that your muscles have certain innate movement patterns. You don't learn to move so much as restrict your movement. So in fact the brain acts as a break. So she would move the leg and foot in the right order to try to re-establish the link the other way. It was a slow process but with the physio moving his legs, gradually she could tell that she was making less and less of an effort to make the movement. He had to be doing some of the work himself.

He walked again for the first time that spring, although curiously enough, to help him stimulate his muscles he sat on the rowing machine and pulled a few light strokes. It was a movement pattern that was well-ingrained and came back to him before he went through the process of re-learning how to walk. But for him that was the most difficult time. He experienced the discrimination of those in a wheelchair as he was 'let out' for the weekend and was taken around the streets of Cambridge. Worse still, he felt like a fraud at Stoke Mandeville.

He was one of the lucky ones – two out of 160 – that would walk out of there. It took him ten days longer to get out of his chair than it should have done. He was afraid to walk in a hospital where nobody else could.

In fact, although he still needed several months' worth of physio, he left hospital rather than feel the guilt of being the only miraculous recovery among his fellow patients. Just how miraculous was clear when the swelling of his spinal column went down and the extent of his injuries became apparent. He had exactly the same damage as a man in the ward above him, who would be paralysed for the rest of his life.

Adrian is now getting on with the rest of his life. He and Siobhan conceived a child in hospital. Isabella was born in the New Year of 1998. They live in in Cambridge, where he secured a coaching post just before leaving hospital. It sounds like everything ended happily ever after. But you'd be wrong to think that he had seen the last of his crisis. When he broke his neck, he was in London, his mates around him, doing an MSc. He was looking forward to a PhD at Cambridge, as well as rowing in the Blue Boat. When he left hospital, he was married with a baby, living in Cambridge, with all his mates in London and doing a job where he wasn't supposed to be rowing. It was as if he just walked through a door and everything had changed. He'd gone away for a while and come back to a different life.

He is still waiting to find out what his 'end-game' will be. Although he will never have the same range of movement in his neck again, he does not yet know when his 'recovery' will stop. Almost every day, Adrian is still moving the goalposts, just like he was in hospital when he was discovering which new muscle he could move each week. He is not satisfied because he still holds this ambition to row in the Olympic Games and win a medal. He says, 'It's an ambition now not a goal,' because he doesn't know if his physiology – or the type of life he leads now – will allow him to achieve it. But at the back of his mind, he holds the dream of the 2004 Games. He will still be only 32.

Just how important a measure achievement in rowing is to him became apparent when he told me, 'Almost my biggest achievement since breaking my neck was finishing the 1998 Head of the River Race.' On the one hand I was struck by his incredible determination and unwillingness to let go of his dream, despite all that had happened to him. On the other I was struck by the apparent impracticability of his goal. After all, he's still living with half his spinal cord severed. He's got a wife and child. Yet this man thinks he can row in the Olympics!

But, of course, it's not about rowing. It wasn't with my 'crisis' and it certainly isn't with his. I had my crisis because I was unwilling, or unable, to let go of a sport that I thought gave me everything in life. To stay involved as I got older, I kept moving my goalposts ever downward, from the aim of a medal to just a final place, and then just to be on the team. In the end there was a kind of mania about it, which most people including Adrian could see but I could not. But Adrian is a driven man too. His life gives testament to Coubertin's words that 'the most important thing in life is not to win but the struggle'. Talking to him, I had the very strong sense that even with an Olympic medal he would still not be 'satisfied'.

For Adrian, the importance of coming back from paralysis was the struggle, not the outcome. It was not that he 'won' his right to walk, let alone row again (although to some it would represent a far greater success than winning an Olympic medal). He doesn't believe that anyway. So although now he may see his gold medal as 'winning', I suspect that the importance for him will be in the struggle to get there. It is not one that he will let go of easily.

Both Adrian and I will never be the same as a result of the crises that we went through, although to an extent we both have moments of trying to pretend that it never happened. For the greater proportion of our lives, we have both sort to justify our sense of self, through success in the sport of rowing. In the middle of it all it is difficult to see what more we needed, other than a few more rowing medals. But, inevitably, life demands much more than that. It is in the midst of such crises that such realisations hit home, with a force that can never be overlooked. Indeed, it is only by going through such traumas that we can learn to grow as human beings. One might almost say that such things were sent to teach us something about ourselves that we needed to learn in order to live the rest of our lives. But perhaps that is a step too far? Whatever, I feel that I have emerged from my experiences as a 'better person' and I suspect that, although he might sometimes not care to admit it, Adrian has too.

As for Henley, for both of us it is still part of our lives. I met Adrian for the first time after his accident at the regatta that year. When we talked in the New Year, he was hoping to row in a Ladies Plate eight that summer with all his old mates. For me, I would be less than honest if I didn't admit to having wistful thoughts of rowing in a fast boat there. But when I walked over the bridge at regatta time and stared down at the boat tents and around the river bend to the course, I felt that I was looking back at a scene from old photograph, of something that I did once and enjoyed. I was grateful for the memory, but felt it was time to try and move on.

Moving On

THE telephone rang in what seemed like the middle of the night. With my eyes still closed, I reached out from under the duvet and fumbled around trying to find the receiver. I was still hung over from the night before. Prothiedin and Chinon do not mix wonderfully well first thing in the morning. Through a haze, an Irish voice sounded in my year. 'Martin, is that you?' I recognised the voice immediately as that of Alan Green, BBC radio's top soccer commentator, my colleague for this week of the World Championships in Aiguebelette. The recognition in itself provided sufficient adrenaline for me to switch my brain into work mode and provide a croaky response.

"Yes Alan, what time is it?' He ignored my question.

'Look, I'm sorry to wake you but something's happened.'

Not again, I thought. The last time he did this to me was the morning before Redgrave and Pinsent's Atlanta final, when a bloody bomb had exploded in Atlanta, throwing the Olympics into chaos. The thought went through my head that BA had at last found his luggage which they'd lost at Heathrow. He'd been walking around in the same clothes for three days now. But it wasn't that.

'Lady Di's dead, Dodi too; a car crash in Paris. It's a massive story, it's on CNN right now. The station will probably go wall-to-wall on it, so I doubt that we'll have much space to do any rowing today, or during the week. They're already talking about a state funeral.'

As Alan went off into his news reporter persona (I suspected that he'd have really liked to have had John Simpson's job more than his own). I thought, 'Shit! They're not going to let us broadcast the rowing.' Instinctively, as Alan carried on analysing the implications of the event, both for the station and the nation, I flicked on the television to see an image of a tangled Mercedes Benz being removed from a tunnel in Paris. I wondered if I'd ever driven down the same tunnel. We agreed to meet over breakfast in an hour or so. It was still only 6am.

One way and another, 1997 was turning out to be a massive year for me: a major mid-life crisis, turning 40, Labour in power at last, and now this.

Down at the rowing course the rowers, out for their early-morning outings, were beginning to pick up the news. Miriam Batten, competing in the double sculls for Great Britain, had a confusing encounter with a half-dressed German on the way to the loo. She couldn't understand his apparent rantings about death and car crashes in Paris. When she got back to the boat her partner, Gillian Lindsay, told her. 'Princess Di's dead... in Paris, she was killed in a car crash.' Miriam felt no immediate emotion. For once, she had a chance to pick up a medal; her thoughts quickly turned back to the outing ahead.

The demands of competing and the distance from events in Britain meant that Miriam was largely divorced from the huge outpourings of public grief that followed in the coming days. To stay focused on the rowing, after a day or so she even stopped listening to the somewhat repetitive television reports. It paid off: the result that Lindsay and her were to achieve that week was to herald a renaissance for British women's rowing.

But more than that, it was to be the start of a momentous time for Miriam. Her emotions would rise and fall with the speed of a roller coaster. At its height, she would realise her heart's desires and lifetime ambitions, but there were moments when she would sink into a deep and dark depression from which there seemed no escape. Although she may not have had the opportunity, or perhaps inclination, to grieve for Diana during the 1997 World Championships, Miriam would soon experience the meaning of sorrow. Yet she would emerge a stronger person from the experience and 'move on' in her life in a way which she never imagined was possible.

You may be wondering where all this fits in with me? Well, from '97 onwards, I felt as if I was moving on in my life and learning all sorts of things about myself that I didn't know. At least, that was how it seemed at the time. In reality it was a period when I was sowing the seeds of further problems. Perhaps I should have guessed as much when, for someone who had 'learnt' that part of the cause of his crisis was an over-reliance on rowing, I was remarkably quick to re-establish my connections with it.

Part of this was the opportunity to pursue a minor career in sports journalism with Radio 5 Live. It seemed a great way to keep in contact with the sport when I was not able to race at that level any longer. I had made a strong play for the Radio 5 Live job in the year before the Atlanta Olympics and after a somewhat traumatic trial at the Lucerne regatta, I was thrown in at the deep end with no instructions, just a contact number. I spent hours writing a 40-second report, during which time I hardly watched the racing. After queuing up at a telephone box to record the piece, I was told that I sounded too serious. I had to read the report with a smile on my face. The next day, I was told that it sounded too much like I was reading a report. I couldn't win; radio journalism was not as easy as I thought it might be. John Leyne, a seasoned radio journalist, did the 'worlds' that year, but when the scale of Redgrave's Atlanta odyssey dawned on the BBC, they decided that they needed a specialist sports commentator to cover the events. Alan Green, one of the corporation's best-known soccer voices, was not perhaps an obvious choice to cover rowing. But his enthusiasm for sport, his availability during the summer and his wish to 'do the Olympics' made him an obvious choice for Bob Shennan, then head of sport at Radio 5 Live. Shennan also knew that if Alan was to present rowing, then he'd need an expert summariser.

We met for the first time over breakfast at Lucerne regatta, just before the Olympics. Green was in the middle of one of his impossible schedules. Just back from England's infamous soccer trip to Hong Kong, he was spending the weekend in Lucerne to acquaint himself with rowing before returning to work on the Euro '96 soccer tournament. Alan had a warm, welcoming smile and a firm handshake. He was much younger than the man whose Belfast brogue I had heard describe so many great soccer matches. I liked him straight away, although I soon became aware that not everybody took to 'Greeny'.

This man was radio sport's 007 – his opinions were licensed to kill. And not many missed their mark. During racing in Atlanta, he was rung up for a comment on Alex Ferguson's purchase of Jordi Cruyff. As the men's quads thundered towards the finish line, Alan immediately launched into a perceptive critique of Ferguson's foray into the transfer market. '... I mean, where does Alex Ferguson think that he's going to play him?' Apparently, Ferguson had been extremely annoyed by Alan's criticism of United.

The fact that Alan's opinions were spoken from the heart and came from a genuine passion for the game cut no ice with Ferguson, or others. There can't be many broadcasters who, in the middle of a Premiership match say, to their audience, 'Listen folks, this game is so dull, I don't know why you're bothering to listen to it. I mean I'm being paid to be here but you at home must have something better to do with your time.'

The man is a consummate professional, a complete natural with the mike. I learnt so much about broadcasting from him. During the Lucerne regatta, Alan was waiting to give his report. Before the presenter came to him there was a little banter between the reporters at other events over the presence of duchesses at their respective venues: the Duchess of Kent at Hickstead, Fergie at the Paris Open. When it came to Alan's turn, he briefly set the scene, then looked over his shoulder to the back of the grandstand. 'You know, John… I don't think we've any duchesses here today.' I asked him why, as it was radio, he had bothered to turn around at all. 'Ah, you see, that way Martin, you get the pause just right.' Where I had agonised for hours over my reports, Alan wrote them intuitively, scribbling off a 40-second report which perfectly summed up the whole regatta in not much more than a minute. The way he used his voice to highlight key words, phrases, or the moods in his piece was a delight to experience.

I loved to spend time with him. Partly because I loved to hear the latest football gossip, but more than that, Alan was a good listener; I felt that what I said and thought mattered to him. What's more, he almost immediately fell in love with rowing at first sight. He contrasted the openness, articulacy and warmth of the people involved in the sport with those in soccer. In particular, he quickly struck up a good relationship with Redgrave, who was mad about Alan's other sport, golf. The mutual respect was revealed just after Redgrave won his medal in Atlanta, when he told a television crew to wait until after Alan had done his post-race interview. 'He's first!' the quadruple Olympic champion had snapped. Between us there was little doubt that during the Atlanta Games rowing received its best-ever British coverage. I was hooked on the adrenaline of working live with the mike and wanted to continue it during the next season.

I was soon given a chance to put what I'd learned into practice and report on all three World Cup regattas in 1997 on my own – Alan being too busy with soccer. It was hectic, especially as I was still FISA's Athletes' Commission representative at all three regattas. As such I needed to keep an eye on the regatta's fairness and safety arrangements as well as get among the rowers and be a sounding board for their opinions as much as possible. It crossed my mind that I was doing too much, particularly in the light of my recent problems. At the first race in Munich most people were surprised to see me anyway, having heard rumours about 'serious illnesses' and being at 'death's door'. In the most, I was pleased to repeat Mark Twain's witticism: 'Rumours of my death have been greatly exaggerated.' While Twain's wit did not come naturally to me on air during regattas, I did feel that I was making progress.

However, for the first time I had to wrestle with the demands of knowing too much. I had a privileged position, being so close to the rowers. Sometimes I got to hear of juicy titbits that would have been better kept silent. In Munich, the story was Foster's injury. From talking to the crew, I knew that there was a good deal of resentment in the boat against Foster. This had not been generally known, or reported in the media. When I commented on air that Foster might find it harder to get back in the boat than he'd imagined, I was immediately quizzed by the presenter about the feeling in the crew. I felt I was close to breaking confidences and immediately felt awkward, balancing my need to sound informed for Radio 5 Live against the loyalty and friendship with former crewmates. Since then, I have always erred on the side of the latter.

By the time the championships at Aiguebelette came along, I was looking forward to working with Alan again, this time with the benefit of experience. Then came the news of Diana's death. We would have no 'live' work that week, so for Alan and therefore me, things would be just that little bit more flat. In fact, most of the key finals would take place during the funeral itself.

I had not remotely appreciated the mood of the nation until I travelled home from France to work for two days at school. There, with word of all weekend sport being cancelled, shops shutting and the unending collection of flowers being deposited at almost any Diana-associated site, the mood was unbelievably sombre. I could not believe the intensity of the feelings being exhibited.

Certainly the British team, far away in the Haute Savoy, had no idea of the mood. David Tanner, the team manager, tried to head off the press from eliciting comments from the team. His worry was that one of the four may let slip that they were far more concerned about their race than the death of Diana, sad though it was. In some quarters there was even talk of the team being forced to withdraw. This, I thought, was nonsense. But when I returned home to work for two days at school, Chris (normally such a level-headed judge of such matters) thought it sensible for the British rowing team not to race.

I thought the whole country had lost its sense of perspective. Even Jonny Searle was deeply affected. He arrived with his girlfriend, Philippa Cross, to watch his brother race. During the finals Cross, herself an Olympic rower with many of her friends rowing in finals, stayed at the hotel to watch the funeral rather than the racing, while Searle joined Alan and myself at our commentary position to watch the racing. Even then, Searle was anxious to catch as much of the funeral service on Alan's headphones, as it was being broadcast on Radio 5 Live.

Of course, to the athletes racing, and to the organisers, the idea that the championships should in any way be affected by Diana's death was wrong. In the end, pressure from the British team led FISA to rather begrudgingly hold a minute's silence. The moment came just after the French pair of Rolland and Andrieux had produced a stunning sprint to win the first French gold medal of the championships (they were to repeat the same burst in Sydney to take the gold).

The crowd was on heat, so the minute's silence was nothing like a minute and the crowd was far from silent. But at least the gesture of the British team in wearing black ribbons did strike a chord with the media. There was little in the way of sport to report on Monday. Redgrave, Pinsent, Foster and Cracknell with heads bowed made the back pages of many national newspapers. Unfortunately, the same level of publicity was not afforded to our commentary, which was a great shame. Alan and I did some good work on some exciting races, many of them involving British crews. With eight medals split evenly between men and women, it seemed that British rowing had moved on massively in the last year.

I felt much the same about myself, although it was clear that I was not 'out of the woods' yet. I enjoyed the championships immensely but had experienced a couple of dizzy spells where my head started to swim. It was a bit unnerving, especially as one happened just before I was due to go on air. I put most of this down to the medication that I was still taking, although I was gradually lowering the dosage. But there was no doubt that my mind needed some attention as well, chiefly to cope with the times where I did feel physically unwell again. I had to allow my body to get illnesses without thinking that each sore throat or dizzy spell was a return of the virus that had hit me in 1996.

It was with this in mind that I decided to go on something called a 'Life Training Weekend'. It was the creation of two Americans, Brad Lewis and Roy Whitten. On the face of it the whole thing sounded a little off-beat and alternative: all weekend on a course, from 6pm on the Friday until Sunday midnight. Thirty-five hours of something – nobody said quite what – and the publicity promised that it would be one of the most rewarding weekends that I'd ever spend. Anyway, it was a message I bought.

The training was based at the unfortunate location – for me at any rate – of Conservative Party headquarters. What I found was a room full of 80 or so people, seated in front of two trainers on the stage where John Major used to take election press conferences and a roving microphone. It soon became clear that, in part, this was some kind of confessional session. Late on the Friday evening the trainers came out with the 'Disciplines'. There was to be no alcohol, non-prescription medicines, caffeine, swearing, lateness, watches, or talking unless asked a question by them.

The realisation of what we'd agreed to dawned fully the next day when those that had arrived late, drank alcohol etc, had to explain themselves to the relentless probing of the excellent trainers. They were only small rules, insignificant really, but that was the point: what did it say about you when you failed to do something that you gave your word about?

During the weekend we went through several processes designed to recognise the welter of emotions and 'mind talk' that can dominate our lives. It wasn't easy; the hardest part was the last evening which involved holding eye contact with five others for 15 minutes. The senior trainer, Sue Oldham, gave me some helpful advice: 'Martin, you're trying so hard, why don't you just relax and let it happen?' At that point she could have been an amalgam of all the rowing coaches that have ever tried to coach me.

So by now you must have gathered that for me, the weekend was an uplifting and emotional experience. I can understand if you may be slightly cringing at the descriptions above – it's not everybody's cup of tea. But the reason that they are there in such detail is because it was the experience of that weekend which made me determined to write this book. Apart from that, the skills I learnt helped me to make some important decisions.

Out of the blue, in February 1998 I was called by Dave Gordon, the executive producer of *Grandstand*. He asked me if I would commentate for BBC television on rowing up until the Olympics in Sydney. Apparently, *Grandstand* had decided to give Garry Herbert the chance to prove that he could hold down a position as a commentator. In 1997, he had been Gerald Sindstadt's summariser, edging out Chris Baillieu whose voice was judged to be too 'posh'. Now, although Sindstadt was judged to be a safe pair of hands, the BBC decided to experiment with a more adventurous approach for Sydney. Garry managed to persuade Dave Gordon that he could move from the role as summariser to that of commentator. Maybe Garry had pretensions to be the next Clive Anderson. But more important, Garry wanted me as his summariser. I was flattered but my instinctive loyalty created barriers in my mind.

Despite being in the same organisation, BBC television had not talked to BBC radio, with whom I felt I had an – albeit informal – agreement to work. More than that, I was not prepared to leave Alan Green 'in the lurch'

St Catherine's, 1999: Garry Herbert and me during a break in commentating on the World Rowing Championships.

with a summariser that he didn't know. In addition to that, although I knew and loved Garry, I wasn't sure that he could move so easily into the role of commentator. For me, it felt a big step going from working with Alan – the top pro in the business – to an untried voice, good friend as he was.

I told Dave Gordon that I would think about his offer, but that I had to talk to those people in radio first and Alan Green in particular. When I spoke to Gordon Turnbill, head of sport at Radio 5 Live, he didn't seem particularly pleased. I left him with the message that unless he was happy for me to go, I would stay with radio. What probably worried him far more than me leaving was the reaction of his senior soccer commentator. Alan was not a man that any of the BBC staff enjoyed upsetting. But Alan was very supportive. He pointed out all the potential pitfalls that could occur in moving to television but only offered me encouragement, saying that I had to take the opportunity.

I still remained to be convinced, though. What if Herbert and I were no good? It was only when I found out that I could do the radio reports together with television commentary for the three World Cup regattas that I agreed to give it a go. In effect, it was a trial. Alan was committed to the soccer World Cup until after Lucerne and would not attend any regattas before the World Championships. The good part of this was it meant that

Garry and I had time to see if we could work together. The downside was that I had loaded on to myself yet another responsibility at regattas. With my role within FISA, as athletes' representative, I now had three responsible and time-consuming jobs at the summer regattas. It was too much, particularly on the finals day at Lucerne that year.

The radio and television commentary positions were on opposite sides of the course and about 1,500 metres apart. Television had an important 'live' slot on *Sunday Grandstand* to take Redgrave's final. Rather than calmly preparing for a demanding afternoon, I used the morning to walk around the rowers' area, trying to gather as many opinions as I could about issues that affected them. In addition, I had to organise attendance at an athletes' meeting immediately after the regatta, a meeting which I was running.

At midday, I moved to the finish trying to organise my radio commitments for the day and file an early report. I was already knackered and late, meaning I had to run round the lake to the television commentary position, set on a hill, high above the finish line. Still the prospect of having to talk on live television to four million people works wonders in reviving tired spirits. Both Herbert and I were very much 'up' for the Redgrave race, not least because our producer, Campbell Ferguson, had made it clear that it was an occasion on which we had to 'perform'.

Then disaster, at least of a sort: the race was delayed for two hours because a boat had snapped its rudder wires, although nobody told us, *Grandstand* or, I suspect, the Swiss television director what was happening. There were Garry and I, live to millions back in Britain, fired up with adrenaline to describe the rematch of the Redgrave four against the Rumanians, their conquerors in Munich, and all we could see on the monitor was pictures of swimmers in the lido at the start, lakeside trees, or ducks and swans along the lake!

Mindful of Campbell's advice always to talk to the pictures, I started extolling some of the Rotsee's virtues as a famous Swiss nature reserve. The problem was the shots went on for over ten minutes before *Grandstand* found out what was happening and decided to show some other sport instead. I'm not sure that our ornithological commentary made the most scintillating sporting coverage that *Grandstand* has ever taken. In fact, viewers who had just switched over could have been forgiven for thinking that this was a trailer for David Attenborough's *The Life of Birds*! What was important, though, was that Garry and I had kept going and hadn't been fazed by the problems. Still, when we went off air, both Garry and I rushed out of the box to let out a few expletives to relieve the tension.

Later in the afternoon we managed to pull ourselves together for the rescheduled final. We did a good job and I felt on top of the race. Garry pulled out all the stops. Even Campbell seemed vaguely pleased.

That done, my ridiculous schedule continued. I rushed back around the lake to interview the victorious four on camera for television and then on tape for Radio 5 Live. Because of the delay, Cracknell had to rush off the medal rostrum to a waiting car. The four needed someone to sit in the boat and paddle the 1,000 metres back to the boating area. David Tanner asked me. I knew I hadn't the time: I had to file the interviews, prepare my voice pieces for *Sports Report*, then there was an Athletes' Commission meeting to chair. But it was an opportunity that I didn't want to miss. And I relished the experience.

Rushing back to the radio point, I filed my report (written and made in just five minutes – à la Alan Green). Then it was the first part of the FISA Athletes' Commission meeting from six until eight. At 8.30pm, I flopped into my hotel bed, switched on the World Cup final and fell asleep during the match.

Just reading back through it now, I think: 'What on earth did I think I was doing? It was an over-demanding schedule which I could have avoided by being more assertive, rather than feeling guilty about letting Radio 5 Live down. Later that season, I made the move to television. Richard 'Radio' Phelps, a crewmate from my Vienna eight, was secured to help Alan Green at the World Championships.

As I began to get on top of the broadcasting, I also began to feel more able to ease myself back towards some level of fitness (I probably needed it for all that running around!). Ian McNuff, my crewmate for so long, asked me to row with him in his veteran's crew. It was a massive step down from the standard of rowing that I was used to, but I was glad of the opportunity, not only to get back behind an oar but also to spend more time with my old friend. Together we won a veteran 'C' fours event at Molesey regatta on 19 July, my birthday. I didn't know whether to be pleased or embarrassed at the standard which I was now racing at.

But bit by bit, I began to push myself a little harder in training sessions (about six or seven a week). It helped that the boys from the first eight at Hampton were of a similar speed to me on their runs and ergometers. It gave me a real incentive to be competitive. What I really wanted was to be fit enough to be able to race at the national squad long distance trials over the winter: not to compete for national selection but just to enjoy the experience of being able to 'mix it' with the top guys once more. Competing in the trials was a promise I had made to myself when I had been 'ill'; a way of marking my recovery.

The chance presented itself when the 'seven' man from the Hampton school eight found himself without a pairs partner. Nick O'Grady was a 'one year junior'; with a birthday the wrong side of January he was not eligible for junior selection. He was a quiet but immensely talented young man, preparing to study history at Oxford. In fact, Nick was one of my 'A' Level history students. Pound for pound he was one of the best boat movers ever to have been through Hampton.

I suppose that he jumped at the chance to row with me, as much as I was eager to race the trials with him. We complemented each other well and so in the national squad trials of February 1999 we produced a very respectable result. I was even chosen for a random drug test, which did wonders for my morale (like I was a 'real' rower again).

So the experience was a boost. The majority of rowers – many of whom I suspect would rather try to avoid the '5K trial' through the featureless fens – will probably find that rather perplexing, if not a little sad. Perhaps it was. In part it was a sign that I had not yet fully let go of the sport. Throughout that year, I tried to keep my fitness.

Things, though, got a little out of hand in the ergometer room at the St Catherine's World Championships in Canada, where Mike Teti and I vied with each other to pull better scores over half an hour on most of the days of the championship. It was my last year as chair of the Athletes' Commission and I had a lot of organising for the end-of-season athletes' meeting. So it won't surprise you to hear that I was still running around with too much to do. Still, the television commentary went pretty well. It was a good warm-up for Sydney. But others didn't have such a great time.

Miriam Batten and her partner, Gillian Lindsay, failed to make the final in their double sculls event. In fact, there were no medals for the women's Olympic boats at all, so the wheels rather seemed to have fallen off the renaissance of British women's rowing that had started in Aiguebelette. I watched Miriam's event with detached interest. It didn't for a minute surprise me that she was at the bottom of one of the loops of the roller-coaster ride of her long career. But I wondered now, if after all that she'd been through, she could still become the first British woman to win a rowing medal in the Olympic Games.

Miriam cuts a striking figure. Her long dark hair ripples down in waves to her shoulders. She is tall and slim, with striking features. One could find no trouble placing her in her first job as a fashion buyer for a major department store. Conversation with her, at one level, was always easy. She is a passionate, articulate and humorous person who almost never seems to be lost for words – the typical extrovert. But if you knew her a little better, you might have a sense that underneath that exterior, hidden by the almost endless stream of words that she pours out, lies a certain nervousness and fragility. Perhaps it was these qualities which sometimes made me feel a little uneasy when I talked to her.

Not that when we meet, we don't slip into an easy familiarity the way that old team-mates and friends often do. But I was never drawn to Miriam, as if I fancied her. Perhaps this was because I saw a similar person to myself. She had staying power in the sport and had achieved some success, while being a vocal supporter of athletes' rights. On the inside, though, lay hidden the same fears and frailties which I knew lurked in the heart of me. So I

knew that Miriam's successes had been won at a price – as mine had – after her own demons had tested her to the limit. It was a profound process, something that, if she could have avoided, she would have done with no hesitation. But that was a long way ahead when Miriam first began her making her mark at Thames Rowing Club in her early 20s.

Miriam, never a person to hide her light under a bushel, had already decided when she arrived in London from Southampton University

Thames Rowing Club, Putney, 1998: Miriam Batten.

that she was going to make the British team. She even promised Dan Topolski that she was 'going to win a medal for her country'. He had gone to Thames to write a piece on a club that seemed to be making all the waves in women's rowing and he came away with what he wanted: a remarkable promise, especially considering that British women had not won any medals for some years. She took a lot of verbal abuse from her clubmates for her audacity. But then, on the surface at least, Miriam was filled with a strong self-belief.

It seemed justified when, in 1990, she not only made the team but was placed in the 'top' boat, the coxless four. Her result in the World Championships was a disappointing last. Then it seemed to me at least that she was a long way from keeping her promise to Topolski. Even in the following year, when she found herself again at stroke, this time a coxless pair with Fiona Freckleton, a crewmate from Tasmania, it seemed unlikely that she would even make the final.

Perhaps this had as much as anything to do with Miriam's nerves. As the big races approached, she became hopelessly nervous and the tension in her body would often build up to an unbearable level, especially while she was sitting on the start of a race. So it wasn't unusual for her to feel drained even before the race began. During the 1991 Lucerne regatta she was 'out for the count on the start'. The pair raced terribly and did not make the final. Mark Lees, who was the chief coach, only selected them for the World Championship team as part of an eight. In fact, it was during the training camp that Miriam pressed her claim to Lees to be given one last chance in the pair. Probably wanting to get some peace from Miriam haranguing him, as much as believing in the pair, Lees relented and allowed them to do a time trial. Without the same tension that she'd felt at Lucerne, it was no problem for Miriam to push the boat to a very fast time and gain the right to race in the World Championships as the coxless pair.

In her heart, Miriam knew that she could never make it in a pressured race unless she got control of her nerves. She sought the help of Liz Ferris, a former Olympic diver. As a psychologist, Ferris was able to help Miriam develop some 'first-aid' techniques to deal with her race nerves. She began to practise autogenics on the bus while travelling to the course. What's more, Ferris's breathing exercises allowed Miriam to feel more relaxed while sitting on the start, ready to race. In addition, the fact that Miriam had to 'double up' in the women's eight meant that she had less time to sit and get nervous about racing in the pair.

It seemed to work and they made the final. During that race she remembers being so intent on her rowing, and oblivious to the other crews, that she was 'completely gobsmacked' when, during the last 500 metres, Freckleton called for her to increase the pace and challenge for second place. The thought went through her head, 'Does that mean we're in third?' They crossed the line in the bronze medal position. Miriam had fulfilled her promise to Topolski, a fact which she reminded him of just after the presentation. It was the first sweep medal won by British women in an open category since 1962. It seemed that an illustrious career lay ahead for Miriam. But that early promise was not to be fulfilled.

This was no surprise to some, who expressed a certain amount of disbelief about the result. To her, it seemed that some people were just waiting for her to fail. Whispers went around that their lane for the final in Vienna was particularly favoured that day with its own 'personal tailwind' blowing down it.

Following her results over the next few years, Miriam started to believe them. Success had brought the inevitable doubts to her mind. She thought that she was 'good' and never stopped telling people so. But to prove it by winning a medal at the World Championships, or Olympics, that was another matter.

She spent the next three years in the pair, although with a different partner. An illness to Freckleton had put paid to her Olympic ambitions. Miriam was paired up with Joe Turvey. On paper it should have been a faster combination. In training it probably was. But once again, Miriam could never deliver in the racing situation.

Perhaps some of this was down to the shortcomings of the women's coaching system. For long periods she would row without ever seeing a coach. Training programmes arrived in the post, and most outings were done in the dark after work. The pair also had a fundamental flaw: when the pressure went on, it didn't go straight. Miriam's natural inclination under pressure was to hit the catch harder, Turvey's was to push the finish. Clearly, Miriam's own nervousness in a race situation didn't help matters.

It was a recipe for disaster. Although they made the Olympic final in 1992, they were never in contention for a medal. At Lucerne in 1993 they were disqualified for coming out of their lane. Despite this, there were strong hopes that they would deliver another medal that year at the World Championships. Once again, Miriam could not deliver under pressure. After taking an early lead, she and Turvey were rowed down in the last 500 metres by a rather rustic-looking American combination and finished fourth.

The following year it was the same story. Miriam's pair was flying in the pre-World Championships training camp. At race intensity they recorded relatively faster times than Redgrave and Pinsent. But at the Indianapolis World Championships, her and Turvey were much slower. Fifth place was the death knell for their pair. They had both struggled to get on with each other at the best of times. Now, each was determined to prove to the other (and to themselves) that it wasn't them who was slowing the pair down in races. Miriam turned to the boat which would settle the issue: the single scull.

It was a boat that her younger sister, Guin, was already starting to make her own. A former shot-putter, she had turned to the single after being told that she lacked co-ordination in a crew boat. In 1995, Guin Batten had already confounded her critics by finishing eighth in the World Championships in the single. Yet, unlike the Searle brothers, whose ambition it was to row together as siblings at the Olympic Games, Miriam made no moves to pair up with her sister.

For all the improvements that she had made in sculling, Miriam, still lacked the confidence in her own ability to change successfully from sculling to rowing. This was despite beating her sister in the singles trials for the 1996 Olympic Games. But despite this, she turned to rowing again, believing that the 'big eight' stood a better chance of a medal. This was to be her last race and she wanted to retire on a high note.

During the summer of 1996, her crew seemed to be moving in harmony. Just before the Olympics her eight, in qualifying at the Lucerne regatta, broke the course record, destroying the talented Australians in the process. It seemed that Miriam's goal was in sight. But for Miriam it was a familiar story. The crew went to pieces during the Atlanta regatta, achieving more fame for hijacking one of the notoriously unreliable Olympic shuttle buses than for their performance on the water. They failed to make the final.

On the other hand, Guin sculled a fantastic race in her semi-final, overtaking Lipa, the Barcelona Olympic champion, in the final few strokes to qualify for the Olympic final. For her, sixth place was a tremendous achievement. What Miriam might have been capable of, had she found the bottle to stick in the single, one can only guess. As it was now, Miriam, taller, seemingly faster and more talented than Guin, had lost the limelight to her kid sister.

At 31, Miriam thought long and hard about stopping. It was time for her to 'move on'. Throughout her rowing career she had been employed by Debenhams as a fashion buyer for women's clothes. They had been remarkably understanding employers, always allowing her the necessary time to train and race. On the face of it, a career path beckoned. She had worked hard, the department was doing well, making a lot of money. But promotion did not seem to come her way (although given the apparent dedication of Miriam to rowing this was not perhaps surprising). In truth, Miriam was uncertain about where she stood with her work. Furthermore, she was deeply uncertain as to how to further her own cause within the work environment. She was aware enough of her own extrovert nature to know that her attempts to attract attention sometimes ended up 'pissing everyone off'.

Ultimately, to battle on in her job Miriam thought she needed the confidence boost that would come if she was successful at rowing. Stopping as another 'also-ran', who had promised much but never delivered, would do nothing for her confidence. At least in rowing, she thought, there was some degree of recognition for the work that she put in during training – unlike in her job. Miriam's psyche needed the 'buzz' that she got from rowing; she needed to be involved, competing or talked about.

In the end, she made no clear commitment either way. On the one hand she played a waiting game, not committing herself to the squad. Rather she kept herself fit by running and single sculling. On the other hand she threw herself back into work, even trained as a rowing coach. However, all the time she was watching the development of the women's squad under their new coach, Mike Spracklen.

There are a few coaches in the world of rowing that have the ability to create success wherever they go and whoever they coach. Mike is such a person. Whether in Britain, Canada or America, his talents have consistently produced gold medals. Uncharacteristically, the Atlanta Games had seen him finish his four-year spell in the States on a low note, his eight finishing a lowly fifth. He was hungry to prove himself again. Furthermore, for family reasons he was looking for a chance to return to his Marlow roots and the vacant position of British women's coach could not have been better timed. Here was an opportunity for Mike to work his own brand of magic with the British women. He soon had the women's squad under his spell. It was only a matter of time before Miriam succumbed.

She was in regular contact with the other women, desperate to know what was going on. Meanwhile, Mike, aware of Miriam's potential and sure of his ability to develop it, took every opportunity to cajole her back into his group. At first he made things easy for her, persuading her to join in weekend training sessions, massaging her ego. But Mike wanted Miriam as a full-time rower. Soon she saw that Mike was running the group differently to any other coach with whom she had worked. He appeared to be immune to the negative bitchy comments that sometimes seemed to be the bane of the women's squad. In the past, the women had been able to manipulate coaches; not now. Mike was both dogmatic and belligerent with a 'take it or leave it' approach. There was no way that he was going to allow any of the women to push him around. It was an attitude that the women quickly came to respect. Miriam felt that if anybody could help her to move on and unlock her potential, then it was Mike Spracklen.

Mike managed to persuade Miriam for the first time to stick with sculling rather than rowing. She found herself in a double scull with Gillian Lindsay, a tall, lithe Scot who had rowed in the Olympic eight with Miriam. Lindsay's sculling skills had blossomed under Spracklen's tutelage. He felt that the older and more experienced Miriam would provide an ideal foil to nurture a young talent. So it proved. At their first international regatta they finished second, being beaten only by the fast German crew. In fact, they were both surprised by just how fast their combination seemed to be going. Miriam had been there before many times, only to fall at the last hurdle. But now she had the benefit of Mike's ultra-tough, very competitive training regime.

Racing at controlled rates during each training session is an essential ingredient of Mike's programme (it differs markedly from the more controlled approach of Jurgen Grobler). With three well-matched scullers – Miriam, her sister Guin and Gill Lindsay – continually racing each other, standards rapidly improved. Miriam began to develop confidence that in a close race she would have far more racing experience than their opposition.

Thus it was in Aiguebelette, where her's and Lindsay's sculling proved to be a revelation. After a slow start they moved extremely fast in the second half of the course. Where before Miriam's nerves had prevented her from moving on in the final 1,000 metres, there was now just focused, relaxed rhythm. The double moved through the field. If anything, Lindsay was the one who needed to be calmed down. But in the end she delivered as the double rowed down the Rumanians in the final strokes to take a silver medal. At last Batten had proved that her first medal all those years ago in 1991 was no fluke.

In fact, the British women had an incredible championships. The coxless four won a gold medal, while the eight took the bronze. Never in their wildest dreams would this have looked likely at the end of the Atlanta Olympics. The four won their race just as Miriam was boating for her final. In doing so, the four became the first British women to win a World Championship gold medal in an open category.

At one time this would have placed extra pressure on her to perform. But now she seemed to relish it. At long last it seemed that Miriam had moved out of the time warp which she had occupied since her one and only medal some six years earlier. It was almost everything that she could have wished for. Life looked rosy once more. Miriam had conquered her demons, or so it seemed.

The fragility of her new-found stability was brutally exposed, however, when she found that her mother's cancer had re-appeared and she had only a few months to live. Where once it seemed so clear that Miriam was moving on, now there only seemed to be a black pit of despair. Both her and Guin were determined to be with their mother as much as possible during her final months. They took their sculling boats away from the squad's Marlow base so as to be able to train near their mother's hospital. It meant that Mike's training group was split. But both sisters were adamant that they did not want to miss out on any time with their dying mother. It was an experience that would leave them both emotionally drained.

It wasn't just the realisation their mother was deteriorating and dying in front of them. Miriam's mother wanted to talk about all the important areas of her own life and try to do what she still could for her daughters. Her mother worried about her daughter's future; pensions, marriage and family. In particular, Miriam had to confront her decision to continue rowing at the expense of the rest of her life. This brought with it stresses all of its own, as Miriam was forced to look at her life in a way she had never done before; almost to justify the decision to row to the exclusion of other things. It was a judgment which before had seemed almost automatic. Her mother's illness forced Miriam to see that she could no longer put her life completely on hold while she rowed.

One of the consequences was that she took a major decision to move on in her life, to get married to her boyfriend Dave Luke. She knew how difficult it was to row and keep a relationship going. Many of the women in the squad did not have partners, or had lost them because of the massive amount of time that it was necessary to spend training. This was even more so in recent years with the advent of National Lottery funding, which allowed squad members to become full-time rowers – or latter-day galley slaves as their partners sometimes saw it. Perhaps this was a lifestyle that a younger woman could live with, but Miriam, approaching her mid-30s, became aware that the biological clock was ticking away. She accepted that a relationship might mean a loss of form, particularly in the early part of the season, but felt it was a price worth paying.

So Miriam still tried to continue her own training through the midst of her mother's illness. Not only was this necessary in order to fulfil the plans which she and Lindsay had for the 1998 season, but it also provided a distraction from the emotional trauma surrounding her mother's hospital bed. However, trying to continue a demanding schedule now added to the problems that Miriam was facing. Her sleep was disturbed with vivid dreams; training, which before she seemed to take in her stride was now much harder. Furthermore, in the context of her mother's death, training and racing became unimportant. Miriam was due to race in trials not long after her mother passed away but angrily thought, 'What's the point of racing in some piddly little race when my mum's just died?'

Ultimately, though, she had been rowing too long just to let it go. The structure that the sport gave her life was, in part, something that helped her recover, although this would be a long process. When she missed a training session, or trained badly, there was a guilty feeling. Moreover, all the pent-up frustration and anger which had built up inside her during her mother's illness had to come out somewhere.

Miriam was on the slippery slope to a breakdown. It manifested itself in the form of over-training syndrome, where an athlete feels in a permanent state of tiredness, lethargy and depression. Complete rest is often the only answer. In fact, Miriam's mind and body needed time to grieve properly, without all the additional strains of her sport. It was her own way of getting through the crisis. She took some time off from the sport, missing the first World Cup regatta of the season in Munich. Meanwhile, she sought help from a doctor who gave her some sleeping pills which helped her at last get some proper rest. The doctor directed her to a therapist, who worked through bereavement issues with her. Slowly, she began to come to terms with her grief and, through this, rediscover her zest for life and for the sport again.

On the surface, the 1998 season seemed like it would be an uphill slog. Miriam's first race that season, at the second World Cup event of the year, saw her and Lindsay well beaten by the strong Dutch double. An injury to Lindsay forced them to withdraw from Lucerne; the last chance to get some much needed race practice before the World Championships in Cologne. To all intents and purposes, improving on their silver medal seemed a remote possibility.

But if you scratched the surface, a different picture emerged. This was a different Miriam who had come through her traumas of those long dark months. The cold, clammy grip of despair had been replaced by a fresh breeze, blowing away the cobwebs in her mind. She had now lost the psychological clutter and baggage which had often stopped her performing in the past. Having faced the fear and pain of her mother's death, she now had nothing to fear in any rowing competition. For once the experience of racing would be one to savour and enjoy.

So for the first time Miriam did not feel nervous for a big competition and her boat progressed smoothly through to the final. For this race she would prepare herself in a different way to that which she had for any other. Before she rowed, she visualised every stroke that she would take, even down to the smallest details of the sensations as the blades were coming through the water.

It was 'virtual rowing'. As she lay on her hotel bed, Miriam could feel the flow of the boat, hear the swoosh of the blades through the water, at the same time as picturing the other crews behind in her wake. But even in her dreams she had not imagined the type of conditions in which they would have to race. The wind was whipping up the Cologne rowing canal into a frenzy of white horses. They were not conditions for the faint-hearted or nervous.

Before her traumas, Miriam might have spent some time worrying about the possible difficulties that racing in such awkward conditions would involve, like catching a crab. But not now. When she arrived at the course and saw the conditions, one thought went through her mind: 'Great!'

As they watched the race before them move off, Miriam, alive to the moment, could see the German pair well out in the lead, ahead of the fancied Australians of the 'Oarsome Foursome'. 'Stop!' she said to Lindsay. 'Look at the German pair, we've got to row like them, go out fast, get in front and have a good lead when the water starts to get really rough at the 1,000 metres.'

It was sound advice. But as Miriam sat on the start, for all her virtual rowing even she could not have imagined the phenomenal speed of their start. The other crews were history after the first 30 strokes. By 1,000 metres they had stretched their lead to nearly three lengths. This was racing of a sort that neither Gill Lindsay nor Miriam had ever experienced before.

I was commentating on the race for BBC television and could not believe what I was seeing. Something was happening which I did not understand. Sure, I knew that they were fast – but not that fast! It was clearly not the smooth relaxed style of Aiguebelette the year before. But on my monitor, as the cameras zoomed into their faces, I could see a steely resolve in their eyes. It somehow told me that they would not be caught, even though I knew that they could not sustain that pace in the second half of the race. They were now in uncharted territory. This had never been part of their race plan. But even as the Dutch began to move back on them and whittle down the lead in the last 500 metres, there was no doubting that the British would stay in front.

As the finish neared, the cameras zoomed on to Miriam's face. Around her mouth was a layer of white froth, matching the flecks on the waves towards the finish. It was a sign of the incredible effort that she had put into this race.

It was a new Miriam that crossed the finish line that day, half a length ahead of the Dutch. For me, that performance was the highlight of the regatta, eclipsing yet another Redgrave gold. But it was not the medal that was important to her; much more was what it signified about how Miriam's life had moved on. In a spontaneous display of joy, her sister Guin dived into the cold water, evaded the German security guards and swam out to hug her exhausted but jubilant sister as she sat in the boat just past the finish line. As they embraced, the sisters were not just celebrating an incredible win but acknowledging what had happened to them both during the past year.

So perhaps it was no surprise to see the world champions dethroned with a vengeance in St Catherine's the following year. On the one hand, she was blissfully happy, her plans for the future already mapped out for Sydney and beyond; a gold medal and then a long holiday in a four-wheel drive round Australia with her husband Dave. She could even think about the first Batten-Luke babies. But behind her happiness lay a burning question: could she still perform when she was happy?

Before Cologne there was a great sadness in her life and she produced the performance of a lifetime. To take a medal in Sydney, could she

Hampton, 2001: It's never that easy to lose a rowing obsession. I'm exercising on my water rower on a February afternoon in our back garden.

manufacture, create, or find the anger that lay behind her victory in Germany?

For a long time the answer seemed to be 'no'. The women's squad was rife with controversy as the pair of Dot Blackie and Cath Bishop rejected Mike Spracklen's coaching methods and looked elsewhere. Following them, the women's eight, whom Mike thought little of, split away too. Of course, As an athlete spokesperson Miriam was very much involved in all this. But she was determined to stay loyal to Mike. Nevertheless, there was bad blood in the air; the effect of it on Miriam was anybody's guess.

There was uncertainty, too, with a new boat type. Mike put Miriam at bow in a quad scull, stroked by her sister Guin. In between them were two new talents, Kath Grainger and Sarah Winckless. Early results were mixed but suggested that a medal was beyond their reach, their boat not having the pace to live with the top crews from Germany and Russia in the first part of the race. It was enough to make Spracklen act with his typical ruthlessness in dropping Winckless and bringing back Lindsay to sit just in front of Miriam again.

As the Games drew closer, it was clear to all that the quad was picking up speed. But would it be enough? That question was answered in a brilliantly-paced final which saw them row through the fancied Russians to take a silver medal by just one hundredth of a second. Miriam had finally delivered in the most challenging of sports arenas. Where the speed came from, who can say? But it would not be fanciful to suggest that the energy in the emotional hug that the two sisters shared on the medal rostrum, as a celebration of their mother's memory, had something to do with it.

Miriam announced her retirement soon after the Games. At the grand old age of 36, this was not a surprise. We talked briefly after the Olympics, of her struggles and experiences. She ended our chat on a prophetic note: 'What was it that Coubertin said? It's not the winning that's important in life but the struggle. Kind of make sense now, doesn't it?'

She fell silent but I saw her face light up in a broad smile. I sensed that behind it, she was already thinking of her drive home that afternoon, to supper with 'Lukey' and the life that lay ahead.

Epilogue

THEY say that all good stories need a beginning, middle and an end. That's how we like things to be in this life and so I find myself writing an ending, rounding things off nicely until the 'present' (or at least the moment that I finally put down my pen and finished this book).

Writing this book has taken up a significant part of the last four years of my life. It's wasn't just the effort involved in writing and redrafting it, but also that of finding the time and energy to do so. For the most part, this process took place in snatched moments here and there, not just in Hampton and Normandy but on various cross-Channel ferries, in assorted cafes, a bed and breakfast hotel, the calm of a retreat centre, even in airport waiting lounges. Before all that, there were the interviews with my fellow travellers. All in all, this amounted to some 30 hours on tape and roughly 70,000 words that needed to be transcribed – and I won't even try to tell you about the angst that went into finding a publisher. But what's done is done. I feel free to move on to other (probably less demanding) projects.

That feeling of 'freedom' is also in response to my experiences over the last year. Suffice to say that things didn't go exactly, or even remotely, as I thought they might. Instead of commentating on the 2000 Olympics in Sydney, I watched on a friend's small television set in Thames Ditton, as Steve Redgrave won his fifth gold. I left shortly afterwards to go home. As I switched on the car radio, I heard Alan Green's voice on Radio 5 Live saying, 'I don't care what you're doing now, go outside and raise the roof.' I broke down and wept.

There had been a lot of 'weeping' that year and much else besides. Without going into too many details, I had experienced a nervous breakdown and descended into a state of deep depression. There were lots of reasons why. If you've read this book they won't surprise you and you'll probably be pleased that I'm not going to list them here. That's another story... Suffice to say that it was the hardest, often the most horrible and ultimately the biggest challenge of my life.

Am I 'better' now? Well, whatever that means I suppose that I am. Although as anyone who has experienced these sort of things may be aware, progress is never measured by straight lines. So I still have my moments. But then so does everybody at periods during their lives. The strange thing is, I never imagined I would one day look back on what happened to me as the most valuable, useful and life-enhancing experience that I have ever had.

Before, I saw my future as a list of things that I needed to do, should do, or had to do. Now there are possibilities. In a way, I suppose that I've rediscovered the sort of person that I really am.

So things are a little different for me now. I say no to things more readily, have begun to take the time to meditate regularly and, among other things, have developed a hitherto unknown penchant for colour schemes and redecorating rooms around the house. My scouse therapist, with a broad grin on his face, wondered how Chris felt now that her husband was becoming another version of Laurence Llewellyn-Bowen. Well these days, she tells me, I'm a 'nicer person', although I've a sneaking suspicion that she thinks I'm spending too much time in Sainsbury's Homebase.

So maybe now you understand why this epilogue is as much about a beginning, as it is about an ending.

One of the things I wanted to achieve by writing was to share my experiences with others, in the hope that this might in some way be helpful for them. Perhaps this seems a touch grandiose. In part I suppose it is. But whatever you take from this book, I hope that it's been able to throw some light on a great sport, recorded a few interesting events and stories, and ultimately explained an Olympic Obsession.

Bushy Park, 2001: A family at ease: the Crosses captured during a Sunday morning stroll. From left to right: Lara, Chris, me (with Sacha), Frank and Natasha.

Appendix I

Common rowing terms and abbreviations used in this book:

'A' final: Race for places 1 to 6. Places from 7 downwards are decided in the 'B', 'C' or even 'D' finals.

ARA: Amateur Rowing Association.

Blade: The thin part at the end of the oar which is buried in the water during a stroke. These days it's usually shaped like a cleaver. Sometimes rowers refer to their oars as 'blades'.

BOA: British Olympic Association

Boat Race: Annual competition between Oxford and Cambridge Universities, raced on the Thames from Putney to Mortlake.

Bow: The sharp end of the boat that cuts through the water first. Rowers and scullers 'do it backwards', so they always row facing away from the bows, looking towards the stern. 'Bow' can also refer to the person rowing nearest the bows of the boat. Often 'bow' is a smooth, technically-adept rower. Towards the end of my career, I often rowed at 'bow'.

Bowside: The rowers who row on 'bowside' have their oars sticking out on their left-hand side. This was because, historically, most boats were made so that the 'bow' man usually had to row with their oar on the left. In America, where perhaps tradition counts for less, bowside is known as 'starboard' side (in other words, if you faced towards the bows, you'd see bowside oars on your right-hand side).

Burst/Burn: A piece of work done at an increased pressure, usually 'bursts' last for between 10 and 30 strokes. Can refer to pieces done in training, or for a tactical push in the middle of a race.

Cadence: American term for rating.

Canvas: The bow, or stern, decking of the boat. In the old days it was the part covered by waterproof canvas. These days, even though the decking is plastic, the term has stuck. Commentators still refer to a leading, or winning margin as a 'canvas'. Generally, it's about 2 metres.

Catch: The name given to the movement of the blade at the beginning of the stroke. Literally, it is the time it takes for the blade to be fully buried under the water. At this point in the stroke, the rower is usually fully compressed (rather as if they were squatting before jumping in the air). The best rowers can perform the 'catch' without any sternward movement of the blade.

Cox: Usually small and light people, coxes steer their boat and give out instructions to the crew over a loudspeaker system. In pairs and fours, the cox usually lies with most of their body under the bow canvas. In eights, coxes sit at the stern. Unlike rowers, coxes face the same way that the boat is moving.

Coxless: Refers to rowing boats without a cox, which are steered by one of the rowers.

Crab: If a rower 'catches a crab' it means that they have lost control of their oar. Often, the blade goes deeper under the water than it should, which ends up with the rower unable to extract it cleanly. 'Crabs' are more common in rough conditions. The most spectacular can stop a boat dead, or eject the unfortunate rower into the water!

Crew: The name given to the rowers in a particular boat. In American colleges, if you 'do crew', it means that you row.

Double: A racing boat constructed for two scullers.

Finish: Name given to the movement by which the blade is extracted from the water at the end of the stroke.

FISA: Fédération Internationale des Sociétiés D' Aviron, or the International Rowing Federation.

Four: A racing boat built for four rowers. There are two types of four: one coxed, the other coxless.

IOC: International Olympic Committee.

IRSC: International Rowers and Scullers Club

Length: Usually refers to the length of a boat and is often used as a measure of a crew's lead (*ie* 'we led them by half a length'). If a coach or cox calls for 'more length', it usually means the rower needs to row a longer arc of stroke.

Lightweight: This class of rowing is limited by weight. Men cannot weigh more than 72.5kg and the average of the whole crew must not exceed 70kg. For women the weights are 59kg and 57kg respectively.

LRC: London Rowing Club.

NOC: National Olympic Committee

Oar: These days, racing oars are made from carbon fibre. They are about 3.5 metres long and have a plastic sleeve and button about 2.5 metres from the tip of the blade. Oars are used by rowers as levers. Held in both hands, the oar rests in a gate attached to a rigger. The gate swivels on a metal pin, usually fixed about 0.85 metres from the centre of the boat. Roughly speaking, the boat is levered past the blade, anchored in the water via the fulcrum of the pin. To do this, the rower exerts pressure on the handle of their oar.

Pair: A racing boat built for two rowers. There are two types of pair, coxless and coxed.

Pairs Matrix: A method of determining the relative speeds of rowers. It consists of a series of races (generally about four or five) in pairs. Each rower on a particular side gets to row with everybody else in the matrix on the same side. Relative differences in time between the crews are noted and selection decisions are made accordingly.

Puddles: These are the whirlpool like swirls, which are created in the water as the rower pulls their oar.

Quad: (quadruple scull) Four scullers row the quad, each uses a pair of sculls.

Rating: The number of strokes rowed in each minute. Light paddling is generally done around '18', mid-race pace at ''36' and off the start anything up to '50'.

Repechage: In international regattas, rowers who don't progress any further after the first heat have a second chance to reach the next round by racing in the repechages. It comes from the French meaning 'to fish out'.

Rigger: A metal or carbon-fibre arm supporting the pin and gate (see 'oar'). Riggers are bolted on to the side of the boat and jut out about 0.9 metres from its centre.

Run: Refers to the movement of the boat through the water. Rowers and coaches are forever trying to improve the 'run' of the boat. One way of gauging this is to watch the stern of the boat as the blades enter the water at the catch. If it tends to bounce, all is not well. If the stern flows smoothly, the boat is said to be running well.

SAF: Sports Aid Foundation.

SANROC: South African Non Racial Olympic Committee.

Scull: An oar of shorter length and with a smaller blade. They are used in sculling. A sculler holds one scull in each hand. It can also refer to the boat used by single scullers

Seat: Refers to the lightweight construction with wheels on the bottom on which the rower sits and moves up and down the slide. Rowers tend to refer rather possessively to their seat in the boat, meaning the position they row in (see stroke).

Seat Race: A direct 'head to-head competition pitting one rower against another. Many coaches (not Jurgen Grobler though) believe that it is the only fair way to select crews. Essentially it consists of a timed series of races between two fours. At the end of the first race a rower in one boat is swapped with someone from the opposing crew. The newly-formed crews then race again over the same course. Any differences in time are noted. This process can continue for several races with other rowers being changed too. At the end, by comparing each rower's times, a winner(s) emerges.

Shell: This is often used as another term for a racing boat. The 'shell' refers directly to the thin skin of the boat which sits in the water.

Single: A racing boat that is built for one person to use.

Slide: Alloy runners on which the rower's seat rolls backwards and forwards.

Stern: Rear of the boat. The cox of an eight sits in the stern of the boat.

Strokeside: The rowers who row on 'strokeside' have their oars sticking out on their right-hand side. Many rowers have a favourite or stronger side. Mine was strokeside. If you've noted 'bowside' you'll have worked out that most boats were made so that the 'stroke' man usually had to row with their oar on their right. In America, strokeside is known as 'portside' (in other words, if you faced towards the bows, you'd see portside oars on your left-hand side).

Stroke[man]: The rower nearest the stern of the boat. They are responsible for setting the rating, rhythm and the pressure for their crew. As leaders, 'strokes' generally excel at either setting a great rhythm, and/or being the 'hardest' rower in the crew. If your 'strokeman' has both qualities then you're on to a winner. Rowers are generally numbered from stroke. In an eight it's 7, 6, 5, 4, 3, 2 and bow. In a four, 3, 2 and bow. A 'stroke' is also the name given to the complete cycle of the rowing action, *ie* from one catch to the next.

TTRC: Thames Tradesmen's Rowing Club

Tub: A wide boat which is often the first craft that novice rowers take to the water in.

USRA: United States Rowing Association.

USOC: United States Olympic Committee.

Appendix II

Martin Cross's notable international wins: Olympic and World Championship results 1975-1996

1975
2nd in the World Junior Rowing Championships, Montreal (4-)
Str. M. Cross, 3. R. Roberts, 2. I. McNuff, Bow. J. Beattie*
Visitors Cup Henley Royal Regatta.

1976
Wyfold Cup, Henley Royal Regatta (4-)
Str. M. Cross, 3. J. Beattie,* 2. I. McNuff, Bow. D. Bond.

1977
Stewards Cup, Henley Royal Regatta
Copenhagen International Regatta (Sat & Sun)
10th in the World Rowing Championships, Amsterdam (4-)
Str. M. Cross, 3. J. Beattie,* 2. I. McNuff, Bow. D. Bond.

1978
Salzgitter International Regatta (Sat & Sun)
3rd in the World Championships, Lake Karapiro, New Zealand (4-)
Str. M. Cross, 3. D. Townsend, 2. I. McNuff, Bow. J. Beattie.*

1979
Mannheim International Regatta (Sat & Sun)
Essen international Regatta (Sat & Sun)
Stewards Cup, Henley Royal Regatta
3rd in the World Rowing Championships, Lake Bled, Yugoslavia (4-)
Str. M. Cross, 3. D. Townsend, 2. I. McNuff, Bow. J. Beattie.*
Mannheim International Regatta (Sun)
Str. N. Christie, 7. C. Seymour, 6. G. Rankine, 5. J. Macleod, 4. M. Cross, 3. H. Bathurst, 2. E. Sims, Bow. L. Robertson, Cox. A. Inns.

1980
Essen International Regatta (Sat)
3rd in the Olympic Games, Moscow (4-)
Mannheim International Regatta (Sat)†
Str. M. Cross, 3. D. Townsend, 2. I. McNuff, Bow. J. Beattie.*
*†**Due to the disqualification of the USSR crew for use of anabolic steroids***

1981
Stewards Cup, Henley Royal Regatta
10th in the World Championships, Munich (4-)
Str. M. Cross, 3. J. Clark, 2. I. McNuff, Bow. J. Beattie.*

1982

Queen Mother's Cup, Henley Royal Regatta (4x)
Str. M. Cross, 3. S. Redgrave*, 2. A. Clift, Bow. E. Sims.
Copenhagen International Regatta (Sat & Sun)
6th in the World Championships, Lucerne (4x)
Str. M. Cross, 3. S. Redgrave,* 2. A. Clift, Bow. A. Whitwell.

1983

Grand Challenge Cup, Henley Royal Regatta
Str. J. Bland, 7. R. Stanhope, 6. T. Cadoux-Hudson, 5. R. Budgett, 4. M. Cross, 3. A. Clift, 2. J. Beattie, Bow. I. McNuff, Cox. A. Sherman.
6th in the World Championships, Duisburg.
Str. R. Budgett, 3. M. Cross, 2. I. McNuff, Bow. J. Beattie. Cox. A. Sherman.

1984

Mannheim International Regatta (Sat)
Str. M. Cross, 3. A. Holmes, 2. R. Budgett, Bow. J. Beattie, Cox. A. Ellison.
Mannheim International Regatta (Sun), Essen International Regatta (Sat), Lucerne International Regatta (Sat)
1st in the Olympic Games, Los Angeles
Str. S. Redgrave, 3. A. Holmes, 2. R. Budgett, Bow. M. Cross, Cox. A. Ellison.

1985

Amsterdam International Regatta (Sat)
2nd in the World Championships, Amsterdam (2-)
Str. M. Cross,* Bow. A. Clift.
Amsterdam International Regatta (Sun)
Str. M. Cross, Bow. A. Clift, Cox. A. Ellison.

1986

Lucerne International Regatta (Sun)
4th in the World Rowing Championships, Nottingham (2-)
Str. M. Cross,* Bow. A. Clift.
1st in the Commonwealth Games, Edinburgh (4+)
Str. S. Redgrave, 3. A. Holmes, 2. A. Clift, Bow. M. Cross, Cox. A. Ellison.

1987

Piedilucco International Regatta (Sat)
Amsterdam International Regatta (Sat) (2- with M. Cross at Stroke)
Str. A. Clift, Bow. M. Cross.*
Piedilucco International Regatta (Sun)
Str. A. Clift, Bow. M. Cross, Cox. P. Sweeney.
5th in the World Championships, Copenhagen
Str. M. Cross, 3. J. Garrett, 2. J. Maxey, Bow. A. Clift. Cox. V. Thomas.

1988

4th in the Olympic Games, Seoul
Str. M. Cross, 3. J. Garrett, 2. J. Maxey, Bow. A. Clift, Cox. V. Thomas.

1989

Unplaced in the World Championships Lake Bled, Slovenia (4x)
Str. C. Andrews, 3. M. Cross, 2. R. Henderson, Bow. R. Stanhope.*

1990

Essen International Regatta (Sat) Brandenburg International Regatta (Sun)
Stewards Challenge Cup, Henley Royal Regatta
3rd in the Goodwill Games, Seattle (4-)
Str. T. Foster,* 3. M. Pinsent, 2. P. Mulkerrins, Bow. M. Cross.
4th in the World Championships, Lake Barrington, Tasmania (4-)
Str. T. Foster,* 3. G. Stewart, 2. P. Mulkerrins, Bow. M. Cross.
Rotterdam International (8+)
Str. P. Mulkerrins, 7. R. Phelps, 6. T. Dillon, 5. M. Pinsent, 4. J. Walker, 3. G. Stewart,
2. T. Foster, Bow. M. Cross, Cox. A. Ellison.
Lucerne Regatta (8+)
Str. P. Mulkerrins, 7. M. Pinsent, 6. S. Redgrave, 5. G. Stewart, 4. T. Dillon, 3. G.
Stewart, 2. T. Foster, Bow. M. Cross, Cox. A. Ellison.

1991

The Grand Challenge Cup, Henley Royal Regatta (8+)
Str. T. Foster, 7. A. Obholzer, 6. J. Singfield, 5. R. Phelps, 4. J. Searle, 3. J. Cracknell,
2. R. Stanhope, Bow. M. Cross, Cox. G. Herbert.
3rd in the World Championships, Vienna (8+)
Str. T. Foster, 7. A. Obholzer, 6. J. Singfield, 5. G. Searle, 4. J. Searle, 3. R. Phelps, 2.
R. Stanhope, Bow. M. Cross, Cox. G. Herbert.
Paris Sprint (8+)
Str. T. Foster, 7. R. Phelps,** 6. J. Singfield, 5. G. Searle,** 4. J. Searle, 3. N. Burfitt,
2. R. Stanhope, Bow. M. Cross, Cox. G. Herbert.

1992

6th in the Olympic Games, Barcelona (8+)
Str. R. Obholzer, 7. S. Turner, 6. J. Singfield, 5. J. Walker, 4. R. Phelps, 3. B. Hunt-
Davies, 2. M. Cross, Bow. T. Foster, Cox. V. Thomas.

1993

6th in the World Championships Racice, Czechoslovakia (8+)
Str. A. Cassidy, 7. R. Phelps, 6. J. Walker, 5. J. Singfield, 4. J. Beherns, 3. M. Parish, 2.
M. Cross, Bow. J. Cracknell, Cox. V. Thomas.

1994

Piedilucco International Regatta (8+)
Str. J. Singfield, 7. J. Searle, 6. G. Searle, 5. J. Walker, 4. R. Phelps, 3. R. Manners, 2.
A. Cassidy, Bow. M. Cross, Cox. G. Herbert.
7th in the World Championships, Indianapolis (2+)
Str. J. Singfield,† Bow. M. Cross, Cox. H. Bass.
‡(with S. Redgrave in the Small Final)

1996

3rd in the Amsterdam International Regatta (Sun) (2-)#
Str. R. Stanhope,* Bow. M. Cross.
#Not a 'win' but worth recording as it was my last international race.

* *Denotes steersman*
** *Denotes horribly drunk at the time.*

Appendix III

A brief chronological summary of some of the things I was involved in when I wasn't rowing.

Education
1962-1979: Full-time education at St James's Primary School, Twickenham; Cardinal Vaughan School, Kensington; Queen Mary College, University of London; The Institute of Education, University of London

Full-time Employment
1979-80: Supply Teacher, St Marks and Lampton Schools, Hounslow; Cardinal Vaughan School, Kensington
1981-82: History teacher, Bishop Thomas Grant School, Streatham
1982-present: History teacher, Hampton School

Sports Politics
1985-1994: Athletes' representative on the National Olympic Committee
1991-1994: Chair, BOA Athletes Council
1992-1999: Member, FISA Council
1992-1997: Chair, FISA Athletes Commission
1985-1994: Member, ARA Council

Broadcasting
1988: C4 TV, summariser Serpentine Regatta
1990: SKY TV, summariser World Championships
1995-1999: BBC Radio 5, Live reporter and summariser
1998-2000: BBC TV, rowing summariser

Other
1987-1994: Secretary, Hampton Labour Party
1989 & 1993 Labour Candidate for Hampton in local government elections
1987-1989: Press secretary and international liaison, Serpentine Regatta
1986-present: Leader of the Folk Group at St Theodore's RC Church, Hampton
1987-1989: Organiser Serpentine International Regatta

Index